Gaelic Scotland in the Colonial Imagination

Gaelic Scotland in the Colonial Imagination

Anglophone Writing from 1600 to 1900

✦

Silke Stroh

NORTHWESTERN UNIVERSITY PRESS
EVANSTON, ILLINOIS

Northwestern University Press
www.nupress.northwestern.edu

Printed in the United States of America

10 9 8 7 6 5 4 3 2 1

Library of Congress Cataloging-in-Publication Data

Names: Stroh, Silke, author.
Title: Gaelic Scotland in the colonial imagination : Anglophone writing from 1600 to 1900 / Silke Stroh.
Description: Evanston, Illinois : Northwestern University Press, 2016. | Includes bibliographical references and index.
Identifiers: LCCN 2016032000 | ISBN 9780810134058 (pbk. : alk. paper) | ISBN 9780810134034 (cloth : alk. paper) | ISBN 9780810134041 (e-book)
Subjects: LCSH: Scottish literature—18th century—History and criticism. | Scottish literature—19th century—History and criticism. | Celts in literature. | Postcolonialism in literature.
Classification: LCC PR8547 .S77 2016 | DDC 820.99411—dc23
LC record available at https://lccn.loc.gov/2016032000

CONTENTS

ACKNOWLEDGMENTS

During the research which underlies this book, and during the gestation process of the manuscript, I have benefited greatly from the advice and support of various people and institutions. Firstly, I would like to express my gratitude to Prof. Dr. Dieter Riemenschneider and Prof. Dr. Frank Schulze-Engler from the University of Frankfurt a.M. for their invaluable mentorship during my first years of working on Scottish postcolonialism. I have also received important encouragement, comments, suggestions, and support from Prof. C. L. Innes, Prof. Dr. Mark Stein, Prof. Carla Sassi, Dr. Michael Newton, Prof. Dr. Christoph Heyl, Dr. Christine Vogt-William, Caroline Kögler, my NUP editors Gianna F. Mosser and Nathan MacBrien, and the two anonymous peer reviewers. Any remaining shortcomings in this book are, of course, entirely my own.

I would also like to thank the friendly staff at Bridgeman Images for supplying the picture reproduced on the cover—this Victorian scrap perfectly captures the ambiguity of the Scottish Highlanders' position in British colonial discourse: on the one hand, the Highlander marches alongside the other (ethnically unmarked) British redcoat soldier as a leader of the pageant, presumably a fellow conqueror of the "exotic" people and animals behind him, but on the other hand he is arguably also part of the pageant of the colonized—ethnically marked like them, and with some "primitive exoticism" emanating from his garb. Recalling the triumphal marches in ancient Rome where victorious commanders and emperors paraded themselves, their troops, foreign captives and spoils, this Victorian procession also reflects Britain's attempts to portray itself as a successor to imperial Rome—with "Celts" as barbarian Others to both empires, and a bridge between them.

Further thanks are due to the German Academic Exchange Service (Deutscher Akademischer Austauschdienst, DAAD) for facilitating my very first stay in Scotland as a scholar of their "Anglistenprogramm" during the academic year 1996–97, which laid the initial foundations for my long-standing fascination with Scottish studies. I have also benefited enormously from a doctoral scholarship granted by the German National Academic Foundation (Studienstiftung des Deutschen Volkes). Furthermore, I would like to thank the National Library of Scotland as well as the libraries of the University of Glasgow, the University of Aberdeen, and Sabhal Mòr Ostaig for their generous permission to use their excellent resources during my research.

Some of the ideas presented in this book were previously published in a different form as parts of essays in the following collections and journals:

Global Fragments: (Dis)Orientation in the New World Order, edited by Anke Bartels and Dirk Wiemann; *Transcultural English Studies: Theories, Fictions, Realities*, edited by Frank Schulze-Engler and Sissy Helff; *Translation of Cultures*, edited by Petra Rüdiger and Konrad Gross; *The Bottle Imp* 10; *Within and Without Empire: Scotland Across the (Post)colonial Borderline*, edited by Carla Sassi and Theo van Heijnsbergen; *Anglistentag 2012 Potsdam: Proceedings*, edited by Katrin Röder and Ilse Wischer; and *Contested Identities: Literary Negotiations in Time and Place*, edited by Roger Nicholson, Claudia Marquis, and Gertrud Szamosi. In terms of theory and historical basics, there are also some overlaps with my earlier monograph *Uneasy Subjects: Postcolonialism and Scottish Gaelic Poetry*—in a way, these two studies complement each other, approaching the Scottish (post)colonial question from different linguistic angles.

I am also immensely grateful for all the love and support I have received from my parents Irene and Werner Stroh, and from my partner Gregor Addison. He is due additional thanks for many inspiring reading suggestions and years of lively intellectual dialogue. It is to these three wonderful people that this book is dedicated.

Gaelic Scotland in the Colonial Imagination

INTRODUCTION

Can Scotland and the "Celtic fringe" be considered as English colonies? Is their experience and literature comparable to that of overseas postcolonial countries? Can international postcolonial theory help us to understand the Scottish predicament? Is Scottish political and cultural nationalism similar to anticolonial resistance overseas? Or are such comparisons no more than Scottish patriotic victimology, attempting to mask complicity in the British Empire and justify initiatives to secede from the United Kingdom? Caught between nationalist rhetoric, an ever-expanding academic "theory industry," and more skeptical perspectives which doubt the value of Scottish and "Celtic" postcolonialisms, these questions have been heatedly debated in recent years. On an international level, the transformation of postcolonial studies from a small academic margin into an increasingly popular, respected, and institutionalized part of the academic mainstream has been ongoing since the 1980s and, despite recurrent theoretical (self-)questioning, the field still remains a trendy academic growth sector. Historically, postcolonialism has close connections to questions of political autonomy, emancipation movements, and nation-building. Hence, debates about extending postcolonial approaches to Scottish studies were to some extent fueled by recent political developments: the devolution process of the late 1990s which gave Scotland its own "regional" parliament within the United Kingdom while pan-British "national" affairs remained with the Parliament in London; the 2007 and 2011 elections which made the Scottish National Party (SNP) the governing power in the Edinburgh Parliament; and the run-up to the 2014 referendum on whether Scotland should become a sovereign nation-state of its own, with full independence from the United Kingdom. When that referendum resulted in a "no" vote, some might have wondered whether nationalist—and postcolonial—questions should now be considered unviable, dated, and discredited: Did not this referendum result confirm an overall satisfaction with being part of Britain, a "sameness" and identification with the English (and other Britons), rather than a sense of being a marginalized Other or an internal colony?[1] These are valid questions, but in reality these issues are much more complex.

Even after the 2014 referendum, the question of Scottish autonomy remained on the agenda. Political campaigning for more powers continued, even if the campaign was supposed to take place within the British state for the time being. Moreover, many refused to give up on independence as a long-term goal. Activism remained vigorous, and the pro-independence Scottish

National Party quadrupled its membership within six months after the 2014 plebiscite. Other pro-independence parties likewise experienced a growth in membership. Desires for stronger representation of Scottish interests within the Union, and for an end of pan-British austerity politics, led to a huge SNP success in the 2015 elections for the British Parliament, when the party gained 50 additional seats and came to represent fifty-six out of fifty-nine Scottish constituencies. The SNP also won the election for the Scottish Parliament in May 2016. The "Brexit" referendum in June 2016 brought a renewed sense of urgency: Although most Scots voted to remain in the European Union, an English-dominated pan-British majority voted to come out. The threat of Scotland being taken out of Europe against its will seemed to underline the difficulties of safeguarding Scotland's interests within the United Kingdom. Suddenly, "indyref2" became a very real possibility, even in the short term, as politicians and grassroots started preparing for a new campaign.

Moreover, postcolonialism cannot be reduced to questions of political autonomy. Cultural concerns are at least equally important, and also pertain in situations where separate statehood is not (presently) on the agenda. One major concern of anti- and postcolonial writing is to criticize the cultural hierarchies set up by the colonizer, discard the sense of cultural inferiority which the colonial system had instilled in the colonized, and develop new ethnic or national cultural confidence. While this is sometimes connected to a quest for political autonomy, it does not have to be: instead, it can also remain limited to the cultural sphere, or pursue sociopolitical goals through a different framework, for instance by pushing for reform within a given state, or by focusing on transnational forms of organization. Strands of postcolonialism which focus on the cultural empowerment of the margins afford various connections to modern Scottish culture, whose energy, achievement, and renewed self-assurance has been widely noted, for instance in the "second Scottish literary renaissance" of the late twentieth century (the first having been launched by Hugh MacDiarmid in the 1920s). This is another reason why various critics have asked whether Scottish studies should take a postcolonial turn.

But although a postcolonial debate already exists in Scottish studies, it is still widely ignored in the international "mainstream" of postcolonial studies which tends to focus on other regions such as Africa, South Asia, or the Caribbean, and does not usually include Scotland in its comparative purview. Thus, the dialogue between Scottish and international postcolonial studies is still relatively one-sided. Moreover, even among Scottish studies specialists, postcolonial inquiry has so far often been somewhat unsystematized. For instance, it has often been limited to specific authors or periods. There is still a marked preference for twentieth- and twenty-first-century literature, without systematic exploration of earlier texts and situations which these modern developments are built on or react against. Lack of historicization might also be one of the reasons why the international postcolonial mainstream is still reluctant to engage with Scottish issues: looking for a "colonized" within a

United Kingdom that has become globally infamous as a colonizer might at first seem counterintuitive. Hence, postcolonial scholars with other regional specializations who approach Scottish issues for the first time, and mainly from a comparatist angle, might need more historical and cultural background information on Scotland in order to understand why Scottish claims to colonial or postcolonial status have been made. There seems to be a need for a more historically oriented study of Scottish (post)colonial discourse which not only tries to provide new insights for Scottish studies specialists (e.g., via detailed analyses of individual texts) but also provides enough background information and surveys to function as an introduction to Scottish postcolonialism for readers who are hitherto unfamiliar with the field. This book aims to facilitate a more intense dialogue between Scottish and postcolonial studies by providing entry points for scholars and students, and perhaps even some general readers, who are approaching these intersections from different directions. Readers who are new to Scottish studies but may already have a background in postcolonial or critical ethnic studies regarding other cultural contexts, such as Afro-Caribbean, South Asian, Chicano, or Native American studies, are provided with sufficient introductory information to make Scottish texts and debates intelligible and meaningful to them. Readers who approach this dialogue from the side of Scottish studies but are relatively new to international postcolonial thought receive pointers to key postcolonial concepts, authors, and texts which provide initial orientation as a basis for further explorations. While this book is thus mainly an introductory survey, even specialist scholars in the (as yet relatively small) field of postcolonial Scottish studies, or in related areas like nineteenth-century literature about the Scottish Highlands, may find that it gives them some new insights, for example into critically neglected authors or into the ways in which texts and tropes already well-known in a more specialized context can be brought into a wider purview through comparison with other national or historical contexts.

Thus, this book tries to chart important foundations of Scottish postcolonial writing by examining how cultural marginalization and resistance are negotiated in anglophone Scottish writing from the first centuries of the dynastic (1603) and political (1707) Union with England. These early texts give crucial insights into the sense of internal hierarchy which was built into pan-British national identity constructs from the beginning, and which contemporary "postcolonial" Scottish literature and criticism writes against. These modern political and cultural debates can only be understood against the background of earlier discursive traditions and social experiences. Furthermore, this book highlights that postcolonial approaches pertain not only to Scottish-English relations, but also to ethno-cultural divisions within Scotland, especially those between the anglophone Lowlands and the traditionally Gaelic-speaking Highlands.[2] The present study focuses on these internal divisions to show the complexity of the Scottish postcolonial question, and to illuminate some of the wider issues which also pertain to Scottish postcolonialism in general. Constructions of the Gaels between ethnic othering and national integration are central to the "internal colonialism" debate. They also play a crucial role in the evolution of colonial and postcolonial moments in Scottish-English relations.

But before engaging with those issues in detail, it may be helpful to give a brief introductory outline of some basic conceptual, theoretical, historical, and disciplinary issues.

Colonialism, Postcolonialism, and Postcolonial Studies: Basic Concepts and Themes

Generally, colonialism is understood as a process by which one country imposes its dominance on a territory which was previously not part of its domain, and often is not even a direct neighbor but lies at considerable geographical distance. Geographical distance can also entail a sense of great cultural difference between colonizers and colonized. Moreover, colonialism often maintains a very strong sense of hierarchy between the colonizer country's "home" population and the inhabitants of the colony. Colonial domination can work on the political, economic, demographic, and cultural levels, and a range of "typical" manifestations have been identified for each of these. Not all of them necessarily appear together in the same place or time, but usually at least some of them are combined.

Politically, colonization can involve the annexation of territories that were previously under different control (either the indigenous population's or another foreign power's), and the subjection of the annexed lands and populations to the colonizer's political, legal, and administrative authority. This can take direct or indirect forms. For instance, French colonialism is often associated with a very direct imposition of French authority and administrative structures on its overseas dependencies. British colonialism, by contrast, is often associated with more indirect forms of control: local political, legal, or administrative structures, and often also local elites, were nominally kept in place, but only under the ultimate authority and control of the colonizer, with the option of more direct interference if local mediating structures and personnel did not deliver the desired results. It is also assumed that colonialism, with its strong intercultural hierarchies and frequent dismissal of the value of local lives, entailed particularly strong clashes of interest between the rulers (colonizers and partly also their local intermediaries) and the ruled (the mass of the colonized population). These strong clashes of interest often necessitated considerable violence, for instance in the form of military subjugation or particularly strict policing.

Economically, colonialism can involve the establishment of small trading outposts in remote regions in order to facilitate the export of the colonizer's homemade commodities in exchange for "exotic" goods. It can also involve the establishment of more extensive territorial control in order to secure the flow of the desired commodities and enforce a monopoly to the exclusion of local and international competitors. Perhaps especially in the latter context, there is a strong sense of power imbalance, and the benefits of the exchange seem to lie rather one-sidedly with the colonizer. For instance, there can be a forcible reorientation of the colony's economy towards a limited range of raw materials for export to the "mother country" (e.g., England) where they are processed and mainly also consumed, whereas local manufactures and even some sectors of local agriculture (even basic foodstuffs) are discouraged so that those products need to be imported at high prices from the colonizer, who thus makes greater profits while the majority of the local population ends up more impoverished than it might have been without this colonial trade. Here, too, colonial systems are often considered to be even more exploitative than other forms of rule, such as precolonial ones or the ones which are practiced within the mother country itself.

Demographically, colonialism can involve considerable movements of population, often across vast geographical and cultural distances. For instance, people from the mother country moved to colonial dependencies, either temporarily or permanently. Sometimes, this happened in smaller numbers to fulfill key positions in "controlling" a labor force which was still largely indigenous, as in British India. Elsewhere, more extensive resettlement was used to rid the mother country of "superfluous" population (criminals or paupers) that might be more profitably settled elsewhere, to stabilize the colonizer's control against the competing interests of indigenous populations or other colonial powers, or to replace local forms of production that were not sufficiently profitable to the colonizer with more lucrative systems imported from the mother country, as happened when certain Native American or Aboriginal Australian hunter-gatherer economies were replaced with European farming systems and imported European farmers. Resettlement can be voluntary, as with some of the European "pioneer" farmers who hoped for better life chances, or enforced, as with deported British criminals, Native Americans resettled on "reservations," or the millions of enslaved Africans shipped to the New World as a colonial labor force. Often enough, colonial demographic displacements grew to the dimension of genocide through loss of land (entailing poverty and starvation), outrageously bad travel conditions (as on the Middle Passage), imported diseases, and outright slaughter. The hierarchization of different population groups was often shored up by the construction of supposedly innate "racial" biological distinctions between them which placed these groups in a "natural" hierarchy and justified the maltreatment of the "lower" orders on this "racial" ladder.

Colonialism also involves the construction of cultural hierarchies: the colonizer's language(s) and cultural forms are claimed to be superior, while those of the colonized are systematically devalued and discriminated against. Sometimes this can be a mere *corollary* of material hierarchies: the dominant power imposes the terms of interaction, and colonizers who were too lazy to learn the colony's language(s) had the means to pressure locals to learn the colonizers' language(s) instead. Here as well, the highly unequal terms of colonial culture contact become obvious. Cultural hierarchies can also help to *legitimate* and *stabilize* material hierarchies. The claim that one culture is worth more than the other can boost the colonizer's sense of supremacy and assuage potential pangs of guilt about the treatment of the colonized, thus deflecting the risk of anticolonial critique within the colonizer's own ranks. If the colonizer manages to instill his ideas of cultural hierarchies among the colonized, the latter can come to believe in their own inferiority, which can reduce the risk of resistance: such colonized subjects may either conceive the ambition to imitate the colonizer and voluntarily discard their own culture, or at least resign themselves to their subordinate status even if imitating the colonizer is beyond their wishes or means (e.g., because they cannot afford a European education). Hierarchies between different population groups can also be shored up by exaggerating the extent of the cultural differences that lie between them: colonial ideologies often construct colonizer and colonized as exact opposites, setting up a binary distinction between self and "Other"; and such claims of absolute cultural distinctness are used to legitimate social distinctions, similar to the way that claims of "racial" distinctions are used. Postcolonial scholarship refers to these and related processes as "othering," often spelling the constructed "Other" with a capital letter.

Colonial ideas of hierarchy are not just imposed *on* cultural products (e.g., by saying that British literature is better than Indian literature); they are also constructed directly *through* cultural products, by what is said within individual texts and visual artworks. For instance, when a great number of novels, history books, and works of art portray people from certain ethnic groups as inferior and the colonial project as a glorious civilizing mission which will ultimately benefit all, people brought up with these cultural products may come to accept colonial hierarchies as natural and justified. This is where the notion of "colonial discourse" comes in—another central term in the postcolonial studies repertoire. Just as colonialism is associated with specific social phenomena, colonial discourse is associated with a range of specific representation patterns which are used to establish or justify colonial power imbalances and hegemonies. These include the devaluation of "native" history and indigenous sociopolitical forms as inferior, chaotic, and barbaric: "natives" are either claimed to be incapable of ruling themselves ("primitive tribal structures"), or the achievements of non-European self-rule are grudgingly acknowledged (e.g., because the size, complexity, and long-standing stability of Asian empires was too evident to deny) but still pronounced to be inferior to Western forms because local states and laws were allegedly more cruel and tyrannous than "enlightened" modern European systems of law and order. Local economic traditions were also deemed inferior to the colonizer's, for example on account of "inefficiency." Colonized people's intellectual, cultural, and moral abilities were likewise frequently ranked as inferior. Local languages, oratures, and literatures were devalued as crude and unpolished; local science was deemed unscientific; local education systems left people "uneducated"; and local moral sensibilities were supposedly corrupted or at least underdeveloped by the imperfections of the barbaric sociocultural systems which nurtured them. Local people's discursive authority, that is, their right to tell their own (hi)story, comment on the colonial encounter from their own perspective, and speak about the world with insight, good judgment, and authority, was denied, since the colonizers claimed all discursive authority for themselves.

A classic study of colonial discourse strategies can be found in Edward W. Said's book *Orientalism*.[3] His critical analysis of Western representations of "the Orient" shows how "the West" and "the East" were constructed as binary opposites, how Westerners set themselves up as the best authorities for speaking about the East rather than letting the East speak for itself, how this shored up Western notions of superiority, and how it legitimized imperialist projects. Said's findings also illuminate more general principles of imperialist ideology which have been at work in other parts of the world as well. For example, the colonizers' arrogation of the right to speak about and for their Others without respecting the Others' own voices can also be discerned in white European discourse about black Africans or Native Americans. Said's work has thus been treated as a major founding text of the entire field of colonial discourse analysis, which often looks at similar ideological strategies employed across different regions.

Nonetheless, colonial discourse does not *only* consist of open devaluation: there is often also an element of attraction, exoticist fascination with the cultural "Other," expressed by Orientalists, tourists, travel writers, and so on. It is also possible to portray the Other not as ignoble savages but as noble savages, for instance by romanticizing the "primitive" as a site of moral innocence and other "simple virtues." But even here, the patronizing, condescending implications of colonial discourse are evident: for example, innocence and "simple virtues" are deemed the result of ignorance, intellectual simplicity, and social backwardness. Attraction to the Other can also take the forms of erotic interest, personal sympathy, or friendship for certain individuals, or even a genuine recognition and espousal of certain "native" cultural features as equal or superior to the colonizer's own. After all, some colonizers were so attracted by the colonized that they "went native." Other colonizers often regarded this as unsettling, a dangerous destabilization of colonial certainties and hierarchies. The mixture of repulsion and attraction which characterized colonial discourse could create considerable unease.

The responses of the colonized to the colonial encounter can likewise entail an ambivalent mixture of attraction and repulsion. On the one hand, colonial inequalities and violence can create anger and resistance. On the other hand, colonial education caused many colonized people to internalize the colonizer's ideologies and develop a sense of inferiority or self-hatred, a "cultural cringe" which made them devalue their own traditions, and a desire to imitate the colonizer. A classical examination of colonial psychology can, for instance, be found in Frantz Fanon's case studies of black Caribbean and African sensibilities affected by French colonialism.[4] But here as well, imitation can also destabilize colonial hierarchies. It is a two-edged sword: on the one hand, colonial ideologies want colonized people to imitate (mimic) the colonizer as an act of assimilation which marks their subjugation, facilitates the functioning of colonial society, and "advances civilization." On the other hand, mimicry can have a subversive dimension. First, imitation requires close scrutiny of the model, and if the colonized scrutinize the colonizer too intensely, they might discern flaws in his logic, contradictions in his social system, or weaknesses in his culture, all of which might call the superiority of the colonizer into question. Second, imitation can be too successful: a complete erasure of cultural difference between colonizer and colonized would again threaten the colonizer's superiority. Third, mimicry can also have a dimension of mockery: imitation can be used for parody, which likewise threatens authority. For all these reasons, mimicry can also make the colonizer uneasy; and the colonized can sometimes use it (consciously or unconsciously) to undermine the colonial hierarchy.

Another, related concept which highlights the ambivalence of colonial discourse between attraction and repulsion, and between binary Othering and the destabilization of cultural boundaries, is hybridity. There are different ways in which this concept has been used. One usage is rooted in biological contexts, for instance regarding the cross-breeding of plants and animals. Here, the hybrid is understood as a mixture between two usually distinct life forms. This understanding of hybridity also informs racist discourse about human "races" and "miscegenation" (the result of erotic attraction to the supposedly repulsive Other, discussed above).[5] Similar essentialism which assumes innate distinctions can be found in texts about "culture clashes," for instance between "East" and "West." Although the idea of a culture clash is ostensibly not based on racial biology but on cultural difference, it assumes an innate essentialism and almost insurmountable differences which are similar to racial essentialism, and discourse on "culture clash" often has an underlying racist dimension.[6] It assumes the purity and separateness of "races" or cultures as the norm, while implying that hybridity is, or at least should be, a mere exception. Such kinds of ethno-cultural essentialism often feature in colonial discourse, but also in certain kinds of popular discourse today, ascribing supposedly innate characteristics to human groups which mark them as insurmountably different, inferior or superior, morally good or morally evil, thus justifying imperialist or neo-imperialist projects, restrictive border regimes, and unequal social systems that privilege certain social groups over others. However, hybridity can also be more than a supposed exception which confirms the essentialist norm of (usually) insurmountable differences: it blurs binary distinctions between "races" or cultures in a way that highlights the *general* constructedness and artificiality of essentialist "racial" and cultural categories. It thus helps to destabilize these categories and the social (e.g., colonial) hierarchies they underpin. Like mimicry, hybridity is another manifestation of ambivalence which can subvert colonial discourse, Othering, and power relations. This non-essentialist, subversive dimension of hybridity is foregrounded in postcolonial scholarship.[7]

Where colonial subjects deploy the subversive potential of mimicry and hybridity intentionally, this leads us from colonial to anticolonial texts. As the name implies, anticolonial writing aims to contest colonial hegemonies. Here too, various typical patterns of representation have evolved. These include a direct critique of colonial political, economic, and social inequalities, as well as practical initiatives to overthrow them, for instance through political resistance. But these direct measures are also complemented and supported by more discourse-centered resistance strategies, such as questioning the colonizer's authority to narrate the story of the colonized, asserting the colonized's own discursive authority, rewriting history from the perspective of the colonized, "writing back" to colonial literature by again retelling stories from the viewpoint of the margins, and vindicating indigenous traditions. There can also be attempts to revive indigenous cultures that were damaged by colonialism. Sometimes, this takes relatively conservative, reconstructionist, "nativist" forms; but it can also involve a conscious embrace of cultural fusion, for instance between "tradition" and "modernity," or between local and international influences.

"Postcolonialism" likewise has different meanings, some of them focusing more on the material and social sphere, and others focusing more on discourse and culture. For instance, used in a sociohistorical sense, based on the literal meaning of "post" as "after," the term "postcolonialism" can be used to mean "after colonialism." Here the term can, for instance, refer to postindependence efforts of a newly created nation state to give itself viable political structures or decolonize and improve its economic infrastructure. Literary and cultural historians might also use the term historically, to refer to postindependence writing, for instance. Here as well, the "post" in "postcolonialism" is understood in a strictly temporary sense of "pastness," as "after." But there is also a looser usage of the term which relies on a desire to *transcend* colonialism, to leave it behind and *make* it a thing of the past. As this does not happen overnight, vestiges of the colonial inheritance often linger for a considerable time after formal independence, so that many efforts at transcending it also take place in the postindependence period. But they do not begin there: these efforts already begin while colonialism still exists, and tend to play an important role in bringing independence about. In this usage, "postcolonialism" as a movement and as a set of resistant strategies of representation can be synonymous with "anticolonialism." Anticolonial and postcolonial strategies are often very similar and contest colonial hegemonies in similar ways. Sometimes, they articulate counter-perspectives which take the side of the colonized rather than the colonizer's, while not questioning the binarism between colonized and colonizer as such. At other times, they attack the binarism itself, for instance by consciously deploying hybridity as a resistance strategy to deconstruct these distinctions. Some scholars express the distinction between different usages of "postcolonialism" by spelling the term without a hyphen when it is used in this looser, discourse-based transhistorical sense as "anti-," and a desire to transcend which starts already in colonial times, and spelling it with a hyphen when using it in the stricter historical sense of "after" colonialism, that is, "postindependence." This useful distinction is also followed in the present study. I also sometimes use the bracketed form "(post)colonialism" as a convenient shorthand for "colonialism and/or postcolonialism."

Postcolonial studies likewise comprises a wide range of different approaches. For instance, a social science approach might focus on the postindependence period, analyzing post-colonial nation-building policies or economic reforms. In literary and cultural studies, the term "post-colonial" is also sometimes used in a historical sense, for instance to discuss period distinctions between pre- and postindependence literary history, or to chart cultural initiatives to support postindependence nation-building. But generally, the field of postcolonial literary and cultural studies is much wider and also takes in the colonial period. This not only comprises the study of anticolonial cultural resistance, but also the criticial analysis of pro-colonial texts, or more ambivalent colonial representations which stand somewhere in between resistance and collusion. Colonial discourse analysis is an important subfield of postcolonial studies.

Like postcolonial literature or postcolonial cultural activism, postcolonial scholarship can sometime take a nativist counter-perspective without substantially questioning binarisms between colonizer and colonized, but most postcolonial scholarship arguably favors a more deconstructive approach. That is, it favors a non-essentialist understanding of human cultural, "racial," and national groupings which recognizes that these group categories are not based on innate features, but are products of social construction which are underwritten by specific institutions and textual practices. This deconstructive approach also underlies the strong interest of postcolonial studies in hybridity as a phenomenon which subverts essentialist categories and boundaries.[8]

The frequently skeptical attitude of postcolonial scholars toward essentialist constructions of social group categories can also lead to a critique of post-colonial nation-states, their claims of national unity, and the fiction that they represent their entire population. Such skepticism towards the nation-state can, for instance, be found in the postcolonial subfield of subaltern studies, which has transferred Antonio Gramsci's concept of the subaltern, which originally referred to lower-class populations, for instance in Italy, to (post)colonial contexts. While this transfer initially emerged in studies on

South Asia, concepts of subalternity have also been applied to other parts of the colonial and post-colonial world, for instance concerning the special marginality of tribal/indigenous, lower-class, female, and/or LGBT populations within colonial and postcolonial hierarchies, and their relationships to anti- and post-colonial nationalism.[9] Spivak's gender-related discussions of subalternity also offer connections to the concept of "double colonization," which has also been applied to the double marginalization of "native" women in terms of both ethnicity/nationality and gender.[10]

The interest of postcolonial studies in deconstructing ideas of national or ethnic homogeneity, whether due to internal inequalities or due to cultural hybridity, is also reflected in the field's enormous interest in themes of migration and diaspora. To some extent, these interests were always part of postcolonial studies, but currently they are a particularly prominent concern in postcolonial scholarship.[11] Experiences of migration and diaspora almost invariably entail an intense concern with cultural hybridity, as well as the need to engage with contemporary ethno-racial hierarchies and exclusion mechanisms which have survived long beyond the colonial period and still characterize the way in which many nation-states, in the West and elsewhere, deal with migrants and diasporic minorities in their midst. Hence, many strategies of anti- and postcolonial criticism can also be applied to the critique of discrimination and cultural essentialism in scenarios which are not (or no longer) "colonial" in the strict, formal sense.

Another contemporary trend in postcolonial studies, which is partly related to the boom in migration and diaspora studies, is the increasing shift of semantic preference from "postcolonial" to "cosmopolitan" or "transcultural."[12] Again, this shift recognizes that phenomena of culture contact or hybridity are not exclusively restricted to colonial contexts, but can also pertain to other contexts, for example contemporary migrations or life in multicultural global mega-cities. Postcolonial studies recognizes that many of its insights can also be adapted to these new phenomena, but reflects the extension of its purview beyond colonial contexts by a change in terminology which likewise moves away from an exclusively "colonial" reference point.

Recent postcolonial criticism has also shown a marked interest in ecocriticism, which extends the field's interest in conquest, hierarchies, and othering between humans to hierarchies between humans and other—or "Other(ed)"—life forms, to human discourse about the "conquest" of nature, and to the critique of those constructions in favor of more sustainable forms of human-human and human-nonhuman coexistence.[13] Another recent growth sector in postcolonial scholarship is trauma studies.[14] Again, these can either refer to the traumas induced by colonialism or anticolonial wars of independence, or to traumas induced by more recent social phenomena, such as post-colonial civil wars or modern racist violence.[15]

As this overview shows, postcolonial literary and cultural studies are often characterized by a very strong thematic interest in the relationship between language, cultural representation, power imbalances, and violence, as well as the critique of those unequal and violent structures. Nonetheless, the engagement of postcolonial studies with these themes often focuses on particular regions of the world, namely those which were on the receiving end of modern European colonial overseas expansion. For instance, this includes former British colonies in South Asia, Africa, and the Caribbean. Former British "settler colonies" like Australia, Canada, or New Zealand are also often included, although there has been some controversy about whether the white people who dominated those societies had any right to claim (post)colonial status.[16] First, their degree of marginality vis-à-vis the British mother country was less pronounced than the marginality of predominantly nonwhite colonial societies like India, Kenya, Nigeria, Trinidad, and so on—a difference still reflected in the fact that former settler colonies tend to be ranked among the "First World" countries whereas many other former colonies are part of the "Third World." Second, the (post)colonized status of white Australians, Canadians, or New Zealanders is arguably compromised by their role in the colonization and ongoing marginalization of their countries' nonwhite indigenous populations. Despite these problems, the inclusion of these countries under the postcolonial studies umbrella has been strongly advocated and is widely accepted.[17] Comparative postcolonial approaches cross not only "racial" and geographical boundaries, but language boundaries as well: former French colonies in Africa or the Caribbean, or former Spanish colonies in the Caribbean or continental Latin America, are also frequently listed as central areas of postcolonial inquiry. Some understandings of "postcolonial studies" not only refer to cultural products from those regions which reflect on such core "postcolonial themes" as colonialism, anticolonialism, hierarchy, cultural difference, or hybridity, but extend the label "postcolonial" to *any* cultural product which comes from a country that was formally colonized, whether it engages with those themes or not.[18] This regional understanding of postcolonialism also means that postcolonial scholarly engagements with migrants and diasporics often focus particularly on those that are rooted in former colonies, perhaps especially if they face ongoing problems of "race"-based othering and discrimination, as is the case with black and Asian British people, for instance. There is often an uneasy oscillation between a regional and a thematic understanding of the term "postcolonialism." The difference between these two usages is not always made explicit, which can cause complications because they can lead to vastly diverging conclusions about the transferability of postcolonial methods to other contexts. Regional understandings of postcolonialism tie the application of postcolonial patterns of textual analysis to regions of the world that were once subjected to European overseas colonialism, and to migrants and diasporics that hail from those regions. A thematic understanding of postcolonialism, by contrast, begs the question whether postcolonialism's thematic interests in the construction and deconstruction of ethno-cultural hierarchies, culture contact, and so on, should really only be limited to formal (ex-)colonies, or whether these themes can also be found elsewhere, so that the analytical tools developed by postcolonial studies can also be usefully adapted to other regional frameworks, such as Scotland. Some implications of this question will be discussed in the following section.

How Do Scotland and the "Celtic Fringe" Fit into the (Post)Colonial Framework? Connections, Ambiguities, and Limitations

Scotland is not the only country which has been suggested for inclusion in an expanded postcolonial canon. A whole range of "new postcolonialisms," as these extensions of postcolonial studies may be called, have been proposed, especially with regard to (largely white) ethnic minorities and marginalized small nations within Europe itself. These include non-Germans in the Habsburg Empire and non-Russians in the tsarist Russian Empire or (post-) Soviet eastern Europe.[19] Habsburg, Russian, and Soviet imperialism are atypical from a standard postcolonial perspective because these imperialisms did not happen far away overseas, but among neighboring countries, regions, and peoples. There have also been postcolonial discussions of the Jewish diaspora.[20] The new postcolonialisms also include the internal "fringe" regions of the British Isles and the English mainstream's cultural Others in Ireland, Scotland, and Wales. Again, these were atypical "colonies" because they were not officially labeled as such but were often considered integral parts of the mother country, for instance due to greater geographic, cultural, and "racial" proximity. They were also atypical because their quasi-colonial experience started long before the modern period, in the Middle Ages or earlier. If it is so atypical, who do people try to include Scotland in the postcolonial canon at all? Is postcolonialism now no more than a trendy academic bandwagon which Scottish studies scholars are trying to jump onto in order to give a fashionable theoretical and international air to their work? Not necessarily. There are arguably some real parallels. Partly, the parallels which have been proposed are open to debate, but are at least worth mentioning. Other parallels are more consensually accepted. This section will sketch a few central points in Scottish, Gaelic, and "Celtic" social and cultural history, compare these to the checklist of "typical" colonial and postcolonial patterns given above, and discuss parallels and differences between Scottish and overseas (post)colonial experiences.

First, it is important to clarify how Scotland, Gaeldom, and Celticity relate to each other. Some use the term "Celtic fringe" to encompass all regions within the British Isles with a non-English ethnic or national identity and, arguably, a certain history of discursive, political, or economic marginalization by English hegemony, sometimes irrespective of how marginalized such territories are today, and irrespective of whether the inhabitants still speak

Celtic languages. In this sense, the term "Celtic fringe" would also include anglophone Lowland Scotland and even its industrial Central Belt, as well as industrial and comparatively anglicized South Wales. Others argue that these industrialized, urbanized, and anglophone areas are "metropolitan" enough to preclude the labeling of these entire countries as either "Celtic" or "fringe." It is thus argued that the label "Celtic fringe" should only be applied to parts of those countries which are indeed Celtic-speaking, economically disadvantaged, and/or marginalized on account of rurality.[21] It could also be argued that, even before industrialization, Scotland was economically or politically far less marginalized than Wales or Ireland. Nonetheless, some degree of marginality has even pertained at a pan-Scottish level, for instance in political relations between Scotland and England. However, a particularly marginalized part of Scotland can indeed be found on its internal "Celtic fringe," in the traditionally Gaelic-speaking, largely rural, and often economically disadvantaged Highlands and Western Isles.[22] The Gaels were long considered as a separate ethnic group within Scotland, set apart not only by their language and their geographical concentration on the mountains and islands, but also by different political, legal, administrative, and economic structures, as well as distinct cultural traditions, for instance regarding literary conventions, dress, music, and partly also spiritual beliefs. This "Celtic" people was often denigrated by anglophone Lowland Scots in terms which resemble colonial discourse. At times, Celts were even considered as racially distinct from Britain's Anglo-Saxon mainstream, despite their geographical and cultural proximity and despite their shared whiteness. Again, this shows that sameness and otherness are a matter of discursive and social construction, and that even a not-so-distant margin can be considered as radically "other"—different enough to appear comparable to overseas colonized subjects.

But the connection between Celticity and what might be called colonial discourse far predates the foundation of the Scottish state, and goes back to Greek and Roman writers of classical antiquity. It is here that the first recorded uses of the category "Celt" appeared. The labels *Keltoi*, *Celtae*, and related terms were applied to various "barbarian" peoples who usually lived to the northwest of the Greek or Roman "centers" of "civilization." Many of these peoples lived in Continental Europe rather than the British Isles. Even the question of whether they were at least united by mutually related Celtic languages is uncertain. Greek and Roman writers often constructed the relationship between "barbarians" and their own cultures in terms of binary oppositions and civilizational hierarchies, using many strategies of textual representation which reappear in modern colonial discourse. There were also concepts of "civilizing missions," for instance in relation to cultural romanization in conquered imperial provinces. The label "Celtic" was presumably imposed from the outside as a blanket label for a range of peoples whose main commonality was that they were northwestern barbarian Others to some Mediterranean center. As such, the concept of Celticity is from the outset intimately related to cultural power imbalances, problems of discursive authority, and "colonial discourse."[23]

When the Roman Empire collapsed, the blanket category "Celtic" likewise fell out of use. In northern Britain, other ancient "colonial discourse" patterns also became rarer. Post-Roman and early medieval political and cultural relationships between different ethno-political groups often seemed too equivocal and devoid of clear lasting hegemonies to evolve such patterns. And the Gaels, who now emerged as one of the identifiable ethnic groups of Scotland and Ireland, were still far from being a margin; instead, they were very much a mainstream. The Gaels were one of the two "founding peoples" of the Scottish kingdom which emerged in the ninth century. The other founding people were the Picts, another presumably Celtic-speaking people, while anglophone population groups only achieved prominence in the later history of the country. Even in the High Middle Ages, Gaelic was at the heart of the Scottish kingdom: the royal dynasty traced its ancestry back to Ireland and used Gaelic at court, and the language was also widespread among the general population—although there were parts of Lowland Scotland where Scots, rather than Gaelic, was prevalent. Gradually, however, the balance of intra-Scottish political, economic, and cultural power relations tipped toward the Scots-speaking population. Scottish Gaels, like other Celtic-speaking populations in Wales and Ireland, now experienced increasing marginalization from internally and externally expansive Scottish and English states.

At some point, the slowly retreating Scottish Gaelic language started to be imagined mainly as the tongue of the mountainous Highlands and the islands in the west, though sociolinguistic realities of its spread were more complex. The region was also associated with wildness and more primitive ways of life. The dichotomy which then emerged between "civilized Scots-speaking Lowlands" and "wild Gaelic-speaking Highlands" (which often tacitly includes the islands off the west coast) is epitomized in the concept of "the Highland line"—a concept which summarizes the idea that the line which can be drawn on a map between Highlands and Lowlands is congruous with the sociolinguistic line between Gaelic-speaking and non-Gaelic-speaking communities, and with the cultural demarcation between "barbarism" and "civilization." With the reemergence of more stable hegemonies and stronger states, classical antiquity's "colonial discourse" patterns and the concept of the "Celtic" northwestern barbarian likewise experienced a revival and came to be used in English or Lowland-Scottish representations of Celtic-speaking margins. Precisely how this was done will be explored and documented in further detail in the subsequent chapters of this book. For the present, a few introductory remarks will hopefully suffice.

The tendency to see the Gaels as an internal barbarian Other within an otherwise civilized, progressive, and anglophone-dominated Scottish nation-state began in the late medieval period, reached its heyday between the early modern era and the late nineteenth century, but partly even survived into the present. This positioning of the Gaels as an internally marginalized Other within Scotland is mirrored on a larger scale by the internally marginalized position of Scotland as a whole in relation to its more powerful English neighbor. This also becomes more palpable in the early modern period, after the dynastic Union of 1603 which placed these still separate, but unequal states under the same monarch. From now on, British monarchs would often be swayed to privilege English interests over the often conflicting, but less powerful interests of their Scottish subjects. In 1707, the Union of Parliaments completely merged the two states into a single pan-British state. However, neither one of these two political Unions was an act of formal colonial conquest. Scotland was never formally an English colony, but officially an equal partner in a merger of states. Moreover, Scotland is geographically and culturally very close to its English quasi-colonizer, and there has often been a sense of racial proximity as well, albeit with exceptions. In all these respects, distances and hierarchies between Britain and its former overseas colonies have seemed much greater than the inequalities between Scotland and England. Scotland was not *only* an alien, peripheral Other to its English fellow Britons, but also a part of the national "Self": otherness was complemented by a sense of sameness. This is not only true for Scottish-English relations, but also for Gaeldom in relation to anglophone Britons. This distinguishes the Scottish/Gaelic experience from that of indigenous populations in overseas (post)colonies who were often portrayed as *completely* "other." Sameness and proximity to the British mainstream also allowed "internally colonized" Scots, even Gaelic-speaking ones, to transform themselves into colonizers by playing important roles in the overseas empire, alongside their English compatriots. In the eyes of some, this overshadows the Scots' "internally colonized" position within Britain. However, it must be borne in mind that even overseas colonized subjects were sometimes given active roles as colonizers (though merely "assistant" ones, since the higher-ranking positions open to Scots were usually barred to nonwhite overseas colonized subjects), to aid in the subjugation of other overseas colonial populations. Moreover, even the otherness of nonwhite colonized subjects was not always thought to be insurmountable: after all, the fiction of a civilizing mission implied the possibility that they, too, could at least acquire *some* degree of sameness, if not immediately, then at least in future.

Critics of postcolonial approaches in Scottish studies might also cite the fact that Scotland's integration into an English-dominated British state and the anglicization of Scottish culture were largely accomplished by Scotland's own elites rather than being coercively imposed from outside. This does not seem to conform to the more direct and brutal domination which is typically associated with overseas colonialism. While this is indeed a very important caveat, it must also be borne in mind that even overseas colonialism often combined direct rule and violent coercion with more indirect and subtle forms of control. As noted above, British colonialism is especially well known for the extent to which it relied on indirect rule. If we recall that indirect rule, the cooperation of local intermediaries, and voluntary self-anglicizations of ambitious colonized subjects were also features of British overseas colonialism, the difference between the latter and "internal colonialism" in Scotland might appear to be a difference in degree rather than a difference in kind. Moreover, more direct forms of subjugation and coercion were not entirely absent in the Scottish context either, as the following chapters will show. In the Highlands in particular, political subjugation under central state authority and the introduction of capitalism had a stronger element of external imposition and often took more violent forms. Here especially, comparisons with overseas colonialism do not seem entirely far-fetched. In addition to the more classical paradigms of (post)colonial studies, Highland history and its textual representation may also afford connections with the more recent subfield of postcolonial trauma studies, for instance regarding the government's punitive measures in the Highlands after the mid-eighteenth-century rebellion.

The Highland economy also took more obviously "colonial" forms than the economy of the Lowlands. The latter remained relatively diversified even after the Union with England and later even became a major center of industrialization and international commerce. In the Highlands, we have a more typically "colonial" scenario: reliance on only a small range of products, mainly raw materials for export, and accordingly a great vulnerability to agricultural misfortunes and price fluctuations. Poverty in the Highlands was often greater, and living standards were lower than in the Lowlands.

There were also initiatives to implant small contingents of Lowland settlers in the Highlands in order to aid the establishment of modern capitalist "civilization" in the region. There was also large-scale dispossession and enforced displacement of Highland farmers from their lands, the so-called Highland Clearances. Often these were cataclysmic experiences which might afford further connections to postcolonial trauma studies. The various agricultural and infrastructural "improvement" projects to "tame" and "modernize" the Highland landscape, and the various literary responses to those projects, can also be studied through an ecocritical lens.[24] Some of the displaced clearance victims were resettled on less desirable tracts of Highland territory (arguably similar to the less desirable lands often used for "Indian reservations" in North America), where they were vulnerable to further exploitation. Others went to the industrial centers of the Lowlands. Yet others were forcibly or (more or less) voluntarily relocated to the "New World," sometimes in so-called coffin ships which were hardly seaworthy so that migrants risked their lives by traveling in them, and which were so tightly packed and unhygienic that some observers were tempted to compare them to the slave ships of the Middle Passage. If they made it, however, even Gaelic migrants from Scotland had the chance to transform themselves from "intra-British colonized" to overseas colonizers of nonwhite indigenous populations and repeat the dispossessions, denigrations, and discrimination they had experienced at home in a different context abroad. Again, this change of roles has justly been cited as a caveat which limits the applicability of the label "colonized" to the Scots. However, the mainstream of international postcolonial studies has already long accepted the application of the labels "colonized" and "postcolonial" to the white people who dominated British "settler colonies" like Australia, Canada, or New Zealand, *although* it has rightly been doubted whether these people had any right to claim colonized status in light of the fact that whiteness still gave them access to a great deal of privilege and power compared to the much more marginalized nonwhite populations in their own countries (whom they often actively helped to suppress) and in other parts of the world. If we accept white Canadians or New Zealanders (many of whom actually came from Gaelic Scotland) as "(post)colonized," then why not accept the application of the same label to Gaelic Scots at home?

In addition to these political and economic ambiguities, there are also cultural ambiguities which are important to the discussion of whether Scotland, or at least its Gaels, can be considered as internally colonized within an anglocentric Britain. As already noted, Scots were not only England's Other, but also a fellow British "Same": the sense of cultural difference was less pronounced than in overseas contexts. Especially the Scots-speaking Lowlands were often considered as an anglophone sister country to England, though perhaps a slightly more rustic and unpolished one. Also, anglicization in Scotland—particularly in the Scots-speaking areas where the change to Standard English was relatively easy to accomplish—was often voluntary and self-imposed, rather than being imposed through direct English pressure. Nonetheless, a sense of linguistic and cultural hierarchy pertained even here, and probably exerted indirect pressure on ambitious Scots to anglicize their accents, habits, and tastes. But again, this does not entirely preclude comparisons with overseas colonies because similar processes of self-anglicization by career-oriented "natives" appeared there, too. In the Gaidhealtachd, the sense of difference from, and inferiority to, Britain's anglocentric mainstream again appeared greater than in anglophone, Lowland Scotland. Here, the pressures for anglicization were even greater, and could also take a more direct form, for instance in anti-Gaelic legislation.

The devaluation of local languages is not the only colonial discourse pattern that is relevant to Scotland. "Ignoble" forms of primitivism were also identified in Scotland's pre-Union history, which was seen as backward and unprogressive, thus justifying the Union as a kind of civilizing mission which opened the way for Scotland's progress. Even more backwardness was projected onto Highland history to justify the region's more energetic integration into the modern central state, first the Scottish and then the British one. There were also dismissals of Highland orature and literature, spiritual beliefs, clothing, and music. External initiatives to bring "civilization" to

Gaels included the introduction of an anglocentric school system, religious missions, and an eighteenth-century ban on Highland dress.

As in overseas colonial discourse, not all local features were seen as ignoble; there were also idealizations of "noble savagery." English or anglicized Scottish elites developed a romantic taste for Robert Burns's Scots poems as an attractive specimen of the simple charms of Lowland rusticity; and kilted Highlanders were romanticized as primitive warrior heroes (and useful, exploitable cannon fodder) or objectified as fascinatingly exotic and wild hypermasculine sex symbols.

Although colonial discourse patterns were applied to both Lowlands and Highlands, the overseas colonial connection is particularly strong in the latter. Celtic and non-European "barbarians" were often discussed in a parallel manner, so much so that various scholars have used the terms "Celticism" and "Highlandism" in analogy to "Orientalism," in deliberate allusion to Said's work, thus underlining the connections between "Celts" and colonial discourse.[25]

If we regard the entirety of Scotland as an internal colony within the borders of the British state, Scotland's own internal Gaelic margin can be termed "doubly" or "multiply" colonized. In international postcolonial studies, the concept of double or multiple colonization refers to various particularly disadvantaged segments of a colony's population, such as women or indigenous populations within white settler colonies. In analogy to the latter, the concept might also be applied to the Gaelic minority within an already marginalized Scotland. For instance, as Michael Newton has aptly put it, Lowlanders often "passed on to the Highlanders the derision they felt coming from the English," and "anti-Gaelic prejudices of the Lowland élite can be seen as projections upon the Highlands of what they rejected in themselves in their efforts to become respectable and . . . 'civilised' in the eyes of the European élite"—including the English elite, which was often the dominant reference point in the British framework.[26] To some extent, Gaeldom can also be viewed through the lens of subaltern studies, since people from this ethno-linguistic minority (and especially from its monoglot, non-English-speaking, and partly also illiterate lower classes) were not only particularly disadvantaged in political and economic terms, but also in terms of representation, as these voices were often completely devalued and silenced, not only by the colonizer but also by their own local elites.[27]

The mixture of attraction and repulsion which often characterizes colonial encounters can also be seen in Scottish people's reactions to single or double "internal colonial" hierarchies. Inferiorization and anglocentrism caused Lowland and Highland Scottish resentment, but there were also internalizations of such ideologies, resulting in cultural cringes and a desire to imitate the "colonizer" through self-anglicization. But here as well, mimicry and hybridity can also have a subversive dimension. Highland writers, for instance, could seize the English language and anglophone literary genres to express Gaelic perspectives through a new medium and create an "anticolonial" counter-discourse.

Issues of hybridity are perhaps especially evident in contexts of migration. Postcolonial insights into migrant sensibilities, diasporic identities, and the relations between diasporic minorities and their host society's mainstream can also illuminate the experiences and textual productions of the many Scottish writers from Highland backgrounds who had moved to the Lowlands or England and wrote for predominantly anglophone audiences. The same applies to Scottish Lowland writers who had moved to England and/or tried to capture the English literary market. Intra-British marginalization also played an important part in overseas migration, transformed "internally colonized" populations into global colonizers, and helped to create an international Scottish diaspora which is already a major focus of interest in contemporary Scottish studies scholarship.[28] Postcolonial theories of diaspora culture can make further useful contributions to this lively field.

Critiques of Scotland's or the Gaidhealtachd's "internally colonized" status were not only articulated in anglophone writings by hybridized Highlanders, but also in other areas of Scottish literature and culture, both Highland and Lowland. Direct critiques of the Scottish-English Union, of the subjugation of the Highlands, and of economic marginalization were complemented by vindications of local history and culture, writing back to the colonizer's literature, and nativist attempts at cultural revival.

If there were so many shared features between representations of Scotland and its Gaels on the one hand and overseas (post)colonial discourse on the other, why is Scotland so often overlooked by the international mainstream of postcolonial studies? First, some postcolonialists still rely too much on a concept of colonialism which assumes very clear dichotomies, hierarchies, differences, and culture clashes. For those scholars, the strong ambiguities of the Scottish case seem to preclude Scotland's inclusion in the remit of postcolonial studies. However, a more nuanced understanding of colonial and imperial sociocultural realities often dismantles simplistic dichotomies between colonized and colonizer, even in overseas contexts, so that Scotland's ambiguities may be less atypical than some may have supposed. In this light, Scotland's ambiguities do not really preclude postcolonial readings: rather, they tie in to postcolonialism's ever-increasing interest in deconstructing binarisms, even in overseas (post)colonial situations. Scotland's internal cultural complexities and inequalities, as well as its Janus-faced position between margin and periphery within the United Kingdom and its empire, are highly pertinent subjects for postcolonial investigation.

A second reason why postcolonial scholars often neglect Scotland may simply be that the first systematic theories about literary negotiations of cultural encounters and hierarchies were developed with an eye to formally (post)colonial contexts, so that it may merely not occur to certain scholars to look for similar discourse patterns elsewhere. Third, and relatedly, there is the aforementioned ambiguity between regional and thematic understandings of postcolonial studies. Postcolonial scholars have often been reluctant to accept Scotland into the (post)colonial fold because they understood postcolonial studies primarily in regional rather than thematic terms, focusing on areas outside Europe which were once formally colonized, a description which Scotland does not fit. Scotland's many thematic and ideological parallels to (post)colonial contexts were thus overlooked. For instance, some postcolonialists are perfectly prepared to regard any aspect of Trinidadian or Canadian literature as postcolonial because it comes from a former official colony, while being unwilling to accept Scottish anti-hegemonic nationalist literature as postcolonial because it comes from the "wrong region" of the world, one that was never officially a colony.[29] Making the problem of the field's dual regional/thematic orientation more explicit might increase awareness of the blind spots which have limited comparative postcolonial studies so far, and may open the path for the inclusion of hitherto neglected regions which can yield fruitful material for thematic comparison. The recent shift in various scholars' terminological preference from "postcolonial studies" to "transcultural studies" might aid this development because dropping the label "postcolonial" bypasses the aforementioned terminological debate about the suitability of "(post)colonial" labels in a Scotland which was never officially an English colony, while a field rechristened from "postcolonial" to "transcultural" studies still retains key postcolonial thematic preoccupations like cultural multiplicity and inequality which are also major themes in Scottish studies.

Comparative investigations of ethnic othering and marginalization not only offer important benefits for the field of postcolonial studies, but for Scottish studies as well. International postcolonial scholarship has developed a plethora of tools for analyzing phenomena which are also central in Scottish studies, such as multi- and transculturalism, the (re)construction of national identities, and correlations between social and cultural power imbalances. Comparative postcolonialism also highlights the complex interconnections between Scottish writing and other "peripheral" discourses further afield.

Skeptics might also ask whether the ever-expanding field of postcolonial studies undermines its own credibility by declaring its theories applicable to more and more different contexts, until its claims become so universal that all specificity and hermeneutic value is lost. But the same might be asked of *any* comparative approach. There must always be a balance between generalization and comparison on the one hand, and specificity and difference on the other. As long as this is borne in mind, postcolonial Scottish studies promises to be a valid approach that can yield many useful insights into both international parallels and local specificities.

So much for the general arguments that can be cited in favor of postcolonial Scottish, Gaelic, and "Celtic fringe" studies, and for the limitations and ambiguities which need to be borne in mind. In the next section, I will give brief pointers to previous scholarly work in this field, identify gaps which the present study is trying to fill, and give some general explanations on its approach.

Postcolonial Scottish Studies and the Rationale of This Book

For a long time, "Celtic fringe postcolonialism" mainly focused on Ireland, while Scotland and Wales remained relatively neglected.[30] Postcolonial approaches to Scottish studies that were more sustained and explicit only emerged belatedly in the 1990s, mainly in the form of isolated essays or themed journal issues.[31] The first few books with expressly postcolonial titles appeared only in the last few years, and even these have not yet provided a sufficient systematic introduction, especially with regard to the large field of anglophone writing.[32] *Scottish Literature and Postcolonial Literature* (2011), edited by Michael Gardiner, Graeme Macdonald, and Niall O'Gallagher, and *Within and Without Empire: Scotland across the (Post)Colonial Borderline* (2013), edited by Carla Sassi and Theo van Heijnsbergen, cover both Gaelic and anglophone texts and contain very helpful analyses, but as multiauthored essay collections they throw spotlights on individual case studies rather than providing systematic contextualization and a continuous narrative.[33] They are thus more useful to Scottish studies specialists than as general introductions to Scottish postcolonialism for those who are unfamiliar with Scottish frameworks and thus need more contextualization and systematization than coedited volumes can offer.

Moreover, the volume by Gardiner et al. focuses largely on the twentieth and twenty-first century, whereas many earlier sociohistorical and literary phenomena to which recent postcolonial Scottish literature and criticism responds are not elucidated. Readers who are not specialists in Scottish studies and approach the field from a comparative perspective might find it helpful to read studies of recent Scottish cultural phenomena alongside an introduction to earlier (post)colonially relevant developments in Scottish society and culture. The present study focuses precisely on those earlier frameworks, thus filling a gap within postcolonial Scottish studies itself. This widening of historical scope also aims to strengthen the position of postcolonial Scottish studies as a whole, as an equally important subfield of "Celtic fringe" postcolonialism alongside the hitherto more established Irish branch. Hence, this book also contributes to filling a gap in "Celtic fringe" postcolonialism. A third gap concerns the relationship between "Celtic fringe" and other postcolonialisms: so far, postcolonial approaches to Scottish, Welsh, and to some extent also Irish culture remain largely confined to the respective regional studies, without much attention from the international postcolonial mainstream.[34] Partly, this one-sidedness might be attributable to a lack of introductory studies which provide sufficient background information to be accessible to international postcolonialists who are relatively unfamiliar with "Celtic fringe" contexts. This book aims to provide such an introduction. To maximize accessibility, this book works within a wide historical, theoretical, and generic framework, combining introductory overviews on sociocultural and discursive developments with more detailed case studies of selected literary and nonliterary texts. These case studies combine lesser-known works like William Sharp's *Green Fire* with highly canonical texts like Walter Scott's *Waverley*. Although this book is mainly conceptualized as an introduction, it also hopes to offer some new insights to more specialized readers, for instance by opening up new ways of reading Scottish authors (e.g., in chapters 2 and 6) who, though well-known and important, have been somewhat neglected by modern literary criticism.

This volume also aims to promote a more interdisciplinary approach, combining postcolonial readings of literature in the narrow sense with discussions of primary texts from many other fields, including political, legal, and administrative documents, writings by missionaries and educators, historiography, journalism, letters, ethnography, and anthropology. Thus, it expands on previous work in postcolonial Scottish studies which largely focuses on literature. This breadth of scope within a single study is a necessary step toward overcoming previous limitations and argumentative deadlocks. So far, most attempts to establish Scottish themes as a subfield of international postcolonial studies have worked on a smaller scale. Acceptance of these initiatives was sometimes hampered by the widespread assumption that the *general* framework of Scottish social and ideological history could never possibly warrant inclusion in colonial or postcolonial categories, and that small-scale Scottish postcolonial case studies must be taking their sources out of context. This again suggests a need for a more wide-ranging single-volume introduction which demonstrates that the examples analyzed by previous Scottish postcolonial scholarship were not isolated exceptions, but form part of a general matrix of colonial and postcolonial themes which surface in Scottish culture again and again. While it is still impossible to give a complete picture of *all* the relevant issues, this book surveys the most important themes and developments over three centuries and combines these with a representative selection of case studies. This hopefully provides a more solid basis for discussing the advantages and pitfalls of incorporating this particular British "fringe" into the postcolonial field.

This book charts the ways in which Scotland's anglophone mainstream constructed and reconstructed its image of the Gaelic margins in the light of two simultaneous developments: the emergence of the modern nation-state with its drive for internal homogenization, and the rise of overseas colonialism which brought British people into contact with a wide range of external cultural Others and entailed intense debates over ethnic differences and hierarchies, civilizing missions, hybridity, progress and regression, expropriation, exploitation, and resistance. Although the earliest manifestations of these developments can be traced back to the fifteenth and sixteenth centuries, a more noticeable impact of modern nation-state-building and colonialism on Gaelic sociocultural realities and their representation in anglophone mainstream discourse becomes evident from the early seventeenth century onwards. Key dates include the dynastic Union between Scotland and England in 1603, legal acts from 1609 and 1616 which aimed to weaken the Scottish Gaelic language and culture through anglicizing education, and the intensification of imperial efforts marked by colonial settlements in Northern Ireland (1609 onwards) and North America (e.g., Jamestown, Virginia 1607; Plymouth, Massachusetts 1620). Thus, this book's main chapters set in around the year 1600. They trace the changing fortunes of Gaeldom in mainstream representations until around 1900—a time which can be regarded as a high point in European certainties about the ethnic nation-state, in Union-British patriotic self-satisfaction, and in imperial overseas expansion. The twentieth century increasingly unsettled ideals of national homogeneity, the unionist consensus, and the frontiers of the disintegrating colonial empires. This also set radically new parameters for the treatment of colonial and postcolonial themes in Scottish literature. These post-1900 shifts cannot be covered within the scope of this one book and, moreover, have already received slightly more attention from previous scholarship in postcolonial Scottish studies. Hence, the year 1900 forms a natural end point for the survey provided in this volume.

To some extent, the discursive trends outlined here with regard to anglophone *Scottish* writing reflect wider British developments that can also be observed in writing from England—for instance concerning romanticism. Hence, some of the issues discussed in this volume can also provide an entry point to English "colonial discourse" about Scotland and its Gaels. But there are also important differences between anglophone discourses in the two countries, for example when they represent rival patriotisms. English texts and their complex interrelations with anglophone Scottish discourse likewise deserve further postcolonial investigation.[35] However, it is impossible to do these complexities justice within a single introductory study. Thus, it has been decided to focus the present inquiry mainly on Scottish authors, with occasional brief cross-referencing to relevant English texts and issues.

Although this book includes a considerable amount of sociohistorical information (e.g., on political debates or economic development), this should not be understood as an attempt to determine whether Scottish *realities* can "objectively" be labeled as "colonial." Neither are these discussions primarily intended as a political intervention in the debates on further devolution, Scottish independence, and greater regional autonomy for the Highlands. Rather, the main purpose of the sociohistorical discussions in this book is to provide background information on key issues around which debates about Scottish and Gaelic marginality and/or coloniality regularly revolve. The sociohistorical sections of this volume chart issues which might be read as (post)colonial or already have been read as (post)colonial to facilitate the understanding of a wider critical debate and of the primary sources that negotiate these realities on the cultural level. The labels "colonial" and "postcolonial" are here mainly used as categories of discourse analysis, and of literary and cultural studies. The main question in this book is how Scotland, its Gaidhealtachd, and their relation to the English and British state have been *represented*, for instance in literary texts which *claim* that the Gaels are comparable to colonized peoples overseas. Whether these representations are historically accurate is not my prime concern, even where I hint at *possible* answers to this question. At times, I also list more than one possible interpretation of the same historical circumstance—again, ways of seeing and traditions of representation are more central to this book than a quest for "objective fact." This ties into Peter Hulme's understanding of the postcolonial as "a descriptive, not an evaluative, term"—an approach which can be extended from the postcolonial to the colonial.[36] Colonial discourse analysis and postcolonial studies have evolved a wealth of conceptual tools which elucidate the relationship between language, cultural representation, and power imbalances in situations of culture contact. Many of these tools can also be applied to intercultural power asymmetries in contexts which are not colonial in the traditional sense—for instance, concerning the relation between majority and minority cultures within the same nation-state, as in the Scottish/British case. That is, the present study assumes the existence of social and cultural power imbalances which have often been *textualized* in ways that resemble the textualization of overseas colonial kinds of power imbalance. These textual parallels do not necessarily require that Scottish *realities* always conform to overseas colonial patterns as well (e.g., in terms of economic statistics). This is why I use the term "colonial *imagination*": it signals that Scotland and its Gaelic margin have often been textualized, represented, and *imagined* in colonial terms, even where the *realities* of Scotland's political or economic predicament also showed considerable differences from overseas colonial contexts. This colonial imagination is responsible for the frequent representation of Scotland through colonial discourse tropes, and often even through direct comparisons to overseas colonies. Thus, I use the term "colonial imagination" to refer to the application of colonial and anticolonial representation patterns to Scotland in creative writing, but also in other genres, between 1600 and 1900. I also use "colonial imagination" to refer to modern Scottish writers and Scottish studies academics who have been drawn to (post)colonial comparisons, again despite the likewise existing differences from overseas (post)colonial patterns.

The concept of the "Celtic" is a particularly interesting instance of the colonial imagination. It implies imagined commonalities between many different "barbarian" Others over vast temporal and spatial distances, from the ancient Roman Empire to the modern British nation-state and its own imperial ventures overseas. One of the themes of this book is how various modern texts about Scotland and its Gaels refer back to ancient Roman writings about "Celtic barbarians," thus imagining connections between Roman imperial civilizing missions and modern British efforts to assimilate its internal Others to form a more homogeneous nation state. At the same time, it shows how images of Scotland and the "Celtic" world functioned as precedents and models for the representation of the British Empire's overseas colonies. In turn, discourse on overseas colonized peoples also influenced the representation of Scots and "Celts," both by themselves and by others. This book demonstrates various instances of such "transperipheral" comparisons in colonial discourse.[37] On this basis, it argues that Scotland and the "Celtic fringe" should not be seen as a mere marginal note to postcolonial studies, but as a highly central part of the field because they form a nodal point where different kinds of (post)colonialism intersect: not only do they form a bridge between premodern and modern (post)colonial discourse, but they also offer reference points for studying the connection between "internal" and "external" colonialism, and the relationship between textualizations of Europe's internal minorities and marginalized small nations on the one hand and the representation of European overseas colonialism on the other.

Paradigms of postcolonial theory which are especially relevant to this study of Scottish representations include internal colonialism within the borders of a given state, as well as double or multiple colonization of particularly disadvantaged segments of a colony's population.[38] Other postcolonial paradigms which are central to the present study include contests for discursive authority, negative and positive stereotypes of otherness (such as "barbarism" versus "noble savagery"), civilizational hierarchies, "civilizing missions," cultural cringes, and writing back. Equally central are essentialist constructs of cultural or national authenticity, as well as contrary manifestations of ambivalence and hybridity which partly reflect the "success" of assimilation projects, but partly also expose the internal instability of colonial discourse by questioning essentialist categories and concepts of otherness. In addition, it is shown how hybrid textual practices (such as anglophone travel writing by Gaelic authors) can be deliberately used for anticolonial counter-representations, criticising the colonizer on his own linguistic and generic turf.

Before embarking on a more detailed overview of the following chapters, it might be useful to add some further clarifications on this book's use of terminology. Wherever essentialist categories and dichotomies, or cultural hierarchizations, are mentioned here, they are not intended as descriptions of actually existing sociocultural realities, but as descriptions of the attempt made by colonial discourse to construct such essences, dichotomies, and hierarchies. For instance, "race" and other problematic terms like "savage," "barbarian," or "civilization" are often cited in this study as important components of the colonial discourse it analyzes. Naturally, these citations should not be taken to imply that I endorse these concepts myself. To emphasize critical distance, I often put these terms into quotation marks. However, to increase typographic simplicity and readability, I have not used quotation marks throughout, but omitted them where the danger of misunderstanding seemed smallest. For instance, in phrases like "notions of barbarism and civilization," the term "notions" seems signal enough that I am merely summarizing others' ideas, rather than expressing my own, so I have not put "barbarism" and "civilization" in quotation marks. However, phrases like "the 'barbarians' of the Highlands" might, without quotation marks, be misread to imply that I myself consider the Highlanders as culturally inferior; hence I have retained the inverted commas in such contexts. While the terms listed above come from colonial discourse and are concepts which I *entirely* reject myself, I sometimes also use quotation marks for terms from contemporary colloquial or academic usage which I do not entirely reject but where I recognize that they are at least *partially* problematic and contested. Such terms include "Celtic," "Celtic fringe," "periphery," "center," "metropolis," "mainstream," and "internal colonialism." At times, these concepts are merely cited as part of other people's positions, but at times I also recognize their usefulness myself, for instance as convenient shorthands in the absence of better terms (e.g., with "Celtic fringe" as a blanket label for Scotland, Ireland, and Wales as the non-English parts of the British Isles, although the respective extent of their "Celticness" or "fringeness" is debatable), or as concepts which have at least *some* analytical validity despite their limitations (as with "internal colonialism"). The concepts are thus used, but their limitations and contested status are often highlighted by quotation marks, though readability has again required that quotation marks are not used in every instance.

Chapter Overview

The general developments outlined in this study can be subdivided into three roughly chronological phases and discursive strands. The assimilationist, progressivist, and "Enlightened" mindset which accompanied the establishment and consolidation of the modern nation-state from the early modern period until about the second half of the eighteenth century tended to see the Gaels mainly in negative terms, as an internal barbarian Other whose culture was inferior to that of the Scottish Lowlands or England. Accordingly, the "improvement" of the Gaels through assimilation was considered desirable. Moreover, it was usually deemed possible—the Enlightenment especially showed an emphatic belief in the potential of education. These two factors—the desirability and possibility of "improvement"—are the main issues around which the distinction of discourse phases revolves.

In the next phase, which mainly began during the second half of the eighteenth century and continued into the first half of the nineteenth, the mainstream's opinion of Gaeldom became more positive—Scotland's Highlanders mutated from "ignoble" into "noble savages." This romantic idealization of cultural difference occurred when the conquest and transformation of the "barbarian" Other was already far advanced, that is, after the possibility of transformation was proven. But the desirability of this transformation was no longer as certain as it had seemed to Enlightenment progressivists.

The third phase is dominated by racial determinism and started with a return to more anti-Gaelic attitudes, with hostility culminating in the mid-nineteenth century. Anti-Gaelic racists would agree with Enlightenment beliefs that there was a universal hierarchy of human cultural achievement, that the superiority of the center in all respects was obvious, and that it would be desirable if all other cultures could transform themselves in the center's image. However, the possibility of such transformations was now questioned: many racists believed that the hierarchy of cultures was fixed in humanity's biological makeup. In the later decades of the nineteenth century, racial determinism was also reinterpreted in the service of *pro*-Gaelic discourse.

These three phases of shifting perspectives on the Highlands are, of course, chronologically not entirely separate: they often coexist, sometimes even within the work of the same author. Nonetheless, the respective overall popularity of Enlightened progressivism, romanticism, and racism varies over time. To reflect these broad shifts, and for conceptual clarity, I have assigned two chapters to each of the three patterns. Chapters 1 and 2 are largely concerned with ideologies of progress, assimilation, and Enlightenment. Chapters 3 and 4 focus on romanticism and "noble savagery," but also on ways in which these conceptual developments can be reconciled with earlier, progressivist notions which endorsed "progress" and "civilizing missions." Chapters 5 and 6 examine the relation between Highlandism (or Celticism) and biologistic racism.

Chapter 1 charts the growing marginalization of Gaeldom, first in the independent early modern Scottish state and then, after the 1707 Union with England, in the British state. Both states pursued a course of internal homogenization which entailed political and administrative centralization; the transformation of residual pockets of feudalism and other premodern forms of economic organization into fully integrated divisions of the new capitalist economy; the assimilation of speakers of "inferior dialects" like Scots and "inferior" languages like Gaelic to anglocentric linguistic norms; and further cultural unification in the fields of religion and education. These projects often used considerable pressure and violence, but were considered legitimate means to advance the "civilizing mission" of uplifting primitive "savages" or "barbarians" into a superior, progressive modernity. Such intra-national "civilizing missions" were frequently compared to similar projects pursued simultaneously in Europe's overseas colonies, for instance in North America. "Colonial discourse" from antiquity (especially the Roman Empire) was rediscovered as a model for seventeenth- and eighteenth-century British approaches to internal and external "barbarian Others." This chapter surveys key sociohistorical and cultural aspects of these developments, and illustrates the pervasiveness of colonial comparisons through a wide range of brief examples from various genres: political and legal documents; historiography; pamphlets; reports by missionaries, educators and administrators; journalism; letters; and poetry.

Chapter 2 follows with a much more detailed reading of two particular sample texts: Martin Martin's *A Description of the Western Islands of Scotland* and *A Late Voyage to St. Kilda*. Like many of the texts surveyed in the previous chapter, these two pieces of travel writing endorse the assimilationist drive of the new capitalist nation-state and discuss the Gaelic world in comparison to other colonial formations. However, Martin's works are particularly interesting because, unlike many of the other texts, they were written by an author who was a Gael himself, albeit a strongly hybridized one who was well-integrated into the anglophone mainstream. In his writings, more straightforward colonial discourse paradigms are complicated by potentially subversive elements such as an uneasy oscillation between "inside" and "outside" identifications, othering and "same-ing," or denigration and vindication. Martin's ambiguous position as a hybridized "native intellectual" parallels phenomena which are frequently observed in overseas (post)colonial contexts.[39] As he relocated from the Gaelic Hebrides to largely anglophone metropolitan environments, he is also relevant to the currently very strong interest of postcolonial studies in migrant and diasporic identities and in diasporic minority writing addressing mainstream readerships.[40]

Chapter 3 charts the growing importance of the concept of the "noble savage" in representations of Scotland and its Gaels in the late eighteenth and early nineteenth century. Again, this is contextualized in relation to key sociohistorical and cultural developments of the time. The different variants of the "noble savage" trope in Gaelic contexts are also discussed in relation to the colonial logic and the permutations of "noble savagery" in overseas colonial contexts. This includes not only a discussion of Gaels as another "colonized" population, but also their transformation into overseas colonizers who were themselves complicit in the subjugation and exploitation of non-European peoples. Analogous to chapter 1, chapter 3 surveys a wide range of examples from poetry and literary criticism, letters, fashion, royal pageantry, historiography, ethnography, tourism, and travel writing.

Chapter 4 provides another close reading of an exemplary and highly influential literary text: Walter Scott's novel *Waverley*. As a non-Gaelic author, Scott projects the perspective of a partly sympathetic outsider. Despite his outside position, there is again ambivalence between nativist vindications of difference and elements of colonial discourse. There is also a synthesis between the two main strands of colonial discourse discussed in the preceding three chapters, namely a denigration of "ignoble savagery" in favor of progressivism and modernization on the one hand, and on the other hand a romantic idealization of "noble savagery" which emphasizes the downsides of "progress," though the latter is often pronounced inevitable. To some extent, Scott endorses and capitalizes on the romantic fashion for noble savagery, but he also ironicizes it, ultimately tending rather towards earlier notions of Enlightenment progressivism—now tempered with a degree of respect for the margins' cultural past which promises a more benign and successful national synthesis on both the pan-Scottish and pan-British levels.

Chapter 5 traces the shift from such integrationism to a reassertion of insurmountable ethnic differences through biologistic race theories. This particular strand of colonial discourse emerged in the late eighteenth century, but only reached its heyday in the Victorian period. Previously, Celticist texts had often provided models for the textual representation of overseas colonial encounters. Now it was the other way round: racialist theories, originally developed mainly with regard to nonwhite overseas colonized subjects, were transferred to the white European mainstream's internal Others such as the "Celtic fringe." An allegedly immutable Gaelic racial otherness and inferiority was cited to justify expropriation, extermination, or expulsion. A survey of key sociohistorical developments which led to this ideological shift is combined with discussions of sample texts from historiography, journalism, and especially anthropology, the focal text being Robert Knox's *The Races of Men*.

Chapter 6 demonstrates that racial categories even permeated texts which aimed to defend and rehabilitate the Gaels or the "Celtic race" as a whole. This is illustrated by a close reading of *Green Fire*—another novel by a non-Gaelic anglophone author, William Sharp, alias "Fiona Macleod"—and of two anthropological essays which were published by a key organization of the Gaelic revival, the Gaelic Society of Inverness: J. Macgregor's "Celts and Teutons" and L. Macbean's "The Mission of the Celt." The latter two also provide further illustration of the Gaels' ambivalent position as both "internally colonized" and overseas colonizers, as the authors redefine the Celts from an inferior subject race into a fellow master race destined to rule Britain's global empire shoulder to shoulder with their Anglo-Saxon compatriots.

The conclusion provides an outlook on the rise of more *radically* anticolonial or postcolonial voices in Scotland, a trend which is mainly observable since the early twentieth century but also had some early manifestations in the nineteenth. This final chapter also summarizes key theoretical points which can be drawn from the analyses in the preceding chapters, and discusses their wider implications for contemporary and future developments in Scottish and international postcolonial studies.

Chapter 1

✦

The Modern Nation-State and Its Others

Civilizing Missions at Home and Abroad, ca. 1600 to 1800

In the early modern period, Scotland's central government authorities increased their efforts to bring the kingdom's geographical and political "fringes" more fully under their control, aiming to align the cultures and societies of these margins with the principles of the emerging capitalist nation-state. Among the various fringes which existed, the Gaidhealtachd turned out to be particularly resilient to such streamlining efforts. Already existing Lowland traditions of representing Highlanders as inferior and potentially hostile Others gained new energy and a new tone. In the Middle Ages, such antagonisms had often been portrayed with a certain playfulness, almost like the good-humored banter one finds between neighboring but slightly rivaling villages or small islands. But early modern Lowland discourse about Gaels appears more earnest, reflecting the modern nation's impatience with alternative ways of life.

The sense of cultural antagonism was also fueled by disputes about the rights of the Stuart royal dynasty. Having ruled Scotland since 1371 and England since 1603, their authority was called into question by the Civil Wars of 1639 to 1651, culminating in the execution of King Charles I in 1649 and the subsequent Cromwellian interregnum. The Stuart monarchy was restored in 1660, but was unsettled again by the Revolution of 1688 which deposed the Catholic king James II and strengthened the role of parliamentary powers. Although the dynasty initially continued to rule through two female Protestant Stuart monarchs, the throne passed to the Protestant House of Hanover in 1714, bypassing Catholic Stuart claimants like James II, his son (also James), and grandson (Charles Edward, alias "Bonnie Prince Charlie"). During and after these various seventeenth- and eighteenth-century disruptions, many (though by no means all) Gaels continued to support the Stuart dynasty, including its Catholic representatives. Supporters of the deposed James II and his Catholic line after 1688 were called "Jacobites" (derived from "Jacobus," the Latin form of "James"). Jacobites existed in all parts of the British Isles and acted from a range of motives. Some believed in the divine right of kings and thus considered deposition by revolution as unacceptable. Some were Catholics themselves and thus preferred a Catholic monarch. Some belonged to other marginalized denominations, such as Episcopalianism, and channeled their dissatisfaction with the current status quo into the hope that a change of dynasty would further their interests. Similar calculations were sometimes made by Gaels who felt wronged by the current government's policies or representatives: Jacobitism offered a chance to avenge themselves on their enemies and a hope of better fortunes under a new status quo. Some may have felt that their ambitions for office, fortune, or lands had no realistic chance under the present system, but that Jacobitism offered a high-risk gamble which, in the event of success, would give them a new monarchy that would gratefully reward their services by granting them the boons they desired. After 1707, certain adversaries of the Union likewise pinned their hopes on Jacobitism, hoping that the restoration of the old line would also restore separate English and Scottish statehood. Furthermore, some patriots objected to the German origins of the Hanoverian dynasty and preferred the Stuarts due to their British background. Jacobitism also became a rallying ground for other kinds of social discontent. Hence, the movement was very diverse, and not all goals were necessarily compatible or realistic. Nonetheless, it was an important social force, and many of its complexities were neglected in the simplistic portrayals it received from both supporters and adversaries. For instance, although Scottish Highlanders played an important role in the movement and provided its military backbone, not all Highlanders were Jacobites, and not all Jacobites were Highlanders. But many hostile representations of the movement simplistically equated its political otherness with the cultural otherness of the Gaelic Highlands. The association with Jacobitism reinforced the notion that Gaeldom was out of tune with the nation's mainstream—a sense of political otherness that lasted until the defeat of the last Jacobite rising in the mid-eighteenth century.

The modern nation-state also saw a need for greater cultural unity. Although the concept of "one nation, one culture, one language" did not come to full fruition until the second half of the eighteenth century, the desire to assimilate the Gaels to "mainstream" cultural norms (as defined ethnocentrically by those in power) is already evident in the sixteenth and seventeenth centuries, if not earlier. Nonetheless, Lowland opinion retained some vestiges of respect for Gaelic culture (though more for its past than its present), for instance because it could be used to underline Scotland's difference from England, thus justifying national independence. This strategy was already used by Scottish historians and propagandists in the Middle Ages. But when the modern period placed a Scottish-English union back on the agenda, the need to bolster Scottish distinctness by reference to its Gaelic traditions declined. Increasing differences between Scotland's Highlands and Lowlands, the desire for intra-national homogenization, and inter-national convergence with England all contributed to a growing sense that Gaeldom was a disturbing internal Other which impeded national unity.[1] Hence, both the Scottish and, later, the British mainstream wished to assimilate these Gaelic "barbarian Others" into a more homogeneous national collective, and launched "civilizing missions" to achieve this end. The belief in cultural hierarchies and civilizing missions aligns Lowland and English images of the Gaidhealtachd with similar perceptions that informed contemporaneous colonial projects in Ireland and overseas. The Lowlanders' colonizing stance toward Highlanders may also have been a response to their own marginalized status in relation to England: by denigrating and "civilizing" the "barbarous" Highlanders, Lowlanders could emphasize that they were not, or not only, England's backward colonized periphery, but also civilized colonizers themselves, thus moving closer to the English center.[2] A similar change of roles from colonized to colonizer was embraced by many Scots, both Lowlanders and Highlanders, who participated in the colonization of Ireland or Britain's overseas territories.

The Quest for National Homogeneity and Progress: Gaeldom, Scotland, and Britain

The sixteenth and seventeenth centuries saw various attempts to strengthen central government control over the Highlands and bring them closer to Lowland standards. However, the initial effect was not law and order, but a destabilization that arguably made the Gaidhealtachd more "disorderly" than before. This perceived lawlessness increased the Highlanders' notoriety in Lowland opinion, which blamed internal Gaelic factors rather than government interference.[3] One reason why the Highlands were associated with disorder was territorial insecurity: James VI attempted to increase royal income by raising rents and renegotiating feu duties, which "led to a demand that the clan elites (*fine*) produce their charters and leases of crown lands in 1598."[4] But written charters and leases did not always exist. A related problem was incongruity between what the modern historian A. I. MacInnes has termed *oighreachd* and *dùthchas*: the *fine* held their estates as individual heritage (*oighreachd*). But their followers often inhabited not only the *oighreachd* but a wider territory (*dùthchas*) for which the *fine* did not have charters. Late sixteenth- and seventeenth-century attempts to bring *dùthchas* and *oighreachd* to congruence caused several conflicts and feuds.[5]

Economic differences also contributed to the increasing perception of Highlanders as "Other." In the Lowlands, pasture and hunting became less important, farming methods changed, and foreign trade and cities grew. Malcolm Chapman's general observations on culture clashes between lowland agriculturalism and highland pastoralism, which was often related to poorer soils, also applies to early modern Scotland: "From the valleys the mountains look like a wilderness, dangerous and insecure, and the pastoralist society, with its mobility, seems to share that insecurity. This insecurity then becomes a figure for logical, moral, and sexual insecurity, with all that these offer in outrage and excitement."[6] This accords with Dawson's remark on cross-cultural misunderstandings related to cattle-raiding: "The very idea horrified many settled Lowlanders, who were often its victims, but within Gaelic society it was an accepted custom . . . carefully regulated by its own . . . rules."[7] This internal logic of Gaelic practices was denied in Lowland discourse where cattle-raiding signified a total absence of rules, an epitome of lawlessness and a threat in need of containment by ordering Lowland hands.[8]

Similar phenomena occur in colonial discourses of antiquity and modern European overseas empires. Gaeldom's real offense, however, was not a lack of rules and authority, but that it posited an alternative system of rules and authority, one which the rest of the nation was trying to transcend, but which still held out on the periphery due to the latter's relative autonomy from centralist state authority.[9] For instance, Womack remarks on cattle-raiding and blackmail, where raiders or their patrons guaranteed individuals the security of their cattle for a certain sum:

> What was particularly offensive . . . was that it was not simply a crime but also a system: . . . the outlaws' protection was so much more worth having than that of the state that even respectable . . . proprietors came to terms. . . . It implied, not just illegality, but an alternative legality—a territorial jurisdiction and a right to tax. In this it resembled, at least from a metropolitan point of view, the old sovereignty of the clan: the blackmailing brigand is a criminalised image of the Chief.[10]

Blackmail seemed so emblematic of Highland otherness that it still informed Lowland depictions of Gaels long after its real heyday was over. By the early eighteenth century it was limited to a few areas, and to broken clans or free-lance reivers rather than "regular" Gaelic social practices.[11]

The emergence of the modern nation-state also altered perceptions of language. The idea that an autonomous nation needed an autonomous and, if possible, single national language gained greater prominence. In Scotland, the dominant voices agreed that this language was Scots or English, but definitely not Gaelic. This Celtic tongue was increasingly perceived and combated as a threat to national unity and progress.

Linguistic and cultural anglicization often began at the top of Gaelic society: partly in response to government pressure and partly voluntarily, Highland elites were increasingly hybridized and integrated into the national mainstream. Chieftains pursued new status symbols like court positions and metropolitan luxuries in Edinburgh and London. Absenteeism increased, patronage of traditional Gaelic arts declined, and chieftains' expenses were greatly increased by their new lifestyles, the many wars of the seventeenth century, taxes, and forced loans. This led to higher rents and sank many aristocrats into debt, creating further upheavals. Anti-Gaelic Lowlanders frequently ignored that it was the very integration of the Highlands, a hybrid society in dynamic transit, into the mainstream which created much of the "disorder" they criticized. Instead, Gael and *Gall* (non-Gael) were often constructed as binary opposites, and Highland disorder was blamed on an allegedly static adherence to barbarous traditions.

One of the people who regarded Highlanders as a threatening Other within was the Scottish king James VI. His 1599 *Basilicon Doron* was a political manual for his son Henry and distinguishes between two kinds of Highlanders with varying degrees of barbarism: "the one, that dwelleth in our maine land, that are barbarous for the most parte, and yet mixed with some shewe of ciuilitie: the other, that dwelleth in the Iles, & are allutterlie barbares, without any sorte or shewe of ciuilitie."[12] King, Parliament, and Privy Council considered Highlanders and Hebrideans as "wild savages" "void of religioun and humanitie" and believed some of them culpable of "maist detestabill, damnabill, and odious murthers, fyiris, reveisching of wemen, witchcraft, and depredatiounis," partly even to the point of being "barbarous cannibals."[13] Already in 1903, the historian W. C. MacKenzie criticized these attitudes and the accompanying policies as being similar to the colonization of Australia's Aboriginal peoples.[14] More recently, fellow historians James Hunter and Edward J. Cowan have likewise drawn colonial comparisons. For instance, Hunter writes:

> These sentiments have a great deal in common with the views which . . . King James's English subjects were just then beginning to express about the Native Americans. . . . It is not surprising, therefore, that there are striking similarities between what was done to Highlanders and what was done to American Indians on the orders of the Scottish and English politicians who, from this point forwards, were looking to gain more and more control over both these sets of "savages."[15]

Although anti-Gaelic othering increased, early modern Lowland Scotland preserved a limited interest in the country's Gaelic past, in continuity with medieval constructions of national identity. Because Gaelic traditions and kings had played a prominent role in Scotland's early history, the Gaelic inheritance was associated with particular antiquity. Antiquity in itself was considered as a source of authority and venerability. Stressing early Gaelic roots also bestowed respectability on the modern nation and its reigning royal dynasty. It legitimized royal authority, boosted patriotic pride, and gave a reassuring sense of continuity.[16] Moreover, the Gaelic heritage embodied Scotland's difference from England, thus legitimizing national autonomy. Such uses of the Gaelic past did not prevent unsympathetic treatment of contemporary Gaels, whose persisting difference was felt to be a thorn in the flesh of national homogeneity, governmental authority, civilization, and order.

Similar ambivalence is observable in religion. Advocates of the Reformation commended early Columban Christianity, supposedly free from the corruptions of the Roman Catholic Church, as a proto-Protestant icon.[17] But even here, the Gaelic dimension was sometimes played down in an attempt to instrumentalize the antiquity of Gaelic Scotland without over-publicizing its distinctness from other parts of Britain or its connections with Ireland, an "inferior" colonized Other and persistently Catholic into the bargain.[18] One author who wrote in this vein was John Spottiswoode (1565–1639). His comments on Saint Columba are also noteworthy for inverting aspects of the saint's biography. Earlier traditions and modern historical consensus claim that Columba lived in Ireland before he moved to Scotland and became a founding figure of Scottish Christianity. But Spottiswoode claims that Columba moved from Scotland to Ireland in order to missionize the pagans there.[19] This illustrates the complicated position of Scottish Gaeldom in colonial discourse. On the one hand, the distortion of Gaelic history and its use by outsiders from the hegemonic Lowlands can be read as an instance of internal colonialism. On the other hand, Scotland's Gaels are implicitly distinguished from, and set above, an external colonized population, that is, Irish Gaels. Spottiswoode's projection of an early medieval Scottish Christian civilizing mission in Ireland parallels the English and Scottish colonial ventures which aimed to civilize the Ireland of his day—this time not only religiously, but also politically, economically, and linguistically. He suggests that Ireland was always more backward than Scotland, and that civilizing missions always moved in the same direction, with Ireland forever a receiver, not a donor country. By implication, casting Scotland's ancient Gaels in the role of cultural donor also includes them among those who were superior to the Irish in the seventeenth-century present: Scotland's Gaels are integrated into the supposedly superior British civilization as a co-colonizer of the Irish. Not all commentators would have agreed. There was considerable insecurity about whether Scotland's Gaels were to be placed on the British or Irish side of the line. The Scottish Gaidhealtachd shared many Irish traits of subalternity, and thus was often cast into the role of internal barbarian Other. De-othering the Scottish Gaels required distinguishing them from the Irish, either discursively as in Spottiswoode's writing, or practically through the political and cultural policies discussed below.

The relationship between Gaeldom and Protestant religious discourse is also ambivalent for another reason. Here as well, espousing real or imagined ancient Scottish Gaelic history did not prevent hostility toward contemporary Gaelic culture. Whereas Scotland's state church was Protestant, in certain parts of the Highlands Catholicism remained stronger than in many other parts of the country, at least for some time. Thus, mainstream discourse could associate the Gaidhealtachd with religious otherness—another threat to the national consensus.

Spottiswoode's comments on religion show a tendency that also occurs in other fields: the urge to de-Irishize the Scottish Gaels by downplaying pan-Gaelic commonalities. Again, this already occurred in some premodern texts, but intensified in the modern period. This was in keeping with the general principles of modern nationhood which implied a basic congruence between cultural boundaries and the territorial boundaries of the state. Ireland was as much a different country from Scotland as England was, and Scotland's autonomous national identity could only be affirmed by distancing it from both these neighbors. Attempts to distance Scotland from Ireland also had a colonial dimension which highlights the ambiguous position of Scotland in (post)colonial discourse: far from declaring solidarity with Ireland as a fellow victim of internal colonialism and English hegemony, many Scots despised the Irish colonized just as much as many English people did and eagerly stressed their country's difference from Ireland.[20]

Scotland's distinctness from England became more problematic as the two countries moved closer together. In 1603, James VI succeeded to the English throne as James I. Both kingdoms now shared the same monarch (Union of the Crowns), but otherwise remained separate independent states with their own parliaments and policies. However, since the monarch still had political power (rather than a purely representative function, as today), there could be problems: if the king was supposed to represent two different countries at once, what was he to do when these two countries' interests clashed? The conundrum is particularly evident in seventeenth-century Scottish foreign policy:

> The Scottish Parliament had never managed to secure much influence over foreign policy before . . . [1603], and an independent foreign policy therefore disappeared over the Border with James after the Regal Union. At the same time, . . . both James and his successor, Charles I, . . . tended to favour the position of England, the senior partner in the dynastic union, especially when any conflict emerged between English and Scottish vital interests.[21]

These problems were among the reasons why some people pushed for a more complete union between the two states. In 1707 Scotland and England merged into a single state, Great Britain, with a Treaty of Union that created a Union of Parliaments, abolishing the Scottish Parliament and giving Scottish delegates seats in the Parliament in London which now served the entire island. But even in this new pan-British state, some distinctions remained: Scotland kept its own state church and its own legal and educational system. Those who espoused the Unions of 1603 and 1707 sometimes downplayed Scotland's Gaelic side in order to make Scotland appear more similar to England. While James VI pursued his claims to the English throne, and after he had attained it, his propaganda machine disseminated unionist iconography with matching origin legends that marginalized the separateness of Scotland's Gaelic tradition in favor of pan-British figures like Brutus or Arthur.[22]

That the Scottish-English rapprochement exacerbated the position of Scottish Gaeldom is also evident in King James's practical policies, for instance concerning the mercenary trade between Gaelic Scotland and Ireland. Tudor colonialism had increased Irish chieftains' demand for hired soldiers from Scotland. Since the late sixteenth century, when Queen Elizabeth's death and James's accession to England's throne drew near, the Scottish king increasingly regarded colonial Irish affairs as his own and tried to curb these intra-Gaelic exchanges. As the mercenary trade clashed more and more with the national interest, it was seen as another sign of Highland lawlessness. The crown's desire to drive a cultural and political wedge between Scottish and Irish Gaeldom was one of the intentions behind the Ulster Plantation which began in 1609 and involved a redistribution of substantial proportions of Northern Irish land to English and Scottish incomers. The withering of the mercenary trade between Gaelic Scotland and Ireland removed one source of "disorder," but created new ones: because surplus Scottish Gaelic manpower could no longer be sent to Ireland, there was an increased pressure on economic resources at home. Sometimes, clan elites resorted to piracy to support themselves.[23]

Despite these negative associations which Gaelicness held for the nation's anglophone mainstream, the Gaelic inheritance was not purged *entirely* from national identity constructs—not even after the Union. Even James VI/I occasionally found Gaelic traditions ideologically useful. In a speech to the English Parliament in 1604, he portrayed himself through the Gaelic concept of a king married to his kingdom(s).[24] Stuart propaganda continued to invoke Gaelic traditions to underline the antiquity of the Scottish monarchy and the legitimacy of the current dynasty. For Charles I's coronation visit to Edinburgh in 1633, William Drummond of Hawthornden devised a spectacle which featured several ancient Gaelic kings, some of whom were real while others were invented. The coronation ceremony for Charles II which took place in Scotland in 1651 relied on early Scottish medieval traditions by taking place in Scone and featuring the recitation of the royal pedigree. The ancient Gaelic kings further resurfaced in the portraits of royal ancestry commissioned by the future James VII/II for Holyrood Palace in 1684.[25]

Another issue which prevented the total erasure of the Gaels from Scottish history was the fact that the Union with England turned out to be more uneasy than had been hoped. Significant sections of society in both countries feared that their own nation might be submerged and disadvantaged. Such anxieties played a key part in seventeenth-century political and religious developments. The Scottish Covenanting movement, which started in the 1630s and whose main pledge was to protect the Presbyterian faith, also criticized royal abuses of power, endorsed parliamentary rights and a constitutional rather than absolute form of monarchy, and even had more radically demotic strains favoring grassroots power. Thus, the Covenanters can be read as a movement which not only aimed to protect Scotland's religious identity, with its Presbyterian Church, against Anglican and Episcopalian inroads, but to some extent also aimed to defend Scotland's political identity in the face of an absentee monarchy. In a climactic phase of the British Civil Wars, between the late 1640s and the early 1650s, England favored republicanism, while Scotland's parliament merely wished to reeducate king and monarchy in line with Covenanting principles. During these disagreements, both countries attempted to impose their principles and interests on their neighbor nation. English imperialism in Scotland is only one side of the coin; similar attempts were made vice versa. A Scottish invasion of England was defeated in 1648. A few months later, the king was executed without consultation of the Scottish Parliament. The latter responded by proclaiming the dead king's son as Charles II, king of Great Britain. It also wanted to presbyterianize this new British monarchy, England included. This amounted to an attempt to reimpose British dynastic Union on *Scottish* terms. Cromwellian England gained the upper hand and conquered Scotland in 1650–51. Scotland was occupied and lost its independence until 1660, when the Restoration of the Stuart monarchy also restored the Union of the Crowns and separate statehood under separate national parliaments. Mutual fears of national disadvantaging persisted until the Union of 1707—and beyond. In Scotland, such anxieties led to reaffirmations of Scottish identity, a great popularity of patriotic epics and histories throughout the seventeenth century, and an interest in symbols which underlined difference from England.[26]

Patriotic invocations of Gaelic traditions can, for instance, be found in *Defense of the Antiquity of the Royal Line of Scotland* (1685) and other writings by Sir George Mackenzie of Rosehaugh, who had Gaelic family connections and some Gaelic language skills, although he was born and bred in the Lowlands. Mackenzie invokes a (nonexistent) Gaelic manuscript from around the birth of Christ, as well as ancient Gaelic oral sources, to substantiate his historical claims. Again, the ancient flavor of the Gaelic heritage is celebrated for patriotic purposes. However, the authority of contemporary Gaelic discourse produced by bards and *seanchaidh*s was dismissed: though Mackenzie paid lip service to the validity of such sources, he did not use them himself. Moreover, like several of his contemporaries, he downplays Scotland's Irish roots and the validity of Irish Gaelic sources. While he does not dismiss the Scottish-Irish link altogether, he stands the traditional narrative on its head by claiming that the Irish were descended from the Scots rather than vice versa. Ferguson points out that Mackenzie launched an anticolonial critique of English historical narratives and to some extent sided with Irish counter-discourse, but only as far as Irish sources were not detrimental to his own objective, which was to assert Scottish nationalism in the face of English hegemonic aspirations.[27] This Scottish self-assertion also involves casting the Scots as an ancient colonial mother country of Ireland. Mackenzie's work again illustrates the ambiguity of Scottish discourse that was situated uneasily between Gaelic roots and anti-Irishness, and between anti-English solidarity and a junior partnership in the ongoing colonization of Ireland.

The Union of 1707 was not just hotly debated at the time, but also by later commentators and right up to the present. The debate is also relevant with regard to Scotland's position vis-à-vis the (post)colonial. Though the Union was nominally a consensual treaty between two equal partners, its critics have argued that it was actually an English hegemonic project achieved mainly through pressure, and that it exacerbated Scotland's political, economic, and cultural marginalization by its more powerful southern neighbor. In the eyes of some, this even went so far as to make Scotland a quasi-colonized country. In 1765 the anonymous pamphlet *A North Briton Extraordinary*, sometimes ascribed to Tobias Smollett, criticised English anti-Scotticism and the Union's harmful economic and political effects on Scotland, culminating in the assertion that "while we scorned to become a province to England, we are in fact become its most valuable colony."[28] And in 1793, the Scottish political reformist Lord Daer argued that, already since 1603, Scotland was "a conquered province," alluding to ancient Rome where a conquered territory which had been firmly integrated into the empire was called a *provincia*.[29] If we accept that Scotland's position resembled that of an imperial colony, this makes the Highlanders doubly colonized: first, by the Lowlanders who were themselves "singly" colonized by the English, and second by the English who colonized both kinds of Scots. However, the Scots were not the only ones who complained about the Union: many eighteenth-century English people were far from seeing themselves as colonial conquerors, let alone profiteering ones. Instead, they were anxious about Scottish economic competition and about government being swamped by an invasion of ambitious and greedy Scots.

Those who stress the Union's benefits for Scotland emphasize that at least some parts of Scottish society had wanted the treaty, and that it had more to do with Scottish ambitions to become a successful global colonizer than with Scottish victimization as an internal colonized. Scotland had already pursued overseas colonial ambitions before the Union, but not very successfully. Its own military and naval resources were not sufficient to protect its economic interests abroad. Scottish overseas ambitions were also undermined by the competition of its more powerful English neighbor. In 1618, an attempt to establish a Scottish East India Company foundered when the king's patent was withdrawn under English pressure. A Scottish Guinea Company for trade with West Africa existed from 1634 to 1639. There were also attempts to establish Scottish colonial settlements in North America: the colony of Nova Scotia was first established in 1629, but abandoned in 1633 and only retaken after the British Union in the eighteenth century. Scottish colonies also existed in East New Jersey (1683–1702) and parts of South Carolina (1684–86). In 1695 a Company of Scotland Trading to Africa and the Indies was founded. In practice, its main venture was the highly ambitious Darien scheme in Central America which began in 1698 and foundered in 1700. This was the most famous Scottish colonial project. It was not only hampered by limited national resources, adverse weather, illness, and internal disagreements but, most importantly, clashed with the mercantile and strategic interests of England and Spain, which used their much greater economic and military clout to undermine the Scottish scheme. The failure of Darien swallowed up a great proportion of Scottish capital and seemed to underline that Scotland's economic, political, and military resources were not enough to compete successfully on an international stage.[30] A more complete Union with its powerful English neighbor offered Scotland access to English resources, and legal access to English colonial markets, which would further Scottish imperial ambitions better than an independent Scottish state could have done. Even if we accept the notion of Scotland as internally colonized within Britain, one might say that Scots accepted this status in order to become colonizers elsewhere. Advocates of the Union could also cite other advantages, such as unhampered Scottish access to English domestic markets. Moreover, it is argued that, even after the Union, Scotland retained sufficient autonomy by preserving its own legal, educational, and ecclesiastical institutions, and was well represented through *informal* political structures, networks, and Scottish politicians who became powerful in the Westminster system.[31]

However, many Scots only came to believe in these advantages with hindsight, several decades later. At first, Scottish anti-Union sentiment was widespread, spanning the Highlands and the Lowlands, and swelled the ranks of Jacobitism which, having initially been based on religious and dynastic arguments, could now also be identified with the cause of Scottish independence.[32] The Highlands were a mainstay of the Stuart camp, which exacerbated their image as a threatening Other. Already during the seventeenth-century revolutions, many Highlanders had supported the Stuarts, sometimes for religious reasons (Catholicism and Episcopalianism were strongest in the Gaidhealtachd and the northeast), sometimes for more material considerations.[33] Some also invoked the divine right of kings and sought to link this to an image of conservative clan values. Jacobitism brought many Highlanders into conflict with those segments of English and Scottish society that supported the revolutionary/Covenanting and later the Hanoverian side, which eventually won out. These segments of society, which represented the new status quo, worried about the Gaidhealtachd's continuing potential as a recruiting ground for insurrection. In addition to widespread Stuart sympathies, the Highland region's geographical and infrastructural isolation from the centers of power would make it a convenient landing place for invasion armies, especially from France, Britain's main rival and home to the exiled Stuart court. Gaelic feudal structures always provided ready contingents of fighting men which might be turned against the government. And the "manipulability of . . . clan musterings" as well as "their relative inaccessibility . . . enabled unhindered mobilization."[34]

In reality, not all Catholics or all Highlanders were Jacobites: Catholic clans were just as divided as Protestant ones. But mainstream perceptions often conflated Gaeldom, religious otherness, and Jacobitism. Among the various Jacobite schemes of the first half of the eighteenth century, the 1715 rebellion had the widest support and the highest chances of success, with a basis not only in Scottish nationalism but also in more general social discontent which comprised even parts of England. When this rising foundered after all, government propaganda downplayed the breadth of its base and retrospectively portrayed it as a case of Highland insurrection.

The acceptance of the Union by the Scottish mainstream in the decades following 1715 might partly be explained by sheer pragmatism or resignation in view of the fact that there were no feasible alternatives. Partly, there was also more genuine espousal of the Union as its economic and career benefits (at least for certain parts of the population) began to show. Jacobitism and/or a fight for independence also seemed unattractive because insurrection and civil war would endanger the regular course of business. Moreover, it was feared that a restored Stuart Britain would be strongly influenced by France, an absolutist state whose example might lead francophile Stuart kings to curtail the liberties of Britain's constitutional monarchy. As France was also Catholic, Britain's Protestant mainstream saw Stuart francophilia as a potential threat to the island's religious identity. France was also a major imperial and economic rival of Britain. Monarchs and their governments were expected to pursue policies which gave their own country advantages against rival powers. But it was feared that francophile Stuart monarchs might not pursue British interests against France with as much rigor as British patriots and businessmen might desire. In all this, the Scottish mainstream was united with the English mainstream, desiring a royal dynasty which would defend pan-British interests against the French Other.[35]

Some people developed a pan-British national identity more easily, while others retained their traditional affiliations to Scotland, England, or subnational regions. Scottish/English patriotism and Great-Britishness could also coexist, even in the same head: many Scottish people felt concentric loyalties toward both Scotland and Great Britain.[36] The respective weight given to these loyalties could change over time and depending on context (e.g., culture vs. politics). But all in all, Scottish support of Britishness and anglicization intensified as the eighteenth century unfolded. This exacerbated Gaeldom's position as an inconvenient internal Other because it represented a part of Scotland's heritage that was definitely non-English and thus threatened unionist identity constructions.[37]

During the next major Jacobite campaign, led by Prince Charles Edward Stuart in 1745/46, the Gaels were again divided. Some fought on the government side, others remained neutral, but those who did support Jacobitism were numerous enough to play a dominant part in the rising and in the way in which the Jacobite movement was represented. Most of their Scottish compatriots had already settled safely and acquiescently into the Union. This seemed to reconfirm the Gaels' position as an internal barbarian Other, an anomaly within an otherwise respectable national collective made up of harmoniously coexisting and rather similar Lowlanders and English people. Once this Jacobite rising was defeated, the British establishment was determined to eliminate any further Highland threat to national stability and unity. It proceeded to eliminate such threats at their cultural roots (see the section on "Religion, Education, Language Policy, and Assimilation" below).

The second half of the eighteenth century saw an economic boom and imperial expansion which further intensified Scottish identification with the Union. In several sectors, Scotland's contribution to the British Empire even surpassed that of the English. First, the Scottish gentry was often poorer than its English counterpart, and thus more willing to accept risks and hardship abroad in pursuit of a fortune. Second, some customary career paths for ambitious Englishmen were less open to Scots because of entrenched networks of intra-English favoritism, as well as anti-Scottish prejudice, for example, in the upper administration. Thus, Scots often opted for career paths where English people and scotophobia were less entrenched, for instance in less fashionable parts of the army and in the overseas colonies. Third, patriotism often urged Scots to help each other in imperial advancement, perhaps to compensate for national handicaps like the small size of their country or English prejudice. The East India Company after 1750 became "a veritable Scottish fiefdom."[38] Similar things could be said about trading companies in eighteenth- and nineteenth-century Canada. Lower-class Scots likewise hoped for colonial career opportunities. Colonial profits were often reinvested in Scotland itself, thus benefiting the domestic economy. It is thus little wonder that "Rule Britannia" was written by a Scotsman, the poet James Thomson. Among Britain's internal peripheral nations, Scotland was arguably the most prominent in imperial projects overseas, although Ireland and Wales also played an important part.[39]

So much for Scotland's post-Union fortunes as an overseas colonizer. But what of the other side of the Scottish experience—that of an "internally colonized" periphery within an English-dominated Britain? In economic terms, the applicability of the label "internally colonized" is debatable in the eighteenth century: in some respects the concept seems to fit, in others it does not. As already noted, a typical colonized economy is often described as focusing on the production of a limited variety of raw materials for export to the "mother country" (e.g., England) where they are processed and mainly also consumed. Within the British Isles, the Irish economy seems to fit this image most closely. The post-Union Scottish economy, at least on the whole, was different: it remained relatively diversified, had its own successful manufactures, and from the late eighteenth century onwards became an increasingly urbanized powerhouse of industralization.[40] Highly vulnerable undiversified economies focusing on raw materials for export existed only in *parts* of Scotland, such as the Highlands and Islands, whose economy James Hunter labels as "neo-colonial" and whose lack of sustained development was lamented even by contemporary advocates of improvement.[41] Devine argues that one of the reasons why Scotland did not develop a typical colonized economy is that economic exploitation in the north was not a prime English interest. England wanted the Union mainly as a guarantee for political stability and military security, which was best ensured by a policy of low interference and by not draining the Scottish economy too much.[42]

This is not to say that people in Scotland from mid-century onwards never felt *any* discontent with the Union. There were always setbacks, and groups that profited less than others. But all in all, the benefits of Union sufficed to create considerable identification with the new pan-British nation.

As eighteenth-century Scotland was increasingly integrated into a united Great Britain, the majority of the Scottish establishment accepted a new identity as "North Britons" and wanted to rid themselves of awkward vestiges of their traditional national difference from England. In practice, this meant not so much mutual hybridization as the cultural anglicization of Scotland. In principle, this logic extended to Highland and Lowland Scots alike. Highlanders were seen as the least civilized population group and had the furthest way to go until they could fulfill "civilized" anglocentric norms. Some Highlanders voluntarily embraced anglicization as a means of social climbing; those who did not were subjected to various forms of coercion (see below). Although Scottish Lowlanders already seemed far more civilized than the Highlanders, they were still often perceived as inferior to the English. Hence, even Lowlanders felt that self-anglicization was the key to social acceptability and a British career. Unlike the often coercive framework of Highland anglicization, cultural pressures on Lowlanders were more indirect, taking the form of career prospects or ridicule, for instance. Indirect pressures and voluntary identification sufficed to make many Scots eager to anglicize themselves. Even aspiring Lowlanders felt a need for linguistic assimilation and tried to purge their English of scotticisms, or, as the Scottish intellectual James Beattie called them, "barbarisms."[43] An anglicizing drive can also be discerned in literary tastes and middle-class behavior.[44]

The ambivalence of colonial mimicry, which can entail elements of both collusion and subversion (as outlined in the "Introduction"), can also be discerned in eighteenth-century Scotland: on the one hand, Scottish self-anglicization reflected and bolstered England's hegemony within the Union; but the very success of these anglicized Scottish sociocultural "upstarts" also caused much English unease about "Scots on the make" who threatened to become undue competition, for instance when they infiltrated the London elites.

The relevance of the concept of colonial mimicry in eighteenth-century Scottish-English relations is also noted by Evan Gottlieb. But he also notes limitations of the "internal colonialism" thesis, for instance because Scots did not simply discard their inherited Scottishness in favor of emulating a ready-made model of Englishness that was entirely defined by others, that is, the English themselves. Instead, Scots also significantly invested in (and *shaped*) a new overarching notion of Britishness which encompassed both Scottish and English people, supposedly on a more or less equal basis, thus allowing both peoples to contribute to the defining and shaping of this new, pan-British national identity and culture. The ideal of Britishness thus offered a compromise: Scots had to give up some of their particularities and "civilize" themselves, but not on exclusively English terms; instead, both peoples were supposed to join in the creation of something new. This allowed Scottish people a degree of recognition and cultural power that was denied to more "typical" colonized subjects.[45] Scots on the make proved their compatibility with an English/British establishment; they were "Same" or at least hybrid enough to be highly successful in a pan-British and even international context, for instance in literature, Enlightenment philosophy, or politics. Scottish playwrights like John Home or David Mallet were successful on London stages. Scottish Enlightenment philosophers like David Hume or Adam Smith made a huge, lasting, and international impact. A significant proportion of London booksellers were Scottish, and the Ossianic prose poems of Scottish writer James Macpherson became international bestsellers beloved by such luminaries as the German poet Johann Wolfgang Goethe and the French emperor Napoleon. Various Scottish intellectuals, including John Home, David Hume, and James Macpherson obtained significant government pensions in recognition of their work. Scottish literati often formed networks to help each other, just as Scottish traders would soon do in the colonial companies. Britain even had a Scottish prime minister for a while, namely the Earl of Bute (1762–63).[46]

However, the self-anglicization of ambitious Scots did not always result from a cultural cringe, but could also be a mere tactic and was often combined with interest and pride in Scotland's own traditions. A limited engagement with Scottish culture could gratify local patriotism in a non-subversive way—it was deemed compatible with British/Hanoverian affiliations as long as it did not question the legitimacy of the British state.[47] In principle, both Lowland and Highland traditions could be acceptable in this framework. Which of the two was more acceptable has been answered differently by different people—both in the eighteenth century and in modern historical debates. As in previous centuries, some eighteenth-century Lowland scholars retained an interest in Gaelic history as an icon of national antiquity (and hence respectability). Some of them were also attracted to Gaelic literature and culture—decades before Macpherson's Ossianic writings of the 1760s inaugurated the Celticist craze of the romantic age. Various non-Gaelic intellectuals discovered an interest in the Gaelic language itself and learned it. This was related to a wider fashion for Celtic linguistics.[48] Dauvit Horsbroch suggests that in some senses the standing of Gaelic as a badge of Scottish identity was stronger than that of the Lowland Scots tongue.[49] However, there is also contrary evidence which suggests that in some areas of discourse interest in Highland and Gaelic tradition actually declined further, whereas Lowland Scots traditions were deemed more acceptable because they were culturally and linguistically closer to England's.[50] Another reason why Gaelic tradition often seemed less compatible with the British status quo is the idea that Gaelic culture was so interwoven with political and economic otherness that neither could be eradicated without the other.

Hence, outside the realm of scholarship, in sociopolitical practice, the desire to assimilate contemporary Gaels into the modern nation clearly won out. In addition to intra-national homogenization, another factor which influenced the image of Gaels at that time was external expansion. We have already seen this with regard to Ireland. Similar things apply to colonialism further afield, for instance across the Atlantic, in Africa, or in the Pacific region. The rise of Britain's overseas empire fueled British interest in themes of intercultural encounters, comparisons, and hierarchies, in "civilizing missions," and also in the history and culture of other empires. This helped to form an arsenal of British colonial discourse patterns which also influenced the representation of intra-British "barbarians" like the Gaels. The Gaels were increasingly seen in comparison to the "barbarians" described by ancient Roman writers, and to the modern "barbarians" encountered by Britain's own imperial adventurers overseas. Even Lowland Scotland was compared to a conquered imperial province. These inter-imperial comparisons in the description of Scottish culture(s) are examined more closely in the following section.

Colonial Visions across Time and Space: Celticity, Classicism, Empire, and Enlightenment

The construction of cultural hierarchies is greatly facilitated by stable economic and political hegemonies. These had existed in Roman times, then disappeared from northern Britain for several centuries, and since the late Middle Ages gradually returned. In the early modern period, this development was intensified by the emergence of the modern capitalist nation-state and overseas colonial ventures. British people increasingly saw the Roman Empire as a mirror for their own supremacy. A classicist vogue had already started during the Renaissance, but gained a further boost from seventeenth- and especially eighteenth-century overseas colonialism. The Roman Empire provided a model for British identity constructions as the center of civilization and a colonizing world power.[51] London was sometimes referred to as "Augusta" to indicate its status as "the heir to imperial Rome."[52] Another model for Enlightenment Britain was ancient Greece, which, though not as outwardly imperialist as Rome, had likewise regarded itself as a navel of civilization. Enlightened Edinburgh was referred to as "the Athens of Britain" or "the Athens of the North."[53] The distribution of these classical urban labels among different parts of modern Britain mirrors internal power imbalances: Greece was incorporated into the Roman Empire as politically subordinate, but its culture often continued to be seen as the epitome of civilization, even in Roman eyes. Applying the name "Athens" to Scotland's capital city likens the entire country to Greece; in relation to London's designation as a new Rome, Scotland is portrayed as a conquered province of an English empire. At the same time, the reference to Athens expresses Scottish cultural pride: it implies that Edinburgh, city of the Enlightenment, is London's equal or superior in civilization, though not in political and economic power. Early in the nineteenth century, *Blackwood's Edinburgh Magazine* voiced similar attitudes:

> While London must always eclipse this city [Edinburgh] in all that depends on wealth, power, or fashionable elegance, . . . and while London is the Rome of the empire, to which . . . [people] resort for . . . pleasure, . . . fortune, or . . . ambition, Edinburgh might become another Athens, in which the arts and the sciences flourished, under the shade of her ancient fame, and established a dominion over the minds of men more permanent than even that which the Roman arms were able to effect.[54]

The general fascination with classical antiquity also encompassed Roman writings about barbarian Others, cultural hierarchies, and civilizing missions, which were reread to inform the modern British mainstream's image of itself and of its "primitive" Others at home and abroad. This also entailed the rediscovery of the Greek and Roman category of the "Celt" as a blanket term for barbarians who lived northwest of the "civilized center." This ancient category of the "Celt" was now recycled as a label for the modern northwestern "barbarian" fringes of Britain and France. This discursive mobilization of "Celtic" as a regional/ethnic identity was facilitated by the discovery of linguistic kinship: the languages spoken on Britain's and France's modern northwestern fringes—Manx, Irish, and Scottish Gaelic, as well as Welsh, Cornish, and Breton—belong to the same language family as ancient Gaulish. These commonalities had already been observed by George Buchanan in the sixteenth century, but mainstream opinion only espoused such notions from the eighteenth century onwards. This language family came to be labeled as "Celtic," subdivided on the basis of a prominent sound shift into the "q-Celtic" Gaelic group and the "p-Celtic" group comprising Welsh, Cornish, and Breton. Linguistic commonalities have also been taken as a signifier of other cultural similarities which set these groups clearly apart from neighboring non-Celtic-speaking peoples, though in reality such correlations are not automatic. The assumption of a distinct "Celtic culture" also associated the speakers of Celtic languages with barbarism, since the label "Celt" originated as an externally imposed blanket label for barbarians of the northwest.[55]

Due to these various associations of Celticity with barbarism and marginalization, ancient and modern Celticism could furnish models for depictions of indigenous peoples encountered by British colonizers further afield.[56] In analogy to Orientalism, eighteenth-century anglophone scholarly interest in Gaelic culture might in itself express a colonizing zeitgeist by reflecting a desire to "own" the "colonized," here the Gaidhealtachd, more completely: material ownership in political and economic terms is rounded off with intellectual "conquest" and guardianship; discursive authority is assumed by anglophone elites while the Gaelic margin's own voices are marginalized. This answer to the question "Who gets to speak?," the privileging of powerful outsiders' voices, constitutes a similarity between Celticism and international colonial discourse on a formal level. There are also similarities at the content level. Just as Greek and Roman texts had done, Renaissance and Enlightened thinkers envisaged the development of human society as progress through several stages, and located their own cultures in the most advanced stage, both materially and intellectually. Usually, the notion of cultural superiority also involved pride in the art of writing and a denigration of oral societies. The representatives of the self-styled centers of civilization measured other cultures by the norms of their own; those not conforming to this model were downgraded as savage or barbarian, that is, as representing earlier stages of development which the civilized center had long left behind.[57] Social theorists of the Enlightenment usually distinguished developmental stages by modes of production, "progressing" from nomadic hunting and gathering via pastoralism to fixed settlement and agriculture, and from there to urban civilizations with their division of labor and lively trade. The synchronous presence of different sociocultural formations was thus seen in terms of uneven development and anachronism: while dominant metropolitan cultures that shaped the general state of the world or the spirit of the age were already at an advanced stage, marginal cultures in the same period still represented a more backward one.[58]

The "civilized center" was associated with order, control, lawfulness, cleanliness, rationality, intellect, reality/realism, constancy, regularity, dynamism, and progress; while the barbarian periphery represented the exact opposite: disorder, lack of control, lawlessness, dirt, emotion, irrationality, unreality, dreams, ghosts, superstition, inconstancy, irregularity, and stasis. In Britain, the position of the civilized center was allocated to anglophone culture in England and often also Lowland Scotland, while the position of the barbarian periphery was allocated to people from the "Celtic fringe," such as the Gaelic Highlanders. Eighteenth-century improvers mainly saw the periphery's side of the binarism in a negative light.[59] However, in contrast to much nineteenth-century racism, even "inferior" Others were accorded the *potential* for progress; they were not doomed to perpetual primitiveness. For instance, "barbarians" were sometimes claimed to possess simple virtues which formed a good basis for further improvement once the obstacle of their traditional culture was out of the way. To some extent, the belief in primitive virtues foreshadows romantic ideals of noble savagery, but while romanticism values primitiveness for its own sake, the main concern of pre-romantic perspectives is to civilize and change the "noble savages": their very virtues are seen as a promising basis for assimilation to the center. The above-mentioned characteristics ascribed to center and periphery in Celticist discourse also appear in Greek and Roman texts about barbarians, and in representations of modern overseas (post)colonies, such as various forms of Orientalism, racist denigrations of black people, or positive reevaluations of negritude.

Despite its associations with colonial discourse strategies, the label "Celtic" was not *only* used by outsiders and for "colonizing" purposes. The adoption of the label "Celtic" as an ethnic self-designation by Scots, Irish, Welsh, and other people also goes back to the eighteenth century. At a time when non-English populations of the British Isles were under political and cultural threat from an expansive, homogenizing anglocentric state, pan-Celticism could offer a rival supra-identity (though cultural rather than political), pride in ancient indigenous ancestry, and solidarity based on shared difference from England.[60]

Universalist cultural hierarchies and other aspects of Enlightenment thought can already be found in the seventeenth or even the sixteenth century, although the Scottish Enlightenment is traditionally seen as belonging to the eighteenth.[61] The pre-Union Scottish state had its own drive towards internal centralization, commercialization, and nation-building, as well as colonial ambitions overseas, all of which warranted ideas about civilizational ladders and Roman parallels. This is also evident in Martin's works, as shown in the next chapter. The center providing the model for the future evolution of the peripheries was not necessarily identified as lying in England or more specifically London, but could also be located in Lowland Scotland and its capital city, Edinburgh.

After the Union, however, many Scottish intellectuals identified England as the hub of civilization. Not only the Gaels were portrayed as barbarians: some commentators depicted the entirety of Scotland as a primitive periphery which was bound to profit from exposure to English culture. The *Edinburgh Review* asserted that the Union had enabled "a disposition to . . . improvement in . . . a people naturally active and intelligent. If countries have their ages with respect to improvement, North Britain may be considered as in a state of early youth, guided and supported by the more mature strength of her kindred country."[62] Here the Scottish populace as a whole, like its Gaelic segment in other texts, is portrayed as being full of good potential, but in need of a superior neighbor to set them on the right path to higher civilization, on a universal ladder of social evolution. Another, related colonial discourse trope is the metaphor of childhood which describes the "inferior" periphery. To realize their potential, children need guidance and education—a role allegedly fulfilled by the benevolent parental figure of the superior, mature colonizer.[63] The emphasis on the Scots' potential to learn and improve also highlights the extent to which the "internal colonization" of Scotland relied on indirect strategies of control, such as cultural assimilation. To some extent, this strategy also played a part in other colonies, but there the relative importance given to more obvious forms of domination was often much greater.

Picturing Scotland as a country which was only just now emerging into the light of civilization meant that many Enlightenment historians were not greatly interested in pre-1688 Scottish history, whether Highland or Lowland. It was considered too full of barbarity, religious extremism, and disorder to merit scholarly study: they wanted to write the history of civilization, not of primitiveness and chaos.[64] Accordingly, they also downplayed the Gaelic heritage and "Dark Age" national origin legends. First, the "Dark Ages" were the epitome of barbarism and thus unworthy of academic attention anyway. Second, the scarcity of verifiable sources from this time made historians too dependent on speculation, which was unattractive to Enlightened scientific rationalism.[65] Thus, Enlightened scholars had little use for Gaelic traditions as part of a progressive national present and future—or even as part of a venerable national past. Nonetheless, they showed *some* interest in Gaelic culture. Though often uninterested in the particulars of national or ethnic premodern histories which diverged from "civilized" norms, they were interested in "barbarian" cultures for a different purpose: the purpose of generalizing from them. From studying specific barbarian cultures they deduced information about the general nature of primitive society and human development. The origins and nature of society were, after all, a favorite subject of Enlightened philosophy. John Millar's account of social evolution drew its examples of savagery from both ancient and modern sources, implying a basic comparability of such diverse groups as Native Americans, Old Testament Jews, the Trojans and Greeks of Homeric times, and "Dark Age" Gaeldom as described in Macpherson's Ossianic publications.[66] As early as 1755, before Macpherson's works appeared, William Robertson had asserted that even in the contemporary Scottish Highlands and Islands "society still appears in its rudest and most imperfect form."[67] Adam Smith likewise assumes a universal ladder of progress. He compares ancient Celts with modern Africans and Native Americans as representatives of the lower stages. Modern Highlanders are placed slightly higher, between nomadic "Oriental" people and advanced mainstream European commercial society.[68] Gaels provided convenient specimens for the study of "primitive" man because they united a sufficient degree of "backward" otherness with geographical proximity and relatively easy access, while overseas "savages" were more difficult to reach. It was only in the nineteenth century, with further imperial expansion and consolidation, as well as improved travel facilities, that many overseas "savage" regions were truly opened up for ethnographic scrutiny.[69]

Thus, Highlanders and other "Celts" could function as *the* paradigmatic barbarian Other in British culture, and even as a substitute for non-European colonial Others when these seemed too far out of reach. In the scholarly, literary, and tourist imagination, Celtic and non-European Others were often mapped onto each other. Notions about Celts could be mapped onto non-Europeans. Later, as non-Europeans moved more to the foreground of the colonial imagination, this could have two different kinds of effect: sometimes, the differences between Celtic and non-Celtic Britons paled into insignificance when compared to the much greater otherness of non-European peoples. This could mean that Celts were now more readily admitted to the ranks of the "civilized," as people who had a valuable part to play in conquering and "civilizing" non-European Others (also see chapters 3 and 6). Sometimes, however, the equation between Celtic and non-European Others was still maintained, so that new ideas about non-Europeans could also reflect back on European Others and affect the way in which the "Celts" were perceived. This will become particularly clear in the examination of biologistic racism in chapter 5.

For Enlightenment thinkers who, like Robertson and Smith, thought that Scottish Highlanders represented an earlier, more primitive stage of society, the Highlanders functioned as "contemporary ancestors": they were living examples of a way of life that the more advanced society of the Lowlands and England had also come through, but which it had already left behind. Thus, the concept of the contemporary ancestor retained a sense of difference, barbarity, and civilizational hierarchy, but it allowed for eventual development: even the "primitives" were capable of attaining a more civilized level in the future. The universal teleology of progress could legitimate assimilation policies as the inevitable corollary of an impersonal course of history.[70] These implications are not only inherent in eighteenth-century scholarly views on social development, as in Robertson's or Smith's work, but also in wider public opinion, as is evident in the various "civilizing missions" that were unleashed to accelerate historical progress in the Highlands (see below). It was thought that the progress of advanced societies could put mounting pressure on neighboring backward ones until the latter were forced to make an accelerated leap forward.[71] The colonizing impetus of Enlightenment theories of society operated not only through othering, but also through same-ing: in a sense, they "samed" *all* human beings by claiming that the entire species follows the same evolutional pattern.[72] This is again exemplified by Smith: while the Highlands are deemed the slowest part of Scotland to advance in civilization, even the more progressive Lowlands have been slower than England or other European countries, but he reckons that Scotland has profited greatly from the Union—despite initial difficulties—and is now on a good path.[73] Similar benefits are envisaged for Ireland and the overseas colonies. While Smith criticizes certain aspects of colonialism, the general principle of empire is still deemed capable of being very beneficial to all concerned, as a great catalyst for progress, trade, and universal material well-being—provided that such an empire is well managed and founded on greater economic and political equality.[74]

The role of Gaels and Celtic-speaking peoples as contemporary ancestors to the more "advanced" imperial centers was also manifested in the notion that the Celtic languages descended from Europe's aboriginal tongue, and could thus reveal information on early history. Jerome Stone (1727–1756) believed that Gaulish once was Europe's common language, antedated Latin and Greek, and had an importance only matched by Hebrew. He even claims linguistic parallels between Hebrew and Gaelic, and suggests that Gaelic might have been spoken in the Garden of Eden.[75] On the one hand, this continues older historiographical traditions by claiming the antiquity of Gaelic tradition as a source of Scottish national pride. On the other hand, the link to early European prehistory and even further back to Eden positions modern Gaels as contemporary ancestors, which denies them coevalness with the center and provides a clear link to colonial discourse. Another link to colonial discourse is the trope of noble savagery: the Garden of Eden is associated with human moral innocence before the Fall. Imagining prelapsarian humans as Gaels suggests that Gaeldom as a whole, even contemporary Gaeldom, consists of primitive people whose simple moral virtues are based on ignorance. While the "primitive" is here celebrated on moral grounds, he (or she) is still patronized on intellectual grounds. Early European colonizers had applied the same trope to Native Americans: here as well, comparisons to the Garden of Eden had been drawn. Thus, Stone's writings about the Gaels constitute one further piece in a larger discursive mosaic which connected Celtic "primitives" to colonial discourse further afield. Stone's image of Gaels as noble savages also anticipates a trend which became more prominent in Scottish literature during the romantic age (see chapter 3).

Stone was not the only scholar of Celtic linguistics whose work implied connections with colonial discourse. Another example is David Malcolm (d. 1748), who drew linguistic parallels between St. Kilda Gaelic, in his view a particularly old form of the language, and Chinese.[76] Here, the comparison is probably not based on an assumption of shared barbarian inferiority but on shared *ancientness*. In the eighteenth century, China was usually considered to be on a par with Western civilizations, while notions of its inferiority only spread in the nineteenth century.[77] Nonetheless, Malcolm's comparison constitutes another connection with colonial discourse because it links Celticism with Orientalism.

Despite the fascination with "primitives" as objects of study and as contemporary ancestors, the main impetus of practical policy was to "civilize" them as far as possible. As was already shown at the beginning of this chapter, the development of the modern capitalist nation-state in Britain initially proceeded primarily from the island's anglophone centers in England and the Scottish Lowlands. As the modern nation-state's central governments and the proponents of capitalism tried to extend their spheres of influence over the entire island, the Scottish Highlands seemed particularly hard to subdue, control, assimilate, and "modernize." They harbored very different socioeconomic and cultural patterns that, for a long time, seemed relatively resilient. Thus, the Gaelic Highlands increasingly appeared as an Other which the nation's anglophone capitalist centralizing mainstream was increasingly unwilling to tolerate. To justify its "modernizing" interference, the mainstream cast Gaelic traditions as backward and savage. Europe's power-hungry modern nation-states were not content with internal centralization; they also sought to extend their influence far beyond their own borders, for instance by establishing colonies overseas. Capitalism's voracious thirst for new resources and markets did not stop at national borders either: here as well, there was an appetite for overseas outposts and dependencies. As in the Scottish Highlands, expansive European states and capitalist business interests encountered social systems overseas which were organized in a different manner. Again, local interests often clashed with the interests of incoming forces. Here as well, subjugation and assimilation were justified by casting local traditions and populations as backward and savage. It is thus little wonder that different kinds of "savages," such as Gaels and Native Americans, were often depicted through the same strategies of "colonial discourse," and that they were also directly compared with each other. This chapter has already given various examples of anglophone mainstream texts which constructed the Gaels as an inferior Other and implicitly or explicitly compared them to colonized populations further afield. All these textual representations could be used to justify practical policies of subjugation and assimilation. The remaining sections of this chapter look more closely at these practical policies themselves, and show that similarities with overseas colonial projects existed not only on the textual, but also on a practical level. These sections also give examples of how individual policies were textualized. It will be shown how "internal colonial" and "civilizing" missions in the Gaidhealtachd were pursued on a wide range of levels: infrastructural, military, political, administrative, demographic, religious, educational, linguistic, sartorial, and economic.

"Colonial" and "Civilizing" Missions in the Gaidhealtachd

As has already been shown, Britain's non-Gaelic establishment in the seventeenth and eighteenth centuries was getting more and more impatient with Gaelic barbarity within its civilized national borders, and launched "civilizing missions" against it. Gaelic difference had to be assimilated. This tied in with Enlightenment theories of social evolution and with a colonial sense of civilizational superiority. In overseas colonialism the educational and missionizing drive only reached its heyday in the nineteenth century.[78] With regard to Scotland and its Gaels, the ideal of a civilizing mission developed already in the seventeenth century. Again, this illustrates that the "Celtic fringe" often set precedents for later colonial discourse about overseas territories. At the same time, the "otherness" of non-Europeans was a reference point for textualizations of "Celtic" otherness. Some authors suggested that Gaels, at least before they could be sufficiently assimilated to the national mainstream, had more in common with the non-European "primitives" encountered in the Orient or on overseas colonial ventures than with their fellow British subjects at home. This view is exemplified by Alexander Pennecuik's poem "A Curse on the Clan M'Phersone, Occasioned by the News of Glenbucket His Being Murdered by Them."[79] The clan's "villainy" is claimed to be "far worse than" that of "Infidel or Turk," and the speaker exclaims:

> Perpetual clouds thro' your black clan shall ring;
> Traitors 'gainst God, and Rebells 'gainst your King,
> Until you feel the law's severest rigour,
> And be extinguished like the base M'Gregor.[80]

The comparison between Gaels and "Infidel or Turk" goes back to the Middle Ages and forms another connection between Celticism and Orientalism. Further comparisons between Gaels and non-European Others—in this case Oceanians—are drawn in Henry Peter Brougham's comments on his 1799 visit to St. Kilda:

> Nothing in Captain Cook's voyages comes *half* so low. The natives are savage. . . . [Locally made] thread and horn-spoons are . . . infinitely coarser . . . , and made in smaller quantity and less variety, than those . . . in . . . the Pacific islands, New Holland . . . excepted. A total want of curiosity, a stupid gaze of wonder, an excessive eagerness for spirits and tobacco, a laziness only to be conquered by the hope of the above-mentioned cordials, and a beastly degree of filth, the natural consequence of this render the St Kildian character truly savage.[81]

Comparisons to Pacific Islanders were not the only colonial discourse tropes in Brougham's account; elsewhere, he even likens the people of St. Kilda to animals: "The only mortals among the . . . inhabitants whom we found in any degree civilized above the brutes, were the priest and his family."[82]

While Brougham could still perceive remote St. Kilda as untouched by civilization, other areas of the Gaidhealtachd had already been exposed to "civilizing missions" for about two centuries. The pre-Union Scottish government, Cromwellian occupying forces, post-Union Hanoverian British authorities, and various religious institutions had all tried to increase their control over the Gaidhealtachd and assimilate it to their standards. Such measures were partly facilitated by scientific and technical advancement, for instance in mapmaking and road-building. Moreover, after the 1707 Union, governmental civilizing missions to the Gaidhealtachd had more clout, as considerable English resources were added to Scotland's own.[83] Belief in integration reached its heyday after 1745—it seemed increasingly likely that Gaelic otherness as the last stand of inner-British barbarism would soon be assimilated into civilization.

Ever since the inception of the modern state, the quest for a unified, centrally controllable nation kindled desires for more knowledge about the internal Other, as well as for classification and discursive containment. This is illustrated by innovations in cartography. The first systematic mapping of Scotland in the 1590s already reflected the wish to unify and control the national territory, although these maps were not easily available and the coastline was not accurately charted before the mid- and late seventeenth century.[84] This also entailed greater integration and internal colonization of the Gaidhealtachd, similar to the function of mapping in overseas colonial discourse.[85] Further parallels to overseas imperialism, but also to colonized Ireland, can be discerned in early modern attempts to colonize Scotland's Highlands and Islands more directly via military occupation or "plantations" of anglophone settlers, as well as indirect attempts to control the Other by assimilating the native population itself to the center's standards of religion, language, education, economics, or dress.

Throughout the British Empire, more direct forms of conquest, control, and coercion were combined with more indirect strategies of rule, like rewarding voluntary self-assimilation with career benefits, and reliance on local intermediaries. However, the proportions in which direct and indirect measures were combined could differ from region to region. In Scotland, "civilizing missions" eventually relied much more strongly on indirect strategies than they did in Ireland or overseas, where more violent and direct coercion played a greater part.

For historian Allan Kennedy, the extent to which the integration of the Gaidhealtachd into the Scottish nation state relied on indirect rule and voluntary assimilation largely devalues the "internal colonialism" or "imperial" model, at least for parts of the seventeenth century. He posits a "collaborative" counter-model which stresses the collusion of local elites and the center's readiness to temper its desire for control and assimilation with a pragmatic respect for local interests and peculiarities. However, his juxtaposition of "imperial" and "collaborative" as binary opposites is problematic, since it implies a simplistic understanding of imperialism as necessarily based on a clear-cut dichotomy between colonizer and colonized where *none* of the colonized population willingly cooperates or profits, and which always aimed for a wholesale transformation of the colonized society.[86] In reality, colonialism very often relied on a degree of local collaboration, indirect rule, and only partial transformation of colonized lifestyles, even in times and places where Kennedy considers "imperial" readings appropriate (e.g., eighteenth-century Scotland or Europe's overseas colonies). Although Kennedy himself admits the possibility of overlaps between the "imperial" and "collaborative" models, he immediately negates the importance of such overlaps and returns to stressing the differences between the two models by reiterating a more simplistic model of imperialism which sees the periphery as an "abject," "passive recipient of an acquisitive centre," while he claims that only a "collaborative" model can accommodate a "vested interest of local elites in strengthening the relationship" with the core.[87] The notion that *any* colony has ever been a completely passive recipient would probably be rejected by most postcolonialists. Hence, while Kennedy's work brilliantly illustrates the complexity of center-periphery relations in the Highlands, I would argue that this complexity does not invalidate (post)colonial readings, especially where these readings focus on discourse, representation, and perceptions rather than sociohistorical realities, since the former often *claim* clear-cut dichotomies even where social realities are more complex.[88]

Nonetheless, even in discourse the position of Scottish Gaeldom could slightly differ from the position of colonized populations elsewhere. For instance, Scottish Gaelic "barbarians" supposedly had sufficient potential for assimilation, while Irish "barbarians" did not. Hence, stupidity as an ethnic trait features more frequently in anglophone stereotypes of Irish Gaels than in depictions of Scottish Highlanders.[89] Even where coercive measures along Irish or overseas colonial lines were *planned* for Scotland, their implementation was often pursued more halfheartedly—possibly one of the reasons why the Scottish Gaelic sense of victimization by (and opposition to) the government was often less unanimous than in more "typical" colonies. But again, this is a difference in degree rather than a difference in kind. Ambiguous "native" responses to colonial governance, mixing acquiescence and repulsion, also existed elsewhere, and the difference is rather in emphasis and proportion. In eighteenth- to twenty-first-century Scotland, the proportion of acquiescence seems higher than in colonies which had to be conquered by military force rather than by treaty, or which ended their colonial dependency with the help of military insurrection.

Despite such differences, the objectives—and some of the practical and representational strategies—of "civilizing missions" in the Highlands show various similarities to more "typical" concepts of colonial projects. This is further illustrated in the following sections.

Military, Political, and Administrative Control; Expropriation and Lowland "Plantations"

An early attempt to exert direct Lowland control over the Gaidhealtachd, in a manner which parallelled—in vocabulary and action—seventeenth-century colonial policies in Ireland and North America, was the attempt to settle Lowlanders in Scottish Gaelic areas, comparable to the plantation of Ulster. Already in 1597, the Scottish government proposed the establishment of burghs and settlements of anglophone Lowland settlers in Kintyre, Lewis, and Lochaber—a project which the king shortly afterwards described as "planting Colonies among them of answerable In-lands subjects, that . . . may reforme and civilize the best inclined among them: rooting out or transporting the barbarous and stubborne sorte, and planting ciuilitie in their roomes."[90] The pacification of the Isles and their inhabitants should be effected "not by agreement with the countrey people, bot by extirpation of them."[91] In practice, however, these schemes met with considerable resistance and setbacks.[92] It was this less successful outcome that set the "plantations" scheme in the Scottish Gaidhealtachd apart from its counterparts in Ireland and North America. Its intentions and colonial mindset were, however, very similar.

The seventeenth century saw several military expeditions, forced expropriations, evictions, and the dispersal or outlawing of certain clans. However, external pressure was not the only relevant factor. Internal disunity of those clans also played a part. Moreover, much of the external pressure came not directly from central government but indirectly via rival Highland families, "frontier clans with a foot in both Highland and Lowland society" functioning as the crown's "Trojan horses in Gaeldom"—such as the MacKenzies and Campbells.[93] Unlike their Irish counterparts, Scotland's Gaelic elites were not destroyed by a big anti-Gaelic scheme of military conquest and wholescale expropriation. Routing Gaelic society and literally supplanting it with Lowlanders was not considered the only solution for the Scottish Highlands. It was believed that this region might also be improved by civilizing the Gaels themselves and integrating them into the national body politic. Direct penetration and plantation of the Gaidhealtachd was complemented by attempts at indirect control through pressuring clan chiefs (who, for example, had to swear oaths of responsibility for their followers' good conduct), commercialization and anglicization of estate management, legislation against the Gaelic language, the assimilation of Gaelic elites into Scotland's landed classes, and their use as local arms of government.[94]

This greater reliance on indirect ways of conquering Scotland, and the smaller proportion of more direct strategies, may be one reason why (post)colonial status is often more readily ascribed to Ireland, where there was a greater proportion of direct coercion in the mixture of strategies. That Irish Gaels were colonized through more uncompromising tactics than the Scottish Gaels also provoked different reactions: in Ireland, political and discursive resistance is considered to have been fiercer, while in Scotland "the stormy relations between the Stewart kings and their Gaelic-speaking subjects were regarded in the same light as quarrels between clans or kin-groups which themselves could easily turn bitter and bloody." Thus, the Scottish Gaels, "though they might portray themselves as sorely oppressed, . . . could not convincingly ascribe their predicament to an alien power which sought to conquer their lands."[95] That Gaeldom was a part of Scotland was never questioned, and it was Scotland's own kings the Gaels were in conflict with. Hence, any Scottish Gaelic sense of oppression was felt to be an intra-national conflict between two Scottish entities. Pre-conquest Ireland, by contrast, was felt to have been its own country, so that English and later British anglocentric hegemony was experienced as a foreign conquest and an imposition from external enemies.

In Scotland, a more obviously alien invasion was the Cromwellian occupation of the mid-seventeenth century which also attempted to increase centralist control of the Gaidhealtachd, for instance by establishing garrisons in strategic places. After 1660, Scotland's own restored government also made efforts to "pacify" the Highlands. For instance, the expansion of the road network facilitated both military control and the intensification of Lowland-Highland trade connections which made their own contributions to integration.[96]

After the failed Jacobite rising of 1715, strict measures for extending centralist control over the Gaidhealtachd were suggested, but implementation was rather halfhearted. Some estates were forfeited but restored after six years in return for assurances of good conduct, and the Disarming Act was not very strictly enforced either. Garrisons were again established, along with a further road- and bridge-building program to facilitate military control, but the government soon shifted its priorities elsewhere.[97] Lynch even argues that "the Union Regime was until the mid-1730s in less control of the Highlands than any government since the late sixteenth century."[98]

The Jacobite rising of 1745 focused government attention again upon the Highlands and strengthened old prejudices about an inextricable connection between this alien, "barbarian" culture and Stuart insurrection. In reality, Jacobite aristocrats were not any more traditionalist than Hanoverian ones, for instance regarding commercialization or patronage for Gaelic culture. Neither did Gaeldom's own marginalized status lead to a *generally* anticolonial attitude: for instance, the Jacobite chieftain Donald Cameron of Lochiel participated in Caribbean trade.[99] Despite such incongruities, Lowland and English perceptions often considered all things Gaelic as irredeemably unprogressive, both economically and politically. Jacobitism was perceived as the expression of a threatening barbarian culture, and the fact that the Highland army had managed to move so far south and even planned a march on London (they got as far as Derby before turning back) had given "civilized" Britain quite a fright.[100] The picture painted of these "barbarians" in Hanoverian discourse is gruesome indeed. The *Scots Magazine* described the Jacobite army as follows:

> Out of the barbarous corners of this country: many . . . are Papists, under the immediate direction of their priests; trained up to the sword, by being practised in open robbery and violence; void of property of their own; the constant invaders of that of others; and who know no law, but the will of their leaders.[101]

The apparent paradox that Highlanders are associated with lawlessness, freedom, and slavery at the same time can be resolved as follows: lawlessness and freedom both relate to the *chieftains'* relative autonomy from centralist state authority. As the centralist state is associated with civic freedom, a weakness of state authority in the Highlands means that the *common* Highlanders, the subjects of the chief, are not free. They are seen as slaves to their chief's tyrannical local power. It is thus no real paradox that later heavy policing of the Gaidhealtachd was described as "extending freedom" to common Highlanders.[102] The portrayal of local Highland traditions as cruel and barbarous makes government efforts to subdue the Highlands appear as a benevolent civilizing mission, and thus legitimates the subjugation of the region.

The same contrast between barbarous local traditions and benevolent plans for civilizing missions is projected in an anonymous text entitled "Some Remarks on the Highland Clans, and Methods Proposed for Civilizing Them" (1746 or shortly after), which likewise considers "the General Savage Character of the people" as capable of the most grisly deeds: "their Barbarous inclinations, which According to Ancient Customs will be the murdering of people of all Sexes and Ages, the Burning of Houses, and Cutting of Cattle to pieces."[103] Again, a major evil is clan feudalism, which in turn induces raiding and laziness.[104] Some English people in 1745 even seem to have believed that Highlanders were cannibals. The memoirs of James Johnstone, who fought on the Jacobite side, contain an anecdote about a terrified Englishwoman who thought that Highlanders ate children.[105]

Following the shock of 1745, the mainstream was now determined to pull out evil by its roots. After the decisive Hanoverian victory at Culloden, the Highlands suffered severe reprisals, and more long-term transformations were set on their way. These were part of a wider effort to increase cultural and ideological integration throughout Britain, which in turn was part of a Europe-wide trend towards national identity-building.[106] But in the Gaidhealtachd, integration had a particular urgency and seemed less like a connection of equally worthy partners than a civilizing mission among primitive barbarians, thus acquiring distinct colonial overtones. The Hanoverian judge and politician Duncan Forbes wrote:

> The inhabitants of the mountains . . . united . . . by the singularity of dress and language, stick close to their antient idle way of life; retain their barbarous customs and maxims . . . ; and being accustomed to . . . Arms, and inured to hard living, are dangerous to the Public peace . . . untill, being deprived of Arms for some years, they forget the use of them. . . .
>
> . . . It has been for . . . many years impracticable . . . to give the Law its course amongst the mountains . . . , for this reason . . . , that the Crown, in former times, was obliged to put . . . Jurisdictions, in the hands of powerful families in the Highlands, who . . . could give

> execution to the Laws within their . . . territories, . . . frequently . . . at the expense of considerable bloodshed.
>
> But as . . . good order and government have been very much improved of late years over all Scotland, excepting the Highlands . . . ; it seems absolutely necessary . . . to restrain and civilize those lawless Highlanders. . . . Whilst the rest of the Country is . . . improving, they continue . . . their accustomed sloth and barbarity. The Want of Roads . . . [and] Accommodation . . . and the difference of language, have proved hitherto a bar to all free intercourse between the high and low lands, and have left the Highlanders in possession of their idle customs and extravagant maxims, absolute strangers to the advantages that must accrue from Industry, and to the blessing of having those advantages protected by Laws.
>
> . . . If the Highlanders can be effectually debarred from the use of Arms . . . , their Successors . . . must be as harmless as the commonality of the adjacent Low Countries; and when they can no longer live by Rapine, must think of living by Industry.
>
> . . . It will require a considerable standing force, . . . for some years, to disarm . . . the rebellious Highlanders.[107]

Forbes also suggests economic civilizing missions to complement the military ones.[108] The Mackay chieftain Lord Reay likewise hoped that military measures would "civilize" the Highlanders by transforming them from "wild" and "idle ignorant people" into "useful subjects"—though this would be difficult, "as it is easier to conquer than to civilize barbarous people."[109]

Post-Culloden penalty measures against the Highlands entailed a period of terror and killings inflicted by government troops upon the local population, as well as formal trials, large-scale transportations to the colonies, and executions.[110] Lynch's evaluation of these events explicitly draws colonial parallels to Ireland, and implicitly also to overseas territories: "it was . . . a repeat performance of the final Elizabethan conquest of Ireland after 1601, . . . bloodletting . . . after forty years of frustration . . . in dealing with a Celtic people. It was one more act in the long drama of the consolidation of an English Empire."[111] The drastic nature of post-Culloden punitive measures in the Highlands also begs the question of whether the emerging field of postcolonial trauma studies might lend useful tools for future inquiries into the impact of those measures on the Highland population and its culture.

Long before Lynch's historical retrospective, parallels to Ireland were already drawn in the eighteenth century: in the aftermath of Culloden it was repeatedly suggested that the Scottish Gaidhealtachd should get the same treatment that Ireland received in the previous century, that is, the complete dispossession of indigenous elites and their replacement by English or Lowland incomers.[112] However, the path eventually chosen was to further assimilate *indigenous* Highlanders. This further confirms that in Scotland hybridity and assimilation were more important, and boundaries between colonizer and colonized less neat, than in Ireland.

Measures implemented after 1745 to control and assimilate the Gaidhealtachd once and for all included a renewal and intensification of earlier measures: increased military control through garrisons, extensions of the road network, and building other infrastructural features like canals, harbors, and bridges. The civilizing potential of military occupation was commended by an anonymous account of the mid-eighteenth century Highlands which is generally assumed to have been written by the Lowlander and government agent David Bruce:

> The . . . Savage Highlanders need to be Bridled . . . by Garrisons and Standing Forces. . . . Those unhappy and infatuated People will . . . Continue Savages if nothing else is done to recover them from their Ignorance and Barbarity . . . ; but as the rest of the People of Britain who are now Civilized were once as Wild and Barbarous as the Highlanders, . . . proper measures would Civilize them also.[113]

A colonial mindset is indicated by epithets like "savage," "wild," and "barbarous," as well as the trope of contemporary ancestry and the universal ladder of progress. The text even draws an explicit comparison between Gaels (albeit not contemporary ones but their forebears before ca. 1730) and "Hottentots," namely regarding their supposed uncleanliness.[114] Again, this illustrates the frequent association of Gaels with overseas colonized peoples. The particular colonized people singled out for comparison here is likewise noteworthy: the "Hottentots," alias the Khoikhoi in southern Africa, were not just seen as one among many other "savage" ethnic communities, but occupied a special position in the European colonial imagination as the most savage people of them all. Such ideas had been current since the mid-seventeenth century, and in the eighteenth century it was even believed that "Hottentots" occupied an interim position between humans and animals. The term "Hottentot" could also be used as a "common slur for someone of congenital stupidity."[115] In addition, it featured as a synonym for a person who was supposedly uncivilized or culturally inferior.[116]

Apart from a general association with primitiveness and stupidity, a more particular reason for comparisons between "Hottentots" and Gaels could have been that the traditional economies of both cultures contained strong elements of pastoralism and had recently been disrupted by the encroachment of "foreign" systems of modernization: Khoikhoi autonomy declined due to European encroachment between the mid-seventeenth and eighteenth century; while the Highland Scottish economy was changed by the rise of capitalism. As a result, many people in both cultures had become landless laborers. Their "belated" introduction to capitalism, and in the Khoikhoi's case even to agriculturalism, also inspired mainstream onlookers with the notion that both Gaels and Khoikhoi were lazy and had remained integral parts of their natural environment instead of becoming proper conquerors and transformers of nature.[117]

However, there were also important differences. One of these was skin color: as white Europeans, Gaels possessed no unmistakable phenotypical differences from the representatives of European mainstream cultures. Another obvious difference between Gaelic and "Hottentot" Others could have been religion: even the most hostile observer would have found it difficult to deny that Scotland's Highlanders were religious, though they were often said to follow the wrong religion: Catholicism as the "wrong" brand of Christianity, or residues of pagan superstition in folk belief. "Hottentots," by contrast, were sometimes deemed too stupid to have any religion whatsoever.[118]

The relative closeness of "Celtic" religion to European mainstream culture was not necessarily a deterrent from Gaelic-African comparisons, even concerning religion: the term "Hottentot" was also used for the disparagement of one kind of Christian by another. This becomes clear from Strother's remark on another "Hottentot"-"Celtic" connection:

> The slur ["Hottentot" as a synonym for stupidity] was often transferred from one colonial situation to another: Ireland. The term was also . . . used to disparage a person's religious understanding. . . . When applied to the Irish, probably both prongs of the epithet were intended.[119]

That Ireland was not the only Celtic country that was deemed comparable to "Hottentots" is illustrated by Bruce's remarks on the Scottish Highlands. The associative connection which Bruce's text forges between Scottish Gaels and the extreme colonial otherness of "Hottentots" shows the extent to which the Gaels were part of the colonial imagination. Despite the Highlanders' phenotypical, geographical, and cultural closeness to Britain's anglophone mainstream, they are likened to an indigenous ethnic group in southern Africa whose phenotypical and cultural features are persistently portrayed by colonial discourse as a case of utmost otherness and "primitiveness." This not only exemplifies the fluidity of race and ethnicity as discursive constructions, but also highlights that the history of constructing the Gaels as colonial barbarians makes postcolonialism a highly relevant analytical approach in Scottish studies.

Bruce not only proclaims Gaels and Hottentots to be *equal* in savagery and in their need of civilizing missions, but even considers the domestic civilizing missions to be *more* urgent than overseas ones: "Has not Britain laid out much Greater Sums on Colonies abroad of not half the Importance of Civilizing and Improving this part of Britain itself . . . ?"[120]

Post-1745 military measures were complemented by legislation: in 1747, the private jurisdictions of clan chiefs were abolished and replaced by royal jurisdiction. Estates of rebel chiefs were forfeited to the crown on an unprecedented scale, which was also considered a starting point for the infiltration of Lowland economic practices (capitalism) into the Highlands. Looking back, the twentieth-century journalist and administrator James Shaw Grant labeled those eighteenth-century military and legal penalty measures, as well as the dispossession of rebel chiefs, as "colonial" measures.[121] The new thoroughness of "civilizing missions" finally promised success. Direct political, infrastructural, and military measures were only one side of the coin. Other "civilizing missions" concentrated on culture and ideology, complementing direct mainstream interference by indirect control through the assimilation of "native" populations. These cultural missions also go back as far as the early seventeenth century, as the following section demonstrates.

Religion, Education, Language Policy, and Assimilation

As important sites of cultural power, the church and education played important roles in missions to "civilize" the Gaidhealtachd.[122] An early attempt to promote cultural assimilation was the legislative initiative known as the Statutes of Iona (1609), which decreed that every gentleman or yeoman owning a certain number of cattle had to send his eldest child to the Lowlands for a Protestant and anglophone education. Chiefs from the central and northern Highlands had already done so for decades, but most on the west coast had not. The statutes aimed to further the transformation of clan elites into responsible members of the Scottish body politic, and probably also aimed to weaken ideological unity between clan and chief.

A significant proportion of the Gaelic elites now spent more time in the Lowlands—for education, and in adult life due to increased involvement in national politics and the pleasures of southern lifestyles. There were also attempts to carry Lowland culture into the Highlands themselves and spread its influence among the Gaelic-speaking masses. The de-gaelicization of elite education was extended to children of lower rank in 1616 through the Act for the Settling of Parochial Schools, although its actual implementation in the Highlands had to wait for several decades. The aim of this act was "that the . . . Inglishe toung be universallie plantit, and the Irishe language, whilk is one of the . . . principall causis of the continewance of barbaritie and incivilitie amongis the inhabitantis of the Ilis and Heylandis, may be abolisheit and removeit."[123] Around 1620, Sir Robert Gordon gave the following advice to his nephew John, 13th Earl of Sutherland:

> Take away the reliques of the Irishe barbaritie which as yet remains in your countrey, to wit, the Irishe langage, and the habit. . . . Ciwilize your countrey and the inhabitants. . . . Plant schooles in ewerie corner . . . to instruct the youth to speak Inglishe. Preasse to ciwilize your countrey and the inhabitants . . . lykwyse in all other things.[124]

In 1626, Charles I renewed the earlier governmental order to establish anglophone schools in all parishes to facilitate the "civilising and removing of the Irish language and barbaritie out of the heigh lands."[125] But a truly thorough implementation of linguistic assimilation had to wait until the eighteenth and nineteenth centuries. For the present, King Charles soon "lost interest in 'civilising' the Highlanders, who were eventually to become his most prominent supporters."[126]

In addition to linguistic missions, there were also religious missions to convert Catholics and Episcopalians to Presbyterianism and to ensure that Highlanders already adhering to the reformed faith would withstand the forces of counter-reformation, such as Jesuit missionaries, among whom, thanks to their Irish connections, Gaelic language skills were—at least initially—more widespread than among their Protestant counterparts. It was also hoped that the extinction of Catholicism and Episcopalianism would undermine the Jacobitism associated with these denominations. Moreover, the eighteenth-century increase of the kirk's disciplinary powers, for example, concerning moral transgressions, meant that clan commons were no longer subject to just one master (their chief), but two. The kirk could thus become a rival authority which broke the feudal chief's regional monopoly of power.[127]

Missions were run by different bodies, such as the General Assembly of the Church of Scotland or the Society in Scotland for Propagating Christian Knowledge (SSPCK, dominated by landlords and lawyers). From 1725 onwards, such missions were also supported by the London government. After 1745, crown commissioners administering annexed estates likewise promoted Presbyterianism. Between the defeat of the rising in 1746 and the final removal of the Jacobite threat through the death of the Stuart prince in 1788, there was also more direct government suppression of Catholicism and Episcopalianism which condemned these creeds to a situation verging on outlawry. During his post-1746 terror campaign, the Duke of Cumberland, commander of the government forces, demanded that Catholic priests should be surrendered and chapels destroyed. Teinds (tithes) were monopolized by Presbyterians, which caused great financial difficulties to the Episcopalian Church while Catholicism as an international denomination could resort to external funding. Educational missions, like the religious ones, were carried out by different—often Presbyterian—institutions: some schools were run directly by local parishes, some by religious charity organizations like the SSPCK.

Perceptions of the Gaidhealtachd as a religious wasteland paralleled similar views on overseas colonies. The title of an SSPCK report even mentions both missions in the same breath: *State of the Society in Scotland, for Propagating Christian Knowledge, Giving a Brief Account of the Condition of the Highlands and Islands of Scotland. . . . Together with Some Account of the Society's Missionaries for Converting the Native Indians of America.*[128] Later, a report to the same organization commented on the Gaels' inadequate theological knowledge and their need for ministers and schools: "They know no more than by hearsay, that there is a God. . . . Were they to be asked anything further they would be found . . . as ignorant as the wild americans."[129] In 1765, the Rev. Dr. John Walker's report to the General Assembly stated that many Gaels retained the "prejudices of an uncivilized state," but that a thorough civilizing mission could improve this situation, as it already had in some parts of the Highlands: "wherever they have access to Schools . . . and the ordinances of Religion . . . they are . . . more civilized in their manners, and in their way of Life."[130] Similar progress had been noted in 1760 by Archibald Wallace, an Edinburgh friend of the Gaelic poet Dugald Buchanan. Buchanan was a preacher in Rannoch, and Wallace praised these efforts as "very dilligent and successful in civilizing one of the most barbarous places in the Highlands."[131]

Civilizing objectives identified by educational bodies fall into different categories. Christian schools emphasized the religious mission: promoting Protestantism. In line with the Protestant tenet that every Christian should be able to read the Bible, schools stressed the teaching of literacy, often using religious class texts only. The second mission of education was economic: already in the early eighteenth century, the SSPCK asserted that greater economic integration of Highlanders was possible, and set up a scheme for establishing "industrial schools." The teaching of crafts and "industry" parallels the objectives and curricula of certain missionary schools overseas.[132] The third and fourth major aspects of educational missions were linguistic and political: during the seventeenth and eighteenth centuries, the Church of Scotland aimed to transform all Highlanders not only into Protestants, but also into loyal subjects of the monarchy (after 1688, this meant the Protestant monarchy, not the Catholic Jacobite line). This objective seemed unattainable without anglicization because the Gaelic language appeared to be inextricably bound up with religious deviation, backwardness, and political unrest. In 1703 the Synod of Glasgow and Ayr wrote about the Highlanders:

> While they continue in their present neglected state Strangers to the Gospell, and bound up to a separate Language and Interest of their own, they are most dangerous to this Church and Nation, ready to assist invading Forrainers, or to break out for plunder in case of Domestick troubles.[133]

But the synod also assumed that Highlanders, "once brought to Religion, Humanity, Industry, and the Low Countrey Language . . . , might yet become a noble accession to the Commonwealth."[134]

It is thus hardly surprising that the church did little to spread the Gaelic Bible, and even in preaching used English wherever possible. Church of Scotland schools and SSPCK schools were similarly unsupportive of Gaelic: as soon as basics in English were acquired, English was supposed to be the sole medium of instruction, and only anglophone texts were to be used for reading. As the SSPCK put it:

> Nothing can be more effectual for reducing these countries to order, and making them usefull to the Commonwealth than teaching them their duty to God, their King and Countrey and rooting out their Irish language, and this has been the case of the Society as far as they could.[135]

Using Gaelic in class was only permissible as a temporary measure to facilitate learning and thus eventually assist anglicization. Teaching literacy in Gaelic was not encouraged.[136] This policy was supported by government officials: crown commissioners who administered estates that had been annexed after the 1745 rebellion likewise recommended the appointment of non-Gaelic-speaking schoolmasters and the prohibition of Gaelic speech in class. Spinning schools for girls established on such estates also taught English. J. S. Grant includes these policies in his list of "colonial" features in Highland history.[137] Although the colonial comparison is arguably justified, it is also important to note differences between internal and external colonialism. For instance, Janet Sorensen points out that "the initial emphasis on linguistic homogenization was much more pronounced in the Highlands (and Wales and Ireland) than in India" because Britain's internal peripheries were not only perceived as a colonial Other but also as a national Same.[138] It seems ironic that precisely this sense of sameness and non-coloniality subjected the Celtic fringe to a linguistic colonization which was more thorough than in many overseas colonies.

Religious, cultural, and economic missions, or even the same kind of mission as understood by different institutions, were not always congruous. While schools wanted to teach Protestantism, English, and economically profitable skills like spinning or weaving, landlords might accept the latter two aims but not necessarily the first: Catholic landlords sometimes protected the Roman faith among their tenants, though this seems to have decreased after 1770. A second incongruity occurred toward the turn of the nineteenth century: while Presbyterian institutions continued to see Catholicism as a form of quasi-paganism in need of missionizing and extermination, the government changed its attitude. Catholicism was no longer associated with a Jacobite menace and had proved its loyalty to the Hanoverian establishment. The number of Highland Catholics had declined anyway, mainly due to emigration, and the government, concerned to stop this population drain, became the main patron of the Catholic Church in the Highlands.[139]

A third incongruity between different "civilizing" objectives lay in the fact that general educational and civilizational aims of uncompromising anglicization sometimes clashed with religious objectives. Reaching the hearts and minds of the flock was easier in their mother tongue. Moreover, it would have been desirable to the locals (clergy, teachers, and populace) if children acquired literacy in Gaelic *and* English, thus being able to read the Gaelic psalms to their illiterate relatives. The educational bodies' central authorities were less eager to provide Gaelic literacy. There were also differences between organizations. The seventeenth- and eighteenth-century Presbyterian Church was more inclined to use Gaelic for religious instruction than its Episcopalian counterpart was, probably because Presbyterianism gave local elders and ministers a greater say and placed more emphasis on the sermon, which needed to use a language that the listeners understood well. The General Assembly showed an earlier lenience toward Gaelic than the SSPCK.

A limited amount of Gaelic religious reading became permissible in schools from the mid-eighteenth century onwards. As the political threat of Jacobitism and chieftainly autonomy was now annihilated, the Gaelic language no longer seemed a great menace to national stability. All these instances of tolerance toward Gaelic did not spring from sudden cross-cultural respect, but were mainly intended as short-term tactics on the way toward long-term anglicization. Nonetheless, these tactical concessions had some unintended positive effects on Gaelic culture: greater tolerance toward Gaelic in schools, as well as bursaries and educational facilities to create a body of Gaelic-speaking preachers, produced a core of people who could contribute to the creation of a modern Gaelic literature. The same developments created a readership for such literature. These policies also prepared the ground for the extensive use of Gaelic by nineteenth-century evangelical religion, an important factor in language maintenance far into the twentieth century.

But the educational "English only" practice still died hard. Again, the sense of a civilizing mission and the parallels to overseas colonization became explicit in the terminology used. In 1760 the Revs. Hyndman and Dick reported to the Church of Scotland's General Assembly about the success of industrial schools:

> The propagation of the English Language appears to be the most effectual method of diffusing through those Countries the advantages of Religion and Civil Society. . . . We observed with pleasure that the English Language is making a very quick progress in the neighbourhood of those small *colonys* which have come from the low Country for the promoting of Manufactures.[140]

"Colony" might be read, firstly, as a relatively neutral general term for a human settlement in a rural area, or, secondly, as it is generally understood today, that is, a settlement of people from a conqueror nation on new territory. The context in which the term is used here, that is, the endorsement of a mission of cultural change, suggests that the second reading is more appropriate. Colonial terminology was also used in a pamphlet from 1809 which reviews the SSPCK's founding objectives from 100 years earlier: before the SSPCK's educational mission took off, Gaelic society was full of "plunderers" and "gross barbarism," "their minds were fierce," "their manners barbarous," "hostile to . . . Government"—while SSPCK schools endeavored to "rescue . . . [them] from . . . barbarism."[141]

All these examples show that the objectives of religious and educational policies in the Scottish Highlands often followed colonial patterns. The next issue which pertains to a discussion of these policies in (post)colonial terms is the question of whether the local population's reaction to the "missions" likewise followed colonial (or anticolonial) patterns. A related issue is the ultimate efficiency of the "civilizing missions."

As to religion, Presbyterianism indeed became more widespread in the eighteenth-century Gaidhealtachd, especially after 1746. However, many Highlanders' allegiance to the Presbyterian Church of Scotland was initially formal and nominal rather than heartfelt, partly because Calvinism's individualist ethic did not easily "appeal to a people for whom work and war were necessarily communal."[142] The real breakthrough for Presbyterianism came not from the mainstream of the national church, but from a new brand of Presbyterianism: evangelicalism. The latter's spread through the Gaidhealtachd was not exclusively due to outside interference, but also to indigenous developments, such as the role of lay evangelicals (*na daoine*, "the men") who combined modern evangelical religion with elements of local tradition, such as speaking Gaelic and fulfilling a seer-like role. Despite their rootedness in local culture, these lay preachers did not support *all* its aspects: similar to Lowland civilizers, they regarded many Gaelic traditions as quasi-pagan and wanted to root them out. The evangelical movement, however, was demotic. It became especially important in the nineteenth century. By restoring a degree of local self-confidence, and through its antiestablishment strain, it laid vital foundations for the anti-landlord protests which happened later in that century.[143] Evangelicalism also transformed outsiders' perceptions of Gaels: while earlier accounts portrayed them as barbarian quasi-pagans, by the 1820s the Highlanders often appeared as sober Calvinists, but sometimes also as religious fanatics—an image which partly survives today.[144]

As to the linguistic mission, Scottish Gaels were not entirely hostile to anglophone education. This illustrates a tendency which has been discernible since the Middle Ages: though Lowland discourse often portrayed the Gaels as outside the nation, the Gaels themselves did not construct an alternative Gaelic nationality, but often felt concentric loyalties to both Gaeldom and Scotland. If their advancement within Scottish society necessitated cultural hybridization and the acquisition of English language skills, this was commonly deemed an acceptable tactic rather than being condemned as a betrayal of Gaelic heritage. As formal education was often only available through anglicizing schools, people were eager to use them.

Despite indigenous complicity in anglicization or at least hybridization, the effects on Gaelic culture were not always favorable. After the indigenous written tradition of premodern Gaelic elite culture had declined (e.g., due to elite anglicization), modern literate mass culture in the Highlands relied largely on English, the language favored by church and schools. "The possibility of a smooth transition . . . from medieval to modern culture . . . was lost."[145] Henceforth, Gaelic culture remained predominantly oral, with long-term effects on linguistic identities. In time, the notion that literacy was a prerequisite for cultural excellence was also internalized by Gaels, who then perceived their largely oral mother tongue as inferior to the only medium of book-learning the schools had taught them: English.[146] This cultural cringe has partly endured into the present, although Gaelic literacy has increased since the nineteenth century (partly due to the evangelical movement), and although the role of Gaelic in schools has improved.

Nevertheless, the efficiency of seventeenth- and eighteenth-century educational missions should not be overestimated. They achieved some of their objectives, such as spreading Protestant doctrines, increasing basic literacy, and giving more Highlanders a smattering of English. But success was not as complete as the "colonizers" might have wished. There were still too many Gaels who had no access to education at all; or if they did, their exposure was not sustained enough. Due to low population density and rough terrain, the way to school was often too far and too difficult, especially in the Isles. Poverty made tuition fees hard to afford and often required children to help with farm labor rather than going to school. The Highland practice of spending long summer months on remote shielings (pastures in the mountains) to graze the cattle likewise made for patchy school attendance. Even where children did go to school, the teaching methods failed to give them a good active knowledge of English. Many ended up being able to memorize or read aloud anglophone religious texts without properly understanding them; and without much ability to form their own sentences.[147] While the education available installed cultural cringes and a belief that Gaelic was not an adequate vehicle for learned discourse, it did not yet succeed in making English replace Gaelic as a community language for everyday topics.

While certain colonial elements existed in the self-understanding of both sides—for example, a sense of civilizing mission among school providers, and the beginnings of a cultural cringe among the local populace—not all aspects of the Highland experience conform to the classical colonial model. For instance, binary constructions seemed somewhat less prominent in the Highlands, while more fluid boundaries and hybridity appear to have been (even) more important than elsewhere.

Religion, education, and language were not the only fields where cultural assimilation policies were implemented. Another significant area was dress. After 1747 Highland dress was proscribed by law—another act of cultural imperialism which is included on J. S. Grant's list of "colonial" elements in Highland history.[148] The Disclothing Act was not always efficiently implemented, especially in the remoter areas and during a period of greater leniency between the 1760s and the formal lifting of the ban in the 1780s.[149] Nonetheless, it managed to abolish the plaid as usual everyday wear. The revival of Highland dress was mostly a matter for special occasions and romantic fancies enjoyed by the privileged.

Economy: Capitalization and "Developmental Aid"

Since the late seventeenth century, extensions of the road network facilitated greater integration between some Highland areas and the Lowland economy, mainly via the cattle trade. Commercialization slowly got under way, often as a result of clan chiefs' own initiatives. However, in Lowland eyes this development was not fast and thorough enough; and certain feudal patterns in Highland social organization inhibited commercialization. After 1745, civilizing missions in the Highlands became increasingly economic in orientation, and several initiatives were launched to support and accelerate commercialization.[150] J. S. Grant again indicts these measures as "colonial."[151] The Rev. Dr. John Walker, having traveled the Hebrides, wrote a report for the Commissioners of the Annexed Estates in which he portrayed the Gaels as occupying a lower rung on the civilizational ladder, but possessing ample potential for improvement—if led by a benevolent outsider's guiding hand:

> Their Soil remains, as it was left at the Creation: The Inhabitants, when compared to their fellow Subjects, with Respect to Arts, are in almost the same Situation as in the Days of Oscian, yet . . . capable of being greatly advanced . . . : and . . . a sensible, hardy, and laborious Race of People.[152]

> Highlanders are as capable to judge of . . . and . . . pursue any innovation that is advantageous . . . as any other People whatever.[153]

> Unassisted Exertions of Industry are not to be expected from a People still in the Pastoral Stage of Society; nor from unenlightened Minds are we . . . to expect the sudden Discontinuance of Bad Customs. But, whatever the Highlands are defective in industry, it will be found . . . to be rather their Misfortune than their Fault. Their Disposition to Industry, . . . if judiciously directed is capable to rise to the greatest heights.[154]

The Board of Commissioners of the Annexed Estates offered this kind of guidance and aimed to become a launchpad for the infiltration of Lowland economic practices into the Gaidhealtachd. "Industrial" schools were established, and Highland boys were apprenticed to Lowland traders. The improvement of traffic infrastructure, partly implemented to facilitate military control, also promised economic benefits. Road inspector Colonel Robert

Anstruther wrote in the 1790s: "Hitherto the Chief Object of Government by making Roads, was to March Troops . . . ; but after the . . . suppression of the Rebellion, the Plan was extended . . . to Civilize and improve the Country, to make the Highlanders . . . Industrious useful subjects."[155]

There were also construction projects for villages and towns. At least one "improver," James Small, believed that these would weaken the Highlanders' notorious hardiness and render them physically unfit for crime: "Proper houses and beding are . . . necessary improvements in the Highlands . . . , for as the people are from their infancy used to lye on the ground in no more than a single blancket, this fitts them for the hardships of their theevish expeditions."[156] Small advocates a civilizing mission and an improvement of the Other's living standards as a strategy of domination. The efficiency of such a strategy had already been pointed out in Tacitus's comments on the introduction of baths and other amenities in Roman England.[157]

To promote loyalty and integration, money from confiscated Jacobite estates was reinvested into the local economy, for instance as subsidies for local industries like tanning, papermaking, fishing, or whaling. Even those chiefs who were allowed to retain their estates were pressured to adopt commercial principles. Initiative from the Gaidhealtachd's own elites carried the commercialization process further after the Board of Commissioners of the Annexed Estates was dissolved and forfeited estates were restored to the heirs of dispossessed Jacobite chiefs in 1784. Now the mission of modernizing estates and "civilizing" their Gaelic inhabitants definitely relied no longer on government interference, but on the native elites themselves. They rose to the occasion with remarkable enthusiasm and relentlessness.

One example of accelerated commercialization after 1745 relates to the tacksmen. Occupying an intermediary position in the landholding system between chieftain and clan commoners, tacksmen were traditionally also military leaders and recruitment agents for the clan. As long as the clans' military autonomy lasted, tacksmen were pillars of chieftainly authority, and chiefs took care not to alienate them. For a while, such calculations forestalled certain unpopular but economically advisable measures, such as excessive rent increases or the replacement of local tacksmen with outside incomers who paid higher prices. But after 1745, law and order were no longer guaranteed by the chieftain's own military and legal authority, but by central state authority. Traditional functions of tacksmen became obsolete, and chiefs felt less constrained in pursuing commercializing reforms.

The commercialization of estates was inextricably linked to the Highland Clearances, which occurred mainly between the second half of the eighteenth and the middle of the nineteenth century. The traditional farming system was not profitable enough to meet modern commercial standards. Far too many people lived off the land, using methods which were too old-fashioned to yield any significant surplus which could be skimmed off as rent to fill the chiefs' coffers. Thus, modernization often took the following forms: good farming lands were cleared of their previous inhabitants and reorganized into profitable bigger farms held by a single tenant. These were frequently sheep farms, a boom sector at that time. Often the people renting or managing these farms were Lowlanders or English people because they had the best know-how about new southern farming methods and imported sheep breeds. Cleared commoners of the clan were resettled elsewhere, often on tinily subdivided "crofts" on land which was not amenable to commercial large-scale farming anyway. In some regions this was virgin ground which had to be broken in for several years, but then became profitable enough to be added to a larger farm as the crofters were resettled on some other patch of virgin land to start anew. In other cases, crofts lay on unsheltered, infertile coastal lands which were permanently useless for serious farming. Crofts were deliberately planned to be insufficient for providing a living, so that people were forced to take up supplementary employment, for example in the kelp industry, in fishing, or as laborers on bigger farms.[158] Usually the landlord was also the employer, which aggravated dependency.

The Clearances and their aftermath caused pauperization, displacement, uncertainty, and enduring trauma. This is another area where the Highland experience can be fruitfully linked to international postcolonial scholarship and its growing interest in trauma studies. Another emerging subfield, postcolonial ecocriticism, is likewise relevant to eighteenth-century (and later also nineteenth-century) Scotland, for instance concerning the material transformations of the "wild" Highland landscape through roads, bridges, canals, and large-scale commercial sheep-farming. The literary representations of this "wild" landscape likewise underwent important changes which can be studied through a postcolonial ecocritical lens.

For the landlords, the profits reaped from modernized estates were enormous. In the second half of the eighteenth century, the Highland economy participated in the general economic boom: cattle prices rose, and cattle trade with the Lowlands expanded further. Other Highland goods were also increasingly exported to the Lowlands: fish, timber, slate, lead, wool, whisky, and later kelp. The "civilizing mission" to integrate the Highlands into the national economy was in that sense successful. This was already announced by the Board of Trustees for Manufactures and Fisheries in 1763:

> The Linen manufacture hath been introduced into . . . the Highlands, the whole Country is thereby greatly civilised & if the same means be continued is likely to become a very useful part of the United Kingdom but if discontinued . . . it will soon relapse into its former Sloth & Barbarity.[159]

Such civilizational "successes" swelled the purses of landlords, but did not necessarily improve the situation of crofters and laborers. One early nineteenth-century traveler even considered the situation of Hebridean landless laborers to be worse than that of slaves in Jamaica.[160] Another comparison to overseas colonialism was drawn by Lord MacDonald, who called North Uist, which was especially profitable in kelping, his "little Peru."[161] This implies that the amount of profit he earned from Hebridean kelp was comparable to the colossal wealth which Spanish colonizers had extracted from America, for instance by looting Inca gold. MacDonald's comment illustrates the integration of Scotland's Gaidhealtachd into the British colonial imagination.

Commercialization of estate management took place in both Lowlands and Highlands, but there were important differences. In the Lowlands, the process was more gradual because land leases tended to be written and ran for longer time spans. In the Highlands, leases were either customary and unwritten, or written but only extending over a short term, both of which facilitated eviction. Moreover, in the Lowlands—and on the southern and eastern fringes of the Highlands—cleared ex-tenants were more easily absorbed by other economic sectors, for instance as agricultural laborers, in rural manufactures, or in the growing cities.[162] In the western and northern Highlands, there were few alternatives to crofting, and when that new economy collapsed after 1815 these regions' inhabitants drifted toward a catastrophe.

Commercialization also had cultural consequences. It intensified the tendency toward chieftainly self-anglicization and the local elites' loss of interest in more traditional forms of Gaelic Highland culture. Anglicization in turn reinforced the commercializing impetus because the more time Highland aristocrats spent in the south, the greater their expenses and their exposure to the example of southerly commercializing trends, such as enclosures.[163] Absentee landlordism increased further.[164] This did not go uncommented. Gaelic poets had criticized absenteeism since the seventeenth century.[165] An early nineteenth-century prose critique can be found in James MacDonald's complaint about "the non-residence of many of the proprietors who drain the poor Hebrides of their wealth and, too often resid[e] in other parts of the empire."[166]

An increasingly common response of tacksmen and clan commoners to the pressures of "modernization" was emigration, especially from the 1760s onwards. This was often a preemptive move to avoid imminent clearance and the hardships of crofting. Many Highlanders eagerly embraced colonial migration as an opportunity to escape the oppressive regime of landlords and obtain a farm of their own.[167] For Catholics before about 1793, the desire to escape religious discrimination could be an additional motivation. Initially, the most popular destinations were areas which are now part of the United States. After U.S. independence, Gaelic migration to North America refocused on British possessions in what later became Canada. Later mythology portrayed these migrants unequivocally as coerced paupers who became colonizers against their will. This, however, is a reductive picture. Many eighteenth-century Gaelic colonizers migrated of their own accord and came from the middling ranks of society, being tacksmen, farmers, and craftsmen with some skills, capital, initiative for self-improvement, and success. Rather than a reluctant flight of passive, wretched victims, these migrations were often proactive strategies of material betterment and social protest. Emigration frequently went against the wishes of landlords, who feared the loss of profitably exploitable tenants. Tenants could also use the threat to migrate as a means to extort concessions from landowners.[168] Naturally, the transformation from internal colonized to eager overseas colonizers further complicates the position of Scottish Highlanders in the global British Empire and the colonial imagination.

The ambivalent mixture of a clear sense of sociocultural antagonism on the one hand, and a remarkable degree of (self-)hybridization and adaptation on the other, can also be discerned in the literature of the period. This is illustrated in the following chapter through a case study of Martin Martin. His travel books are an example of anglophone "colonizing" discourse, but this is seriously complicated by the fact that Martin was a native Gael, whose hybrid position is palpable at various points in these texts.

Chapter 2

✦

Anglophone Literature of Civilization and the Hybridized Gaelic Subject

Martin Martin's Travel Writings

Many discursive trends outlined in chapter 1 are also reflected in two central texts chosen for more detailed analysis in the present chapter: Martin's *A Late Voyage to St. Kilda* (*SK*; written ca. 1697, published 1698) and *A Description of the Western Islands of Scotland* (*WI*; probably mainly written in the 1690s, published 1703).[1] These two pieces of travel writing and geographical description cover a wide range of subjects, including topography, botany, zoology, ethnography, economy, history, archaeological remains, and other sights such as special features of church design, personal anecdotes, folklore, and traditional medicine. While this broad scope is in line with other work in European geography at that time, it is also tempting to compare Martin's wide-ranging works to the early modern colonial encyclopedias discussed by Walter Mignolo in a Latin American context.[2] Again, the modern nation-state's efforts to extend its knowledge and control of its own territory—even its most remote internal fringes—employ discursive and practical strategies which resemble those of overseas colonial conquest and knowledge production.

Martin's books are two of the earliest sustained descriptions of the Hebrides which found their way into print. They are also among the most influential. For instance, Martin's writings helped to increase scholarly interest in Gaelic, and accompanied the English intellectual Samuel Johnson and his friend, the Lowland Scottish writer James Boswell, on their own famous Hebridean journey (1773), which likewise became immortalized in book form.[3] Martin has also been a key reference point for many later authors on Hebridean travel, history, and traditions.[4] He remains well known today, though surprisingly neglected by literary scholars. Another factor that makes his works particularly relevant to the present study is their ambivalent perspective which reflects key colonial and postcolonial themes. Like many later texts about the Gaidhealtachd, they often speak from the viewpoint of a "learnèd gentleman of the world," in English and to an anglophone audience presumably located mainly in the Lowlands or England. However, unlike many other accounts, Martin's were written by a native Hebridean and Gaelic speaker. As such, Martin could offer an inside perspective, while at the same time his education, class, and experience of living in non-Gaelic regions set him apart from many of his fellow Gaels. This results in a thoroughly hybridized perspective on Scotland's western periphery.[5] Martin's work is central to a postcolonial history of Scottish identity and literature, as a powerful reminder that simplistic binarisms between colonizers and colonized (problematic anywhere) are particularly unsuited to the complexities of the Scottish situation, even at this relatively early date. The interstitial position of Martin's works as Hebridean self-representations partially influenced by, but also in critical dialogue with, metropolitan discourse, and aimed at a mainly metropolitan audience, makes them noteworthy examples of what Mary Louise Pratt has termed "autoethnography."[6]

Martin is aware of his own hybrid position. Issues of border-crossing, cultural translation, and liminality surface in various forms. Often he consciously embraces the position of a cultural mediator, explaining and vindicating merits of Gaelic life to an anglophone mainstream audience at a time when this mainstream was generally rather hostile toward Gaeldom. This vindication occasionally resembles anti- or post-colonial "writing back" strategies, but other aspects of his work are more similar to (pro)colonial discourse. For instance, he perceives himself as standing not only on a cultural, but also on a historical threshold: he subscribes to a universalist, hierarchical concept of progress and civilization which takes the anglophone mainstream as the norm, judges deviant models of social organization as deficient and primitive, and believes that the "primitives" should follow the mainstream's lead on the path to progress. Thus, Martin—despite his sympathy with Gaelic otherness—also supports the margin's assimilation and integration into the national collective. Although he was writing before the Union of 1707, his review of previous national integration measures is not limited to intra-Scottish initiatives, but takes in England as well: due to the dynastic Union of 1603, his discussion of crown policies already has a pan-British dimension; and he also discusses private investors from both sides of the border. This pan-British outlook and some of the measures he suggests for future modernization in the Isles already anticipate the intensification of assimilating endeavors that set in after 1707.

The integration of Gaeldom into the national mainstream appears as a civilizing mission, an impression reinforced by Martin's occasional tendency to read concepts from Caesar, Tacitus, and modern overseas colonial discourse into his own Gaelic culture. Sometimes Martin seems remarkably ahead of his time: several ideas he uses did not become prominent in mainstream discourse until several decades later. For instance, his recycling of classical antiquity's concept of a universal ladder of progress anticipates ideas popularized by the Scottish Enlightenment in the mid-eighteenth century; and his use of the "noble savage" trope anticipates romanticism. Thus, on the one hand, Martin's works are integral parts of an anglophone, colonizing canon of texts on Gaelic "barbarity," while on the other hand these particular colonizing texts were written by a son of the colonized culture. As a result of this liminality, the boundaries between self and Other, as well as the value judgments set up within the text, constantly fluctuate and frequently appear on the brink of breaking down altogether.

Martin was born in the 1660s on the Isle of Skye, apparently into a family of good social standing. Surviving biographical information is limited.[7] He attended Edinburgh University and from about 1681 to 1692 worked as a tutor for the island's aristocracy. Subsequently, he apparently spent time in Scotland's Western and Northern Isles, Edinburgh, London, and Continental Europe. He was involved with various members of Britain's scientific establishment for whom he acted as a "geographical field agent . . . , directly observing and reporting upon things and transmitting specimens and facts about unknown parts of Britain."[8] One of the scientific hubs with which Martin was involved in this manner was the Royal Society, to whom he presented two papers.[9] Martin's services as a field agent were also used by the geographer royal, Sir Robert Sibbald, who was working on a Scottish atlas. Some of Martin's travels were made in the employ of the Lowland-born geographer John Adair, who was engaged in a major mapmaking project to chart the Scottish coasts, sanctioned by the Scottish Parliament and funded by the state. At the inception of the project in 1686, an avowed parliamentary motive was to provide added security and stimulus to incoming foreign traders.[10] This applied to all of Scotland, but with regard to its Gaelic western periphery it also meant opening up the region to the new capitalist system and integrating the area more closely into the nation-state and its international economic interests. In 1695, a second parliamentary act on Adair's project makes special mention of the Western and Northern Isles.[11] Adair's 1698 expedition to those islands also aimed to collect other information on the region, for instance on botany, and was accompanied by native guides whose local knowledge was to help with navigation and the Gaelic language. Martin was one of those native informants, and also received a direct payment from the state in recognition of his services on Adair's expedition. This involved Martin directly in the process of "internal colonial" exploration, economic "civilizing missions," and national integration even before he published his own writings on these subjects. Moreover, Martin evidently used some of the observations he made during the Adair expedition as a basis for his own publications. Later, Martin apparently did further work as a tutor between 1704 and 1710, and studied medicine at the universities of Leiden and Rheims. He seems to have spent most of his final years in the London area, practicing as a doctor and styling himself a "gentleman." He died in 1718.

This biographical background goes some way toward explaining why Martin's attitude to metropolitan influences was less hostile than that of many other Gaelic-speaking authors of the seventeenth and eighteenth centuries, who often retained a rather conservative and partly even nativist outlook.[12] Martin's personal experiences of travel, migration, and state employment made the center's cultural perspective partially his own. Another crucial factor is literary genre: while many nativist Gaelic poets were steeped in highly conservative values and genre conventions inherited from medieval traditions, Martin wrote in a different genre which did not consign him to conservatism. His social position was different as well: his legal and medical training gave him the progressive outlook of the newly ascendant Scottish professional middle class. He was an islander who had *profited* from a metropolitan education, a hybridized subject whose own achievements induced him to think that hybridization would prove similarly beneficial to the rest of Gaeldom, even those of lower rank. Nonetheless, Martin's position ultimately eludes fixture, constantly oscillating between the perspective of a sympathetic Gaelic insider on the one hand, and that of an outsider from a "civilized" and "civilizing" anglophone mainstream on the other. This flexible self-positioning also makes clear that the underlying categories ("pre-modern Gaelic margin" vs. "civilized anglophone center") are themselves unstable: the binary opposition between them is a social construct, not the result of innate essential properties. Martin's hybridity can thus contribute to a postcolonial deconstruction of the essentialism and othering which so frequently characterizes colonial discourse.

Narrative Perspective: Inside/Outside

Martin's narrative perspective is itself ambivalent. The preface to *A Description of the Western Islands of Scotland* deliberately positions him as a bearer of local knowledge and native viewpoints when he complains that, although some previous accounts exist, the Western Isles "have never been described till now by any man that was a native of the country or had travelled them."[13] Martin further emphasises his indigeneity when expressing his hope that readers will forgive

> what defects may be found in my style . . . : for there is a wantonness in language . . . to which *my countrymen of the Isles* are as much strangers as to other excesses which are too frequent in many parts of Europe. *We* study things there more than words, though those that understand *our native language* must own that *we* have enough of the latter to inform the judgment and work upon the affections in as pathetic a manner as any other languages. (*WI* 62, italics mine)

The first-person pronouns imply identification with the inhabitants of the Western Isles. However, adopting the pose of a "simple islander" need not necessarily reflect a complete ethnic alignment, but may refer to literary style alone—and even that appears rather coquettish, a display of modesty not entirely sincere, for Martin's writing style is literary and educated, though free from excessive rhetorical flourishes. Casting himself in the role of a native informant may also be a marketing strategy: it presents Martin's account as different from previous texts and as particularly well-informed.[14]

Once this position has been established by the preface, the main text continues in a slightly different vein, placing more emphasis on the distinction between the author and the locals. For instance, when Martin cites a Gaelic expression from Lewis in literal English translation, he adds: "For so it signifies in their language" (*WI* 88) instead of ". . . our language." In this particular case, it might be argued that the third-person pronoun need not imply that Martin poses as a non-Gael. Instead, it might merely refer to an intra-Gaelic dialect difference between Martin the Skye man and the Lewis people. Elsewhere, however, Martin's posing as a non-Gaelic outsider is unmistakable, for instance when he refers to Gaelic as "*their* language" (*WI* 168–69). Similarly, he often refers to all kinds of islanders, even those from his own island, as "the natives" instead of "we." The shift between the first-person pronouns of the preface and third-person pronouns here illustrates again how hybridity highlights the instability of "us"/"them" categories. This is, however, not merely a matter of cultural difference and Martin's partial assimilation to the non-Gaelic mainstream. It is also a matter of class: Martin as a university-educated "man of the world" stands apart from the uneducated "rustics," and when he speaks of local society he mainly refers to the lower ranks. Although middle-class individuals like stewards and clergymen are also frequently mentioned, they mainly appear as witnesses corroborating information given by lower-class people, lending the latter additional credibility (e.g., *WI* 146; *SK* 424–25). The middle class's own lifestyle and outlook is not usually mentioned, or at least not distinguished from that of the masses. Aristocratic life is not described in any detail either, apart from a few references to medieval feudal traditions, most of which have already disappeared, and to aristocratic patronage of poets. Most references to aristocrats are limited to half-sentences explaining who owns which tract of land.[15] Hence, Martin's focus is clearly on the lower social orders.

The way in which Martin presents Gaelic traditions might try to play on the expectations of his intended audience, for instance concerning the exotic and the "curious": both books explicitly aim to cater to the contemporary appetite for travel narratives and other descriptions of remote, strange, or unknown places (*WI*, preface, 62; *SK*, preface, 397), which accords with the establishment and expansion of British colonies. The texts Martin identifies as fashionable include those on overseas territories: for example, in *St. Kilda* he mentions "the Indies" (*SK* 397). *Western Islands* does not give a regional specification—he may again think of the colonies, but probably not exclusively, as the allusion might also extend to growing interest in intra-European travel.[16] Sometimes Martin deliberately exoticizes the Western Isles, for instance by drawing attention to things which his readers might find "curious," that is, new, strange, or Other. Already the title page—which in typical eighteenth-century fashion gives an extensive list of the main contents—promises this when referring to "Curiosities of Art and Nature."[17] Similar references to "curiosities" occur on pp. 83 and 370 (*WI*).[18]

The same logic dominates Martin's account of how inhabitants of smaller and remoter islands reacted when first traveling to the bigger islands, the mainland, or even Glasgow (*WI* 317–19, *SK* 462–64): their naturally slightly bewildered perspective is labeled as "strange"—already in the table of contents (*WI* 81; also see p. 462 of *SK*'s main text). Thus, the city-dweller's perspective is established as normal, while the diverging viewpoint of the country bumpkin is "strange." Similarly, the main text of *St. Kilda* comments: "their opinion of foreign objects is . . . remote from the ordinary sentiments of other mankind" (*SK* 464). Martin even makes fun of those inexperienced travelers, exposing their views for the metropolitan reader's amusement and for a laugh at the islanders' expense (*SK* 462–64).[19]

The text takes the perspective of its intended audience: the metropolitan is "normal," the Western Isles are marked as "Other" alias "curious." On the one hand, the intended readers have been invited to trust Martin's discursive authority precisely because he is a "native." On the other hand, in order to make things intelligible, enjoyable, and interesting to his readers, Martin must "other" his native culture and describe it at least to a certain degree in terms laid out and expected by his audience. This may partly be just a tactical move and partly represent Martin's own beliefs, the latter perhaps influenced by his mainstream education and socialization. Martin's (self-)marketing as a native informant, albeit a metropolitanized and thus intelligible one, is comparable to the packaging of contemporary diasporic or otherwise westernized postcolonial authors for the Western metropolitan market. Such marketing issues have also become an object of postcolonial critical analysis, for instance by Graham Huggan, Sarah Brouillette, and Sandra Ponzanesi.[20] Divergences between their approaches notwithstanding, all three critics highlight that commodification and cliché, despite their problems, can also be handled strategically and subversively, for instance when authors play on their hybrid status as both insider and outsider, or when they expose the stereotypes and power relations which underlie their position in the global market.[21] Similar things can be said of Martin's hybrid self-positioning between primitive otherness and civilized metropolitan authority, and his use of the returned gaze to expose the limits of metropolitan self-righteousness. Thus, despite his occasional pandering to mainstream prejudices, Martin also counters them by presenting a more positive and sympathetic account of the Gaelic world than was usual in anglophone texts of his time. He explains his mediating intentions as follows:

> I am not ignorant that foreigners, sailing through the Western Isles, have been tempted from the sight of so many wild hills that seem to be covered all over with heath . . . to imagine that the inhabitants, as well as the places of their residence, are barbarous; and to this opinion, their habit, as well as their language, have contributed. The like is supposed by many that live in the south of Scotland, who know no more of the Western Isles than the natives of Italy, but the lion is not so fierce as he is painted, neither are the people . . . so barbarous as the world imagines. (*WI* 356)

One way to enforce this point was to counter assumptions of spatial otherness: mainstream assertions of the Western Isles' remoteness, strangeness, and primitiveness, to which Martin partly subscribes himself, are tempered by hints that the Isles are not entirely cut off from the world. Even the particularly remote island of St. Kilda, with its sometimes exotic and archaic measurements, calculates at least the years and months in the same way as the rest of Britain does (*SK* 462). Thus, othering is complemented by same-ing. The other Western Isles are shown to have even more links and parallels to the rest of the world: a second instance of same-ing occurs when Martin notes a custom which is observed similarly in Uist and Aberdeenshire (*WI* 136). He also acknowledges economic links to the mainland (though still too few; see below) and even to the overseas colonies. He mentions the wool trade between most of the Western Isles, Moray, and Aberdeen (*WI* 354–55); as well as the fact that "beef is transported to Glasgow, . . . and from thence . . . to the Indies" (*WI* 139). He also refers to four islanders who spent time in Barbados (*WI* 347). Thus, Martin partially reintegrates the supposedly remote and alien Western Isles into the national and international space by reporting their connections to the outside world.

Martin also counters the mainstream's anti-Gaelic prejudices by displaying respect for the islanders' intelligence, discursive authority, social organization, and cultural achievements.

Respect for Native Voices and Achievements

Contrary to colonial images of Gaels as ignoble savages, several passages in Martin's books portray the islanders as very intelligent, though somewhat uneducated. The author makes clear that, considering the limited resources at their disposal, it is amazing how much they make of them. With remarkable skill and invention they can tell their nautical position from the flight of seabirds as precisely as the visitors' compass (*SK* 405). Similarly, they calculate the time by watching tides and sky (*SK* 460–61). Martin also praises their good memory (*SK* 438). He asserts that they are "reputed very cunning" (*SK* 438) and that "there is scarce any circumventing of them in traffic and bartering" (*SK* 438). Already the contents pages contain hints like "natives sagacious" (*WI* 76), "ingenuity" (*WI* 81), and "capable of acquiring all arts" (*WI* 82). Likewise, the main text of *Western Islands* asserts that "the natives are generally ingenious and quick of apprehension; they have a mechanical genius" (*WI* 95) as well as "a genius for all callings and employments" (*WI* 260). "They are generally a very sagacious people, quick of apprehension, and even the vulgar exceed all those of their rank and education I ever yet saw in any other country" (*WI* 240). The latter passage even asserts the islanders' superiority over the inhabitants of other regions.

Martin's respect for native intelligence and native voices is reflected in his use of language. An important feature of cultural imperialism—whether ancient Roman or modern anglophone British, whether in the "Celtic fringe" or overseas—is the power of naming. Renaming in the colonizer's or mainstream's language and the marginalization or utter silencing of indigenous terms have also affected the Scottish Gaidhealtachd, where Ordnance Survey maps and road signs with anglicized place-names have carried this problem forward into the twentieth and twenty-first centuries.[22] Martin has a more ambiguous approach to the names of places, people, animals, things, and techniques: some names are given in the established English version. Some are directly translated from Gaelic, for instance in his remarks on "Seapork" (from *muc-mhara*, meaning "whale" or "porpoise," *WI* 88), or the English/Latinate rendering of Bearnaraidh Beag and Bearnaraidh Mór into "Bernera Minor" and "Bernera Major" (*WI* 96). Other names appear only in Gaelic, though occasionally in anglicised spellings like "Timiy" (*WI* 86). Yet other names are given in both languages. Now and then he translates only half of a name, as when he gives "Eilean Mór" (*eilean* = "island," *mór* = "big") as "Island-More" (*WI* 98). Martin's linguistic syncretism and his awareness of onomastic variations highlight gaps between cultures and languages.[23] Here he places Highland and Lowland systems next to each other, without privileging either. This underlines the bilingual, hybrid nature of both the author and the society he writes about. This effect might be unintentional—although it may be legitimate for modern audiences to read the text this way, and although readings against the grain can prove highly fruitful, assuming consciously subversive intentions on the part of the author might go too far in projecting postmodern agendas onto an early modern consciousness. But even if the effect of highlighting gaps is unintentional in Martin's text, it nonetheless exists as a revealing intra-textual fissure which illustrates the deeply hybrid and ambiguous nature of the Highland "colonial" experience.

Martin's respect for the Gaelic language is further expressed by the inclusion of rationalizations and etymologies for Gaelic names, for example, for places like Skye (*WI* 190), Arran (*WI* 154), and Iona (*WI* 286). The following passage is especially revealing:

> The Island of Lewis is so called from Leog, which in the Irish language signifies water, lying on the surface of the ground; which is very proper to this island, because of the . . . fresh-water lakes that abound in it. . . . It is . . . distinguished by . . . several names: by the islanders it is commonly called, the Long Island, being from south to north 100 miles in length. (*WI* 85)[24]

Here the linguistic gaps and variations acknowledged concern not only differences between Gaelic- and English-speaking people, but also differences within Gaelic discourse, as Martin discusses *two* Gaelic names: Leòdhas (or "Leog") and An t-Eilean Fada (the Long Island). He asserts that indigenous names are rational, not only by giving their etymology, but also by emphasizing that the toponyms reflect the nature of the object they name. This emphasis on Gaelic rationality sets Martin's text apart from many other anglophone writings which portray Gaelic as primitive, irrational, inappropriate, ugly, and intrinsically unintelligible gibberish. Martin's insistence on the appropriateness of local names could also be read as a more general defense of the rationality of indigenous voices, while many other descriptions of marginalized cultures assume that rationality belongs exclusively to the center or colonizer.

Another feature of Martin's text which highlights the bilingual character of Scottish society, as well as the linguistic gaps which impede cross-cultural understanding, is a subchapter that reproduces a complete Gaelic prayer in the original language over one and a half pages, followed by an English translation (*WI* 186–89). The full inclusion of the original expresses Martin's respect for the Gaelic language and shows that the intended audience is not an *exclusively* anglophone one: "I have set down the original for the satisfaction of such readers as understand it" (*WI* 186). Bilingual textual elements, and the envisioning of a target audience comprising both metropolitan outsiders and educated, part-metropolitanized "natives," are further characteristics of autoethnographic texts.[25]

Respect for indigenous voices also surfaces in Martin's comments on the role of native informants for his own research.[26] The precedence of local voices over those of outsiders is affirmed not only in the prefaces, where he poses as a native informant himself, using authenticity as a marketing tactic, but also in the main text, which abounds in phrases like "the natives assure me that . . ." (*WI* 87) or "I was told by the natives . . ." (*WI* 88, 116, 174).[27] Martin frequently affirms his informants' general integrity and, more particularly, their discursive reliability (*WI* 126, 135, 173, 180, 227, 332).[28]

Sometimes, Martin also assures his readers that local accounts have been confirmed by his own observations (e.g., *WI* 63; *SK* 427). At first, this seems to imply a hierarchization of discursive authority, since Gaelic accounts, mostly from "ordinary" lower-class people, need a stamp of approval from a more authoritative observer, in this case Martin himself as an educated, part-anglicized middle-class man. Similarly, he sometimes makes class-based distinctions among local informers when he has ordinary people's accounts confirmed by middle- or upper-class residents such as ministers (e.g., *WI* 342) or landowners (e.g., *WI* 118). However, such apparent hierarchizations of reliability should not be overemphasised because the more illustrious witnesses usually concur with folk opinion—which thus turns out to be just as reliable as higher-class voices. Moreover, Martin's invocation of more educated or better-placed witnesses need not mean that he is prejudiced against folk culture or lower-class people himself: he might merely make concessions to prejudices held by some members of his intended audience—prejudices he may be trying to refute.[29]

It is also noteworthy that Martin believes in aspects of folk tradition which many outsiders from the mainstream would probably have despised as superstition. For instance, he reports that certain nuts are believed to have talismanic powers against witchcraft and change color as a warning. Martin affirms this to be "true by my own observation," though he "cannot be positive as to the cause of it" (*WI* 116), and he even admits to owning such a nut himself.

Respect for folk tradition also informs his remarks on the "second sight." How important this subject is to him can be seen from its appearance on the title page, and from the fact that he devotes an entire chapter to it (*WI* 321–48). Martin believes the second sight to be very "common" (*WI*, title page) among the people of the Western Isles, though apparently less common elsewhere. Thus, to most of Martin's intended audience the phenomenon would appear as an alien curiosity. This can also be inferred from the fact that Martin's chapter starts by defining what second sight is, which would be unnecessary if all readers could be expected to know (*WI* 321). He does not give explicit reasons for this regional difference in supernatural sensitivity, but it might be inferred that a difference in "civilizational stages" plays a part. As also suggested by his use of the "noble savage" trope (see below), he seems to think that the relatively "primitive" people of the Western Isles enjoy a close relationship with nature which their more "advanced" Lowland and English compatriots have lost. This closeness might be extended from the natural to the supernatural world, so that second sight appears more at home in a society which is relatively unadvanced in rational science. This accords with Martin's assertion that in recent years the second sight has somewhat declined (*WI* 330, 348). Though he does not give an explicit reason, it can be plausibly assumed that the reason lies in the onset of modernity and centralization, which Martin elsewhere names as recent phenomena in island life that have weakened other folk traditions. In addition to Scotland's Western Isles, he mentions three other places where the second sight remains relatively common, and two of these are likewise "backward" inner-British peripheries: Wales and the Isle of Man.[30] Although he seems to consider progress and second sight to be in mutual opposition, Martin does *not* take the side of "progress": he staunchly defends his belief in the second sight against rational skepticism and Protestant clerical objections (*WI*, e.g., 65, 326–28, 344).

In this context, he even privileges local oral accounts over the canonized written reports of historians—a remarkable feature in an educated author of his time, considering that many anglophone mainstream intellectuals tended to despise oral cultures:

> Such as deny those visions [second sight] give their assent to . . . strange passages in history upon the authority . . . of historians that lived . . . centuries before our time, and yet they deny the people of this generation the liberty to believe their intimate friends and acquaintance, men of probity and unquestionable reputation, and of whose veracity they have greater certainty than we can have of any ancient historian. (*WI* 328)

This leads us to another important trope in Martin's work: history. Colonial discourse about "primitive" cultures (whether the latter are ancient or modern, colonial or noncolonial, "noble" or "ignoble") often perceives indigenous populations as living not only out of space, remote from the centers of the world, but also out of time, as people who have no history or progress of their own, or at least none which is worth mentioning—not before they came into contact with the dynamic culture of the colonizer/center, at any rate.[31] Martin, however, deems local history significant enough to be mentioned in his books, though parts of this history had little to do with Scottish, English, or European "centers." The historical sources he quotes include not only written ones such as inscriptions (*WI* 287, 289–91) or the works of Bede (*WI* 292–93), but also local oral traditions—for instance about the neolithic standing stones of Calanais: "I enquired of the inhabitants what tradition they had from their ancestors concerning these stones; and they told me" (*WI* 91).[32] It seems strikingly modern that he frequently even provides his informants' names, sometimes along with additional data such as occupation, place of residence, and even the time when his information was collected.[33] Perhaps he merely meant to bolster the credibility of his account, as if to say: "if you don't believe me, go there and ask for yourself." However, this feature might also be read as a respectful recognition of the way oral tradition works, for instance as regards subjectivity, multivocality, and the possibility to modify an account with each retelling to reflect shifting perspectives or the requirements of different occasions and audiences. This kind of individuation extends not only to Martin's direct informants, but also to other locals he writes about: while many other texts about "primitive" and/or colonized populations use sweeping generalizations about "the natives" which reduce or entirely ignore internal differences of class, time, gender, individual interest, and so on, Martin's account of "native" customs and experiences often emphasizes the specificity of each case, for instance concerning illnesses, omens, and second sight. And again, he frequently personalizes by name and address.[34]

Past events which Martin considers worth mentioning despite their "merely" local significance include an earthquake (*SK* 423), shipwrecks (*WI* 171), agricultural misfortunes (*WI* 104), inter-clan feuds (*WI* 340), religious conversions, and heresy (*WI* 108, 312). He also devotes considerable space to the history of Iona Abbey (*WI* 286–93) and makes a few references to the medieval Lordship of the Isles (*WI* 155, 273, 288). Here, the more common anglophone title "Lord of the Isles" is used alongside the epithet "king" which alludes to the Gaelic title *rìgh nan eilean*, thus again suggesting respect for indigenous traditions.

Many authors interpret other cultures' divergence from their own society's rules as a complete absence of rules and logic of any sort.[35] Martin, however, is at pains to demonstrate that local customs follow a very elaborate set of indigenous rules and have an internal logic of their own. For instance, he does not think that Anglo-British modernity invented law and order after a dark, chaotic medieval quagmire. He recognizes that medieval Gaelic feudal society likewise saw a need for order and devised means for achieving it—he calls certain medieval customs "necessary to prevent disorder and contention" (*WI* 170) and stresses a high degree of regularity in the appointment of officers, hereditary positions, the organization of meetings (*WI* 166–71), and feudal duties (*WI* 175–76). His comments on cattle raiding are especially remarkable. Many anglophone onlookers had, ever since the Middle Ages, perceived cattle raiding as *the* epitome of Highland lawlessness and disorder because in the eyes of Lowlanders (who had different socioeconomic practices) it looked like theft and a perpetual threat of military action or upheaval. By contrast, Martin knows that, within the internal logic of Highland society, cattle raiding made perfect sense and was not lawless or chaotic at all. He sympathetically explains that the mutuality of raiding maintained balance and order: "This custom being reciprocally used . . . , was not reputed robbery; for the damage which one tribe sustained . . . was repaired when their chieftain came in his turn to make his specimen" (*WI* 165).[36]

Martin's respect for local forms of knowledge and organization also extends to contemporaneous island law—another largely oral tradition. He is far from considering a society as lawless just because its rules are not codified in writing. Describing how leases are contracted without a written document, through the ceremonial passing of straw and a stick between lord and tenant, Martin asserts: "then both parties are as much obliged to perform their respective conditions as if they had signed a . . . deed" (*WI* 184). This emphasis on law-abiding and regularity even extends to elements of local life which are pre- or noncapitalist, such as disregard for high profits—although Martin would probably prefer a capitalist system (see below): "they covet no wealth . . . ; though . . . they are very precise in the matter of property among themselves; for none of them will . . . allow his neighbour to fish within his property; and every one must exactly observe not to make any encroachment on his neighbour" (*WI* 102). Regularity is also observed in the scrupulous and punctual delivery of dues and payments (e.g., *WI* 163; *SK* 408, 447). St. Kilda seems to be especially punctilious (*WI* 314; *SK* 416, 422, 424, 438, 443–44, 451–53, 458–59), although in this case regularity also has its drawbacks, as it can lead to undue inflexibility: "there is not a parcel of men in the world more scrupulously . . . punctilious in maintaining their liberties and properties than these . . . , being most religiously fond of their ancient laws . . . ; nor will they by any means consent to alter their first (though unreasonable) constitution."[37]

Another sphere of achievement is agriculture: although island agriculture leaves much to be desired in efficiency (see below), Martin does not consider the local farmers entirely devoid of merit. In Lewis he even notes a very efficient local method of working fields which "produces a greater increase than digging or ploughing otherwise" (*WI* 86).

He also remarks on native art, music, orature/literature, and learning, noting not only achievements already made (e.g., *WI* 241) but also additional ones attainable with some extra help. Already the table of contents identifies the islanders as "lovers of music" (*WI* 76), and the main text elaborates by mentioning "men who could play on the violin pretty well without being taught" (*WI* 95, also see 240–41). Martin also notes that the Gaelic language is just as expressive as other European languages (see the passage from *WI* 62, quoted above).

His respect for Gaelic eloquence does not, however, extend to traditional court poetry: "they furnish . . . a style . . . understood by very few . . . and if they purchase a couple of horses as the reward . . . they think they have done a great matter" (*WI* 177). If "understand" is taken to mean the poets' ability to master the complex and difficult Classical Gaelic meters, the passage might be read as a statement of admiration. But "understand" might also refer to the audience's ability to comprehend the contents of such poems, and in this light Martin appears to criticize the remoteness of the traditional Classical Gaelic literary language from the modern Scottish Gaelic vernacular.[38] This interpretation is corroborated by Martin's assertion that the poets "*think* they have done a great matter" (italics mine), which suggests that he considers their self-satisfaction to be unfounded. Elsewhere, an account of the traditionally high prestige of Gaelic poets concludes: "but these gentlemen becoming insolent lost ever since both the profit and esteem which was formerly due to their character" (*WI* 176). Martin apparently thinks that the poets' behavior was above their proper station—an opinion which had already been expressed by another anglophone Scottish author over 200 years earlier, that is, Richard Holland in *The Buke of the Howlat*.[39] Martin lays all the blame for the decline of the bardic order on the poets themselves; the role of wider social changes is not mentioned. Nonetheless, Martin's lack of admiration does not necessarily stem from a Lowland, anti-Gaelic, or colonizing attitude. For instance, he never suggests that his dislike of Gaelic court poetry is founded in its "primitiveness." Neither does he claim that the poets' "unreasonable" demands reflect a *general* unreasonableness of Gaelic society. Rather than reading Martin's critique of these poets as an outsider's colonial contempt for Gaelic culture as a whole, we may read it as an insider's critique of just one particular aspect of a culture which he nonetheless considers very much as his own. And why should such criticism not be legitimate, without immediately forfeiting the critic's membership in the society he criticizes?

Martin's continuing identification with, and appreciation of, Gaelic culture, is also evident in the fact that his reservations about court poetry do not extend to folk poetry. Quite the contrary: contents pages and main text stress the islanders' "genius for poetry."[40] Martin writes: "Several . . . have a gift of poesy, and are able to form a satire or panegyric *ex tempore*" (*WI* 95, italics in original). In addition to his respect for the predominantly oral genre of folk poetry, Martin acknowledges the existence of a learned Gaelic manuscript tradition (e.g., *WI* 292) and even its awareness of the mainstream European canon: "Fergus Beaton hath the following ancient Irish manuscripts in the Irish character; . . . Avicenna, Averroes, Joannes de Vigo, Bernardus Gordonus, and several volumes of Hippocrates" (*WI* 155).

Martin's vindication of local culture and local knowledge displays various features commonly associated with anticolonial discourse. But this is not the whole story: his perspective shifts back and forth between a Hebridean insider's and a metropolitan outsider's view, as well as between respect and condescension.

The Metropolitan View and Colonial Discourse Patterns

Historical Stasis

In spite of Martin's partial respect for local history, he sometimes betrays a more colonial viewpoint, for example when local history, though of interest, is presented as having been rather static for a very long time until the recent encroachment of the anglophone center. Martin's belief in stasis is so strong that he discerns historical continuities between the medieval or even early seventeeth-century Western Isles and Caesar's Gaul, for example, concerning inauguration ceremonies for clan chiefs (*WI* 166–69).[41] It seems that Celtic society during those long, slow centuries did not produce many noteworthy historical changes, nor does it seem to have had much contact with the dynamics of the wider world outside, at least not before the seventeenth century. Martin's anecdotes on local history include only one pre-1600 event which formed a link between the Western Isles and "major" European history, that is, the destruction of a ship of the Spanish Armada near Mull in 1588 (*WI* 283–84). Such wider contacts are presented as having increased rather suddenly during the seventeenth century through the growing impact of central government authority and the Reformation. It is to such external impact that Martin attributes the gradual crumbling of ancient static Celtic traditions and their replacement by dynamics and progress. If indigenously generated progress is mentioned at all, it appears to have been but slight, as the Western Isles seem to need catalyst energy from outside to realize their full potential. Thus, Martin's description of Eriskay notes that "the natives begin to manage it better, but not to that advantage it is capable of" (*WI* 154).

While Martin also shows an interest in historical events of more limited, local significance, now that the Isles are touched by national and international developments he deems those wider connections especially noteworthy—thus coming closer to a colonial view of indigenous history which assumes that proper history can only be brought to the periphery from outside, by the colonizer/center. Events in which national and local history are intertwined include the destruction of Stornoway Castle by Cromwell's army (*WI* 90) and the wreck of a Cromwellian ship "sent there to subdue the natives" (*WI* 152). Other examples are English investments in herring fisheries (*WI* 128–29) and an omen about the death of a local at the battle of Killiecrankie which had been fought between Hanoverian and Jacobite troops in 1689 (*WI* 209).

Martin implies that the Gaidhealtachd only began its proper integration into history and progressive dynamics in the seventeenth century. He devotes an entire chapter to "The Ancient and Modern Customs of the Inhabitants of the Western Islands of Scotland," in which he often juxtaposes traditions and recent developments. In this view of island history, change appears to be a very recent phenomenon whose arrival is dated varyingly between within the last thirteen years and within the last sixty years. Sometimes Martin also refrains from explicit datings, instead merely noting that many traditions are only maintained by the old (e.g., *WI* 154, 179), or preserved in old people's memories of yet earlier—and already dead—generations. Customs which Martin reports to have "been laid aside of late" include cattle raiding (*WI* 166), heavy drinking (*WI* 169), some aristocratic household rituals (*WI* 170), the building of a special kind of cairn (*WI* 205), Catholic customs in now reformed areas (*WI* 106), and a number of folk "superstitions." For instance, he mentions the "ancient custom . . . to hang a he-goat to the boat's mast . . . to procure a favourable wind; . . . not practised at present; though . . . it hath been done once by some of the vulgar within these 13 years last past" (*WI* 171). As usual, Martin envisages change as emanating from the middle or higher strata of society, while the lower classes are considered as more conservative. Another superstition—already gone completely, even among the "vulgar"—is the custom of consulting a certain oracle which "was . . . practised in the night, and may literally be called the works of darkness."[42] Martin also notes the demise of certain feudal duties (*WI* 175–76), though others are shown to have survived into his own time, so that in this field the juxtaposition between past and present is not strictly binary. It is also noteworthy that some dynamics have even reached the particularly remote and "static" island of St. Kilda, where they have occasioned changes in local government (*SK* 450–51) and dress (*SK* 455).

Noble Savagery

Another colonial discourse pattern in Martin's work is the motif of the noble savage living closer to nature and displaying greater moral virtue than his metropolitan contemporaries. Martin might have imbibed and internalized this trope in the course of a classicist education which exposed him to Roman discourse on both Celtic and non-Celtic "barbarians." This may be inferred not only from implicit parallels between Martin's works and such classical texts, but even from explicit references, for instance to Caesar's writings on Gaul: "Every great family in the isles had a chief Druid. . . . Caesar says they worshipped a deity under the name of Taramis, or Taran, which in Welsh signifies Thunder; and in the ancient language of the Highlanders, Torin signifies Thunder also" (*WI* 168). As Caesar never seems to have written about the Western Isles of Scotland, Martin appears to be one of the first modern authors to assume pan-Celtic cultural links between those islands and ancient Gaul. References to Livy's work on Gaul and to Tacitus's report on the Germans occur on page 168. An additional, though implicit, echo of Tacitus might be discerned in Martin's account of an incident when the steward of St. Kilda, who came from another island, demanded new taxes in addition to what was traditionally his due, but was repealed by armed resistance from locals. This outcome seems to find Martin's approval: "by this stout resistance they preserved their freedom from such imposition" (*WI* 313)—a remark which recalls Tacitus's praise of noble savages' readiness to defend their ancient freedom by force of arms. Additional sources for Martin's use of the "noble savage" trope may have been modern European texts on overseas exploration and colonized populations.

Despite the general antiquity and wide popularity of the "noble savage" trope, its application to Scottish Gaels is unusual for Martin's time, as anglophone discourse between the Middle Ages and the mid-eighteenth century usually preferred to treat them as ignoble savages. Martin's early readers might have expected the description of a Gaelic Other, and they received one, but this was probably not the kind of Other they expected: Martin writes back against the derogatory type of othering, only to replace it with another (though more idealistic) one. He anticipates the general European romantic revival of the "noble savage" trope, as well as its development into the dominant way of seeing Gaels, by several decades. Although Martin might have resented the application of the term "savage" or "barbarian" to the Western Isles (as the above quotation from *WI* 356 suggests), the attributes associated with this concept do pertain to his description of the area. The purest form of Hebridean noble savagery is located on Rona and St. Kilda, and is, for instance, reflected in the inhabitants' lack of materialism: the people of St. Kilda "have neither gold nor silver, but barter . . . for what they want" (*WI* 313). The same scenario is given for Rona:

> They . . . live a harmless life, being perfectly ignorant of most of the vices that abound in the world. They know nothing of money or gold, having no occasion for either; they neither sell nor buy, but only barter for such little things as they want: they covet no wealth, being fully content . . . with food and raiment. . . . They concern not themselves about the rest of mankind. . . . They take their surname from the colour of the sky, rain-bow, and clouds. (*WI* 102)

As Martin had not visited Rona in person, his account is based on information given by Lewis people who have done so, especially the minister. Thus, it is not entirely clear whether the opinion quoted is entirely Martin's own or someone else's. Nonetheless, the fact that Martin leaves it uncommented suggests that he finds it plausible. The islanders are so "primitively" at one with nature that even their names reflect natural phenomena. They have not yet come to live in opposition to their natural environment or to "primitive" moral virtues—unlike the more "advanced," but also more "decadent" metropolitans. Thus, the natives of St. Kilda are described as honest and chaste (*SK* 438, 445, 471), a virtuousness allegedly based on ignorance. Native self-sufficiency and indigenous life in general appear rather idyllic, for instance when Martin states that St. Kilda folk "live contentedly together" (*WI* 313). This recalls the Arcadian bliss of classical texts, as well as modern ideas of a tropical paradise overseas—in the Pacific, for example.[43] What sets the Hebrides apart from these is their rough non-Arcadian climate, but this rougher variant of "noble savage" life likewise has classical precedents: Tacitus, for instance, also described a rough climate as a begetter of virtue, for example, in the case of the Germans.

While the purest forms of "noble savagery" are found on the particularly remote isles of Rona and St. Kilda, at least some elements of noble savagery also pertain to Martin's description of other Western Isles. But with regard to the latter, the "noble savage" trope is less consistent: there, Martin is more ready to concede that the inhabitants have already left the state of nature—see the agricultural metaphor in *WI* 63–64, cited below, which portrays them as active, progressive cultivators of nature, not as passive and integral parts of nature. For Martin, the level of development on smaller and more remote islands differs from the level reached by bigger and more accessible ones. Instead of a simplistic dichotomy between a monolithically constructed western Scottish island world and an anglophone center, he envisages a *continuum* of marginality and civilization.

St. Kilda not only represents the most genuine type of noble savagery in the Hebrides, but even worldwide: "people so plain, and so little inclined to impose upon mankind, that perhaps no place in the world at this day, knows such . . . true primitive honour and simplicity, a people who abhor lying tricks and artifices" (*SK* 398). This claim that St. Kilda represents the very superlative of noble savagery may again be an advertising tactic, especially as it occurs in a preface, a part of the paratext likely to contain marketing arguments. Advertising often uses superlatives to outstrip competitors, and Martin's claim that St. Kilda represents the most extreme primitiveness may be an attempt to outstrip competing texts about "primitives" who live further away, that is, in the overseas colonies.

The idea that St. Kilda's primitiveness exceeded even that of remote overseas cultures might have seemed implausible to some readers, considering that the Hebrides were so much closer to the "centers" of world civilization. To counter such skepticism, Martin repeatedly stresses how very inaccessible St. Kilda is. This contrasts with his comments on many other Western Islands of Scotland, where he emphasizes accessibility because he wants to attract investors for "improvement" (see below). But he seems to envisage no such improvement for St. Kilda, whose description seems exclusively geared to satisfying the audience's taste for exotic otherness. This island appears very evasive from the outset, through Martin's emphasis on his difficulties of reaching it because of bad weather (*SK* 404–7). Once there, he again stresses the general inaccessibility of St. Kilda and the surrounding rocks (*SK*, 410–11, 423). Moreover, there are special places on the island which only the "natives" can reach while strangers cannot (*SK* 414, 421). Despite its inaccessibility, the place is not seen as generally hostile or depressing: Martin praises its simple assets such as good spring water (*SK* 414–15, 423), good soil (*SK* 416), and abundance of fish (*SK* 419). It should also be noted that the island's inaccessibility is merely blamed on its difficult weather and topography, not on any hostility from the "natives":

> There is a little old ruinous fort. . . . It is evident from what hath been already said that this place can be reckoned among the strongest forts . . . in the world; Nature has provided the place with store of ammunition for acting on the defensive; that is, a heap of loose stones . . . directly above the landing-place; it is very easy to discharge vollies of this ammunition directly upon the place of landing, and . . . this I myself had occasion to demonstrate, having for my diversion put it in practice, to the great satisfaction of the inhabitants, to whom this defence never ocurr'd hitherto.[44] They are resolved to make use of this for the future, to keep off the Lowlanders, against whom of late they have conceived prejudices. (*SK* 411–12)

This is ironic in several ways: first, the "natives" are originally not as hostile as their surroundings, as this military option has never occurred to themselves. However, this might not only be owed to the natural peaceableness of these "noble savages," but also to the fact that their island is so poor in resources that no stranger ever thought conquest worthwhile. A second moment of irony arises from the fact that it is Martin, an outsider (though no Lowlander, but a Gael from a different island and with a Lowland education) who shows them a defense against other outsiders, that is, proper Lowlanders. Third, this advice—given by an outsider who lives in a more warlike, less "noble" world, and who is equipped with a sense of civilizing mission—"corrupts" their natural peaceableness, and thus their virtue, to some extent. Fourth, the "natives" in their local patriotism suddenly believe that someone *would* consider their island worth attacking, so that they now do begin to think of military defense—while of course it is still unlikely that outsiders would deem an invasion of St. Kilda worth the effort. Thus, readers are possibly invited to smile at the locals' naiveté.

Nonetheless, again in line with classical concepts, the metropolis also has a moral lesson to learn: its decadence, artificiality, superfluous luxuries, and moral decay are juxtaposed against the honest and simple virtues of "primitive" life. Martin contrasts the stately buildings, new trends, and "painted beauties" of fashionable foreign travel destinations with the Western Isles, which "afford no such entertainment" as "the inhabitants . . . prefer conveniency to ornament both in their houses and apparel, and they rather satisfy than oppress nature in their ways of eating and drinking; and not a few among them have a natural beauty, which excels any that has been drawn by the finest Apelles" (*WI* 62–63).[45] In addition, Martin recounts a St. Kilda man's first reactions to Glasgow. Though his naiveté is mostly exposed as funny, his views are also cited as an implicit critique of lazy and affluent city-dwellers: "He thought it foolish in women to wear thin silks, as being a very improper habit for such as pretended to any sort of employment" (*WI* 319). Other passages express similar attitudes:

> The garb in fashion [does not] qualify him that wears it to be virtuous. The inhabitants have humanity, and use strangers hospitably. . . . I could bring several instances of barbarity and theft committed by stranger seamen in the isles, but . . . not one instance of any injury offered by the islanders to any seamen or strangers. (*WI* 356)

> The inhabitants of these islands do for the most part labour under the want of knowledge of letters and other useful arts and sciences; notwithstanding which defect, they seem . . . better versed in the book of nature than many that have greater opportunities of improvement. This will appear plain upon a view of the practice of the islanders in the preservation of their health, above what the generality of mankind enjoys, . . . merely by temperance and the prudent use of simples. (*WI*, preface, 63)

Or, to return to St. Kilda: "there is not one instance, or the least suspicion of perjury among them. . . . They never swear or steal, neither do they take God's name in vain . . . ; they are free from whoredom and adultery, and . . . other immoralities that abound . . . everywhere else" (*WI* 311). The islanders' simplicity also extends to religion: their Christianity is "much of the primitive temper," which keeps them from perjury and popish vices (*SK* 442). On the other hand, their naiveté once led them to follow a profit- and power-seeking heretic religious impostor (*SK* 466–75), a false prophet who "had no true mission" (*SK* 471). But Martin does not blame them too heavily, laying the main responsibility at the door of the man who uncharitably abused the locals' credulity: "The impostor continued . . . to delude these poor innocent well-meaning people" (*SK* 471). Presumably, one of the factors which made Martin so ready to absolve these credulous natives from the sin of heresy is the promptness with which they resubmitted to mainstream authority: after a strict but benevolent rebuttal, they soon saw the errors of their ways and again became good, orthodox members of the fold.

> We reproved the credulous people for complying implicitly with such follies and delusions . . . ; and all of them with one voice answered that what they did was unaccountable; but seeing one of their own number and stamp . . . endued, as they fancied, with a powerful faculty of preaching so fluently and frequently . . . they were induced to believe his mission from heaven. (*SK* 475)

The combination of strictness and benevolence casts Martin and the accompanying minister into the role of firm but loving parents, while the locals appear to act like children—a trope which, as noted above, is also common in overseas colonial discourse. Martin also implies that the natives themselves believe that they are ignorant—so much so that none of them is thought capable of eloquence without divine help. But all's well that ends well, and order is restored: "They are now overjoyed to find themselves undeceived, and the light of the Gospel restored to them. . . . We . . . delivered him [the impostor] to the steward's servants in . . . Harries, where he remains still in custody in order to his trial" (*SK* 476).

Another passage which shows the locals in awe of outsiders' learning, while unable to trust their own native capacities, runs as follows:

> [They] have a great inclination to novelty; and . . . anything . . . different. . . . A parcel of them were always attending the minister and me, admiring our habit, behaviour; and . . . all that we did or said was wonderful in their esteem; but above all, writing was the most astonishing to them; they cannot conceive how it is possible for any mortal to express the conceptions of his mind . . . upon . . . paper. After they had with admiration argued upon this subject, I told them,

> that within . . . two years or less, . . . they might easily be taught to read and write, but they were not of the opinion that either . . . could be obtained, at least by them, in an age. (*SK* 461–62)

Again, Martin has more confidence in the abilities of these "noble savages" than they have themselves.

Ignoble Savagery

So far, it has been shown that Martin often displays considerable respect for local traditions, either because he does not think them uncivilized or irrational at all, or because he perceives certain moral virtues in their "uncivilized" state. But there are also local customs which receive a less respectful treatment. One example is Martin's comment on the tradition of marriage on trial, which entailed the right to reject a wife and send her back to her parents during the first year: "this unreasonable custom was long ago brought into disuse" (*WI* 175). Most of the local beliefs and customs he criticizes are related to—or at least blamed upon—Catholicism (e.g., *WI* 205). Although the popish connection is not explicitly specified for each individual superstition, the preface contains a general statement which implicitly pertains to the individual cases outlined elsewhere:

> There are several instances of heathenism and pagan superstition . . . , but I would not have the reader to think those practices are chargeable upon the generality of the present inhabitants, since only a few of the oldest and most ignorant of the vulgar are guilty of them. These practices are only to be found where the reformed religion has not prevailed; for it is to the progress of that alone that the banishment of evil spirits, as well as of evil customs, is owing, when all other methods proved ineffectual. . . . The islanders in general . . . in religion and virtue . . . excel many thousands of others who have greater advantages of daily improvement. (*WI* 65)

Martin assumes the mainstream position of a member of a sober Protestant church which distances itself from all sorts of heathenism. But the dividing lines between Self and Other are drawn in a way that differs from many other contemporary mainstream texts about Gaels: while many construct binary juxtapositions of civilized Lowlands and barbarous Highlands, Martin redraws the dividing lines to let them run within the Gaidhealtachd itself. Intra-Gaelic divisions could already be discerned in Martin's juxtaposition of remote and nobly savage Rona and St. Kilda against other, more accessible islands. Further intra-Gaelic differences are reflected in his distinction between the true and the wrong faith: he ranks the Protestant and already partly enlightened majority of Gaels among the civilized, presumably alongside the Protestant rest of the nation, including the anglophones. Only a small and dwindling old, popish, and lower-class segment of the Gaelic populace remains in primitive ignorance.[46]

This, at least, is Martin's opinion of the Gaels of his own time. However, his comments about the onset of progress in the seventeenth century suggest that barbarism has only very recently started to recede from the Gaidhealtachd. In other regions—such as, presumably, the Lowlands or England—barbarism belongs to a much more remote past. This echoes the trope of the contemporary ancestor, but in the case of religion the Gaidhealtachd is not lumped together with other geographical peripheries, such as non-European colonies, and juxtaposed to a more "advanced" geographical center. Instead, the "quasi-pagan" Catholic Other, the contemporary ancestor, is envisaged as populating Europe's metropoles as well: the complaint that Catholicism retains too many heathen survivals, and the denunciation of both popery and paganism as superstitions, are part of the standard repertory of Protestant discourse, from whose perspective *any* Catholic, not just a Gaelic one, is a contemporary ancestor whose mind ought to be colonized and civilized by implantation of the only true faith, that is, Protestantism.

Martin hardly ever forgets to mention which islands are Catholic and which are Protestant, and scrupulously notes the exact size of religious minorities. But sometimes he has to admit that clear-cut dichotomies cannot be maintained. For example, he records an instance of confessional hybridity where Protestant women celebrate a festival of the Holy Virgin (*WI* 280). However, with regard to religion the author always makes clear where his own sympathies lie: they lie with the Protestant ministers. With regard to second sight, Martin contradicts the ministers, but when it comes to more exclusively Catholic "superstitions" and pagan survivals in folk religion he rigorously and self-righteously adheres to orthodox Protestant doctrines. This is illustrated by his description of a Hallowtide ceremony in honor of a sea god which entails almost orgiastic revelry, from which the author distances himself by ironically labeling the drunken rout as "solemn."[47] Martin shares the disapproval shown by the local ministers, who "spent several years before they could persuade the vulgar natives to abandon this ridiculous piece of superstition; which is quite abolished for these 32 years past" (*WI* 107–8).

Protestantism is clearly recognized to have a civilizing mission in the Western Isles. Usually, Martin leaves the role of religious missionary to others, without aspiring to being one himself, or at least without making the fight against superstition the main objective of his travels. But sometimes he cannot resist trying his luck as a civilizer himself. His personal sense of civilizing mission is not purely religious, but that of an enlightened, educated, scientific, rational man of the world fighting against (selected) superstitions or even against ignorance in general. For instance, in one place he encounters the rule that men must be buried in one chapel and women in another, or else the corpses might return above ground. "I told them this was a most ridiculous fancy which they might soon perceive by experience if they would but put it to a trial." Martin secures the help of a more enlightened local who shares his views, "to undeceive the credulous vulgar." The undeceivers have the next corpse buried in the "wrong" spot, "contrary to the ancient custom . . . , but his corpse is still in the grave. . . . This . . . has delivered the credulous natives from this unreasonable fancy" (*WI* 123–24). Similarly, the first two times that Martin takes a boat from Jura to Colonsay, the superstitious boatmen row sunways (clockwise) to ensure a safe passage—a practice which runs contrary to Martin's wishes and convictions: "I forbade them to do it" (*WI* 179). The rowers' superstitious actions are shown to be of no avail: "by a contrary wind the boat and those in it were forced back" (*WI* 179). Martin's "enlightened" approach is more successful:

> I took boat again a third time . . . and forbade them to row about their boat, which they obeyed, and then we landed safely . . . , which some of the crew did not believe possible, for want of the round; but this . . . hath convinced them of the vanity of this superstitious ceremony. (*WI* 179)

Again, Martin seems rather proud of his achievement. The reasons for the change of weather are not specified. He might wish to imply that there is no connection whatsoever between the ceremony and the weather (or supernatural benevolence)—meaning that the first two times the wind was unfavorable despite the ceremony, and good the third time although there was no ceremony. Alternatively, Martin may wish to imply that God himself interfered, that is, that the weather first was bad because the ceremony took place (and incurred God's displeasure), and later improved because there was no longer a ceremony (i.e., God was pleased about this defeat of unchristian superstition).

A third instance where Martin missionizes against superstition, though this time unsuccessfully, is his report on a folk belief that supernatural presences in a local glen must be asked for protection:

> I told the natives that this was a piece of silly credulity as ever was imposed upon the most ignorant ages, and that their imaginary protectors deserved no such invocation. . . . They answered that there had happened a late instance of a woman who went into that glen without resigning herself to the conduct of these . . . [supernatural beings], and . . . became mad, which confirmed them in their unreasonable fancy. (*WI* 153)

The regional, that is, spatial, specificity of a custom is reinterpreted to fit into a linear, universalist vision of history by being recast as the equivalent of a different time ("age") in civilizational development—a trope which is familiar from many colonial contexts. Again, the island Martin describes is dominated by Catholicism, a factor which seems to lie at the root of the Protestant author's incredulity and condescension.

His missionizing pose also entails economic aspects: he aims to spread more wealth among the locals. A small-scale example is Martin's account of how the only inhabitant of St. Kilda to own steel and flint for kindling fire charged all his neighbors for using this crucial resource, until Martin showed them that certain easily available local stones fulfill the same purpose (*WI* 315; *SK* 458). The author claims that the natives then started "accusing themselves of their own ignorance" (*SK* 458), and again seems proud of his philanthropic interference (*WI* 315). The most important aspect of Martin's economic mission is infinitely more ambitious: he hopes to secure outside investors and patrons for the large-scale "improvement" of the Western Isles' economy and the latter's integration into mainstream capitalism.[48]

The Road to the Future: Extraneous "Modernization" as an Economic Mission

Despite his considerable sympathy with Gaelic island culture and indigenous perspectives, Martin's ultimate vision for the future of the Isles is one of externally induced "improvement." Here as well, his perspective resembles colonial discourse. But how does this resemblance to colonial projects fit in with his sympathy for native culture, and with the fact that, unlike many later descriptions of non-European colonies, Martin's landscape is not emptied of people?[49] It might be argued that he, too, discursively empties the landscape of its native inhabitants by compartmentalizing the latter in a separate "manners and customs" chapter; but this would overlook that other chapters likewise contain much information on people, folk beliefs, oral history, and so on, so that Martin's landscape is clearly animated throughout. The type of improvement scheme he envisages is compatible with the animation of the margin's landscape and a certain respect for the local population. Complete belittling of the "natives," or their discursive removal from the landscape, makes sense if the colonial project is genocide or at least very thorough geographical and economic marginalization of indigenous populations (for instance, removing them to less valuable ground or crowded reserves) and the resettlement of their original territory by a large incoming population of settlers from the colonial center. But this is not what Martin plans: he does not want to supplant the natives but, under the guidance of just a few outsiders, "improve" and hybridize/assimilate them into profiting and profitable subjects of the centralized British monarchy. Apart from the few incomers needed to initiate and supervise the modernization process, he also envisages the influx of a more numerous labor force from the opposite Highland mainland and from the north. But even these are not supposed to replace or marginalize native labor. Martin expects an economic boom great enough to satisfactorily employ all the natives *and* incoming laborers (*WI* 353). This particular type of "colonial improvement" scheme does accord with his belief in local virtues.

In fact, one reason why he stresses the merits of the indigenous population so emphatically might be his desire to convince his readership—which includes potential investors and patrons—that improvement schemes are both possible and desirable. They are possible because the locals already provide a sound basis of virtues and achievements to start from, and desirable because such decent people with such great potential could form a valuable pool of human resources for the crown (see below). Sometimes he even implies that only "improvement" can help the natives to realize their natural morality most fully. For instance, he stresses their hospitality, but notes that it has now declined because of poverty (*WI* 95)—a poverty whose removal through economic civilizing missions is envisaged elsewhere in his book. Martin's belief in improvement without large-scale resettlement, as well as his conviction that the natives are incapable of implementing the desired progressive policies without paternalistic help and instruction from outside, become clear from the following passages:

> Those places need not to be planted with a new colony, but only furnished with proper materials, and a few expert hands, to join with the natives to . . . advance . . . fishery. (*WI* 353)

> If the natives were taught and encouraged to . . . improve their corn and hay, to plant, enclose, and manure their ground, drain lakes, sow wheat and peas, and plant orchards and kitchen-gardens, &c., they might have as great plenty . . . for the sustenance of mankind as any other people in Europe. (*WI* 350)[50]

Michael Newton has plausibly suggested that Martin's emphasis on the Gaels' virtues and their amenability to civilizing missions might have been motivated by a conviction that some form of colonization was unavoidable, and that he wanted to cushion the effects of colonization by at least avoiding its worst forms, such as large-scale expropriations of locals and their replacement by "plantation" settlers from outside.[51] Martin may have believed that Gaelic self-marketing as tractable and profitable was a lesser evil than an otherwise inescapable dispossession or extermination.

The paternalist ideology which Martin employs to sell the idea of civilizing the Gaels is again obvious when he describes the farming methods of the Western Isles as an "infant state of agriculture" (*WI* 350). Once more, this asserts a linear view of historical development, and the colonial-style childhood metaphor casts indigenous populations as inferior to the mature center which is responsible for the margin's education. The benefit of this hierarchial relationship is, however, envisaged to be mutual: both outsiders' and local opinion is invoked to confirm the desirability of "improvements" (*WI* 358–59).

> The north-west isles are . . . most capable of improvement . . . ; yet by reason of their distance from trading towns, and because of their language, which is Irish, the inhabitants have never had any opportunity to trade at home or abroad, or to acquire mechanical arts and other sciences; so that they are still left to act by the force of their natural genius and what they could learn by observation. They have not yet arrived to a competent knowledge in agriculture, . . . Tracts of rich ground lie neglected, or . . . but meanly improved in proportion to what they might be. This is the more to be regretted because the people are as capable to acquire arts or sciences as any other in Europe. If two or more persons skilled in agriculture were sent from the lowlands, to each parish in the isles, they would soon enable the natives to furnish themselves with such plenty of corn as could maintain all their poor and idle people; many of which, for want of subsistence at home, are forced to seek their livelihood in foreign countries, to the great loss, as well as dishonour of the nation. This would enable them also to furnish the opposite barren parts of the continent with bread. (*WI* 349)

The Gaelic language was widely considered a main reason for the Gaidhealtachd's "backwardness." Martin partly shares this opinion, but unlike many of his contemporaries he does not ascribe this to an intrinsic inferiority of Gaelic language and culture—as shown above, he considers Gaelic to be very expressive and on a par with any other language. Instead, Martin presents the problem as a merely practical matter, that is, the difficulty of communicating with potential trading partners. He states that the islanders would do wisely to acquire English. The table of contents promises the "language of the inhabitants" to be "no obstacle" to improvement (*WI* 82), but the relevant chapter reveals that the reason why it is no obstacle is the Gaels' capacity for learning English in future (*WI* 353–54). Some change in this direction is already acknowledged: Stornoway's school teaches Latin and English (*WI* 109). Martin also notes that anglicization is partly a matter of class (*WI* 275, 285). Although English is recommended more on pragmatic grounds than out of disregard for Gaelic, a slight cultural cringe may underlie even Martin's perspective, as he never suggests that the same interest in mutual communication might induce outside improvers to learn Gaelic in return. Such mutuality does not even seem to occur to him, which suggests a slight bias in favor of English.

If Martin's reference to those who "seek their livelihood in foreign countries, to the great loss, as well as dishonour of the nation" is to be taken as an allusion to overseas colonialism rather than intra-British or intra-European migration, the passage suggests that the author is opposed to overseas colonialism in favor of domestic development, for instance as regards the European herring industry. This accords with the following passage: "If the Dutch . . . call their fishery a golden mine, and . . . affirm that it yields them more profit than the Indies do to Spain, we have very great reason to begin to work upon those rich mines, not only in the isles, but on all our coast" (*WI* 359). Though Martin recommends foreign trade in general, the main partners advocated here are not overseas colonies but the geographically proximate regions of Britain, Ireland, and Europe (*WI* 352).[52] His critique of overseas ventures is not based on solidarity with foreign colonized populations, but on economic motivations: intra-European trade seems more profitable to him. There is also a sense of inter-peripheral competition: he might feel that investments are drawn away from domestic peripheries like Gaelic Scotland, to favor economic and civilizing schemes in overseas colonialism; and as a Hebridean who believes in the beneficial potential of such investments, Martin wants to redirect these benefits away from the overseas colonies to use them back home.[53]

Attracting investors and other supporters for "improvement" schemes seems to have been one of Martin's main motivations for writing his *Description of the Western Islands*. The title page promises "A Brief Hint of Improving Trade in That Country," and an entire chapter is dedicated to "The Advantages the Isles Afford by Sea and Land, and Particularly for a Fishing Trade" (*WI* 349–59). A third hint in this direction is the dedication to Queen Anne's husband, Prince George of Denmark. The dedication more or less claims to speak in the islanders' name. At first, one might assume that Martin's shifting persona here leans toward the insider role, speaking as one of the locals. However, it seems more plausible that he means to speak *for* the "natives," like an ombudsman standing *between* the parties involved, without a personal stake in the matter. His own economic welfare is not as dependent on improvement schemes as that of, say, local fishermen. Martin, as an educated English-speaking member of the middle class, is more mobile and can seek employment elsewhere if necessary. That he sees himself more as a mediator than a native petitioner is also suggested by his use of the pronoun "they" instead of "we":

> The islanders . . . presume that it is owing to their great distance from the imperial seat, rather than their want of native worth, that their islands have been so little regarded; which by improvement might render a considerable accession of strength and riches to the Crown, as appears by a scheme annexed to the following treatise. They have suffered hitherto under the want of a powerful and affectionate patron.[54]

A person who may become such a patron has now been found: Prince George. "Providence seems to have given [the islanders] a natural claim" on him, apparently because of their historical links to Scandinavia: "They . . . now . . .

pay their duty to a Danish Prince, to whose predecessors all of them formerly belonged. They . . . are honoured with the sepulchres of eight Kings of Norway" (*WI* 59). In earlier centuries, this Scandinavian connection would have been a source of political and cultural otherness rather than an argument for closer integration into a British polity.[55] It had given the Western Isles alternative options for alliances, which local magnates tried to exploit for their own interests, for instance playing the Scottish and Norwegian crowns against each other. By Martin's time, the Isles were subject to political authorities in Edinburgh and London, and a Danish prince consort served the British crown. Martin thus reinterprets the history of the connections between Scandinavia and the Scottish Islands: instead of regional autonomy, they signify the Islands' loyalty to their overlord at the "center"—the Scottish (and through personal union with England also British) crown. Martin seems to hope that the prince consort might secure additional patronage from Queen Anne herself: "protection . . . they hope for from two princes" (*WI* 59–60). That Martin's reinterpretation jars with earlier history shines through when he states that the islanders' respect to a Danish prince can "now" be paid "without suspicion of infidelity to the Queen of England" (*WI* 59), implying that formerly things were different.

Martin's commendation of "native worth" seems slightly at odds with another passage which says that patronage is prayed for "though it be almost presumption for so sinful a nation to hope for so great a blessing" (*WI* 59). Sins against God might include the persistence of Catholicism and "pagan" superstition in parts of the Isles. In addition, the passage may allude to political sins: the "disloyalty" which parts of the Gaelic community had, at various points in history, shown to the crown.

To alert future patrons and improvers to the Western Isles' good potential, Martin praises not only the inhabitants, but also the natural resources: he gives detailed accounts of soils, products, and fisheries, thus informing investors about tradeable goods and their profitability—he always stresses the fruitfulness of the soil and the abundance of fish.[56] Even St. Kilda is noted to possess "plenty of cod and ling of a great size . . . , the improvement of which might be of great advantage" (*WI* 308). One reason why Martin discusses climate and soil conditions is their relevance to the question of which crops—and thus, trade goods—could be grown.[57] Martin also stresses that native produce is not inferior to that of other regions (e.g., *WI* 92). Already the contents pages (especially 82) announce the exploitability of the Isles with regard to soil fertility, costs of living, trade and fishing prospects, and minerals, for instance from the lead mine "recently discovered" on Islay which, however, "has not turned to any account as yet" (*WI* 272). Elsewhere, his assessment of profitability is more modest, but even there he advises investors to give it a try:

> I shall not . . . assert that there are mines of gold or silver . . . , from any resemblance they may bear to other parts that afford mines, but

> the natives affirm that gold dust has been found. . . . There is a good lead mine, having a mixture of silver in it, . . . and . . . Lismore affords lead; and . . . Islay. . . . If search were made . . . , it is not improbable that some good mines might be discovered. (*WI* 351–52)

Prospective improvers of the Western Isles also receive practical information on how to get there: Martin includes detailed shipping information, for example concerning anchoring places. This valuable practical information is already announced on the title page, at the very top of the list: "Full Account of Their [the Western Isles'] Situation, Extent, Soils, Product, Harbours, Bays, Tides, Anchoring Places, and Fisheries." Both books also contain maps, drawn by Martin himself.[58] In *Western Islands* the map is also advertised on the title page, as a means to describe "the Harbours, Anchoring Places, and dangerous Rocks, for the benefit of Sailers." Presumably, this is aimed primarily at sailors from outside the Isles, since local ones would know these things from experience, even without the new map. Mapping the Isles is an act of symbolic and material incorporation into the Scottish or British nation. There had been a strong correlation between centralization and Scottish mapmaking since the sixteenth century. Communicating detailed local information to a nonlocal audience helps to integrate the mapped area into the imagination of the national community; moreover, it promotes material integration by facilitating trade.[59]

Martin's storehouse of practical information also includes outlines of previous attempts at modernization and external investment which now lie abandoned but may be revived. For instance, he describes a loch which "hath been famous for the great quantity of herrings yearly taken in it within these fifty years last past" (*WI* 128):

> There had been 400 sail loaded in it with herrings at one season; but it is not now frequented for fishing, though the herrings do still abound in it; . . . natives sit angling on the rocks . . . it is strange that in all this island there is not one herring net to be had; but if the natives saw any encouragement, they could soon provide them.

Similar remnants are found in another place nearby:

> There is still . . . the foundation of a house, built by the English, for a magazine to keep their casks, salt, etc., for carrying on a great fishery which was then begun there. . . . King Charles the First had a share in it. This lake . . . is certainly capable of great improvement; much of the ground about the bay is capable of cultivation. (*WI* 128)

More general comments on the archipelago and the fishing industry follow later:

> The advantage that might be reaped from the improvement of the fish trade in these isles, prevailed among considering people in former times to attempt it. The first . . . was by King Charles the First, in conjunction with a company of merchants; but it miscarried because of the civil wars. . . . The next attempt was by King Charles the Second, who also joined with some merchants; and this succeeded well for a time. . . . The fish catched by that company . . . were reputed the best in Europe of their kind . . . ; but this design was ruined thus: the king having occasion for money, was advised to withdraw that which was employed at the fishery; at which the merchants . . . also withdrew their money. (*WI* 352–53)

The latter passage may be read as an implicit plea to the crown for renewed investment. Apart from suggesting the revival of old improvement schemes, Martin also suggests new ones, such as administrative reform. He advocates the creation of a new, separate sheriffdom in the Western Isles because they are too remote to be controlled from Inverness (*WI* 358). He also suggests the creation of new centers for industries, a new royal borough, and a free port—and recommends his native Skye as the best location (*WI* 355, 358).

Martin's book on the Western Isles also contains a chapter on the Northern Isles, Orkney and Shetland—culturally different from the Gaelic Western Isles, but similar in their peripheral, "underdeveloped" economic status.[60] However, the north seems slightly ahead in development, thus being a model for what can be done in the west. Orkney's herring industry is as derelict as that of the Western Isles, but at least Orkney already exports some other goods (*WI* 365). The forefront of peripheral development is Shetland:

> Shetland is much more populous now, than it was thirty years ago; . . . owing to the trade, and particularly . . . their fishery, so much followed every year by the Hollanders, Hamburgers, and others. The . . . people at Lerwick is . . . increased to about three hundred families: and . . . few . . . were natives of Shetland, but came from several parts of Scotland. . . . The fishery in Shetland is the foundation both of their trade and wealth; and though it be of late . . . less than before, yet the inhabitants by their industry . . . make a greater profit of it than formerly. (*WI* 385, also see 386)
>
> This fishing-trade is very beneficial to the inhabitants, who have provisions and necessaries imported . . . ; and employment for all their people, who by . . . selling . . . products . . . , bring in a considerable sum of money. . . . The proprietors of the ground are considerable gainers also, by letting their houses . . . as shops to the seamen, during their residence. (*WI* 387)

An envoi at the end of the book incites people to improve Shetland further, which may be read as an implicit call for similar initiatives in the other isles: "The great number of foreign ships which repair hither yearly upon the account of fishing, ought to excite the people of Scotland to a speedy improvement of that profitable trade; which they may carry on with more ease and profit in their own seas, than any foreigners" (*WI* 391).

Martin's advocacy of improvement schemes and his frequent display of a colonizing outlook place him, to some extent, alongside other texts which present the anglophone mainstream as the center of civilization. But for Martin the inhabitants of the peripheries are not merely passive objects, recipients, or imitators of the center's discoveries. Instead, he emphasizes mutuality.

Mutuality and the Returned Gaze

Martin greatly admires traditional Gaelic folk medicine. Even the title page of *Western Islands* highlights the locals' "Admirable . . . way of Curing most Diseases by Simples of their own Product." These medical methods, described in great detail, are clearly meant to set an example for imitation by non-islanders. Civilization is perceived as a two-way process: while Martin wants the center to bring trade and education to the Western Isles, the human genius of the islanders also has something to teach the center—it even contributes to what is often considered the very motor of Western modernity and progress, and an exclusive domain of the metropolitan center, that is, natural science.

> Human industry has of late advanced useful and experimental philosophy very much. Women and illiterate persons have in some measure contributed . . . by the discovery of some useful cures.[61] The field of nature is large, and much of it wants still to be cultivated by an ingenious . . . application; and the curious, by their observations, might daily make further advances in the history of nature. (*WI* 63–64)

At first, cultivation seems more than a general agricultural metaphor: it is reminiscent of colonial texts assigning the task of cultivation exclusively to people from the hegemonic center, while the natural resources to be cultivated include not only plants, soil, and animals, but also indigenous human populations that are envisaged as parts of nature, not as cultivators in their own right who are able and entitled to master both nature and their own destiny. However, on closer inspection it seems implausible that this particular passage should be read in such a colonial sense: his references to native discoveries imply that, here at least, he does not categorize the islanders as a mere part of nature. Instead, he sees them as part of a wider human community of cultivators who in mutual cooperation advance a common stock of learning and exploit nature (in this case the local flora and fauna which natives use, that is, "cultivate," for making medicines) for the general benefit of mankind.[62]

Mutuality is also significant in Martin's descriptions of cross-cultural communication. As already shown, several passages proclaim local discursive authority, while other passages imply the superiority of the anglophone mainstream. But his work also contains sections where islanders and non-islanders are portrayed as being strange *to each other*, without either side being privileged. Sometimes, mutuality takes the unproblematic form of reciprocal admiration, as when the natives of St. Kilda admire Martin and his companions for crossing the sea in unfavorable weather, while Martin in turn admires the locals' nimbleness and courage in moving about on a dangerous cliff (*SK* 406). Other descriptions of mutuality and "returned gaze" demonstrate a clear awareness of the potential problems and conflicts that cross-cultural communication entails. His awareness of, and interest in, these issues may well be intensified by his own hybrid position. Martin tells of a stranded English seaman whose incomprehension and misinterpretation of life on Boreray is offered as a target for ridicule. This reverses the perspective presented in other passages, which ridicule the islanders' reactions to Glasgow. In the chapter that returns this gaze toward the "center," the English sailor finds it difficult to understand certain activities of Hebridean women:

> [The women] were employed (as he supposed) in a strange manner, viz., their arms and legs were bare, being five [women] on a side; and between them lay a board, upon which they had laid a piece of cloth, and were thickening . . . it with their hands and feet, and singing all the while. The Englishman presently concluded it to be a little bedlam, which he did not expect in so remote a corner; and this he told to Mr. John Maclean who possesses the island. Mr. Maclean answered he never saw any mad people in those islands; but this would not satisfy him, till they both went to the place where the women were at work, and then Mr. Maclean having told him that it was their common way of thickening cloth, he was convinced, though surprised at the manner of it. (*WI* 129–30)

This thickening process, accompanied by rhythmical work songs, is known as "waulking." Martin's account of this intercultural encounter shows incomprehension and bewilderment to be mutual: islanders wonder at the (to them) unusual sights of Glasgow, and the Englishman wonders at island customs, finding them "strange." The sailor tries to overcome his bewilderment and make sense of the scene. In itself, the urge to make sense of the world is a basic, ubiquitous human need not restricted to colonial or cross-cultural encounters. It is likewise unavoidable that humans interpret new experiences against the background of their previous knowledge, which can limit their conclusions, and that they supplement gaps in their knowledge by conjecture, which might mislead them. But the particular way in which Martin's Englishman deals with such cognitive insecurities does show features which might be characterized as symptoms of a colonial consciousness: the seafaring Saxon jumps to his conclusions very quickly, without retaining any insecurities about the correctness of his interpretation. The self-assurance with which he assumes discursive authority is reminiscent of the thought processes Edward Said identified in *Orientalism*.

Martin, by relating this anecdote, exposes and ridicules such metropolitan complacency. His use of the word "presently" might be an ironic sidesweep at the rashness with which such presumptions are made. The only rationalization the English stranger can think of is that there is none: he concludes that all the women must be *ir*rational, that is, mad. This recalls the frequent use of epithets of irrationality in cross-cultural contacts in general, but also more particularly in modern overseas colonial discourse, for instance in Orientalist texts labeling Eastern religions as less rational and more mystic than Western ones, or in Joseph Conrad's description of Africa in his novella *Heart of Darkness*.[63] However, Martin questions self-assured assumptions of hegemonic discursive authority: he shows that the center is by no means able to fully comprehend the margin and to explain it better than the natives can. The Englishman's urge to diagnose madness reflects his need to reestablish the security of his authority to understand and explain even those things which his limited experience has not yet taught him to comprehend. This urge is so powerful that it even overrides the doubts emanating from his own common sense: even to him it appears unlikely that such a remote place would have a bedlam. But if he accepted this objection, he would be left without any explanation—unless he condescended to ask the women themselves, something that does not occur to him, either because he does not expect them to speak anything other than Gaelic, or because they appear too lowly in ethnicity, rank, or gender. Later the Englishman talks to Mr. Maclean, the tacksman, but even he cannot be trusted at first, presumably because he is still a native, albeit an upper-class one. Since the sailor apparently cannot bear the existence of anything he is unable to accommodate within his own sense of rationality, he prefers the bedlam hypothesis. That such diagnoses of irrationality and madness are based on the outsider's incomprehension is highlighted by Martin's account of Maclean's answer, that is, that no cases of madness are known.[64] Both Martin and Maclean are islanders themselves, and thus know the internal logic and rationality of local codes. Even when Maclean provides the answer to the riddle, the Englishman is unwilling to give a local voice precedence over his own uninformed conjectures. It is only later that he accepts this new item of knowledge and succumbs once more to wonder.

Readers might feel invited to smile at the Englishman's misconceptions, but the *way* in which Martin presents this invitation is significant: he does not explain the women's activity before he relates the anecdote—instead, readers experience it mostly through the Englishman's eyes. Most members of Martin's target audience would likewise have been strangers to the island, and might have reacted in a similarly uncomprehending way. No solution to the riddle is given at the outset—the only clue that there might be an underlying logic to this "strange" and perhaps "mad" sight is the phrase "as he supposed." Initially left rather clueless, readers are invited to either walk into the same logical trap as the Englishman in the story, or to keep wondering or make conjectures of their own. The readers' knowledge would not be superior to that of the Englishman (apart from that one subtle clue), which might make them aware of their own ignorance. When the riddle is finally solved, they might smile not only at the Englishman, but also at themselves—and hopefully become more wary of the problems of cross-cultural understanding, and of the pitfalls which metropolitan assumptions of discursive authority can entail.

Another story about mutual communication problems tells how a "foreign priest" happened to arrive in Barra on the anniversary of the local patron saint (Saint Barr), about whom he was asked to preach, "according to the ancient custom of the place" (*WI* 163):

> The priest was surprised, . . . never having heard of Saint Barr before . . . ; and therefore . . . could say nothing concerning him: but told them that if a sermon to the honour of St. Paul or St. Peter could please them, they might have it instantly. This answer . . . was so disagreeable to them, that they . . . told him he could be no true priest, if he had not heard of St. Barr, for the Pope himself had heard of him; but this would not persuade the priest, so that they parted much dissatisfied with one another. (*WI* 163–64)

It is not entirely obvious what Martin's own opinion is. One possibility is that he recounts the story merely to emphasize the remoteness of the place from all mainstreams, as the natives reject the central saints Peter and Paul in favor of a local saint who is so peripheral that he is unheard of elsewhere. Another possibility is that Martin's intentions are less neutral in this case, insinuating mild censure and mockery of the islanders' parochialism. However, though not necessarily intentionally, his report again betrays the limits of metropolitan self-centeredness: metropolitans may believe that the rest of the world looks to them for guidance in all things, but the episode shows that this is not true. Although the islanders still recognize the authority of the pope, they place themselves at the center of their theological views, and look down upon the ignorant visitor who has not even heard of the crucial Saint Barr. Moreover, the displeasure is noted to be mutual.

Sometimes the returned gaze is even discernible in passages where Martin's own disapproval of the locals is explicit—for instance when he explains local taboos: although he calls them "superstitious," he acknowledges them to be based on an intricate system of norms, rather than on random chaos (*SK* 498–99). Elsewhere, a faint indigenous counter-voice against his disapproval can be heard in his remark on taboo-breaking which "they reckon a great barbarity, and directly contrary to ancient custom" (*WI* 98). The choice of the word "barbarity" for the *periphery's* disapproval of the *center* might show momentary awareness that all societies perceive divergences from their own rules as barbaric—as if the natives now return the colonizing gaze to the outsiders, or to incredulous half-insiders like Martin, and throw the label "barbaric" back at them. The same happens in Martin's account of French and Spanish ships coming to St. Kilda in 1686: "Both seamen and inhabitants were barbarians one to another, the inhabitants speaking only the Irish tongue, to which the French and the Spaniards were altogether strangers" (*SK* 444). The word "barbarian" is apparently not used in an exclusively linguistic sense, but also extends to behavior, as a few sentences later Martin records the natives' astonishment and resolute interference when they saw the foreigners work on a Sunday (*SK* 444–45). A third example refers to the more recent landing of another ship:

> They told me of a ship . . . and that the Lowlanders aboard her were not Christians. . . . They said . . . they knew this by their practices[:] . . . working upon Sunday, . . . taking away some of their cows without any return for them, except a few Irish copper pieces; and . . . the attempt . . . to ravish their women. (*SK* 445)

Here, Martin's sympathies obviously lie with the locals. Other passages likewise show awareness that not all visiting outsiders are benevolent: he notes further cases where incoming seamen attempted cattle theft (*WI* 104) or otherwise abused the trust, hospitality, and generosity of islanders (e.g., *WI* 146, 356; *SK* 464). He even records an attack and rape carried out by government troops on Eigg (*WI* 346)—although the attack is reported in a rather neutral voice, Martin more clearly disapproves of the rape.

Occasionally these negative experiences have led the islanders to become suspicious of strangers, and sometimes this distrust even turns against Martin himself, for instance when the local constable does not grant him a sightseeing tour of Kismul Castle: "the constable was very apprehensive of some design I might have in viewing the fort, and thereby to expose it to the conquest of a foreign power, of which I supposed there was no great cause of fear" (*WI* 157). While this anxiety may indeed have been unfounded, the following fears in the same Catholic area were not (as evident from Martin's "enlightened" lecturing to Catholics on other occasions):

> The natives have St. Barr's wooden image standing on the altar. . . . I came . . . with an intention to see this image, but was disappointed; for the natives prevented me by carrying it away, lest I might take

> occasion to ridicule their superstition, as some Protestants have done formerly; and when I was gone it was again exposed on the altar. (*WI* 158)

A third example relates to a "superstitious" custom already in decline (a fire ritual connected to childbirth): "I inquired their reason for this custom, which I told them was altogether unlawful; this disobliged them mightily, insomuch that they would give me no satisfaction.[65] But others, that were of a more agreeable temper, told me" (*WI* 177–78). Again, the text notes the evasiveness of indigenous tradition as the locals try to shield it from Martin's eyes, which lets an indigenous counter-perspective shine through and allows it to comment on Martin's arrogance.

These instances of mutuality and returned gaze are among the most noteworthy aspects of Martin's work, and of special relevance for postcolonial readings. His writings also reflect other themes which are familiar from anti- and postcolonial contexts, such as the "writing back" paradigm. But, significantly, Martin is also deeply implicated in procolonial thinking, at times reflecting common seventeenth-century preoccupations, but also anticipating ideas which became dominant later in the eighteenth century, such as Enlightened optimism about the feasibility of fully integrating the Gaidhealtachd into the nation, or the romantic application of the "noble savage" trope to the Gaels. Of course, Martin was not the only author from the Gaidhealtachd who responded to the social, cultural, and ideological developments of this period. Further responses, sometimes equally ambivalent, can be found in the poetry produced in the Gaelic language itself.[66] The Gaels' complex responses to the nation-state and its colonizing endeavors at home and overseas highlight that Britain's "internally colonized" Highlanders and Islanders were, despite their marginality, also an integral and integrated part of the British nation—not only an Other, but also part of the nation's Self. This integration intensified in the second half of the eighteenth century and at the beginning of the nineteenth. The implications of these developments for the representation of the Gaidhealtachd in anglophone writing are discussed in the next two chapters.

Chapter 3

✦

The Reemergence of the Primitive Other?

Noble Savagery and the Romantic Age

As previous chapters have illustrated, endorsements of Scottish Gaels as noble savages and valuable parts of the nation were not invented by the romantic age. There are several instances from earlier periods. But in the second half of the eighteenth century, when romanticism appeared on the horizon, such images became much more widespread. Civilizing and homogenizing missions within Britain appeared fairly successful by this time, both as regards the integration of Scotland as a whole into Britain and its empire, and more particularly the integration and "taming" of the Gaels. Capitalism was firmly established, and urbanization and industralization were well under way. It was precisely the success of these "modernizations" which cleared the path for a partial rehabilitation of the "premodern." This general romantic tendency also affected the image of "premodern" populations: once they were no longer a threat, "ignoble savages" could become "noble savages."

In the Scottish context, the new idealization of cultural difference could pertain to both Highland and (still sufficiently non-English) Lowland Scots traditions. Where diversity was valued for its own sake, a limited endorsement of local culture could offer harmless ideological compensation for any remaining grudges held by some Scottish nationalists against the Union, or by Gaelic traditionalists against capitalization and assimilation.

Elsewhere, difference was freed even from these moderately antiestablishment associations and was deemed directly beneficial to the British "center" itself. Partly, this is related to Britain's self-image as the heir of Roman supremacy. This proud analogy could also entail anxieties: it was thought that the Roman Empire, spoiled by success, became placid and decadent; civil and military virtues declined; its sheer size made the realm difficult to govern and defend. Thus weakened, the empire finally fell victim to the "barbarian" onslaught; the forces of the primitive had apparently won out. These issues loomed large in late eighteenth-century thought, as illustrated by Edward Gibbon's *The History of the Decline and Fall of the Roman Empire*.[1] Modern Britons wondered if their own state and empire had to fear the same fate as

Rome. Another English scholar, Edward Wortley Montagu, gave the following warning about contemporary Britain:

> To . . . universal luxury . . . we must impute that amazing progress of corruption, which seiz'd the very vitals of our constitution. If therefore we impartially compare the present state of our own country with that of Rome and Carthage, we shall find, that we resemble them most when in their declining period.[2]

Civilized imperial decadence was juxtaposed to the laudable frugality, virtue, and military valor of more "primitive" peoples, both ancient and modern.[3] Britain sought a synthesis: could the simple virtues of internal barbarian fringes like Highland Scotland be integrated into the moral and military arsenal of the center, in a way which would make the center and its empire more resilient? The celebration of Highland loyalty as a good example to *all* British subjects and an antidote to social revolution, and the recruitment of innumerable Highland soldiers into the British Army, were two experiments in this direction. Here, "primitive" assets were directly placed at the service of the British state and its expanding empire. Again, this illustrates the ambivalent position of Scotland and its Gaels: as colonized, their romanticization was premised on the successful conquest of their traditions, and as colonizers their very "barbarism" offered moral and military capital for the establishment of British world power. Imperial benefits had long been a key factor in Scottish unionism, and eventually helped to integrate even the Gaels into the nation, especially via the army.[4] The following sections chart the permutations of Highland noble savagery, both as a tool and as a counterbalance to the status quo, in more detail.

Difference as a Harmless *Counterbalance* to the Status Quo

General Frameworks: Romantic Zeitgeist and Celticism as Wider Phenomena

Sufficiently well-established capitalist societies tend to entail urbanization, the increase of human control over nature—often connected to the destruction of natural resources—and the mechanization and standardization of labor. In response, many people develop a liking for (and propensity to idealize) less densely populated places, "unspoiled" countryside, rural life, "tradition," and simplicity.[5] They often romanticize the supposedly more individualist, natural, and non-standardizable work rhythms of agriculture which depend more on the irregularities of weather and seasons than on the regular pace of clock and machinery. But the relation between individualism and tradition can also be interpreted differently: feudal agriculture may seem to embody laudable community spirit, while capitalism is criticized for destroying such solidarities—personal liberty can also mean an atomization of society until everyone is left to fend for him- or herself, and thus more at risk if any difficulties should befall. All these critiques of capitalism have found use for cultural Others: actual or supposed alternative ways of life become objects of desire, projection screens for social or moral fantasies, and sources of temporary escapism. The Other can be viewed as a relic from a better past—a past that may be irretrievably lost or dying, but radiates a light of fading glory that can still be seen and enjoyed. Alternatively, it may be an object of moral study for those who search for a better kind of human nature, and/or the original state of morality. Temporary escapism may be gained by reading about these alternative worlds or physically visiting them oneself: the romantic age also saw an increase in tourism. The inhabitants of these "different worlds" are often portrayed as noble savages.[6]

Another factor in the new idealization of nonmainstream cultures was aesthetic, and a consequence of the general mutability of fashions. Some people simply seemed saturated with classicist aesthetics and Enlightened rationalism and were on the lookout for something new, something different from what they were used to. Apart from sheer unusualness (at least to mainstream eyes and ears), emotionality, dreams, mysteriousness, and the supernatural were also highly sought after. It was thought that the savage's deficiencies in the field of rational thought bred an overabundance of metaphor and unusual, that is, potentially creative, turns of mind. Moreover, "primitive" peoples were allegedly prone to particularly strong, unrestrained feelings and passions. Thus, "savages" might be bad scholars, but they made fantastic poets.[7] Historicity and traditionality were again valued for their own sake, while Enlightened progressivist scholars had discarded large parts of history as too barbarian to be interesting. Where "Enlightened" historians had shied away from subjects about which there were too few reliable written sources to yield scientific results, this very mysteriousness of remote cultures and ages was now endorsed as a field for speculation, creative imagining, and fantasy.[8]

Through the centuries, these roles of remote projection screen, noble savage, or alternative aesthetic model have been assigned to many different Others: "Celts," Scots, Gaels, indigenous populations of overseas colonies such as North American "Indians," or Maori; medieval ancestry; or even the contemporaneous peasantry and folk culture of the respective mainstreamers' own national or ethnic collective. For England's eighteenth-century urban middle or upper classes, even an English peasant could be different, "traditional," and "authentic" enough to serve as a noble savage.[9] Despite this wider context, the particular ways in which the "noble savage" trope has been applied to Britain's internally marginalized ethnicities (whether Scottish, "Celtic," or Gaelic) as well as overseas colonized cultures establishes discursive links between those regions and validates the examination of noble savagery in the postcolonial context of the present study.

Here, it is particularly important that subjugation and control function as prerequisites for romanticization, and romantic images of Scots or Celts show many commonalities with other, more overtly hostile variants of colonial discourse. The idea that primitive peoples can possess moral virtues despite, or even because of, their primitiveness also occurs in predominantly "Enlightened" texts which embrace assimilation and "progress." But "Enlightened" respect for "simple virtues" does not prevent those texts from regarding the assimilation of "noble savages" into the "civilized" mainstream as the most desirable course. After all, simple virtues were often invoked as a promising *basis* for the civilizing mission. Enlightened perspectives thus lay more stress on the beneficial aspects of culture contact and homogenization. By contrast, romanticism often values cultural difference for its own sake, professes a desire to preserve it, or at least laments its passing. Such texts tend more toward a traditionalist or nativist stance. Frequently, however, sociocultural change was already a fait accompli—romantic nostalgia only set in after the "noble savages" were under control, that is, when the Other was no longer dangerous and the civilizing mission had already been partially successful.[10] The same was true for nature: it had to seem reasonably tameable before the last "wildernesses" could be romanticized.

Colonial discourse is not the only field where Enlightenment and romanticism are closely connected. A neatly chronological periodization between the two is impossible. Ian Duncan stresses that "in Scotland . . . 'Classical' and 'Romantic' cultural forms occupy the same moment, rather than defining successive stages."[11] Michael Baridon argues that Enlightened cosmopolitanism, Gothic gloom, cultural nationalism, and emotionalism were not only chronologically synchronous, but also conceptually inseparable, as an interest in emotions, cultural origins, and traditions was central to many Enlightenment achievements.[12] In various ways, the Enlightened "modern" center's self-understanding and universalist rationality depended on the peripheral or bygone/vanishing "primitive" Other and its particularized subjective experience, or what was constructed as such.[13]

Concerning the center's views on marginalized or colonized cultures, the kinship between Enlightenment and romanticism is also evident in their reliance on similar binarisms, for instance when associating the "civilized metropolis" with rationality, order, and progress, and the "barbarian periphery" with irrationality, chaos, and stasis. Such binarisms also link imperial discourses of antiquity to modern ones, and intra-European fringes like the "Celtic" ones (ancient or modern) to colonized populations overseas. Advocates of civilizing missions evaluated the periphery's supposed attributes in mainly negative terms and wanted to improve the "savage" condition, while romantic discourse reinterpreted the same alleged attributes in positive, but still patronizing, terms. For instance, intellectual simplicity no longer connoted deplorable stupidity but laudable emotional intuition and/or moral innocence. In an inner-British context, the most uncontested candidate for the position of the center was England, while the position of the barbarian periphery could be occupied by "Celts" or even the partly non-"Celtic" subordinate nation of Scotland. Within Scotland, such role structures could be reproduced internally, with anglophone and especially Lowland Scottish culture as the center and Gaelic traditions as the barbarian periphery.

Celticism thus found itself on the rise throughout Britain, and to a certain extent also in Europe. Mainstream interest lighted upon contemporaneous "Celts" and their remote ancestors. Critics of neoclassicism could be drawn to "barbarians" of old who had (really or supposedly) rebelled against "original" Roman or Greek classicism in antiquity. These barbarians were not all Celtic: there was also an interest in Germanic cultures. But the Celts had an important advantage:

> The German or Goth was not . . . apt to British romanticism, which took the form of a revolt against the established forms of *England*: the Anglo-Saxon, at the centre of England's conception of itself, was first cousin to the Goth . . . ; moreover, a German dynasty was on the throne of England. These were reasons . . . to discourage a romanticism of the barbarian Anglo-Saxon. There *was* such a romanticism, but it was . . . feeble compared to that of the Celt. . . .
>
> Indeed, the Anglo-Saxon came to represent . . . the opposite of the Celt.[14]

Despite the numerous parallels between modern and ancient images of Celts, there are also differences, for instance regarding nature and spirituality. Some ancient authors depicted the Celtic lifestyle as being closer to nature than Greek or Roman habits were, for example because the barbarians ate from the ground instead of using tables. But unlike many modern authors, ancient writers did not claim a special *emotional* connection between Celts and their natural surroundings. Neither did they claim a special Celtic propensity for spirituality and visions. Although "various Classical writers were fascinated by the druids, their etymological connection with the oak tree, their use of mistletoe, and their sinister activities in their sacred groves," they did not treat this exceptional priestly section of "Celtic" society as a metonymy for Celtic sensibility in general.[15] But romantic and post-romantic images would do exactly that: henceforth, all "Celts" would be suspected of a special closeness to nature, visions, and the spiritual world. Druidism became—and remains—a fashionable trope in Celticism because it seems to illustrate the naturalness, spirituality, fascinating otherness, and mysteriousness (as opposed to more established, well-known religions like Christianity) which romantically inclined mainstreamers like to perceive as a general feature of indigenous cultures.

The assumption that Celts and other "primitive" peoples enjoy a privileged relationship with nature and spirituality also ties in with romantic concepts of poetic and musical talent which laid heavy emphasis on natural genius. Material primitiveness was considered to foster creativity as well as poetic and musical tastes, both among the populace in general and in the specialists it brought forth: its bards.[16] In a footnote to his long poem *Rona*, the Scottish poet John Ogilvie asserted: "the inhabitants of the Hebrides have been distinguished from the earliest times, by a talent for poetic composition, and an exquisite feeling of its beauties. . . . The most admired productions in this art have appeared in the least cultivated ages."[17] The timelessness assumed here can also be found in descriptions of overseas colonized populations. By contrast, the assumption that Celts have a special talent for art is not always paralleled in overseas colonial discourse. Some Orientalists acknowledged aesthetic merit in Asian art, for instance in India. But other colonized people, such as black Africans or Aboriginal Australians, were not as readily credited with artistic talent until the early twentieth century—when, for instance, expressionist visual artists in Europe discovered the merits of African art and its geometric forms.

Some of the supposed qualities of romanticized Celts were also ascribed to women, such as sensitivity, emotionality, and an inferior capacity for rational thought. Both were disempowered social groups, and the qualities attributed to them converged accordingly, implying a need for patriarchal (or "masculine" Saxons') guidance and protection, thus justifying disempowerment. Some non-European colonized populations—"Orientals," for instance—were likewise feminized, and for the same reasons. While "Orientals" were not only feminized but also supposedly effeminate, this was not the case with Scotland's "Celts": the Highlanders supposedly possessed intellectual and emotional propensities which were conventionally "feminine," but they were also invested with extraordinary masculinity as soldiers and sex symbols.[18] This other, masculine, extreme likewise has parallels in overseas colonial discourse: though "Orientals" were often considered effeminate, other "natives" like Zulus or certain Pacific Islanders were portrayed as the exact opposite and supposedly possessed greater manliness than "civilized" European men.[19] Such manliness could concern general physical fitness attributable to a less mechanized state of economy and warfare, or it could focus on sexual potency and sexual freedom. Partly, Frantz Fanon's observation on sexual relations in colonies also applies to Gaelic Scotland:

> Since he is the master and . . . the male, the white man can allow himself the luxury of sleeping with many women. This is true in every country and especially in colonies. But when a white woman accepts a black man there is automatically a romantic aspect. It is a giving, not a seizing.[20]

In anglophone popular songs, the same romance is attached to sexual relations between Highland men and anglophone, sometimes middle- or upper-class women.[21]

Another parallel between romantic Celticist fashions and a colonial mindset is the potential link to a conqueror's guilt complex. The "civilizers" saw how well their colonizing project was going, and they also saw the social problems which this process generated within Gaelic society. Symbolic celebration of the victims' culture might be an attempt to appease occasional stirrings of conscience. Moreover, appropriated "Celtic" symbols lent the conquerors an aura of ownership, rootedness, and legitimacy. Parallels could be drawn to nativist fashions in North America, Australia, or New Zealand where white cultures have appropriated certain icons of the indigenous cultures they colonized, thus attempting to create a sense of rootedness and national authenticity.[22]

Hegemonic outsiders or "colonizers" were not the only ones who indulged in romantic Celticism: idealized notions of Celtic and rural traditions as counter-constructs to industrialization and urban life also appealed to the increasing number of native "Celts" who had migrated to anglophone centers and often expressed nostalgia for home and the past.[23] Moreover, Celticity came to occupy significant functions in regionalist or nationalist resistance, not only during the romantic era but also later. In the late eighteenth and especially in the nineteenth century, a wave of ethnic renaissances swept all over Europe—particularly through minorities and small nations suffering cultural, political, and economic marginalization. Celticism was part of this wider trend, (re)affirming pride in local specificities in places like Galicia, Brittany, or Ireland. Moreover, from the nineteenth century onwards there was increasing pan-Celticism across national borders, for instance through claims of common genealogical and cultural roots, or through mutual imitation.[24] This destabilized dominant ideologies about a congruity of national and ethnic boundaries. Sometimes, claims to a distinct national character were used to justify wishes and initiatives to gain political or economic autonomy from a centralist state, and the celebration of past ethnic achievements could fill resistance movements with confidence in their potential to attain other successes in the future. But Celticism and similar ethnic ideologies also flourished in regions which did not possess a sufficient material basis or promising political chances for autonomy, for instance due to their lack of a bourgeois class, their weak infrastructure, a frail economy, or an all too powerful and unlenient "center" entirely unprepared to make concessions. In such conditions, past ethnic greatness and present cultural resurgence could be a mere compensation for a lack of more material autonomy in the political or economic realm.[25] Such compensatory dimensions predominated in Scotland for a long time—though the Scots had arguably less to compensate than many other submerged nations, for example considering Scotland's relatively high degree of integration and success.

The Scottish Context: Marginalized Ethnicity/ Patriotism and Cultural Resurgence

Scotland was thoroughly integrated into the British state and its empire since the second half of the eighteenth century—not as a passive victim but as an active participant drawing considerable profits from these arrangements. Nonetheless, there was a degree of discontented patriotism which led to a resurgence of Scottishness in northern British identity discourse. The very success and thoroughness which (self-)anglicization had shown by that time was one of the reasons for the reawakening of Scottish patriotism as a sort of counterreaction. Another factor might have been *English* intransigence to pan-British identity constructs: initially, Scottish people had appeared more eager to discard their old national identity in favor of a larger British one than their southern neighbors had been. Continued English popular insistence on the differences between English and Scottish Britons, as well as anti-Scottish sentiment, prompted several "North Britons" to return to traditional Scottish identifications and reassert their distinctness from the southerners. Moreover, several controversial issues in the 1760s and 1770s caused some disillusionment with Scotland's treatment in British politics. This might also have contributed to a renewed interest in Scottish traditions.[26]

But identification with the Union remained strong enough to forestall practical separatism. The Union had by now shown considerable economic success. Since the end of serious Jacobite aspirations there was also political and military stability. As political resistance seemed undesirable, Scottish nationalism and Highland pride in the late eighteenth and most of the nineteenth century was mainly restricted to the cultural sphere, where a certain degree of difference could be articulated and celebrated without jeopardizing the material status quo of modern Britain. For instance, there was an intensification of the general post-Union trend to collect bits and pieces of Scotland's own traditions.[27] Anticolonial or early postcolonial culture in overseas (ex-) colonies likewise showed antiquarian, folkloric, and revivalist interests in re-excavating native traditions which had been submerged by English imperialism. It also emphasized indigenous cultural continuities across the historical disruption lines created by colonialism. But in eighteenth- and early nineteenth-century Scotland, this cultural "anticolonialism" was unaccompanied by practical political nationalism.

Even non-secessionist and merely cultural articulations of national difference could be problematic: previous successes of self-anglicization had undermined the Scottish distinctness which was so crucial to patriotic resurgence. Difference became ever more elusive, especially in anglophone or Scots-speaking Scottish culture and among the educated middle and upper classes.

An especially convenient source of Scottish distinctness and "authenticity" was the Highland and Gaelic tradition, which had fulfilled this function in

Scottish patriotic discourse since the Middle Ages. In unionist and progressivist discourse of the sixteenth to eighteenth centuries, the tradition of using Gaels as a patriotic symbol of the difference between Scotland and England had declined because Gaelic otherness was seen as a threat to the homogeneity of the nation-state or to the emerging capitalist economy. By the later decades of the eighteenth century, Gaelic political and economic otherness had been obliterated or minimized. Thus, the use of Gaelic cultural otherness could again become more popular. Though even Gaelic culture was becoming more hybridized, this process was not as far advanced as in Lowland Scots culture. Hence, Gaelic traditions were, perhaps more than ever, redefined as a pan-Scottish heritage and a marker of national distinctness.[28] However, this is not to say that such exploitation of Gaelic symbols equated to actually supporting the survival of Gaelic as a living language for the present and future—far from it: the decline of Gaelic speech and Gaelic traditions as viable sociocultural alternatives that could challenge anglocentric norms were often a prerequisite to their romantic mainstreaming.

A major catalyst for the mainstreaming of Celtic noble savagery was provided by James Macpherson's Ossianic works. Like Martin Martin before him, Macpherson was a native Gaelic speaker whose anglophone education and aspirations as a middle-class professional linked him firmly to the urban worlds of the Lowlands and England—and his works reflect this ambivalence, combining elements of nativist vindication, autoethnography, exoticist self-marketing, and a "colonial" anglicizing drive. Macpherson's collections *Fragments of Ancient Poetry* (1760), *Fingal* (1761), and *Temora* (1763), mainly consisting of prose poems, purported to be English translations of Gaelic poems from, and about, the third century AD recounting the exploits of the mythical King Fionn and his warriors. Most poems claim to be the works of Fionn's son Ossian, warrior and bard, who supposedly composed them in his old age, woefully commemorating the heroic deeds and dead companions of his youth. Macpherson claimed to have collected the poems from oral Gaelic tradition as well as Gaelic manuscripts, and to have separated the original elements from later corruptions, so that his "translations" represented an authentic third-century voice.

In reality, Fionn and Ossian (Oisean) were indeed part of Gaelic tradition and supposedly lived between the third and fifth centuries, but our oldest sources on them seem to date back no further than the Middle Ages, at least in the form we know. Macpherson did use Gaelic oral and written sources, but his "translations" are often remarkably free, as he adapts his materials to eighteenth-century needs and the tastes of his mostly anglophone target audience, often making substantial additions of his own. For instance, he takes the Ossianic material closer to Greek and Roman standards of epic poetry, thus satisfying mainstream classicist tastes. Elsewhere, the feeling and conduct of his heroes combine supposedly primitive assets with modern virtues more reminiscent of the eighteenth-century literature of sensibility.[29]

Macpherson's Ossianic publications were a big success, satisfying contemporary mainstream tastes for "primitive" poetic genius, "nobly savage" virtues like bravery, and "ancient" pieces of national heritage.[30] These texts also influenced contemporaneous discourse about early social history, not only in Scottish and "Celtic" contexts, but even elsewhere. Notions of ethnic continuity ensured that Macpherson's image of ancient Gaeldom also influenced mainstream ideas about *modern* Highlanders and *their* "noble savagery."[31] Again, it is clear that romanticization is only possible if the Other is no longer menacing: Macpherson's Fenian heroes are safely contained in the "Dark Age" past, and even then they are dying out. Ossian, who preserves their memory, is the last survivor, and even the later Gaelic culture which succeeded them is now, in the eighteenth century, in rapid decline, which is why its poetry needs to be transferred into English for consumption by the modern audiences that own the future.[32] In this safe form, it can be an object of sentimental retrospection, aesthetic enjoyment, and patriotic pride. Lowland Scottish endorsements of a celticized national image also resemble constructions of national identity in settler (post-)colonies overseas as analyzed by Nicholas Thomas: there, too, the (white) mainstream has appropriated elements from the cultures of indigenous populations in order to distinguish itself from "merely impoverished versions of Britishness."[33] Macpherson's influence on the Celtic image is still discernible in today's popular culture, which often associates Celticity with romantic melancholia, a close link to the supernatural, for instance via spectral visions, and a particular talent for poetry and music.

Despite Macpherson's national and international popularity, there were also many critics. For instance, the "Dark Age" authenticity of his publications was questioned in various quarters, which sparked a lively debate over several decades. Macpherson's attempt to position his thoroughly hybrid texts as pure primitive artifacts can be read as a strategic use of a metropolitan colonial gaze which has an appetite for "native authenticity." The subsequent controversy exposes, and partly subverts, such exoticist demands. This can be related to similar issues discussed by Graham Huggan with regard to twentieth-century postcolonial Australian debates about authors who laid claims to Aboriginality that were later exposed as "fraudulent."[34] While those Australian authors were "frauds" because they did not come from the ethnic (Aboriginal) community in question, Macpherson actually did come from the "right" (in this case Gaelic) community, but there was still an element of fraud because his texts came from the "wrong" time and the "wrong" Gaelic author, being his own rewritings from a range of sources, rather than reconstructions of a "Dark Age" epic by a single bard called Ossian. The reception of this eighteenth-century Scottish literary hoax was similar to the reception of modern Australian hoaxes discussed by Huggan: both controversies were fueled by a desire for indigenous authenticity in a context of unequal cultural power relations.

The authenticity question was only one of several fields where the reception of Macpherson's Ossian became a veritable battleground of conflicting patriotisms and ethnic identities. There were bursts of Highland regional and Scottish national pride; Scottish-Irish rivalries about who had the strongest claim to the Fenian/Ossianic heritage; English critiques of "overinflated" Scottish claims to literary eminence; and disgruntled non-Gaelic Scots who felt that Highlandist fashions obscured the Lowland or Teutonic element in the national heritage.[35]

Although "modernization" and the loss of "authentic" Scottish traditions were more advanced in the Lowlands, even here there was a search for such traditions. One solution was to concentrate the search more on the past than on the present, for instance by collecting older material from less anglicized times. Another valuable repository of national distinctness was located in folk tradition past and present: Lowland Scots customs and language seemed better preserved among the lower classes than among the more anglicized and cosmopolitan middle and upper ranks of society. "Celts" were not the only locals who functioned as noble savages, contemporary ancestors, or markers of Scottish national distinctness—Lowlanders, especially peasants, could serve just as well. One example is the reception of Robert Burns's (1759–1796) supposedly untutored "peasant poetry" by the Edinburgh literati. Sometimes Burns even assumes such an "untutored noble peasant" persona himself, perhaps as a tactical move and marketing strategy. A further Lowland poet whose humble origins as a farmer's son entitled him to primitivist reception was William Wilkie (1721–1772)—despite his university education.[36] The vogue for Lowland Scots folk culture is also reflected in the efforts to collect ballads, for instance from the Borders, as in Walter Scott's *Minstrelsy*.[37] Other authors who had a share in the fashion for Scots as a literary medium were James Hogg and John Galt. But there was a sense that Lowland cultural distinctness was dwindling, even among the "simple folk," so that its status as a national marker was problematic. Scott implies that he collected the Border ballads precisely because "the peculiar features" of his culture "are daily melting and dissolving into those of her sister and ally."[38]

"Authentic" traditions and cultural distinctness from neighboring countries gained added importance as new concepts of "organic" national identity spread across Europe. In several other countries, such ideas of nationhood soon influenced political practice, for instance in the German unification movement. By contrast, Scottish national resurgence long remained confined to the cultural arena, without major political (e.g., separatist) correlatives. The subjugation of Scottish otherness, Gaelic or otherwise, remained a prerequisite for its romanticization. Distinctness from England had to be stressed in terms which did not renounce the status quo of post-Union Britain. It was thus expedient to locate Scottish distinctness in the *margins* of Scottish society—there was a separation between mainstream social practices on the one hand and an ideological celebration of the periphery on the other. The romanticization of the margins was largely confined to spiritual and moral issues. It was also heavily historicized: it seemed as if a progressive Scottish mainstream ran forward into the future while throwing affectionate backward glances over its shoulder to look upon a Highland culture doomed to obsoleteness. Quintessential, unadulterated Gaelicness was frequently located in the times before the great watershed of 1745. This emphasis on pastness, spirituality, and morals helped to depoliticize and de-antagonize Scottish patriotism. A romanticized, distinct past provided ideological compensation for a more homogenized unionist present.[39]

Contemporaneous Highland society had likewise ceased to be a threat. Jacobitism no longer posed any political or military danger. This made it possible to readmit the Gaels into the national community and pity them for the traumas of Culloden and the subsequent penalty measures. Such feelings are reflected in Tobias Smollett's poem "The Tears of Scotland" (1746).[40] While Jacobitism itself is condemned as a "baneful cause" that divided the nation and even individual families, the nation is reunited in postwar mourning as the Highland penalty measures are transformed from a regional into a pan-Scottish tragedy. There is also a hint of anti-English or antigovernment sentiment, not only in the critique of the penalty measures as overly cruel, but also in the reference to Caledonia's "insulting foe" whom the poem defies through its patriotic statement.

Further unease with the post-Union continuation of intra-British national antagonisms, prejudice, and power imbalances, for instance between England and Scotland, is negotiated in parts of Smollett's novels *The Adventures of Roderick Random* (1748) and *The Expedition of Humphrey Clinker*.[41] However, there is also hope of enhancing mutual understanding and of making Highland or pan-Scottish merits better appreciated in the south, that is, the Lowlands or southern Britain, though much of the North-South mediation in *Humphrey Clinker* happens between Scottish and Welsh, rather than Scottish and English, characters.[42] That this novel traces a journey through England and Scotland is significant in itself. The voyage enhances the characters'—and readers'—knowledge of different parts of the national community, gives opportunities of negotiating prejudice, forges connections, and facilitates cultural dialogue, thus contributing to pan-British nation-building.[43] Critique of post-Culloden reprisals—here mainly the Disclothing Act—resurfaces in *Humphrey Clinker* through the comments of a compassionate Welsh traveler. He also seems to note signs of collective trauma among Highlanders, observing "manifest marks of dejection."[44]

For other texts, the recent "pacification" of the Highlands provided a safe vantage point from which the region's former violence could be recounted as a source of harmless excitement. Moreover, it was now safe and increasingly commonplace to sympathize with the defeated Jacobites emotionally, and to acknowledge a degree of moral value in their loyalty, bravery, and sense of honor, though these virtues had unfortunately been deployed in the wrong cause—if these Gaelic merits had served the right master, all would have been well.[45] There was hope that all would be well in future, when the Gaels would be finally transformed into dutiful subjects of the Hanoverian state. Economic integration also seemed to make progress, as "backward" feudal structures were replaced by more "productive" capitalist arrangements. Previously, much anti-Gaelic prejudice had been based on a conflation of Gaelic culture with undesirable political and economic agendas. Now that politics and economics were under control, the language and culture of the Highlands seemed less menacing. Moreover, even in this sphere regional distinctness was on the retreat, so that its remaining vestiges were more easily tolerable. Religious and educational integration were underfoot, many Gaels migrated away from the Highlands, and those who remained at home seemed to anglicize rather fast. English was learned with eagerness, and the percentage of Gaelic speakers among Scotland's population was shrinking.[46] Indigenous (bardic) traditions of Gaelic learning were also in relative decline.

This very decline seems to have boosted the interest of Lowland scholars in Gaelic tradition. Patriotic anxiety may have played a part: an important segment of the nation's distinct culture seemed about to vanish forever, which made Lowland literati feel that it was now *their* task to preserve what was left.[47] There may also have been an urge to complete material economic and political conquest and "colonization" with intellectual appropriation. A third motivation could have been the romantic need for a counterculture to the mundane, "banal" industrializing society of the urban middle class. All three factors are intimately related to subjugation.

The new belief in the harmlessness of Highland culture not only stimulated academic and literary Lowland interest, but also facilitated more lenient government policies. The 1780s saw the re-legalization of Highland dress and the restoration of forfeited Jacobite estates to the families of the original owners. Capitalism and the appropriate mentality were now perceived to have spread far enough among the clan gentry to let assimilation proceed by itself without extra centralist compulsion. Many landlords had shown themselves willing and able to implement the capitalization of their estates themselves. This trend continued after the restoration of the forfeited estates.

Assimilation did not go so far as to make the Highland economy indistinguishable from the Lowland one. Rather, the Gaidhealtachd entered into a "phase of super-exploitation" inflicted by Highland landlords upon their tenants.[48] Instead of being "modernized" according to the principles of liberal capitalism, social relations in the area became more archaic, for instance when recruitment methods during the Napoleonic Wars revived the feudal pattern of exchanging military service for rights of land use.[49] The main modernizing exception to this "bastard feudalism" was the more truly liberalist system of capitalist sheep farming, but the entrepreneurs who implemented the latter in the Highlands mainly hailed from elsewhere.[50] Moreover, it was frequently impossible to reinvest profits locally in a way which was capitalistically productive and which strengthened the region's economic structure in the long term: often, cash influx was immediately swallowed up by the need to pay off previously accumulated debts on estates. This phase of super-exploitation bears several similarities to a colonial economy, for instance as regards its failure to extend liberalist principles to increase the personal freedom of local populations and its failure to reinvest profits in the region to build a viable, diversified local economy.[51] Nonetheless, this colonial type of economy was highly compatible with capitalism, which traditional Gaelic feudalism had not been.

Here as well, exploitation and "progress" went hand in hand with cultural (pseudo-)conservatism. Even "improvers" and anglicizers now proudly wore Highland dress—"the kilt . . . moved from being the dress of the most poverty-stricken at the periphery, to being the party-dress of the most priviliged at the centre."[52] Discussing how tartan cult and noble savagery often coexisted with ongoing contempt for other aspects of Gaelic culture, Newton draws parallels with "other marginalised peoples whose cultures have been harvested for profit," citing an overseas colonial example from the Native American context.[53] Bagpipes likewise came into fashion. Previously common throughout Europe, the instrument had long disappeared almost everywhere except in the Scottish Highlands, and even there it had come close to extinction earlier in the eighteenth century. But in the romantic era, such "atavisms" suddenly appeared valuable precisely because they were rare and old-fashioned. This ensured the Highland bagpipe's revival.[54] Various Highland or Celtic societies were founded in anglophone cities, and further illustrate the close connection between "noble savage" romanticism and (quasi-)colonialism. On the one hand, they celebrated idealized clanship, pipe music, Highland dress, or other elements of Gaelic culture. On the other hand, their cultural pursuits often focused on antiquarian dimensions or attempted to remold contemporary Gaelic cultural expressions in the image of their own romantic notions. The clientele often belonged to the elite; many were outsiders to Gaelic culture or anglicized Highland aristocrats. For instance, most members of the Celtic Society of Edinburgh were landowners, lawyers, or intellectuals like Walter Scott. These organizations supported "improvements" like the economic missions outlined in chapter 1.[55] This schizophrenia of cultural romanticism and material colonization did not go uncontested. An anonymous newspaper article complained:

> If the Celtic Society confine itself to such parades as flatter only the ancestral pride . . . of the proprietors of the soil, without doing anything to relieve the . . . heavy distresses of the population, . . . the Society is worse than mockery; for what can be more absurd than to see Highland landlords assembling . . . to revive the dress of a people, whom they are either driving from their homes . . . or allowing them to be so expatriated without making one effort in their favour.[56]

One of the Celtic Society's own founders, David Stewart of Garth, held similar views, although he was persuaded to soften his critique when publishing his views on the Highlands in book form.[57]

The Celticist vogue even reached royalty itself. King George IV's visit to Scotland in 1822 was full of Highlandist pageantry, which was emphatically presented as a pan-Scottish national symbol. His royal highness honored his Scottish subjects by symbolically becoming one of them through wearing a kilt himself—though he did not expose his legs as traditional Highland fashion required: for decency's sake the king wore a flesh-colored hose underneath. Most other men at the event likewise sported Highland dress.

> The iconography of the Highlander, adopted as a badge of national identification by the Lowland Scot in the nineteenth century, is not the iconography of a separate Scottish identity: it is . . . the iconography of the unity of the British state. George IV's visit . . . was . . . a symbolic re-admittance into the British *Geist* of that part of the nation which had alienated itself by the 1715 and 1745 uprisings, but had paid its debts by dying profusely on the Heights of Abraham and Waterloo.[58] It is . . . the symbol of a unifying British identity . . . able to integrate all the differences . . . in . . . harmony. All subjects are equal in the eyes of the monarch and . . . find their status mirrored in the monarch's adoption of their symbolic dress.[59]

The ceremonies of 1822 helped to make Highlandism and the transformation of Gaelic symbols into pan-Scottish icons even more popular than before, although some contemporaries were critically aware of the "inauthenticity" of such reinventions.[60] But primitivist reconstructions did not always come from complete outsiders—sometimes they were endorsed by members of the indigenous population itself, for instance in order to gain social advantages in metropolitan circles through fashionable self-exoticization.[61]

McCracken-Flesher provides a highly informative reading of the complex ways in which the royal visit negotiated the power relations between Highland, pan-Scottish, English, and pan-British identifications.[62] She places particular emphasis on the subversion of discursive and cultural hierarchies, for instance when a metropolitan king was clothed in the dress of a supposedly peripheral culture and coveted the sympathy of his subjects in "peripheral" Scotland to validate his authority. I agree that this exposes certain instabilities on the semiotic and symbolic level—we might take this to exemplify the complexities and anxieties of colonial discourse. And it may indeed have given some Scots a share in defining British national identity, thus partly reversing their subjugation under English discursive authority. For instance, this might have been true for Lowland culture brokers like Scott, or anglicized Highland elites masking as romantic noble savages. But their gain was arguably based on the continued discursive and social colonization of other Scots, that is, Gaelic commoners and their traditional everyday culture, for instance on the linguistic or economic level. Even the dwindling remains of this culture, stripped of their subversive potential, were submitted to mainstream redefinition and appropriation, as a mere symbol in the identity discourse of their colonizers—arguably the last capstone of their subjugation. *They* seem to have profited very little from the subversive play of signs which McCracken-Flesher identifies on the level of national relations between (elite/Anglo-)Scotland and England. And even on that level, the pageantry of the royal visit left many *real* power imbalances intact, and arguably stabilized them, for instance through compensation. Against this background, romantic surface emblems, however unstably employed, appear considerably less subversive.

Despite this non-subversive dimension, several contemporaries objected that this pageantry gave the Highland dimension too much power. Some protested that the popularization of Highland symbols as pan-Scottish icons happened at the expense of Lowland tradition, so that standard hierarchies between Scotland's two cultures were reversed. Several of those who advocated Lowland traditions as preferable national emblems celebrated Robert Burns as an antidote to gaelocentric Ossianism. Some patriots resented the representation of the entire Scottish nation as a horde of Gaelic barbarians.[63]

These disagreements notwithstanding, Highlandism remained a key component of Scottish national iconography throughout the nineteenth century, and even until today. These Scottish romantic constructs of national distinctness and "authenticity" could be tolerated and even actively supported by the nineteenth-century British establishment precisely because they were politically non-subversive. This is another point where Scotland significantly differed from Ireland, where the old Jacobite potential for unrest was soon followed by another: radical nationalism. Moreover, this nationalist movement used Ireland's cultural distinctness as a political argument and did not content itself with invocations of the culture's past—instead, it laid considerable stress on revival. This sets Irish pro-Gaelicism apart from its "museumizing" and depoliticized Scottish counterparts. The continued role of Ireland as a source of turbulence long forestalled the romanticization of its cultural traditions by an anglophone unionist British mainstream.[64]

Romanticizations of the Gaels were not limited to discussions of Scottish national identity. They could also feature in scholarly reflections about the general nature of primitive human society, as discussed in chapter 1. Concepts of noble savagery played an important part in this context. Many intellectuals considered traditional Gaelic society as a specimen of archaic "patriarchal society" which had long vanished from other parts of the globe where it could only be studied from books, like the the Old Testament or the works of Homer. Surviving "archaisms" and "noble savagery" were found both in the Gaidhealtachd and among indigenous populations of overseas colonies.[65] However, Gaels could be more easily studied because they were geographically closer to the center. Moreover, the Highlands had already been subjected to enough "civilizing" activity to become relatively safe to travel, while retaining enough "exotic" difference to remain interesting, and "primitive" enough to function as contemporary ancestors. Highlanders thus occupied an intermediate position between Lowland Scots peasants and overseas indigenous peoples. Although Lowlanders were sometimes cast as noble savages as well, they often seemed too close and too similar to the center to make such constructs credible. "Natives" of other continents, by contrast, were still beyond the reach of most: travel was difficult, and tourism to Asia, for instance, only developed in the nineteenth century. Furthermore, overseas terrains and societies were often so "wild" and unintelligible to Europeans that they were unsafe to visit.[66]

Eighteenth-century discourse on Gaelic noble savagery ignored the probability that many Highlanders would have happily become prosperous capitalist citizens if they had had a choice, and that their freedom from luxury and "corruption" was not so much a consequence of moral superiority as of a lack of opportunity. Their enforced exclusion from the prospering capitalist community was, in the comments of outside observers, often interpreted (and idealized) as a voluntary rejection of materialism on moral or sentimental grounds.[67]

Highland noble savagery not only performed important functions in discourse about national identity and the general origins of human society, but also in the more personal realm of individual dreams, lifestyle, and recreation. Here as well, the marginalized Other was constructed as a binary opposite of the mainstream's urban capitalist life-world and became a site of temporary escapism via fancy-dress occasions, contemplation, reading, or tourism. For instance, in romanticizations of Highland dress,

> the bare . . . knee became a piece of noble savagery, and the freedom of movement of the . . . Highlander became a laudable escape from the unnatural constraints of urban industrial civilisation. The kilt suggested an apparently ready access to Highland masculine sexuality, and so to passion and violence; these also changed from being deplorable to desirable features.[68]

The appeal of the "wild" emanated not only from the Highlanders and their be-kilted bodies, but also from the country they inhabited: from about 1760 onwards, this landscape started to be considered worth seeing and provided a welcome change from the all too cultivated landscapes of the Lowlands and England. Initially, most travelers restricted themselves to the "tamer" southwestern and central parts of the Highlands, picturesque wildernesses already half-domesticated through estate "improvement" but still offering a pleasant contrast to the *fully* domesticated centers of Britain and Europe. This half-tamed Highland landscape complemented and confirmed the viewer's sense of human superiority over nature, rather than challenging it. The more thoroughly "wild" regions of the northwestern Highlands and Islands did not become popular travel destinations until a little later.[69]

Primitiveness, though not necessarily of the "wild," dangerous variety, was also ascribed to those Gaels who were, even by metropolitan standards, highly educated, such as the Aberdeen scholar and poet Eòghann MacLachlainn (Ewen MacLachlan). An anonymous obituary on MacLachlainn, published in the *Aberdeen Journal* on April 24, 1822, initially admits that the deceased had "extensive . . . knowledge of the Greek and Roman Classics."[70] But soon, the text denies MacLachlainn's intelligence again: "Ignorant of men and manners and passing through life with the innocent simplicity of childhood, he lived in a world of his own creation."[71] This view is probably influenced by an implicit belief that all Gaels as noble savages were by definition possessed of a childlike intellect which gave them moral innocence but also a degree of naïveté and simple-mindedness. This notion of noble savagery is even more obvious in one of the two anonymous anglophone poems which accompanied the obituary: "in him primeval manners shone / And friendship dwel'd with simplicity."[72] As already noted, the comparison with children is also familiar from overseas colonial contexts.

While the "innocence" of children and "savages" can give them moral superiority over more "debased" adults or metropolitans, *leaving* the children/colonized in their state of innocence without trying to educate and "develop" them can also be to their—and the center's—disadvantage: "Had he known how to avail himself of the vast resources of his genius and industry, few could have made so conspicuous a figure in the republic of letters as he might have done."[73] The vocabulary suggests that this statement could be extended from MacLachlainn the individual to Gaeldom in general, and from the "republic of letters" to a community which was more literally a "state," though not a republic but a constitutional monarchy: Britain. The Gaidhealtachd was seen as a reservoir of human and economic resources which had hitherto remained largely unexploited because the natives in their simplicity had never known how to do so. Moreover, they were supposedly too idle for innovation and capitalist success, which in contemporary language was frequently dubbed as lack of "industry." These failings had long prevented them from making prominent contributions to the British national community. Whereas MacLachlainn, like many other Gaels of the past, supposedly died without fulfilling his potential, the Gaidhealtachd of the future faced a brighter fate: intellectually better-endowed onlookers from the center had seen the Gaels' good potential and sent help to set regional development on its way, so that Highland assets would not be lost to the world.

Despite such apparent relish in progress, MacLachlainn's death could also be linked to "dying race" romanticism: the first poem which accompanies the obituary sentimentally demands: "wrap him in his Highland plaid— / No other shroud were half so dear."[74] The anglophone author admires the plaid especially for its picturesqueness, as the reference to "its chequered folds"[75] indicates. But the idea that tartan cloth is highly suitable for shrouds suggests that, although the Gaels' economic potential may be developed, their culture faces not progress but decline. This is reinforced in the following stanza:

> Since he is gone, now man must fail
> To rescue from oblivious night
> The language of the Gael.[76]

Whereas the previously outlined romanticizations of Highland noble savagery tended to serve as harmless ideological *counterweights* to (and compensations for) certain lingering discontents with the economic, political, social, and cultural status quo, these romantic concepts could also function as direct *tools* of the status quo, as the following sections show.

Difference as a Tool of the Status Quo

Romantic Concepts of National Identity

During its formation and consolidation, the modern nation-state had taken care to homogenize internal cultural differences on its territory. Homogenization and modernization had eliminated or at least weakened many local traditions. But by the late eighteenth century it was feared that modernization might have gone too far. The fiction of a national community needed tradition and organic continuity as ideological cement. It also needed a degree of local particularity to distinguish itself from other nation-states. The urban, modern, and to a certain extent cosmopolitan culture which carried so much prestige among aspiring eighteenth-century national subjects was not the best source of social cement because it belonged to a privileged, educated minority. Moreover, it was too new to boost the fiction of a historically continuous national culture, and too cosmopolitan to clearly distinguish one nation from the other.[77] Thus, national identity in the late eighteenth century came to a point where it felt a need to fall back on some of the very traditions, localisms, and folk cultures which it had previously devalued as vulgar counter-images to national elite culture, or which it had tried to obliterate altogether as superannuated obstacles to national progress.

The romantic age saw the emergence of national identity concepts which stressed cultural organicism rather than pragmatism, materialism, and progress. The German philosopher and poet Johann Gottfried Herder was a key figure in this context. The central tenets of organic nationalism included the historical continuity of national or ethnic character, and the clear distinguishability of national or ethnic groups from each other. This favored deterministic concepts of history which claimed that inherited characteristics and geography shaped national/ethnic psychology and distinctness. Where significant historical ruptures and sociocultural changes were difficult to deny, landscape and nature could be seen as vehicles of continuity which stood above the mutabilities of human society, such as shifting borders and power structures. The search for evidence of continuity fanned interest in ancient history, for instance in Stone Age monuments, often interpreted as druidic. There was also increased interest in early literature from the "Dark Age" or medieval period, as well as in folklore and the search for an indigenous aesthetic. In early history, cultural communities had supposedly been more sheltered from foreign influences or other forces of hybridization and change. Thus, older cultural artifacts and traditions represented the greatest "authenticity" and "purity," the very essence of the national or ethnic spirit which distinguished societies from each other.[78]

In light of these new concepts, Scotland and the rest of Britain were in search of roots and essences. Even in England, there was some interest in the "Celts" because their aura of exceptional ancientness promised access to the earliest history of the entire British island. Moreover, many Scots seem to have felt that a complete assimilation into a united Britain no longer appeared satisfying because North Britishness was too recent and "artificial"—especially in view of frequent English refusals to embrace them as brethren. An emotional component was deemed crucial to national happiness, but attempts to emotionalize the pragmatic Anglo-Scottish Union by fostering mutual sympathy had been only partially successful. Those who felt that the Union had left an emotional void often shifted the focus of their affections back to more homely traditions which had been Scotland's very own. Non-subversive ethnic self-assertions which helped Scots to feel at home in the United Kingdom were actively encouraged by the monarchy.[79]

Highlandism, Social Cohesion, and the Cult of the Monarchy

It was thought that Highland society possessed several noble virtues which, despite their savage provenance, could be turned to direct advantage for the modern civilized British polity. If Celtic sensibility, high morality, and family values could be adopted by their Saxon compatriots too, these values would provide useful moral glue to hold civil society together and prevent it from degeneration.[80]

In addition to civil society, the political sphere could also benefit from "Highland values." Previously, Highland royalism and loyalism had often been perceived as an obstacle to modern nation-state formation because many Gaels' fidelity to the Stuarts had set them at odds with the bourgeois revolutions which had dethroned that dynasty. Gaels had been reviled as representatives of anti-nation-state, antibourgeois, and anticapitalist forces, such as feudalism and absolutism. But around 140 years after Britain's first bourgeois revolution—when another, much more radical bourgeois revolution swept over France—British people feared that the French precedent might unleash social unrest in the United Kingdom, overthrow the constitutional monarchy, and erect a republic. As in the above-mentioned anxiety about over-civilization, modern British society was afraid of being destroyed by an over-radicalization of its own internal logic, for instance concerning bourgeois anti-feudalism. In search of ideological antidotes against this danger, it re-embraced the very traditions it had once combated. Highland social conservatism was now commended as a model which other, potentially more rebellious Britons should emulate.

In this way, Jacobitism became a symbol of monarchism in general.[81] Similarly, there was a partial rehabilitation of chieftainship and clan feudalism: a clan could be seen as an extended family with the chief as the father of his people—ideally a benevolent one. It was thought that social relations in a clan were softened by family affection, and that the Gaels' loyalty to their superiors and the entire social structure had a pre-political, natural, immutable aspect which set clanship apart from the more impersonal and unstable bourgeois society of the mainstream. Historical discourse about pre-1746 Jacobitism now often minimized the political motivations of the rebels, instead ascribing the risings to purely moral and emotional reasons or to innate ethnic character. Allegedly, the Gaels' general instinct for loyalty, or their rules of hospitality (another commonly acclaimed ethnic virtue) had compelled them to help "Bonnie Prince Charlie" in 1745–46 without leaving them any choice. Such explanations downplayed intentionality and guilt. Moreover, the instinctiveness and generality of Gaelic loyalty seemed to make this loyalty easily transferable—from the Stuarts or the chiefs to the Hanoverian kings. As Hogg's song "Donald MacDonald" puts it:

> What though we befriendit young Charlie?
> . . . .
> Had Geordie come friendless amang us
> Wi' him we had a' gane away.[82]

Apart from the French Revolution, another factor which soon threatened to destabilize the status quo was the emergence of class consciousness and socialism. Here too, idealized pictures of a stable clan society promised an ideological antidote to the anxiety of the privileged, and perhaps a means to create loyalty among the lower ranks. One event which associated the Gaidhealtachd with the cult of the monarchy was the royal visit to Scotland in 1822. Romantic images of royalism and feudalism also drew other Anglo-British aristocrats to the Highlands, which became a fashionable hunting ground from the 1830s and 1840s onwards. The trend also spread to the lower gentry and middle classes. Since about the 1840s, Highland tourism also profited from improved communications and travel facilities.[83] Buying or renting Highland estates became a status symbol for Britain's elite. In 1852,

Queen Victoria herself purchased such an estate at Balmoral and decorated the castle with tartans of her husband's own design. Highlandism acquired increasingly aristocratic associations, and became more and more dissociated from the Gaelic language—unlike in Wales, where cultural and linguistic distinctness remained more strongly linked. Its aristocratic connotations were another aspect of Highlandism which met with criticism from some Scottish patriots, who desired more demotic national icons. Again, Burns could be embraced as an alternative symbol of Scottishness, this time not because he was a Lowlander but because he stood for a more demotic (and democratic) heritage.[84]

"In the Army Now": Savage Virtue and Imperialist Warfare

Highlanders had been belittled physically, morally, culturally, and mentally in order to justify outside control. Despite this supposed inferiority, they had also been seen as a menace. The latter was strongly linked to their prominent military role in the mid-seventeenth-century Civil Wars and in Jacobitism. The contrast between their alleged primitiveness and their considerable military potential to threaten a powerful state could be rationalized through an analogy with the hardy barbarians of antiquity who threatened and eventually smashed a Roman Empire which excessive luxury had spoiled into degeneracy. Partly through direct influence from Roman texts and partly through mere "analogy of viewpoint," the modern British mainstream saw the Gaels as natural-born soldiers who could be a danger, but also a good example to its government troops.[85] Gradually, the negative aspects of "primitiveness" decreased in importance, and the Gaels' roles as soldiers were central to these redefinitions.[86] Early examples can be found in anglophone Jacobite and Episcopalian discourse from the 1690s onwards: as the Stuart cause relied heavily on Highland armies, its anglophone supporters saw Gaels in more positive terms than was customary in the Anglo-Scottish or English mainstream. Highlanders could now be seen as the most patriotic of Scots, as heroes and potential saviors of their country from English occupation. Alternatively, for instance in English Jacobites' eyes, Highlanders could appear as the most patriotic of Britons who would save Britain from a usurping dynasty.[87]

An example of pro-Highland sentiment in anglophone Scottish patriotic discourse is a Jacobite drinking song which begins with the words "Come let uss go drink boyes":

> Let the brave loyal Clans
> the Stuarts ancient race
> restoar with sword in hand [?——]
> and al there foes displace
> the union overturn boyes

which makes our nation m[?ourn boyes]
like bruce at bonic burn [?boyes]
the english home weell Ch[?ase.][88]

This anticipates several attributes which recurred in later portraits of Gaelic noble savagery: extraordinary loyalty, martial valor, and antiquity. There are also anglophone Jacobite songs about love between Lowland lassies and Highland laddies where the woman personifies Scotland or more specifically its Lowlands. Sometimes she is portrayed as having once lapsed into unfaithfulness, which symbolizes Scottish complicity in the Union with England, but the true love to whom she eventually returns is the strong, virile, and patriotically ever-loyal Gael.[89]

The trend for the future, however, was set by the employment of Gaelic soldiers not on the Jacobite side, but in the British government army. This already started on a small scale before 1745, most famously in the Black Watch Regiment. In 1725 the Black Watch was established as a rural police force, mainly to prevent cattle theft and contain the Jacobite threat. In 1743 it was first sent outside the Gaidhealtachd, to train in England for service on the Continent. Rumors that they were intended for the Caribbean led to mutiny, but later the reconstituted regiment was more successfully employed, both in Europe and overseas.[90] Hiring Highland warriors for the British Army again had a precedent in the Roman Empire, which likewise recruited "barbarian" soldiers to use their savage hardihood for the "civilized" center's own purposes. One of the earliest mainstream eulogies on Highland bravery in the British Army is a popular print recounting the heroism of a Black Watch soldier fighting against the French around 1740. An eyewitness account of a Highland regiment in London around 1743 explicitly invokes imperial parallels—in this case not ancient Roman, but modern overseas ones. Interestingly, the othering gaze is also playfully inverted, with a detachment and self-consciousness reminiscent of certain passages in Martin Martin's work:

> When the Highlanders walk'd the streets here, . . . there was more staring at them than ever was seen at the Morocco embassador's attendance, or even at the Indian chiefs. . . . The amazement expressed by our mob was not greater than the surprize of these poor creatures; and if we thought their dress and language barbarous, they had just the same opinion of our manners; nor will I pretend to decide which was most in the right.[91]

Soon, however, the Londoners came to regard the Highlanders with respect—namely, when they learned of their military successes.[92] The Highlanders' gradual ascent in mainstream opinion to the position of national military heroes was delayed by the 1745 rising which ensured a temporary resurgence of older, more negative notions about Gaels. These subsided after the victory of "civilized" forces over "barbarism" at Culloden, but even afterwards the mainstream retained enough belief in the Gaels' primitive martial valor to harness the latter for Britain's government army with increased eagerness.[93] Highland elites played an active part in this, raising regiments and deliberately marketing the region to create a "recognizable brand in a lucrative [military] marketplace."[94] During the Seven Years War (1756–63), Highlanders were recruited on a considerable scale. Scottish losses during this and several other wars were disproportionately heavier than English ones, similar to the "disproportionate losses . . . [later] repeated among other 'white' colonies," as Murray Pittock remarks.[95] Their usefulness as soldiers abroad greatly contributed to a more positive evaluation of Highlanders by the mainstream. The Seven Years War was only the beginning. Even more Highlanders were recruited during the American War of Independence and the Napoleonic Wars.

Gaelic noble savages appeared as ideal soldiers, thanks to their hardihood-inducing physical environment and the loyalty allegedly engendered by clanship. Together with the hierarchic principles outlined above, Highland regiments were another factor in clanship's rehabilitation. These regiments were often organized on a clan basis, which was regarded as an ideal asset. One reason was the supposedly natural and unlimited Gaelic loyalty to their chiefs and commanders, and by extension to the crown. Second, the soldiers had known many of their comrades from childhood, which increased cohesion. Devotion to their superiors was sometimes more myth than reality: the Clearances had created considerable anti-landlord sentiment and weakened feudal loyalties among the clan commoners, and there were several mutinies in eighteenth-century Highland regiments. Nonetheless, the myth was powerful, and the Gaels' prominent role in Britain's European and colonial wars contributed to their ideological integration into the national mainstream and the burgeoning empire, as well as to the transformation of Highland dress and bagpipes (though not the language) into widely accepted symbols of national and imperial pride. This "militarism and imperialism . . . distinguished Scottish Celticism . . . from its pacifistic Welsh and rebellious Irish contemporaries."[96] Devine points out that the military contribution of Lowland—and, for that matter, Irish—soldiers to the British Empire was also considerable, but their ideological and iconographic profile was less conspicuous, while Highland troops were distinguished by their particular dress and "clan-based" organization.[97] In 1745 armed Highlanders had still been mostly perceived in negative terms as forces of Catholicism and autocracy. Only two decades later, they were considered a "bulwark of British liberties."[98] This is reflected in the popular song "The Highland Character." Penned by Sir Harry Erskine (ca. 1710–1765), the lyrics were allegedly translated from a Gaelic text by a Black Watch soldier. The song is also interesting for its overt Roman references:

In the garb of old Gaul, wi' the fire of old Rome,
From the heath-cover'd mountains of Scotia we come,
Where the Romans endeavour'd our country to gain,
But our ancestors fought, and they fought not in vain.[99]

[Chorus:] Such our love of liberty, our country, and our laws,
That, like our ancestors of old, we stand by Freedom's cause;
We'll bravely fight like heroes bold, for honour and applause,
And defy the French, with all their art, to alter our laws.

No effeminate customs our sinews unbrace,
No luxurious tables enervate our race,
Our loud-sounding pipe bears the true martial strain,
So do we the old Scottish valour retain.

. . . .

We sons of the mountains, tremendous as rocks,
Dash the force of our foes with our thundering strokes.

Quebec and Cape Breton, the pride of old France,
In their troops fondly boasted till we did advance;
But when our claymore they saw us produce,
Their courage did fail, and they sued for a truce.[100]

The qualities of ancient colonizers and colonized are amalgamated, and the virtues of both are projected onto the modern Gaels. Here, the invader who threatens Gaelic liberty is not an intra-British enemy (e.g., Lowlanders, English people, the anglocentric British state), but France. This external menace strengthens British intra-national cohesion. The Celtic defenders of freedom do not fight *against* their immediate "colonizers"—Rome or the British state—but *for* them, protecting the United Kingdom's interests against a rival empire.

The military virtues fostered by "primitive" Gaelic traditions are also noted in Smollett's novel *The Expedition of Humphrey Clinker* and Adam Smith's economic treatise *The Wealth of Nations*. But their endorsement of the primitive is not unqualified: they also identify grave problems in traditional clanship, such as local autocracy, disorder produced by chieftains' disregard of central government authority, and lack of productivity. Moreover, Smith argues that the valor of Highland-style militias is still surpassed by that of modern standing armies—to which, however, they are a helpful supplement that also counteracts the risk of authoritarianism entailed by standing forces.[101]

The army has also been associated with the revival and maintenance of piping traditions.[102] This connection has survived into the present, as can be seen from the annual Royal Edinburgh Military Tattoo where pipers from all over the Commonwealth (and beyond) display their skill. Apart from these imperial associations, Highland dress also acquired a more domestic symbolic function: especially during the Napoleonic Wars, it became an emblem for defending the whole of Britain against republican and revolutionary threats. Early nineteenth-century eulogists of Gaelic noble savagery and martial valor include David Stewart of Garth: "nursed in poverty, he [the Highlander] acquired a hardihood which enabled him to sustain severe privations"—"the simplicity of his life gave vigour to his body."[103] The ways in which Enlightened and romantic thinkers acknowledged the presence and usefulness of the noble savage in the midst of their own, generally more "advanced" society is one way in which the primitive can anachronistically irrupt into a model of linear social development which normally assumes a clear succession of mutually distinct historical stages. It thus highlights the complexities of Enlightenment concepts of history and of the Highlands' role in the construction of modern Scotland and Britain.

But "even as the local colour grew brighter, it was reduced to the function of tinting an imperial outline."[104] The romanticized Highland soldier became an iconic symbol of Scotland's junior partnership in Britain's global empire. Military recruitment drained the Highlands of fighting men, thus reducing the risk of internal disorder at home. As an incentive, the state offered cash grants to chieftains who raised regiments. Moreover, the army offered promising careers for Highland aristocrats. Partly, however, especially as regards the commoners, the Gaels' complicit role in imperialism was based on direct or indirect compulsion: for many Jacobites, joining the British Army was the only way of gaining pardon and social rehabilitation, and such recruits often "remained openly cynical about the British cause."[105] Others were induced by the fact that their home districts offered few ways of earning a living. There was also more directly enforced recruitment, for example during the Napoleonic Wars, via press gangs or chieftainly blackmail: some landowners gave land leases only to families who gave a son for the chief's regiment.[106] The modern British capitalist mainstream had long fought feudal relics in its midst as obstacles to progress and liberty. But now, after the commercialization of estate management and the end of private clan armies, it was happy to use a feudal pattern (exchanging land for military service) in the wars fought by the central government to establish capitalism in overseas colonies and beat competing European powers.

Not all military participation in imperialism was enforced, of course: even commoners developed considerable identification with the nation and its empire. Military Highlandism could flatter Gaelic ethnic pride. This may have been especially important in the early years when Gaelic traditions at home and in civil contexts were still regarded with suspicion, for instance during the time of the Disclothing Act. Even then, the army allowed the otherwise prohibited Highland dress as uniforms, which offered Gaels legitimate space for practicing and displaying their traditions. A similar attraction may have been that the Highland regiments were organized in a way which retained some semblance of traditional military clanship. This may have appealed to those who regretted the decline of the old Gaelic society, especially to the tacksmen whose traditional privileged status and class confidence had greatly relied on their military role within the clan, but who were now losing their status at home through the decline of clan feudalism. A "revival" of military clanship in the government army might have seemed an interesting option. Other factors which increased national and imperial identification among higher- and lower-class Gaels alike were successful careers in the colonial army and administration, a share in the honor and spoils, and the advantages which the wars had for the domestic economy of the Highlands. The need to clothe and feed the armies, as well as restrictions on Continental imports, increased the demand for Highland goods like wool, cattle, and kelp. Military recruitment temporarily eased demographic pressure: there was less of a "population surplus" which had to live off small, infertile patches of land, or compete for a limited number of tolerable local jobs. Soldiers' wages and pensions sent home to their families or brought back by survivors increased capital influx.

Their military usefulness also promoted the establishment of Gaels as colonial settlers. Sometimes the government rewarded disbanded soldiers with land grants overseas. As early as the 1730s, Highlanders who had fought in the government army were promised land in Georgia. Further land grants were offered to those who had fought in the wars of 1756–63 and 1776–83. Nonetheless, there were occasional attempts to curtail migration. In the early 1770s, for instance, there were rumours that as many as 20,000 Gaels were preparing to emigrate. This caused fears in government circles because hopeful overseas "pioneers" might be less likely to join the military than Highland tenants threatened by clearance, crofting, and chieftainly pressure. Several members of the political establishment were Highland landlords who had an additional interest in retaining Gaelic tenants as a profitable labor force. Sometimes, there were clashes of interest between London politicians and the provincial governments in the colonies, since the latter could show a more immediate interest in encouraging migration.[107] All in all, the usefulness of Highlanders as soldiers and settlers implicated them considerably in the colonizing process.

The advantages which the Gaels drew from their complicity in army and empire do not necessarily preclude a postcolonial approach to the Highland experience. First, military recruitment often relied on direct or indirect coercion. Second, the Gaels were not the only colonized ethnic group that came to serve in the imperial army:

> The Gaels' experience of gaining a measure of "respectability" through military service was later shared by ex-slaves and their descendants in the United States; and the long and distinguished service of the

> Highland regiments . . . [was] setting an example for Sikhs and Gurkhas, other conquered races of "warlike" character who joined the British cause.[108]

Third, the material and ideological integration of the Gaels did not last forever: after the Napoleonic Wars had ended, many Highland soldiers and Highland-produced goods were no longer required. This contributed to a general economic crisis in the Gaidhealtachd, and the resultant pauperism caused another change of discursive trends: Highlanders again became more of a despised colonized than a celebrated colonizer (see chapter 5).

But for the time being, the new respectability of the Gaels also found its way into—and partly even emanated from—anglophone literature. And although the image of Gaelic noble savagery would face a serious backlash as the nineteenth century progressed, it never entirely disappeared, as romantic perceptions exerted a lasting influence. One of the most important novels from the latter end of the romantic period—though not a *completely* romantic text itself—was Walter Scott's *Waverley*. Like James Macpherson at the start of the romantic era, Scott played a crucial role in shaping perceptions of the Highlands, and of Scotland in general. The next chapter provides a case study of *Waverley*, charting the interplay of romantic and Enlightened colonizing discourse strategies, as well as elements which could be read as anticolonial.

Chapter 4

✦

From Flirtations with Romantic Otherness to a More Integrated National Synthesis

"Gentleman Savages" in Walter Scott's Novel *Waverley*

Begun in 1805 and first published in 1814, *Waverley* is a historical novel set around the time of the 1745 Jacobite rebellion.[1] Several aspects of Walter Scott's work which concern us here—that is, the presentation of traditional Highland culture as noble but savage and ultimately doomed to oblivion, and the absorption of selected "Highland" features into the anglophone mainstream of a unified, pacified nation—have already been addressed by previous studies. Some of those even make explicit recourse to postcolonial theory and terminology.[2] Nonetheless, it seems expedient to readdress *Waverley* here, not only because well-known canonical texts furnish accessible entrance points for readers of introductory surveys like this one, but also because extant postcolonial analyses of *Waverley* are not necessarily very detailed and often do not take account of all its intricacies. Conversely, more detailed studies which are not explicitly postcolonial although they address postcolonially relevant themes do not always bring out the full theoretical implications or overseas colonial parallels in a form which is sufficiently accessible to readers from the international postcolonial mainstream. Thus, it seems desirable to bring both strands together in detail, elucidating the (post)colonial aspects of *Waverley* in a more stringent form, at the same time introducing enough specific textual analysis as well as highlighting overseas parallels more clearly.

The story of *Waverley*'s fictional protagonists is interwoven with historical information about the rising, as well as about Scottish manners, customs, and culture of that time.[3] This information appears partly in the main text and partly in footnotes, introductions, and postscripts. The book aimed not only at Scottish audiences, but also at a wider British and international readership. One reason might have been the relative smallness of the Scottish market, so that an ambitious author would naturally look to a wider public.[4] There may also be patriotic reasons: Scott apparently wanted to increase mutual understanding between the various parts of British society, for instance between English and Scottish people. His footnotes and ethnographic explanations not only recover aspects of national history for a home audience, but also undertake intercultural mediation and translation.

All this links Scott's work to various novels produced in former overseas colonies which likewise aim to recover aspects of a national past in order to assist nation-building and come to grips with harsh experiences of externally induced "modernization" and rapid historical and cultural change. There as well, such inward-looking interests and the aim to reach an audience in the author's own country are complemented—or, as some have argued, compromised—by a need or wish to address overseas audiences from very different cultural backgrounds and render one's own culture intelligible to them. Both in Scott and in those overseas authors, this dual orientation toward inside and outside audiences can render literary production a precarious balancing act. It can incur violent criticism from nationalists who are anxious about a potential sellout and commodification of national culture for the needs of outsiders, about a related danger of distorting national reality, about sacrificing cultural autonomy or distinctness, and about over-adaptation to foreigners' literary forms, tastes, and expectations. In a Scottish context, similar concerns have been raised about James Macpherson's Ossianic prose poems.

In the case of *Waverley*, such problems of cultural translation are not only evident in its mixed target audience or in passages concerned with ethnographic background information, but they are also built into the novel's plot and the characters of its protagonists. Its deep concern with intra-British cross-cultural communication is one of the reasons why this novel is so pertinent to this study, especially as it does not restrict its treatment to a simple Scottish/English or Gaelic/Saxon dichotomy, but instead has a tripartite structure that reflects the separate identities of the Highlands, Lowland Scotland, and England, further complicated by mutual intermingling as well as foreign, especially French, influences. Another factor which makes *Waverley* an interesting subject for postcolonial analysis is that it discusses cultural differences not—or at least not always—in order to vindicate cultural heterogeneity, but also in order to contribute to pan-British national integration. In some respects, *Waverley* voices postcolonial concerns about prejudice and cross-cultural communication problems. But in other respects, for instance concerning its justification of the Union and assimilation, it can be regarded as a master text of British internal colonialism.

The plot revolves around the adventures of Edward Waverley, the young scion of a wealthy English family of mixed political loyalties: his uncle and aunt are Jacobites, while his father is a Whig. Edward himself starts out as a Whig, but his literary tastes (e.g., for tales of chivalry) and general disposition make him susceptible to backward-looking romanticism. Edward takes up a commission in the government army in Scotland in 1744, and after a while takes temporary leave from his regiment to visit his uncle's friend, the Jacobite Baron of Bradwardine, and his daughter Rose. Their Perthshire home belongs to the Lowlands but is close to the Highland line. During this visit, Edward makes the acquaintance of a neighboring Gael and is invited to spend some time with his clan to experience the Highlands and their way of life. He befriends the Jacobite chieftain Fergus Mac-Ivor and unrequitedly falls in love with Fergus's fervently Jacobite sister Flora. When Fergus tries to convince the well-connected English visitor to join the insurgents, Edward is tempted, hoping that this might help him gain Flora's affection, but he is still reluctant to break his soldier's loyalty to the Hanoverian government. However, due to a chain of unfortunate events, misunderstandings, and the intrigues of one of the clansmen, Edward is dismissed from the army, and the authorities' misplaced suspicions of his loyalties hurt his pride. This, together with personal enthusiasm for Flora and the charismatic Stuart prince, sways Edward to join the rebels. Gradually, as the misunderstandings underlying his dismissal come to light, showing that his former superiors in the government army were free from blame, and as Edward perceives the foolhardiness of the Jacobite endeavor, he regrets his enrollment in the rebel forces. Moved by such feelings, he saves the life of an English soldier, Colonel Talbot, and their growing friendship further contributes to Waverley's change of loyalty toward the Whigs, as well as his disenchantment with the Gaels. Accidentally separated from the troops, Waverley misses the Jacobites' final defeat. Nonetheless, he is outlawed along with the Baron and Fergus, who have forfeited their estates. Talbot gains Edward a pardon and helps him to purchase the Bradwardine estate, which is afterwards restored to its former owner. Fergus is captured and executed, and Flora prepares to join a convent in France. Edward has meanwhile fallen in love with Rose, marries her, and comes into his English inheritance.

Waverley's spatial and intellectual journeys offer Scott ample scope for exploring differences within the nation and its population. (Anglocentric) Britain, (Lowland-dominated) Scotland, and Highland Scotland form "Russian dolls" of otherness: the larger units encapsulate the smaller ones, but each is a separate entity; and as Waverley gets further and further "inside," the spatial units become smaller while otherness becomes greater.[5] Otherness in this novel provokes a variety of reactions. Partly, it is represented in a relatively neutral fashion, for instance where factual information about local customs is recorded without obvious attempts at evaluation. This accords with James Chandler's argument that writers of the romantic age—despite indebtedness to Enlightened theories about universal historical stages—not *only* spoke in abstractions supposedly valid for all humanity, but also acknowledged the need to understand historically or spatially different cultures on their own terms, as well as acknowledging intra-cultural contradictions. There was a sense of balance, or dialectic, between particularity and generalization.[6] Chandler also stresses romantic thinkers' skepticism concerning the objective knowability or judgeability of the past, and their awareness that their own subject position might influence their perceptions.[7] In *Waverley*, frequent reluctance to set up absolute hierarchies is combined with an emphasis on multivocality.[8] There is a marked interest in exploring and combating prejudice between Britain's various subjects, both on the plot level and, presumably, among the novel's readership. Partly, this happens on the emotional level: Edward's friendship with Fergus and his romantic affections for Flora and Rose create English-Scottish sympathy which is not merely personal, but also affords a metonymy and blueprint for increasing mutual understanding between Britain's different ethnic and national groups.[9] Prejudice is also countered on the cognitive level, through increased knowledge. Englishmen are shown to be especially prone to prejudice and to be gravely ignorant of Scottish matters. This is even true of Waverley himself, at least at the beginning, but in the course of the story he gradually gains a deeper understanding of the country. Readers share this learning process.[10]

Elsewhere, reactions to otherness in *Waverley* are less "neutral" and more reminiscent of colonial discourse. This also takes different forms: partly, there is primitivist romanticism and an idealization of the Other, and partly there is a more critical attitude based on Enlightened progressivism. This underlines that romanticism and Enlightenment—perhaps especially in frameworks of internal and external colonialism—need not be diametrically opposed to each other, but were essentially two sides of the same coin. In *Waverley*, all the usual tropes of romantic Highlandism are skilfully played on and exploited, but at the same time they are often ironized. However, such irony does not necessarily aim to deconstruct all discursive colonizations of the Scottish or Gaelic Other: often, deconstruction is only aimed at romantic primitivism, while equally colonizing discourse of "improvement" receives less censorship.

Another connection between *Waverley* and colonial discourse is its concern with mapping. The protagonist's journeys and the ethnographic paratext chart different geographical and cultural segments of Britain's more or less "barbarian" north. The English and, with regard to the Highlands, also the Lowland Scottish colonizing eye gains knowledge about the Other, complementing material conquest by intellectual conquest. For David Richards, mapping is an issue where *Waverley* does *not* conform to colonial patterns. He argues that spaces which are mapped must always be previously unknown, whereas the Highlands had already been mapped since at least the sixteenth century and thus did not constitute a previously unknown space when Scott wrote his novel in the early nineteenth century.[11] However, it seems legitimate to ask whether the longer history of mapping automatically disqualifies readings which identify colonial mapping in *Waverley*: Although maps of the Highlands had indeed existed for a long time, many Lowland and English readers in the early nineteenth century still envisaged the *terra* of the Highlands as sufficiently *incognita* and "other" to *them*, so that mappings of an "exotic" Highland space—in Scott's novels, but also in travel writing—were consumed with eager interest. Waverley's maps were indeed useless to practical "colonial" projects of the government or of economic investors, who had long reconnoitered and conquered that space through earlier mapping and infrastructure projects. But the imaginary colonization of the Highlands in the minds of the wider British reading public—whose role as patriotic citizens gave them an ideological stake in the colonization of internal others—was still a very contemporary project in Scott's time, so that it still seems possible to speak of *Waverley* as a piece of colonial discourse. Moreover, even where people feel that a territory is already somewhat familiar to them, for instance through previous reading or map use, this does not necessarily cancel out the need for further reading and mapping. Richards overlooks that narration and maps can also have a performative function: national identities and colonial discourse both rely on frequent reiteration, for instance to combat anxieties.[12] Hence, even the rereading of familiar maps, or the production of new maps for well-known lands, can contribute to a colonizing discourse.

The treatment of cultural difference in *Waverley* is also noteworthy because most of the boundaries are portrayed as permeable.[13] David Richards seems to assume that both colonial discourse and postcolonial scholarship are necessarily premised on the assumption of very clear boundaries and binarisms between colonizer and colonized, and of internal homogeneity within these groups. The lack of clear binarisms, as well as the existence of strong internal heterogeneity in the Scottish case in general, and in Scott's novel in particular—for instance concerning the ambivalent role of the Lowlands—is thus, for Richards, a main reason why postcolonial readings are questionable.[14] In reality, however, even overseas colonial discourse, even where it indeed aims for such binarisms, struggles with the messily complex realities of cross-cultural encounters and social hierarchies which do not fit into neat binary frameworks. Hence, the importance of ambivalence and hybridity in *Waverley* (and Scottish culture in general) speaks for, rather than against, its pertinence to postcolonial studies. Partly, this novel actively constructs cultural boundaries, and partly such boundaries are systematically undercut. Ambivalence can also have a specific function in internal colonialism, since the deconstruction of internal boundaries can be motivated by a wish for the ideological unification of Britain's national community. Boundary-crossing can show the feasibility of amalgamation; and the preservation of selected differences goes hand in hand with their neutralization as a politically disruptive force.

Mapping Difference: The Lowlands

Even the Scottish Lowlands often appear "other" enough to be classified as primitive and to be described through colonial discourse tropes. Sometimes, such tropes are only used by certain characters, while the narrator seems to distance himself from them. In other cases, the narrator himself partakes of the colonizing impetus. Where possible, the following analysis will take account of this distinction. But even where a character's colonial viewpoint is relativized by narratorial comment, the use of a colonial trope reflects divisions within British society and aspects of popular opinion, as well as contributing to the general ideological matrix which often positioned Scotland among the international ranks of the colonized in the colonial imagination.

When Waverley first arrives at Tully-Veolan, the Bradwardine estate, his initial reaction resembles denigratory kinds of colonial discourse. He focuses on the squalor and primitiveness of lower-class life in the village and voices his critique in the language of Enlightened progressivism:[15]

> The houses seemed miserable in the extreme, especially to an eye accustomed to the smiling neatness of English cottages. They stood, without any respect for regularity, on each side of a straggling . . . unpaved street, where children, almost in a primitive state of nakedness, lay sprawling. (*Waverley* 74)

The houses are "miserable cells," the locals are "sunburnt loiterers" (74), communal agriculture is "unprofitable" (76), the income of landlords is based on "scanty rents" (78), and the estate is only "half-cultivated" (87).[16] Waverley perceives the squalor but almost instantly attempts to romanticize it as picturesque, while the narrator remains more critical of the lack of "improvement" in mid-eighteenth-century rural Lowland life.[17] But even Waverley cannot banish progressivist thoughts, even at the height of picturesqueness:

> Village girls . . . formed more pleasing objects; and, with their thin, short gowns and single petticoats, bare arms, legs and feet, uncovered heads, and braided hair, somewhat resembled Italian forms of landscape. Nor could a lover of the picturesque have challenged either the elegance of their costume, or the symmetry of their shape; although, to say the truth, a mere Englishman, in search of the *comfortable*, . . . might have wished the clothes less scanty, the feet and legs somewhat protected from the weather, the head and complexion shrouded from the sun, or perhaps might even have thought the whole person . . . considerably improved, by a plentiful application of . . . soap. The whole scene was depressing; for it argued, at the first glance, . . . a stagnation of industry, and perhaps of intellect. . . . Yet the physiognomy of the people, when more closely examined, was far from exhibiting . . . stupidity: their features were rough, but remarkably intelligent. It seemed . . . as if poverty, and indolence, its too frequent companion, were combining to depress the natural genius . . . of a hardy, intelligent . . . peasantry.
>
> Some such thought crossed Waverley's mind. (75–76, Scott's italics)

This description of the Lowlands uses a trope which Martin Martin had previously applied to the Gaels of the Western Isles: the concept of a noble savage whose good qualities are perceptible even in a primitive state, but would shine more brightly if the rough diamond were polished by a civilizing mission. Another motif in this passage which is comparable to Orientalist and overseas colonial discourse is the eroticization of exoticized indigenous women. Their mode of dress is unusual to English eyes and reveals more of their bodies than English fashions would, which connotes sexual promise. Later examples of the eroticization of Highland women and their exposed legs can be found on late nineteenth- and early twentieth-century postcards, which often showed Highland women doing the laundry, treading the washing with their skirts hitched up—a sight considered extremely daring by the strict standards of Victorian and Edwardian morality.[18]

The otherness of this Lowland Scottish scene to Waverley's eyes is highlighted when he compares the locals to foreigners: in the passage just cited he feels reminded of Italy, while in another passage he thinks of Greeks (75). The foreigners to whom Lowland Scots are compared are "other" and perhaps also somewhat more "primitive," but they are still fellow Europeans. The Gaels, by contrast, are usually compared to non-European foreigners, especially Orientals or the indigenous populations of overseas colonies.[19] This distinction is related to the fact that the Lowlanders in *Waverley* are constructed not as an essentially Celtic, or at least ex-Celtic, population sharing the same descent as the Highlanders, as James Macpherson or James Hogg claimed, but as people of Saxon stock. For instance, the surname of the Bradwardine family, and the first name of its founding father Godmund, sound un-Celtic and even un-Scottish.[20]

Although the Lowlanders share a common ancestry with the English, they are shown to be less "advanced" than their southern neighbors. The Lowland Scots of the mid-eighteenth century are placed in an intermediate stage of development between old feudal traditions which are more completely preserved in the Highlands, and the modern society already found in England. This intermediary position becomes clear when Highlanders commit a cattle raid upon Tully-Veolan. The Baron's first impulse is to retaliate in a feudal manner by following the raiders and recover the booty by force of arms, but Rose thinks this inadvisable in a modern polity: "we cannot defend ourselves as in old times, for the government have taken all our arms" (124, also see 125–27, 129). This refers to the post-1715 Disarming Acts which had succeeded in disarming the Lowlands and perhaps some Hanoverian Highland clans, but had not been thoroughly implemented in large parts of the Highlands (125). *Waverley* shows a Lowland region halfway on the peace-path toward a modern civil society where the use of violence is only permitted to state authorities. Temporarily, the Lowlanders are the worse for it, since they observe rules which their unruly Highland neighbors do not respect: they can no longer defend themselves, and the state cannot protect them either, as its power or interest does not sufficiently reach the Gaidhealtachd as yet. From a Lowland perspective, it would thus be desirable to either return the whole country to the feudal system of petty armies and constant private warfare, or propel the Highlands forward into disarmed modernity as well. It later becomes clear that the novel advocates the latter path.

The idea of linear development is expressed in metaphors which liken social evolution and history to the course of a human life. The first metaphor is that of old age: several Jacobite characters are advanced in years, such as Waverley's aunt and uncle, their chaplain Mr. Pembroke, or the Baron of Bradwardine. This suggests that Jacobitism is an outdated political stance, whereas the future lies elsewhere. Apart from physical old age, the Jacobites seem intellectually old-fashioned, for instance because they are preoccupied with dry antiquarian matters and styles, reflected in the excessively bulky and boring theological manuscript which Mr. Pembroke bestows on Waverley for spiritual edification on his journey (which he never reads due to said boringness), and the Baron's profusion of Latinate quotations.[21]

The other metaphor relating Jacobitism to a human life span is, at first sight paradoxically, youth. But this is not the youth of newly adult people who take over society from retiring elders and proceed to develop it further according to the needs of the times. Instead, it is the earlier youth of childhood and adolescence—the stage of development before youngsters take on major responsibilities, and before their actions have serious consequences. At this age, people are free to play, and feed on tales and dreams of romance and adventure, without having to be overly concerned with potentially harsh social realities. It is exactly this kind of reading and adolescent romanticism which makes Waverley susceptible to Jacobitism; and it might also play a part in shaping the attitudes and actions of another young Jacobite in the book: Prince Charles Edward Stuart.

Jacobitism is not the only aspect of Waverley's Scottish experience which is associated with youth. Metaphors of youth are also used to comment on Scottish society in general, as a colonial discourse trope symbolizing the immaturity of indigenous society at an earlier stage of development. In *Waverley*, Scotland with its residues of feudalism is socially less "mature" than England. The association between feudalism and childlikeness is discernible, for instance, when Waverley finds that the Baron—both a Jacobite and a Scottish feudal landlord—as an elderly man still looks very much like the portrait of his ten-year-old self.[22]

The portrayal of Scotland as a less advanced country which, despite its primitive virtues, needs improvement can even be discerned in the description of Rose:

> She . . . showed a natural taste, which required only cultivation. . . . [In] music . . . she had made no proficiency further than to . . . accompany her voice with the harpsichord, but even this was not very

> common in Scotland at that period. To make amends, she sung with great taste and feeling, and with a respect to the sense of what she uttered that might be proposed an example to ladies of much superior musical talent. Her natural good sense taught her. . . . Her singing gave more pleasure to all the unlearned in music, and even to many of the learned, than could have been communicated by a much finer voice and more brilliant execution, unguided by the same delicacy of feeling. (111)

Waverley colonizes Rose's mind by lending her books, interesting her in English poetry, endeavoring to "explain difficult passages" (120), and helping her to study Italian (378). However, this does not go uncriticized—the narrator observes: "the wild romance of his spirit delighted a character too young and inexperienced to observe its deficiencies" (120). Another complication is that Rose's intellectual improvement is not entirely owed to Edward, but also to Flora (367)—the French-educated Highland woman appears more cultivated than the Lowland girl, and plays a part in the civilizing mission aimed at Rose's mind.

Waverley does not always deconstruct colonial tropes and interethnic prejudices—some of them remain unquestioned throughout the book. Nonetheless, it is instructive to look into further instances where this novel emphasizes deconstruction, multivocality, and the contextuality of perceptions. English prejudices about Scotland are frequently exposed as contrafactual or exaggerated. On the eve of Edward's departure, his aunt warns him "against the fascination of Scottish beauty" (71):

> She allowed that the northern part of the island contained ancient families, but they were all Whigs and Presbyterians except the Highlanders; and respecting them . . . there could be no great delicacy among the ladies, where the gentlemen's usual attire was, as she had been assured, . . . very singular, and not at all decorous. (71)

The phrase "as she had been assured" highlights that her opinions are entirely based on hearsay. That rumour can distort reality is shown when Edward (and with him the reader) arrives in Scotland: the Baron is a Jacobite although he is a Lowlander; and Flora is an elegant, sophisticated woman although she is a Highlander.

Waverley himself also has prejudices, but it becomes increasingly clear that his English ways of looking at the world do not necessarily apply in Scotland, whose society follows a different logic. After hearing about the cattle raid and Fergus's involvement in the "blackmail" or raid-and-ransom system, Edward asks "whether this Fergus, with the unpronounceable name, was the chief thief-taker of the district. 'Thief-taker!' answered Rose, laughing; 'he is a gentleman of great honour and consequence; the chieftain of an independent branch of a powerful . . . clan, and is much respected' " (127). She further explains that "he is a very polite . . . man, . . . and his sister . . . is one of the most . . . accomplished young ladies in this country" (128). This is one of many passages which emphasize a plurality of perceptions and systems, as well as the contextuality of social values.[23] Other examples can be found in the novel's concern with names as signals of value judgments and metonymies of entire sociocultural systems, and with the clashes and shifts of cultural values implicit in the plurality of names. For instance, Charles Edward Stuart has multiple designations: Jacobites call him "the Prince," Whigs call him "the Pretender," and where both search for neutral ground they call him "the Chevalier" (e.g., 386). Another person with multiple names is Fergus: Edward initially labels him "Mr Mac-Ivor," only to be corrected by Rose about the niceties (and plurality) of local usage:

> That is not his name; and he would consider *master* as a sort of affront, only that you are an Englishman, and know no better. But the Lowlanders call him . . . by the name of his estate, Glennaquoich; and the Highlanders call him Vich Ian Vohr, that is, the son of John the Great; and we upon the braes here call him by both names indifferently. (128, Scott's italics)[24]

Referring to a gentleman by the name of his estate is apparently related to feudalism; hence, representatives of Lowland feudalism likewise partake of this custom: "The Baron of Bradwardine . . . was generally so called in Scotland (although his intimates, from his place of residence, used to denominate him Tully-Veolan . . .)" (66).

Multivocality is also reflected in the emphasis on multilingualism. The Baron frequently intersperses his utterances with French words (e.g., 116), which hints at his Jacobite sympathies since France was the asylum of many exiled Jacobites. Although his way of expressing himself is sometimes an object of ridicule, it draws attention to multivocality in a way which ultimately questions the notion that objective standards of cultural evaluation exist. Further multilingualism can be found in the occasional use of Scots, not only in dialogue (e.g., 119) but even by the narrator himself: besides using certain Scottish words, he expressly draws attention to linguistic differences and gives explanations, so that Waverley and the readers increase their linguistic competence together. Chapter 9 ends with the words: "Waverley learned . . . that in Scotland a single house was called a *town* and a natural fool an *innocent*" (85, Scott's italics). Subsequent occurrences of the word *innocent* are still italicized but no longer explained (105): the reader is now expected to know the term. Further examples of linguistic mediation between Scots and English appear on p. 99 ("the hallan, or earthen partition of the cottage"), or in the Baron's use of the word *sorners* (bullying beggars) which is explained in a footnote (125). English people's occasional reluctance to be drawn into non-English linguistic universes is taken up in Waverley's own initial reluctance and bafflement, but his subsequent development shows that such difficulties can be overcome. At first, Scotland appears to Waverley as an Other which is hard—and sometimes even impossible—to understand, let alone imitate, as when he asserts that he will never learn to pronounce *Glennaquoich* or *Vich Ian Vohr* (128), but eventually his linguistic and cultural competence grows as both he and the reader learn some Scots and Gaelic words.[25]

Although Waverley's knowledge of and sympathy for Scotland increase, he does not lose his English prejudices completely: temporarily imprisoned, he fears trial in a Scottish court because he is ignorant of and prejudiced against Scottish law, while the narrator implicitly questions this attitude (256). The two countries' traditions are shown to be different, but equally meritorious.

Concern with prejudice is not confined to antipathies between Scottish and English people, but also takes in intra-Scottish ones. Gael and *Gall* pursue their mutual rivalry even when campaigning on the same (Jacobite) side: Lowlanders look "with a jealous eye on the Highlanders' avowed pretensions to superior valor, and utility in the Prince's service" (394). This can also be read as an allusion to a later period, between the 1760s and Scott's own time, when Lowland opinion developed anxieties that the new prestige of Gaeldom—in literature, the British Army, and the symbolization of Scottishness—might eclipse Lowland achievements. Scott is less simplistically pro-Lowland, as he is concerned to show the strengths and weaknesses of both sides. He counterbalances mid-eighteenth-century Lowland prejudices about the Highlanders' alleged tendency toward fanaticism and violence by showing that some Lowlanders could be just as fanatic and dangerous as the Gaels (304)—although other parts of this novel seem to corroborate the notion that Highlanders are particularly prone to these failures. It is in the description of Highlanders that *Waverley*'s preoccupation with prejudice, and the use of colonial discourse tropes, is most intense.

Mapping Difference: The Highlands

Again, a geographical divide also represents a historical divide—Waverley travels in both space and time. While England represents the state of the art in modern social organization and truly belongs to the eighteenth-century present, the Lowlands are partly stuck in fourteenth-century feudalism, and the Highlands appear even more medieval, or even pre-medieval.[26] The Highlanders' status as contemporary ancestors becomes explicit in Scott's "General Preface" to the 1829 edition of the Waverley novels, where he talks of "the ancient traditions . . . of a people who, living in a civilised age and country, retained so strong a tincture of manners belonging to an early period of society."[27] Before Edward leaves home to join the government army, his

Jacobite uncle regrets that the feudal system of military recruitment is no longer customary in England (65). However, Edward soon finds out that feudal military structures persist in the Scottish Highlands. This helps to make Jacobitism and Highland ways attractive to the young Englishman who has been nurtured on chivalric tales from or about the Middle Ages, and whose education was partly colored by the (in England anachronistic) notions of his uncle. In Scotland, he can live out his chivalric and historical fantasies where they are still part of everyday reality. In Tully-Veolan, he finds it interesting that the region preserves such ancient practices as cattle raids, and "might have said . . . , 'I am actually in the land of military and romantic adventures, and it only remains to be seen what will be my own share in them' " (129). Waverley again romanticizes Gaels as contemporary ancestors when he encounters an old Highlander who represents a precapitalist, tradeless subsistence economy: "In this person . . . Edward admired a relic of primitive simplicity. He wore no dress but what his estate afforded . . . , nor did his table . . . offer an article but what was of native produce" (193).

At first he is astonished that primitive customs can still be found so close to his civilized home: "It seemed like a dream to Waverley that these deeds of violence should be . . . happening daily in the immediate vicinity, without his having crossed the seas, and while he was yet in the otherwise well-ordered island of Great Britain" (130). It is implied that such barbarism can usually only be expected in remote history or contemporary foreign lands, for instance among Orientals or indigenous populations of overseas colonies.[28] Associations with remote history occur when the abode of the cattle raider Donald Bean Lean reminds Waverley of a "Scythian camp" (146), which alludes to ancient Greek discourse on barbarism. Another link to ancient history appears in a scene at Glennaquoich when Edward is "offered the patriarchal refreshment of a bath for the feet" (162). As the epithet "patriarchal" suggests, such refreshments are also mentioned in the Bible. This echoes James Macpherson's attempts to conceptualize Highland culture as developmentally coeval with the world of the Old Testament. However, Scott's description juxtaposes romance and reality in a way which immediately punctures Waverley's inflated literary dreams of entering ancient worlds: "he was not . . . so luxuriously attended . . . as the . . . travellers in the Odyssey . . . , not by a beautiful damsel . . . but by a . . . skinny old Highland woman, who did not seem to think herself much honoured by the duty imposed upon her" (162). Her lack of enthusiasm also deconstructs romantic ideas about the supposed "natural" and voluntary devotion of "primitive" peoples to their social superiors. But most things can be bought for a certain price—a degree of commercial spirit has even penetrated this remote and otherwise precapitalist region: "A small donation . . . amply reconciled this . . . handmaiden to the supposed degradation; and . . . she gave him her blessing, in . . . Gaelic" (162). The illusion of a devout native/lower class can be restored with the help of money.

In addition to associations with antiquity, Gaels are also likened to more contemporary "barbarian Others." Waverley exoticizes the Highlands when a scene at Donald's camp reminds him of "an Oriental tale" (139). Highlandwoman Flora is complicit in the exoticization of her own culture when she calls herself (as translator of Gaelic poetry) a "dragoman" (174), which originally denotes a translator of Oriental languages. Another connection between Gaelic and Muslim Others appears in the title of chapter 58: "The Confusion of King Agramant's Camp" (395), which here refers to the Jacobite army. Agramant was the king of the Moors in Ariosto's *Orlando Furioso*. Comparisons move even further afield when Waverley accompanies the clan on a hunting trip and sustains an accidental injury. A shelter which the Gaels erect for him is called a "wigwam" (189), which likens Highlanders to indigenous North Americans.[29] The clan physician is described in terms which evoke white people's descriptions of Native American or African "medicine men": "The surgeon . . . appeared to unite the characters of a leech and a conjuror" (189). His work is accompanied by ceremonies which, to the "modern" outside observer, appear impractical and superstitious:

> He observed great ceremony in approaching . . . ; and though our hero was writhing with pain, would not proceed to any operation which might assuage it until he had perambulated his couch three times . . . according to the course of the sun. . . . Edward was given to understand that . . . the ingredients [of the medicine] had been gathered . . . during the full moon, and that the herbalist had . . . recited a charm. (190)

When he finally attends to the injuries, he is "never failing to murmur prayers or spells" (190). When the cure takes "speedy effect," Edward ascribes this "to the virtue of the herbs," while the Gaels ascribe it to the spells and rituals (190). Another connection between Highlanders and overseas colonial subjects is established when Gaelic soldiers are described as moving "in single or Indian file" (280).

Othering goes even further: Gaels are not only compared to "exotic," "primitive" humans, but also to animals. In colonial discourse, the same strategy of dehumanization has been applied to non-European indigenous peoples. In *Waverley*, a Highlander steals a dead English soldier's cloak and hides it with "the caution of a spaniel hiding a bone" (329). Another Highlander, who is involved in a clandestine military mission, merges not only into the animal world but even into the inanimate nature of the very soil as he "snuffed the wind like a . . . spaniel, . . . stooped down upon all-fours, wrapped up in his plaid, so as to be scarce distinguishable from the heathy ground on which he moved, and advanced in this posture to reconnoitre" (280). Waverley's nose is worse than the Highlander's (280), suggesting that the civilized Englishman is more remote from the animal world than the uncivilized Gael is. Later, this Highlander moves out of the animal world to reenter the realm of overseas colonized humans: "crawling on all fours with the dexterity of an Indian" (281).

Primitiveness is also suggested by other passages. The attendants of Evan Dhu, a member of the clan gentry, are labeled as "wild Highlanders" (134), the dinner at Glennaquoich "was simple, even to rudeness" (i.e., primitiveness, 162), and clan commoners on the Jacobite campaign are described as follows:

> The grim, uncombed, and wild appearance of these men, most of whom gazed with all the admiration of ignorance upon the most ordinary production of domestic art, created surprise in the Lowlands, but it also created terror. So little was the condition of the Highlands known . . . , that the character and appearance of their population, while thus sallying forth as military adventurers, conveyed to the south-country Lowlanders as much surprise as if an invasion of African Negroes or Indians had issued forth from the northern mountains of their own native country. (324)

Here, however, the narrator reports other people's views rather than his own, for his own feelings are dominated by pity rather than condescension or terror (324–25). A similar report of other people's prejudices, while the narrator seems more distanced, occurs when the Jacobite army comes into contact with English people: "the ignorant gazed with astonishment, mixed with horror and aversion, at the wild appearance, unknown language, and singular garb of the Scottish Highlanders" (390).

Variations occur in the way Gaelic otherness and "primitiveness" are evaluated. Sometimes the Highlanders appear as noble, sometimes as ignoble savages. The latter is exemplified by Callum Beag, who displays the negative side of clanship and its fierce loyalties: an equally fierce aggression toward people from outside the clan.[30] At times, negative associations are also evoked by the otherness of the Gaelic language, which can form an insurmountable barrier for communication between Highlanders and people from other parts of the country. This in turn can create anxieties and feelings of helplessness in the uninitiated stranger. On first coming into the Highlands, Waverley is left with a guide who hardly speaks any English, whereupon he feels vulnerable and becomes suspicious of the Gaels' intentions (137). Although in this particular case his fears turn out to be ungrounded, the use of Gaelic, and the gaps of communication and comprehension it occasions, are stressed so frequently throughout the novel (e.g., 143, 190, 195, 273) that it is difficult to avoid the impression that linguistic heterogeneity within a country can pose a serious problem. For instance, when Waverley participates in a Highland hunt, he is almost overrun by a herd of deer because he cannot understand a Gaelic warning (189).

One of the most completely and unsettlingly "Other" scenes he encounters takes place at the camp of Donald Bean Lean, who is othered in a way which not only illustrates Waverley's perspective, but also plays on the likely expectations of contemporaneous readers. The sensationalist title of chapter 17—"The Hold of a Highland Robber" (139)—might be intended to tickle the reader's fancy and give a pleasant thrill. Donald is another ignoble specimen of savagery, not only because he is a cattle raider, but also, as readers learn later, because of his intrigues which aim to alienate Waverley from his Hanoverian regiment. Donald himself, however, does not wish to be seen as a savage and tries to wear a civilized mask to impress his guest from the English center. This act of mimicry does not have the intended effect, as in Waverley's eyes this is worse than honest plaid-wearing barbarity:[31]

> He had served . . . in the French army, and in order to receive his English visitor in great form, . . . he had laid aside the Highland dress . . . to put on an old . . . uniform, and a feathered hat, in which he was far from showing to advantage, and indeed looked so incongruous, compared with all around him, that Waverley would have been tempted to laugh, had laughter been either civil or safe. (141)

The description and the "civilized" outsider's reaction are reminiscent of Marlow's reaction to the African wearing European dress in Joseph Conrad's *Heart of Darkness* more than eighty years later: Marlow feels reminded of "a dog in . . . breeches and a feather hat, walking on his hind legs."[32]

At Glennaquoich, Waverley also encounters primitiveness to boot, but of a less sinister kind. Moreover, Flora and Fergus are French-educated and multilingual—unexpected elements of "real" civilization in the midst of a primitive culture, as opposed to the sham and incongruous civilization of Donald Bean Lean. Despite his "civilized" traits, Fergus sometimes appears as a picturesque specimen of Highland noble savagery, with the usual aesthetic trappings of colorful garments and weapons which underline his military role and competence:

> Peculiar grace and dignity . . . , above the middle size, and finely proportioned, the Highland dress . . . set off his person to great advantage. He wore the trews, or close trowsers, made of tartan, . . . a dirk, very richly mounted with silver. . . . His countenance was decidedly Scottish, with the . . . northern physiognomy, but . . . had so little of its harshness and exaggeration, that it would have been pronounced in any country extremely handsome. The martial air of the bonnet . . . added much to the manly appearance of his head, which was besides ornamented with a far more natural and graceful cluster of close black curls than ever were exposed to sale in Bond Street. (153–54)

As in Martin Martin's comparison between urban and island women, the natural beauty of the noble savage surpasses the artificial beauty of fashionable metropolitans. The same applies to Fergus's sister Flora, whose "hair was not disfigured by the art of the friseur, but fell in jetty ringlets round her neck" (167). Thus, *Waverley* at least sometimes exploits the stock conventions of romantic Highlandism, either because characters, narrator, or author partly subscribe to these notions as well, or in order to play along with the expectations and tastes of contemporaneous readers. The iconography of Gaelic noble savagery also informs the description of Evan Dhu (131): again, it emphasizes not only picturesqueness, but also the physical fitness which seemed to make the Gaels ideal raw material for Britain's imperial army, once their pacification had progressed far enough to make them trustworthy. Plaid, tartans, armor, and physical fitness are stressed throughout the novel.[33] Other aspects of Highland life which appealed strongly to anglophone audiences of Scott's time and appear frequently in *Waverley* are Gaelic music, especially pipes (e.g., 192, 219, 321), as well as the beauty of the landscape and its ruins (e.g., 135, 139, 283).

While *Waverley* uses various tropes of primitivism and noble savagery, it also frequently ironizes them. For instance, it reveals the simplistic and sometimes even entirely fictional nature of such constructs, and points out the negative sides of "primitive" life or of the Jacobite past which serve as a warning against over-romanticization. While Evan represents mainly the good qualities of "barbarism," being "unpolished" but good-natured and unselfishly loyal, his moral integrity is by no means shared by all his fellow Gaels. Donald does not even display the loyalty to his chief which romantic Highlandism regarded as so typical (363). Fergus's morals are not entirely noble, either: despite good qualities like "openness and affability," he also shows self-importance, rashness, authoritarianism, and vindictiveness. While the omniscient narrator hints at these flaws almost from the outset, he notes that Waverley himself as a more romantically minded onlooker would not recognize those faults until later (154). As Fiona Stafford observes, "despite the romantic atmosphere, . . . Fergus and Flora . . . are flawed by pride, intolerance, and political obsession while there is a clear suggestion that their tragedy has as much to do with the character of the race as with external forces."[34]

Apart from "racial character" and post-1745 missions of externally induced assimilation, internal social factors also play a part. The narrator qualifies romantic clichés of Gaels as valiant and picturesque ideal soldiers by pointing out that, while the clan elites were indeed of formidable valor and appearance, their commoners seemed a pitiable, poor, half-naked, and insufficiently armed rabble (323–24). This poverty is linked to the unimproved state of the feudal Highland economy: "he crowded his estate with a tenantry, hardy indeed, . . . but greatly outnumbering what the soil was calculated to maintain" (157). Fergus's Highland home is similarly unimproved as the Lowland estate of Tully-Veolan:

> There appeared none of that attention to convenience, far less to ornament, which usually surrounds a gentleman's habitation. An inclosure or two . . . were the only part of the domain which was fenced; . . . scanty crop of barley, liable to constant depredations from the herds. (160)

Romantic idealizations of barren Highland landscapes are criticized: "the hills were high and heathy, but without any variety of surface; so that the whole view was wild and desolate rather than grand and solitary" (160). Such passages still display an undertone of colonial discourse, but now of the Enlightened progressivist rather than romantically primitivist kind.

Enlightenment perspectives on the primitive are also echoed in the representation of Fergus's attitudes to women. He thinks it completely legitimate to use women and marriage as pawns in political and dynastic schemes, without paying much attention to love or the will and needs of the lady. His own heart is not suited to domestic comforts, as his main pursuit is politics, and he wants a wife mainly as a bearer of children to continue his line, rather than as a beloved companion. In his opinion, matches should be made between the prospective husband and the male guardian of the bride-to-be, such as a father or brother. This does not conform to the modern bourgeois sentimental ideal of love marriages, here represented by the attitude of Englishman Waverley (184, 206, 209, 301–2, 368–69, 373–74, 377, 391). In practice, this ideal has been frequently disregarded even in bourgeois spheres, where women have likewise been married off for material reasons without consideration for their feelings. But in bourgeois *ideology*, the love marriage served as a marker to distinguish the older "feudal" order, supposedly more coercive and unemotional, from the allegedly more humane morality of the bourgeois age. Fergus's attitude to women appears as a morally brutalizing, old-fashioned stance springing from the primitive Gaelic feudal order, or from his education in France (205, 302, 368). France, though some kind of "civilized" center, is marred by its absolutist and essentially pre-bourgeois political system which in English eyes appeared feudal enough to seem dated as well. Certain Scottish Enlightenment thinkers, such as John Millar, considered the treatment of women as an important indicator of social development: the more respect a culture paid to females, the higher it stood on the civilizational ladder. In a debate with Fergus, Waverley says: "I am ignorant of the customs of the Highlands in that particular. But . . . I would not take the hand of an angel, with an empire for her dowry, if her consent were extorted by the importunity of . . . guardians, and did not flow from her own free inclination" (391). This can be read as a comment on the barbarity of Highland culture.

A further aspect of *Waverley*'s portrayal of Highlanders which is reminiscent of colonial discourse is, again, the eroticization of exoticized local women. The short-skirted Lowland girls noted earlier find their Highland counterpart in Donald's flirty (and rather lengthily described) daughter Alice:

> She had secured time . . . to arrange her person in her best trim . . . , a petticoat, of scanty longitude . . . ; but . . . clean, and neatly arranged. . . .
>
> Her form, though rather large for her years, was very well proportioned, and her demeanour had a natural and rustic grace. . . . The smiles, displaying . . . teeth of exquisite whiteness, and the laughing eyes, with which . . . she gave Waverley . . . greeting . . . , might have been interpreted . . . as meant to convey more than the courtesy of an hostess. (146)

> Flinging her plaid around her, she advanced up to Edward, and, with the utmost simplicity, taking hold of his hand, offered her cheek to his salute. (147)

However, the novel's stance toward the primitive is not entirely a colonizing one. There are also passages on Highland culture which display considerable respect for difference. The discrepancy between native and (unreliable) outside perceptions is highlighted when Waverley encounters a Gael for the first time: as the latter enters Tully-Veolan in full Highland costume, to which weaponry is integral, Edward is inclined to be alarmed, whereas the locals are used to the sight and treat it as a harmless matter of fact (131). Another attempt to evaluate different cultures on their own terms is made in the description of the encounter between Highland Jacobite rebels and government troops: "the two armies, so different . . . , yet each admirably trained in its own peculiar mode of war" (332).

Although this novel was written by a Lowland author describing Highland society from the outside, it repeatedly takes care to reproduce the insiders' perspective as well, for instance displaying awareness of the indigenous logic of cattle raiding. Knowledge of Gaelic norms also extends to poetry: one passage reports that a panegyric by the clan bard ended with a complimentary reference to Flora (170), which reflects the genuine Gaelic convention of ending panegyric poems with a short praise of the lady of the house.

Multivocality is also reflected in an emphasis on linguistic pluralism. In Scott's novel, even Highlanders who are rather fluent in English use a peculiar kind of English which is neither the Lowland Scots nor the Standard variant. Partly, this Highland English seems an artificial invention for literary characterization, but other elements appear relatively genuine, for example when characters use a considerable amount of Gaelic proverbial wisdom in their English utterances.[35] The text also includes utterances by characters who know very little English, and whose use of this language is so "broken" or pidginized that it seems hardly intelligible to anglophone characters or readers. A local guide once says to Waverley: "Ta cove was tree, four mile; but as Duinhé-wassel was a wee taiglit, Donald could, tat is, might—would—should send ta curragh" (137). Many readers might share Waverley's puzzlement as attention is drawn to problems in cross-cultural understanding as well as gradual learning processes: "This conveyed no information. The *curragh* . . . might be a man, a horse, a cart, or chaise. . . . But . . . Edward began to conceive his meaning when . . . he found himself on the banks of a . . . river or lake" (138)—the *curragh* is a boat, which soon arrives.

Further Gaelic expressions are introduced throughout the book. Sometimes snippets of Gaelic are given in a linguistically "authentic," "correct" manner, as in *deoch an doruis* (drink of the door, 94). At other times, such snippets are at least recognizable, though they appear in rather adventurous spelling, as in *Duinhé-wassel* for *duine-uasal*, "gentleman." Despite such limitations, the use of Gaelic in this novel draws attention to linguistic and cultural gaps. It also displays basic respect for an indigenous language which might not be perfectly understood by author or readers, but which is nonetheless deemed worthy of representation, as a metonymy for a more extended indigenous discourse in the background which forms a discursive universe of its own that can only be partially known and represented by an outsider. This becomes particularly clear in the postscript, where the narrator shows awareness of his linguistic shortcomings, stressing that he was "not born a Highlander (which may be an apology for much bad Gaelic)" (492).

Although Scott's Gaels are merely fictional characters in an English-language novel by a Lowland author, his emphasis on multivocality allows the "natives," at least to a certain extent, a voice of their own. Constructed or not, Scott's fictional native voices highlight the existence and validity of such voices outside this text. However, such tolerance might only have become possible because by Scott's time the Other was no longer menacing.[36]

Another aspect of *Waverley*'s quest for tolerance toward Highland otherness is, again, the deconstruction of prejudice. One strategy is to show that prejudice and ignorance are mutual: Gaels and English speakers are equally biased toward each other. The romantic cliché that Highland noble savages are physically fitter than their anglophone southern compatriots is not only believed by outsiders like Waverley, but even by insiders like Evan Dhu: Edward "was anxious . . . to remove the opinion which Evan seemed to entertain of the effeminacy of the Lowlanders, and particularly that of the English" (136). Initially, Evan's condescension towards Waverley's hardihood seems justified as the young Englishman is unaccustomed to so much exercise and rough terrain (136), but later Edward shows himself adaptable through training. Another Gael who is ignorant and prejudiced about southerners is Flora: one reason why she is so little impressed by Edward is his shyness, "which, as she had been educated in the first foreign circles, and was little acquainted with the shyness of English manners, was, in her opinion, too nearly related to timidity and imbecility" (317). Further evidence that Highlanders can be as biased and self-righteous as their southern neighbors is afforded by Fergus's conduct while the Jacobite army occupies Edinburgh:

his attempt to convert his Presbyterian Lowland landlady to Catholicism or at least Episcopalianism (311) could be interpreted as a colonizing mission in reverse.

Not only is othering portrayed as mutual, but boundaries are also shown to be permeable. This novel constantly emphasizes border crossing and cultural mediation. At times, boundaries not only seem permeable, but threaten to dissolve altogether: various instances of hybridity illustrate the artificiality of cultural categories, which are thus exposed as highly unstable constructs.

Deconstructing Difference? Border Crossers and Mediators

While the purest instances of Highland primitiveness are encountered among the lower ranks of Gaelic society, the principal representatives of its elite, Fergus and Flora, are cultural hybrids, partly still anchored (or re-anchored) in traditional Gaelic society, and partly shaped by the "high civilizations" of Europe's metropolitan cultures through education at the French court. This French connection makes even their metropolitan features alien to the British mainstream, but they are undeniably "cultured." They are also relatively familiar with British metropolitan culture: both speak flawless English, and Flora is well versed in English literature, such as the works of Shakespeare. Fergus's hybridity, which sets him apart from most of his "primitive" clansmen, is reflected in the fact that he, like his fellow Jacobite the Baron of Bradwardine, often intersperses his English utterances with French words (e.g., 353, 376). Where Fergus uses Gaelic traditions, he does so selectively, and only when it suits his purposes. When Waverley arrives, Fergus's monocultural clansmen want their chief to present himself according to Gaelic custom with a large feudal retinue. Judging from their own experience, which is limited to the Highlands, they think that such a retinue would impress not only local chiefs, but also an English outsider. By contrast, Fergus is a man of the world who estimates an outsider's reaction more realistically and refrains from using Gaelic tradition in an inappropriate context:

> He was well aware that such an unnecessary attendance would seem to Edward rather ludicrous . . . ; and while few men were more attached to ideas of chieftainship and feudal power, he was . . . cautious of exhibiting external marks of dignity, unless . . . when they were most likely to produce an imposing effect. Therefore, although, had he been to receive a brother chieftain, he would probably have been attended by all that retinue . . . , he judged it more respectable to . . . meet Waverley with a single attendant. (153)

Fergus, similar to the Lowland Baron, is midway between two civilizational stages:

> Had Fergus MacIvor lived Sixty Years sooner . . . , he would . . . have wanted the polished manner and knowledge of the world which he now possessed; and had he lived Sixty Years later, his ambition and love of rule would have lacked the fuel which his situation now afforded. (157)

He is already half-civilized, but his authority (and some of his character) is still that of a feudal chieftain. Traditional, and perhaps cliché, Gaelic features include his belief in supernatural apparitions.[37] Fergus's ambivalence is evident in his dismissive remarks to Waverley about the Highland traditions of which he partakes: Fergus speaks of "my rude mansion" (161), calls the clan feast "the barbarous ritual of our forefathers" (171), and "apologised for the confusion" created by the great number of clansmen at the festivity. He seems to regret that his position binds him to respect rude and unprofitable traditions: "I must find them beef and ale, while the rogues will do nothing . . . but practice the broadsword, or wander about the hills, shooting, fishing, hunting, drinking, and making love" (164). It is not entirely clear how much of this critique is sincere and how much is tactical mimicry to establish common ground with his English guest by affecting to share an outsider's perspective. Elsewhere in the novel, Fergus is evidently fond of certain feudal traditions, such as his unquestioned authority as a chieftain. Perhaps he wants the best of both worlds: loyal feudal followers, grand titles, independence, and a sense of his own greatness, plus a modern landlord's freedom from obligations to his tenants, and a capitalistically maximized income. Fergus's attitude toward Gaelic poetry likewise appears ambivalent: he asserts that he has no interest in it (169, 171–72, 181), while Flora claims that he does (172).

Fergus's ambivalent position as a perpetual border crosser also becomes clear from the fact that he and his foster brother Evan, now Jacobites, have only recently served in the Black Watch of the government army (150, 157). Fergus does not correspond to conventional romantic images which portrayed Highlanders as figures who fought for the Stuarts out of pure unselfish loyalty and moral righteousness. The chief of the Mac-Ivors is a calculating opportunist who changes his allegiance as its suits his own interests.[38] The narrator highlights this deviation from the cliché, stating that Fergus "was too thorough a politician . . . that we should term him the model of a Highland Chieftain" (170). The rest of his clan does seem to fight for loyalty alone—but a loyalty which looks to the chief, not to kings or the nation at large. Concerning their change of allegiance from King George to the Stuarts, Evan says: "you must ask Vich Ian Vohr about that; for we are for his king, and care not much which of them it is" (150). This suggests that the Gaelic commoners are not really to blame for the Jacobite uprising, as the guilt lies with the chiefs who abused the clansmen's loyalty for rebellious purposes. It also implies that, once Jacobitism is defeated, the clan commoners have just as much potential to be loyal servants of the Hanoverian regime.[39] This had become the dominant interpretation of Jacobite guilt and Highland loyalties by Scott's time.

Flora, too, is a hybrid figure between tradition and modernity:

> The dress of the lady . . . partook partly of the Parisian fashion, and partly of the more simple dress of the Highlands, blended together with great taste. (167)

> She was highly accomplished, and had acquired those elegant manners to be expected from one who, in early youth, had been the companion of a princess; yet she had not learned to substitute the gloss of politeness for the reality of feeling. (169)

Flora partly appears as a noble savage highly suitable for romantic idealization. But such associations are also deconstructed—while the enraptured Waverley often romanticizes Flora and "primitive" Gaeldom, the narrator is more distanced. When Flora sings to Edward by a waterfall, this appears to him as a real-life, unpremediated materialization of the kind of scene one would otherwise only encounter in stories. The narrator, by contrast, tells us that the scene has been carefully landscaped and prepared by Flora, so that it is not the result of a "natural," unaffected Highland environment and culture, but the manufactured product of artful stage management (174–77, 502). This contrast between apparent naturalness and actual artificiality is underlined by the labeling of the glen in which this performance takes place as a "sylvan amphitheatre" (175)—"sylvan" connotes forests, unsettled country, wildness, and an absence of civilization, whereas "amphitheatre" evokes the "high" civilizations of ancient Greece and Rome. The illusory nature of romanticized images is also exposed when the narrator points out that Waverley's idealization of Miss Mac-Ivor results from the absence of the object of desire—only distance allows us to distort reality and forget its faults:

> Distance . . . produces in idea the same effect as in real perspective. Objects are softened . . . and rendered doubly graceful; the harsher and more ordinary points of character are mellowed down. . . . There are mists too in the mental as well as the natural horizon, to conceal what is less pleasing in distant objects, and there are happy lights . . . upon those points which can profit by brilliant illumination. (225–26)[40]

This applies not just to Edward's idealization of Flora, but also to early nineteenth-century readers' romanticization of the Jacobite era, which by then had become distant in time.[41] Scott's language in this passage also suggests applicability to romanticizations of *anything* Highland, as mists and striking light effects are both an actual part of the Highland landscape and a conventional element of its representation in romantic discourse.

Another instance where Flora appears as an intermediary between barbarism and civilization, and where it is possible to identify another jibe at romanticism, occurs when she is presented as a translator of Gaelic poetry into English. The terms in which this role is described humorously allude to Macpherson's Ossian—Fergus tells Waverley that his sister dabbles in poetic translation, and asks her to provide a sample for their guest, to which she replies: "You know how little these verses can possibly interest an English stranger, even if I could translate them as you pretend" (172). The same scruples were initially felt by Macpherson. Another parallel is Fergus's supposition that Flora had a hand in the original Gaelic text of the poem the clan bard presented on that night. To counter suspicions of forgery, Macpherson had prepared Gaelic versions of his Ossianic works, but instead of being his original sources (as claimed), these were largely retranslations of his English texts.[42] Skeptics soon suspected this, too, though conclusive proof was only published later.[43] *Waverley* also alludes to Macpherson when Flora claims that Fergus considers his bard a greater poet than Homer (172), and that, if these poems "are ever translated into any of the languages of civilized Europe, cannot fail to produce a deep and general sensation" (173). Later, the narrator refers to feasting as "the joys of the shell, as Ossian has it," and says that the Gaels were "probably as deeply engaged in the discussion of politics and news, as Milton's spirits in metaphysical disquisition" (188)—*Paradise Lost* had been a reference point for Macpherson when he positioned his "translations" in an epic framework. Although *Waverley* is set long before Macpherson published his Ossianic texts, these passages ironically foreshadow the translations and debates of the 1760s.

Another, though more implicit, jibe at romantic Ossianism can be discerned in the reference to a Highland girl at Glennaquoich who sings a "burlesque elegy of a countryman on the loss of his cow" in "comic tones" (182)—which undermines post-Macphersonic mainstream clichés which pictured all Gaelic poetry as melancholic and sublime. One of the most explicit deconstructions of romanticism comes from Flora herself, although she is the very character who at first glance seems most suited to be a romantic figure. Talking to Rose, she perceptively and ironically says:

> High and perilous enterprise is not Waverley's forte. He would never have been his celebrated ancestor Sir Nigel, only Sir Nigel's eulogist and poet. I will tell you where he will be . . . in his place—in the quiet . . . domestic happiness, lettered indolence, and elegant enjoyments of Waverley-Honour.[44] And he will refit the old library in . . . Gothic taste, . . . and gaze on the deer . . . in the moonlight—and he will repeat verses to his . . . wife . . .—and he will be a happy man. (370–71)

"'And she will be a happy woman,' thought poor Rose" (371)—on whom the irony is entirely lost.

Occasionally, Evan likewise features as a border crosser: sufficient competence in Lowland culture enables him to speak "in good English," though this English is unidiomatic, being heavily interspersed with translated Gaelic metaphors which to an outsider would sometimes render his speech unintelligible (132). Callum Beag is also capable of cultural border crossing: when he accompanies Waverley to the Lowlands, he quite successfully mimics Lowland speech in order to conceal his Highland background which, if discovered, could result in capture by radical Whigs (229). Further border crossing occurs in the following passage:

> Our hero . . . endeavoured to address them, but was only answered with "*Cha n'eil Beurl' agam*," *i.e.*, "I have no English," being as Waverley well knew, the constant reply of a Highlander, when he either does not understand, or does not choose to reply to, an Englishman or Lowlander. (273)

The first border crossing is accomplished by Waverley himself, who has now picked up enough Gaelic to understand simple sentences like this one, though not enough to gather the information he desires without recourse to English. The second border crossing is the narrator's provision of a translation for the reader—who thus learns some Gaelic, just like Waverley has before. Third, many Gaels are here said to know some English. A fourth border crossing occurs in the mimicry performed when they tactically cross back from their actual bilingual and hybridized state into the fake purity of an entirely "uneducated," monoglot Gaelic Other when it suits their purposes.

While these passages highlight the existence of border-crossing Gaels, there are also characters that cross the Gael-*Gall* boundary from the other side, that is, Lowlanders who have a limited competence in Gaelic culture. The Lowlanders of Perthshire, as inhabitants of a border zone, are multilingual or at least use Gaelic loanwords in their English, for example in "what they technically called *deoch an doruis*, a stirrup-cup" (94, Scott's italics). Again, the reader is invited to participate in the border crossing by learning about the Other's language and culture, helped by a footnote which explains the *deoch an doruis* custom in more detail (497–98). Here, a further Gaelic loanword is used and explained: "the clachan or village" (497). Neighboring Lowlanders' partial competence in Highland culture is also evident in the dealings between the Baron and Evan when the latter comes as a post-cattle-raid ambassador to negotiate terms: "the Baron . . . well knew their customs, and the proper mode of addressing them" (132).

One of the most important border crossers is Waverley himself: an Englishman who goes native and becomes highlandized. Even his surname marks him as an in-between figure: with his "wavering and unsettled habit of mind"

(73), he is torn between cultures, women, and political opinions. His indecision makes Edward an ideal site for the projection and exploration of different cultures and attitudes, where their conflicts can be negotiated and finally resolved.[45] Waverley's shifting cultural identities are often externalized through dress. Symbolically reclothed in tartan, he temporarily becomes a Highlander. This first happens at the start of a hunting trip shortly before the Jacobite rising: "Waverley complied so far with the custom of the country as to adopt the trews (he could not be reconciled to the kilt), brogues and bonnet, as the fittest dress for the exercise . . . , and which least exposed him to be stared at as a stranger" (187). Later, when the Highlanders rescue him from captivity among the Whigs, they again clothe him in Highland dress, this time in a plaid (273–74). The Stuart Prince ritualistically affirms Waverley's admission into his service by arming him "after the Highland fashion" with a broadsword which is an heirloom of the Stuart family (298). Soon afterwards, Fergus has Edward clothed in trews and a plaid of Mac-Ivor tartan, one of Fergus's own cloaks, and "a blue bonnet of the Prince's pattern" (300). This reclothing is a symbolic act of political and cultural appropriation which makes Edward a Jacobite and an honorary Gael—in Fergus's words: "you will be a complete son of Ivor" (300). This point is repeated when the chief calls Edward "an adopted son of Ivor" (313). Waverley himself still has practical difficulties with his new identity, for instance needing assistance in handling his new garments (320). Nonetheless, he has sufficiently gone native as a barbarian—"our hero having now fairly assumed the 'garb of old Gaul' " (305) alludes to the primitivist song quoted in chapter 3 of this study.

When the Baron learns of Edward's gaelification, he takes umbrage, as he would gladly have offered Waverley a different kind of scottification as a Lowlander through a position among the Bradwardine contingent of Jacobites (303)—as in Edward's wavering romantic inclinations, Lowland and Highland Scotland vie for his sympathy. Initially, the Highlands have the upper hand in his heart and imagination, as they give him the opportunity to live out his romantic fantasies. To his enjoyment, being part of his friend's Highland regiment gives him firsthand experience of the loyalty normally only shown to a chief (326). Nonetheless, Edward never goes completely native: at least inwardly, he always remains skeptical about certain Highland attitudes, such as the belief in second sight. Despite his romantic inclinations, he is never totally "irrational."[46]

Waverley's hybridity enables him to mediate between Britain's ethnic and political factions. How far he has moved away from the anti-Scottish stance of many of his English compatriots becomes clear when he meets Colonel Talbot, who is a much more uncompromising specimen of the "prejudices which are peculiarly English" (366). Talbot calls the Gaels "a gang of . . . cut-throats" (366) and staunchly refuses to be impressed by the beautiful and accomplished Flora. He puts his dislike down to her allegedly affected airs, but the narrator gives a different reason, namely that to the biased Colonel "the white cockade on the breast, . . . and the Mac at the beginning of a name, would have made the devil out of an angel" (366). Talbot is also prejudiced about the Gaelic language: "your Highland friend, Glen—what do you call his barbarous name?" (386). He exclaims:

> Let them stay in their own barren mountains . . . : but what business have they to come where people wear breeches, and speak an intelligible language? I mean intelligible in comparison with their gibberish, for even the Lowlanders talk a kind of English little better than the negroes in Jamaica. (387)

This is juxtaposed to the opinions of the now much less biased Waverley, who tries to temper his fellow Englishman's xenophobia: "For shame, . . . you swell at sight of tartan, as the bull . . . at scarlet. You and Mac-Ivor have some points not much unlike, so far as national prejudice is concerned. . . . You judge too harshly of the Highlanders" (387).

Despite the novel's emphasis on tolerance and mediation, it becomes clear that Waverley's infatuation with Highland culture is related to his personal immaturity, and must be overcome in a process of growing up. As in the presentation of the Lowlands, personal immaturity and social primitiveness go hand in hand and are frequently expressed through images of childhood or adolescence, which must inevitably be transcended by personal and social maturation. Waverley's repeatedly emphasized youth and his romantically immature, unrealistic, and irresponsible reading play an important role in making him susceptible to Jacobite, primitivist, and gaelicizing influences—he attempts to reenact fantasies based on literature. Though intelligent, Edward is inexperienced, does not yet trust his own judgment, and defers to the advice of others, such as Fergus (201–2). When Waverley loses his commission in the Hanoverian army, his hurt pride makes him cry like a child and seek consolation: "he . . . threw himself into Mac-Ivor's arms, and gave vent to tears of shame and indignation" (202). Childlikeness makes him open to manipulation, for instance when Fergus, after comforting him, tries to use his hurt pride to steer him into the Jacobite camp (203).

Sometimes Fergus himself also displays attributes of immaturity, childishness, or adolescence, as he is proud, stubborn, and easily offended.[47] His willfulness may also be encouraged by his absolute power as a feudal chief. Thus, his personal flaws and immaturity also stand for the immaturity of the "primitive" society he lives in. The connection between the Gaelic "primitive" Other and immaturity is also reflected in Scott's own reaction to Macpherson: first, he was enthusiastic, but later came to think that "Ossian . . . has more charms for youth than for a more advanced stage."[48]

In *Waverley*, the protagonist's individual growing up—becoming a little older, but also, as is repeatedly stressed, physically stronger—is linked to social and political maturation.[49] During this process, the Hanoverian order and its representative Talbot become ever more likeable.[50] Waverley's maturation culminates in his becoming a de-highlandized pro-Hanoverian subject, getting married, and coming into his inheritance, accepting adult responsibility as the head of a family and as a landlord. His particular choice of wife underlines the superseding of individual, political, and civilizational "immaturity." His first love, Flora, stands for social immaturity, representing "primitive" Highland culture and an equally dated and fated Jacobitism. She also highlights Waverley's personal immaturity by being slightly older than himself, and intellectually at least his equal, if not even superior. Rose comes from a less "backward" society, and makes Waverley feel and appear more mature than he would have seemed next to Flora: Rose is slightly younger and much more dependent on his intellectual influence. The marriage between Rose and Edward reenacts the Union of England and Scotland on a personal level, unionism being an important part of "mature" progressivist Whig attitudes. Significantly, this marriage is a union between England and *Lowland* Scotland, while the Highlands ultimately play no great part: they must be neutralized, marginalized, or even killed off before the union can take effect—Jacobitism is vanquished, Fergus is executed, and Flora is neutralized by ceasing to be an object of desire for Waverley, and later retreating into the loveless, childless celibacy of a nunnery.[51] In view of the parallels between Edward's individual maturation and national maturation, Murray Pittock appositely calls *Waverley* a "*bildungsroman* of nations."[52]

Read in this way, *Waverley* appears essentially as a narrative of progress. A different reading is proposed by Cairns Craig, who argues that the linearity of progress is destabilized by underlying skepticism. For him, Waverley as an Englishman initially represents a more "advanced" stage, while his highlandization exposes the civilization process as reversible. Although the end of the novel shows that this reversibility is only temporary and is again superseded by a forward-looking narrative of progress, Craig argues that *Waverley*'s beginning poses unsettling questions, for instance whether progress really is inevitable, whether it can last, or whether it can be reversed, both personally and socially.[53] While plausibly pointing out potential anxieties of progressivists, such a reading might overemphasize the reversability of progress in this novel because Edward's highlandization might not really be a civilizational regression: although Waverley the Englishman comes from a *society* which on the whole seems more advanced than the Scottish/Gaelic one, his *personal* stage of development is that of an adolescent and, moreover, an unrealistic romance reader. As such, he is from the outset, even when still in England, linked to a "backward" mindset. An adolescent will inevitably grow up, and once this has happened, the childhood metaphor of progress usually does *not* allow a lapse back. In this light, progress seems less insecure and reversible than Craig assumes.

The inferiority of Jacobite and Gaelic otherness is expressed not only through the childhood metaphor, but also through the metaphor of femininity:

like children, women have often been assumed to be intellectually inferior, or at least more prone to emotionalism, dreaming, romanticism, and fantasy. This was linked to the notion that women and children could afford to dream more than adults and men could, because it was with the latter that social power and responsibility lay, so that their tasks forced them to be more rational and pragmatic. For women and children it was supposedly quite safe to dream, as less depended on their actions and choices. Hence, it seemed safe to commend or tolerate attitudes in women and children which would be less acceptable in an adult male. In practice, male adult authority was supposed to overrule social inferiors like women and children. Such familial images furnished basic metaphors of power which were also highly popular in colonial discourse, where subject populations were both infantilized and feminized.

In *Waverley*, admirers of Gaelic poetry are either unsophisticated clan commoners (guests at the feast), women (Flora, 169–72, 181), or outsiders who do not understand the language and are childishly romantic (Edward). Gaelic literature is designated as a pursuit for the powerless or the intellectually inferior. Fergus, by contrast, does not seem to share this admiration—unless he is merely unwilling to admit it, as Flora suggests. *Waverley*'s association of Gaelic culture with dependence and femininity anticipates the progressive feminization of the Celtic image in the further course of the nineteenth century.

Feminization can also be observed in relation to Jacobitism: Fergus's Jacobitism is shown to be opportunistic and morally flawed, while Flora's Jacobitism is a fitter subject for unqualified romanticization, as hers is really idealistic and unselfish (168–70, 184–85, 206–7, 216). She shares her first name with a devoted female Jacobite from real history who after Culloden played a crucial role in helping the Stuart prince escape from his pursuers, and who has featured prominently in romantic images of Jacobitism ever since: Flora MacDonald. It was safer to romanticize Jacobitism in a woman than in a man because women had less social power, whereas male Jacobitism posed political and military danger.

As the "immaturity" and flaws of his Jacobite and Highland involvements become more obvious, the newly hybridized but gradually maturing Waverley embarks on a reverse course of de-gaelicization. Even before he meets Colonel Talbot, Edward starts to see his hybridized position as unnatural and hears the calling of his own "race"—when he perceives the approaching English government soldiers at Prestonpans, his cultural allegiances waver yet again:

> Waverley could plainly recognise the standard of the troop he had formerly commanded, . . . the English dialect, . . . the commanding officer, for whom he had once felt so much respect. . . . Looking around him, he saw the wild dress and appearance of his Highland

> associates, heard their whispers in an uncouth and unknown language, looked upon his own dress, so unlike that which he had worn from his infancy, and wished to awake from what seemed . . . a dream, strange and terrible, and unnatural. (333)

For a while, Waverley has represented the intersection of two cultures and historical stages within himself, but now this ambivalence unsettles him—his lately acquired Highland features seem increasingly alien to him, and the lost unity of his identity has to be restored.[54] Increasingly disenchanted with, and suspicious of, his Gaelic comrades, he eventually dismisses his Highland attendant and hires a servant from Edinburgh (365), apparently because a Lowlander seems less alien to him than a Gael, and thus more trustworthy. Edward's appreciation of English virtues also increases, for instance when he endorses Talbot's approach to military activity, which is "in every point" that of "the English soldier," as opposed to the apparently inferior approaches of Fergus and the Baron (365). When Talbot advises Edward to leave the Jacobite army as soon as possible, he again clothes this matter in the symbolic language of dress: "Unplaid yourself on the first opportunity" (388). Lacking such an opportunity, Edward perforce remains highlandized for a while, so that eventually he "equalled any Highlander in the endurance of fatigue, and was become somewhat acquainted with their language" (389). After a quarrel with Fergus, however, Edward takes the first step to complement his inward de-gaelicization by an outward one. When the Jacobites left Edinburgh, he initially intended to follow the custom of English military elites and ride on horseback, but was immediately pursuaded to follow Fergus's example and march on foot at the head of his clan (320). Now, however, Edward mounts a horse and decides to ask the Baron for a place in his regiment (393), that is, he leaves the innermost of the Russian dolls of otherness, de-highlandizes himself, and joins a Lowland troop, which is culturally closer to his English roots. As Buzard puts it: "Waverley undertakes the ethnographer's double journey: he undergoes immersion in the alien culture in order to achieve a greater . . . withdrawal from it, to that final distance from which one can assert authoritative apprehension of the whole."[55]

After the reconciliation with Fergus, Edward joins the Gaelic infantry once more, but now this apparently stems more from personal affection for Fergus than from a primitivist romanticization of Gaelic culture (408)—essentially, Waverley has become an outsider again. This process is completed after his separation from the Jacobite army and his ultimate reintegration into the English establishment. Nonetheless, even after the final pacification of the country, he retains at least some Highland habits, which can now be relished in a peaceful, harmless context. He clings to the Highland custom of traveling on foot when he journeys through Scotland, and the narrator reemphasizes that "his campaign had considerably strengthened his constitution, and improved his habits of enduring fatigue" (432). Residues of Waverley's hybridity and partial Gaelicness are reinvoked shortly before Fergus's execution, when the chief implores Edward: "You are rich, . . . and . . . generous. When you hear of these poor Mac-Ivors being distressed . . . by some harsh overseer or agent of government, remember you have worn their tartan, and are an adopted son of their race" (472). Fergus asks Waverley to alleviate Gaelic suffering by the only method which remains possible: through alms given by a man who had once been one of them, but now acts from the position of a paternalistically benevolent, wealthy English outsider who is not persecuted by the government, unlike many Scottish leaders. Edward honors Fergus's plea.

Through these developments, cultural hybridity loses much of its subversive potential and survives only in a politically neutralized form, as part of an essentially unionist, assimilative, and thus arguably "internally colonialist" vision.

The End of Otherness? Unionist and Hanoverian Conclusions

Waverley cements this ultimately pro-establishment message by emphatically suggesting that the victory of unionism, Hanoverianism, assimilation, and progress was inevitable. This is already evident in the childhood metaphor which implies an inescapable growing-up. The inevitability of "progress" is also expressed in the suggestion that the flaws of Gaelic traditions and Jacobitism made them self-destructive, or so destructive for the rest of society that their disappearance was necessary.

Clanship must disappear because it is destructive to the national community: it makes people unreliable patriots, as their loyalties to the crown are always indirect and mediated through the chief. Clansmen are loyal to a king as long as the chief commands them to be, but can turn swiftly into insurgents if the chief changes his mind. This is also noted by Waverley's Lowland servant Alick: "there's mony o' them wadna mind a bawbee the weising a ball through the Prince himsell, an the Chief gae them the wink" (395). The disruptive force of clanship also creates rivalries within the Jacobite camp, whose smallness in the face of a far more numerous enemy means that any additional problems arising from internal fragmentation are disastrous (e.g., 399). The heterogeneity of this army is underlined through language, in a Babelian confusion of Scots, Gaelic, French, and English: "The Baron lectured, the Chieftain stormed, the Highlanders screamed in Gaelic, the horsemen cursed and swore in Lowland Scotch" (398). The confusion becomes even more hilarious when the Prince commands a French officer to call the Scottish troops to order—the Frenchman speaks none of the local languages sufficiently well, so that the soldiers can barely understand his commands (399–400): "'Messieurs les sauvages Ecossois—dat is—gentilmans savages, have the goodness d'arranger vous.' The Gaels, comprehending the order more from the gesture than from the words . . . hastened to dress their ranks" (400). Notably, when the Frenchman addresses the Lowlanders, he varies his address from "gentilmans savages" to "Gentilmans cavalry" (400), reflecting the widespread perception that Lowlanders were less barbaric than Gaels. Presumably it is just as well for the Jacobite army's discipline that the Gaels have *not* understood the Frenchman's words: had they realized that he called them "savages," they might have created further uproar in indignation, instead of obeying the order. The linguistic cacophony is metonymic of the general heterogeneity of pre-Union Scotland or pre-Culloden Britain. Destroying clanship and at least partly assimilating Scotland is inevitable if British nation-building is ever to be completed.

The fated and partly self-destructive nature of the Gaels is also reflected in a lack of successful love stories, of marriages, and of children. In Macpherson's Ossian, one reason why the "Dark Age" Gaelic heroes die out is the fact that their "mating patterns were too destructive."[56] In *Waverley* there is no successful Gaelic mating either: Evan loves Alice, but is executed before serious wooing can take place. Fergus is denied even the (by bourgeois romantic standards unsatisfactory) feudal dynastic marriage he desires; death without heirs awaits him instead. His sister highlights the exchange of the one for the other while she works on his shroud: "I am sewing his bridal-garment" (469). Flora herself asserts from the beginning that her heart is not bent on marriage at all, as she lives only for the Stuart cause (214). After Jacobitism's final defeat she seals her—and her whole lineage's—fate of infertility and heirlessness by retiring to a convent.

The extinction of the Mac-Ivor chieftainly line is also linked to the devastations which its clan (and by implicit extension, Gaeldom in general) has wrought upon its non-Gaelic compatriots: for centuries, Mac-Ivor chiefs when close to death have been visited by the ghost of a Lowlander killed by one of their ancestors. Fergus is no exception and sees the ghost before his capture by government forces and his resulting execution. That this ghost is a Lowlander might be significant. It appears as if the sins which generations of Highlanders have committed against their Lowland neighbors and against the peace of the realm are being revenged upon them. This national dimension is emphasized in connection with Fergus's own death as the last of his line and one of the last traditional Highland chieftains. This element of revenge, now completed with the death of the "last of the race," is hinted at when Fergus asks the ghost: "art thou come to . . . enjoy thy triumph in the fall of the last descendant of thine enemy!" (473).

While earlier sections of this novel give much space to plurality, and even show it respect, in the end none of this plurality escapes the now ubiquitously valid and enforced law of the British state. This is made clear by the proclamation of the verdict over Fergus and Evan, which carefully takes in every single one of their multiple names: "Fergus Mac-Ivor of Glennaquoich, otherwise called Vich Ian Vohr, and Evan Mac-Ivor, in the Dhu of

Tarrascleugh, otherwise called Evan Dhu, otherwise called Evan Maccombich, or Evan Dhu Maccombich—you, and each of you, stand attainted of high treason" (464–65). Although the narrator condemns the mercilessness of the law against Fergus, this condemnation is uttered not in the name of Highland difference, but in the name of British national unity: "Such was the reasoning of those times, held even by . . . humane men towards a vanquished enemy. Let us . . . hope that, in this respect . . . , we shall never see the scenes, or hold the sentiments, that were general in Britain Sixty Years Since" (464). One negative aspect of the Union was the extension of the harsh English law on high treason to Scotland, whose own legislation on the subject had been less cruel (474)—in this respect, Scotland seems to have been more civilized than England and was forced to regress into more primitive practices by its southern neighbor. However, unified Britain can again ascend on the scale of civilization and mercy after the country has been sufficiently pacified: Fergus prophesies that the harsh treason law will be abolished "when there are no longer any wild Highlanders to benefit by its tender mercies—they will blot it from their records, as levelling them with a nation of cannibals" (474).

The "vanishing race" is not the only motif *Waverley* has in common with Macpherson's Ossian. A related trope, likewise used by both, is the imagery of ruins: when Waverley contemplates Fergus's and the Baron's loss of position—and potentially also of life—he worries about "those who clung for support to these fallen columns, Rose and Flora" (429).[57] Another metaphor shared by the two authors, and by various later nineteenth-century writers on Celticity, is twilight: "the success at Falkirk had thrown a faint and setting gleam over the arms of the Chevalier" (429).[58] The gleam implies a certain amount of moral luster which indicates that historical change, though unavoidable and ultimately beneficial, also entails regrettable losses. Stafford suggests that this very "ability to accept the inevitability of change, while retaining a deep affection for the superseded, . . . made Scott's work so influential in the nineteenth century."[59]

Apart from Fergus, his clan has another "last of the race" figure in Edward Waverley, since he, though not a native Gael, was temporarily an "adopted" one. Like Macpherson's Ossian, Waverley stands at the interface between clashing historical periods and cultures, and survives the death of his companions. Edward's perspective, however, is less bleak, as he is not a full member of the vanished Gaelic world and can thus reemerge from his Highland phase into his modern English self, surviving as part of the new order with a happy future and offspring.

Besides clanship, another Other which must disappear is Jacobitism, whose mid-eighteenth century manifestations are referred to as "that unhappy period" (159) by the narrator. Jacobitism is likewise presented as self-destructive, for instance when, elated by their victories, Jacobite soldiers fire their guns at random in celebration and one bullet grazes Flora's temple. Though she, in equal high spirits, dismisses the injury as unimportant

(358–59) and thus comes off as laudably high-minded, the incident also highlights a negative trait of Jacobitism, presenting its followers as so imprudent that they disregard the safety of people from their own party, and even their own lives. Further critique is expressed through ironic treatment of the Stuarts' claim to royal authority, and of the Jacobites' hopes that they would fare better under the old dynasty than under the new. The Stuarts' support for Britain's Jacobites is exposed as a sham, consisting of little more than grand empty gestures (159). After the Prince's arrival, there is an overinflation of high-sounding titles without substance, and of high-ranking military commanders without enough troops to direct (e.g., 286–87, 297–98, 322, 356). *Waverley* also deconstructs the Jacobite notion that the contemporary Stuarts were more native to Britain than the originally German House of Hanover, and had more affection for their Scottish subjects than the Hanoverians had. The deconstruction of these ideas is most obvious when the Stuart Prince as a skilled diplomat tries to pacify internal quarrels in his army:

> Charles Edward . . . rode to the head of the Mac-Ivors, threw himself from his horse, . . . marched about half-mile along with them, inquiring into the history and connections of Sliochd nan Ivor, adroitly using the few words of Gaelic he possessed and *affecting* a great desire to learn it more thoroughly. He then mounted his horse once more, and galloped to the Baron's cavalry, . . . examined their state of discipline; . . . enquired after their ladies . . . ; rode about an hour with the Baron . . . , and *endured* three long stories. . . . "Ah, Beaujeu, mon cher ami," said he as he returned to his usual place . . . , "que mon métier de prince errant est ennuyant, par fois . . . ."[60] (402–3, italics mine)

This is tactical transculturalism: the Prince pretends interest in the cultures and concerns of all his subjects because he presently needs their support to establish his power. He talks to all of them about what interests them most: genealogy for the Gaels, discipline and ladies for the Lowlanders—a difference which again shows the latter's higher civilization.[61] But in truth he remains a foreigner. His usual place is with the French friend he has brought from exile. French is the language in which he feels most comfortable and reveals his true feelings. This debunks the myth of Stuart nativeness, showing the Prince as just another power-mongering hypocritical foreign politician. In fact, he is portrayed as being *more* foreign than King George, who in Talbot's description is not a German outsider, but a scion of a dynasty gone native: "*my* prince can be as generous as *yours*. I do not pretend . . . that he confers favour with all the foreign graces . . . of your Chevalier errant; but he has the plain English manner" (456, italics Scott's).

When Flora laments the debased state of the disaffected Scottish elites, she hopes for "a brighter day . . . when a Scottish country-gentleman may be a scholar without . . . pedantry . . . ; a sportsman without . . . low habits . . . ; and a judicious improver of his property without becoming a boorish two-legged steer" (183). For her, this future is linked to the restoration of the Stuarts. The narrator, by contrast, implies that even the hopes of the Jacobites are ultimately fulfilled by the Hanoverian triumph, so that there can be no just qualms left to smolder among the populace: "Thus did Flora prophesy a revolution, which time indeed has produced, but in a manner very different from what she had in mind" (183).

After the Jacobite peril is neutralized, as many (ex-)Jacobites as possible are reintegrated into the victorious body politic. Their political motivations are downplayed and substituted with more excusable ones. The Whig Major Melville makes a statement which proves prophetic for the respective fates of Fergus and Waverley, and for the future rehabilitation of other (ex-)Jacobites who had merely been misguided: "He whom . . . hope of personal advantage, has led to disturb the peace . . . , let him fall a victim to the laws; but . . . youth, misled by the wild visions of chivalry and imaginary loyalty, may plead for pardon" (252). In Edward's case, the excuse for rehabilitation is his youth and romantic reading. Most clan commoners are—as often in romantic Highlandism—exculpated as victims of misplaced loyalty for their blameworthy chiefs, by whose "arbitrary authority" they had been "forced into the field" (323). Numerous characters became Jacobites for all sorts of reasons *except* for political ones. Many are desperadoes who feel that they have no other choice: Waverley himself is barred from a lawful career in the right army due to ungrounded government suspicion (e.g., 350). Another Jacobite soldier hopes to pay off his debts with the money his laird pays him for military service (288). A farmer follows his laird to war in order to ensure the renewal of his land lease (289); and a jealous lover joined the Jacobites because his sweetheart danced with a Hanoverian soldier (365). The Jacobite side also includes Englishmen with "broken" fortunes and nothing to lose (390), and an Edinburgh woman who sympathizes with the Stuart cause because she is so taken with the dashing, gentlemanly Highland soldiers (307, 430–31). Later, readers are told that her case was symptomatic: "The ladies . . . of Scotland very generally espoused the cause of the gallant and handsome young Prince, who threw himself upon the mercy of his countrymen, rather like a hero of romance than a calculating politician" (312).[62] *Waverley* exculpates most Jacobite characters from political guilt, emphasizing that they could just as easily become good Hanoverian subjects—and soon did so, as history had shown in the intervening "Sixty Years." Talbot observes:

> So many unfortunate gentlemen . . . [were] lately in arms against the Government. . . . Their treason . . . is . . . arising from mistaken virtue, and therefore cannot be classed as a disgrace, though . . . highly criminal. Where the guilty are so numerous, clemency must be extended to far the greater number. (424)

The majority of Highlanders are vindicated because it is assumed that they were primitive and unenlightened, and thus not fully responsible for having chosen the wrong course of action—unlike the more civilized chief Fergus: "that he was enlightened and accomplished made his crime the less excusable. . . . He had been the means of bringing many hundreds of men into the field who, without him, would never have broken the peace" (463). Scott's "General Preface" to the 1829 edition of the Waverley novels again reflects on the exculpation and recent rehabilitation of Highlanders:

> The sufferers of that melancholy period have, during the last and present reign, been honoured both with the sympathy and protection of the reigning family, whose magnanimity can well pardon a sigh from others, and bestow one themselves to the memory of brave opponents, who did nothing in hate, but all in honour. (530)

After the most dangerous elements of mid-eighteenth-century British society are eliminated (Highland clanship, the vestiges of Lowland Scottish feudalism, and the principal Jacobite leaders), the United Kingdom can finally complete the process of national integration and build a better future characterized by progress, law and order, and an internally peaceful civil society.[63] Of course, progress also entails certain losses: the Jacobite party "has now almost entirely vanished . . . , and with it . . . , much absurd political prejudice—but also many . . . examples of loyalty which they received from their fathers, and of old Scottish faith, hospitality, worth, and honour" (492). Several colorful and picturesque Scottish customs have also been lost.[64] But when gains and losses are weighed against each other, the end of romance ultimately appears as a good thing. This, at least, is the opinion of the protagonist, and perhaps also of the narrator, when Waverley "felt, in . . . confidence and mental dignity, a compensation for the gay dreams which . . . experience had . . . dissolved" (432–33). The end of the clan system also inspires relief, as the modern forms of social organization which supplant it appear—at least on the whole—less cruel, less arbitrary, and more humane.[65]

The humaneness of the new order is highlighted by Rose's position. Her critique of the rising is not based on political motivations, but on personal ones—she is only interested in the safety of those she loves (219–20), which is endangered by any kind of civil war. This is why she, already at the start of the rebellion, writes a letter to Waverley which expresses her longing for a settled civil society after the English model: "I hope . . . you will get safe home to England, where you used to tell me there was no military violence nor fighting among clans permitted, but everything was done according to an equal law that protected all who were harmless and innocent" (220, also see 221). The Baron represents the old Scotland, with its feudal spirit, militancy, and Jacobitism, whereas Rose represents the new Scotland, eager for modern law and order. Significantly, her enthusiasm for civil society has been aroused by the Englishman Waverley, who can be said to have colonized her mind and later marries her in a symbolic reiteration of the Treaty of Union.

The unionist national allegory can also be discerned in Waverley's worry that, after the Jacobites' defeat, Fergus and the Baron can no longer protect and support their female dependents Flora and Rose. Thus, Edward thinks about his own role: "It might be still his fate to supply the want of those guardians they had lost" (429). Scotland has lost its own native sovereigns and feudal elites, but is adopted by the paternalistically benevolent superior power of England which becomes Scotland's guardian. Any kindness now bestowed on the Scots is bestowed on English terms, at the discretion of the hegemonic south: the Hanoverian dynasty grants pardons to some ex-rebels like the Baron; Waverley and Talbot buy the forfeited Bradwardine estate and later restore it to its previous owner; Waverley marries and supports Rose as well as giving substantial alms to the survivors of Clan Mac-Ivor. English superiority and seniority are also reflected in the fact that Rose and Edward's first son will inherit the English estates, while their second son will inherit the Scottish possessions—this reiterates a metaphor of regional hierarchy which is at least as old as Geoffrey of Monmouth, who had depicted Britain's eponymous founding father Brutus as dividing the island among his sons, giving England to the oldest and Scotland to the youngest one.[66]

In *Waverley*, both Highland and Lowland Scotland come under English guardianship, but the Lowlands are accepted on more lenient and more equal terms, though not *entirely* equal ones. Fergus, representative of Highland feudalism and Jacobitism, must be executed; but the Baron, representative of Lowland feudalism, is soon reintegrated into society and regains his estate. The shared Saxonness of the Lowland Scots and the English is conducive to British integration.[67] The different degrees to which Gael and *Gall* are amenable to cultivation are also reflected in the names of the female protagonists. Flora's name evokes not only the Jacobite heroine Flora MacDonald, but also the entirety of plant life, the flora. This might be taken to signify nature: full of splendor and grandeur, but untameable. The rose, by contrast, is only one particular kind of plant, and mainly associated with domesticated garden flowers rather than wild varieties. Moreover, it is the heraldic flower of England. All this underlines Rose Bradwardine's receptiveness to English standards of cultivation. The colonizing impetus in this marriage is captured in Talbot's comment on Waverley's change of affection from Flora to Rose: "simplicity may be improved, but pride and conceit never" (426). Again, this can be interpreted as a national allegory on the relative virtues and "civilizability" of Highlands and Lowlands.

Although the wedding between Rose and Edward casts feminized Scotland as the officially subordinate and weaker partner, at second glance she is revealed to be quite resourceful and in control, sometimes even more so than Edward, for instance when it comes to light that she was secretly responsible for his rescue from captivity among outlaws and for the healing of his injuries. She has saved his life and for a while clandestinely steered it (446–50).[68]

This role of being officially the subordinate, female, weaker partner, but unofficially in charge, parallels the way in which Scotland's role in the Union has often been evaluated: supposedly the weaker partner, but actually playing important roles, for instance in Britain's government and administration under the Earl of Bute and his protegés, and in overseas imperialism.

The Union envisaged by Scott need not entail *complete* assimilation: instead of a total leveling of differences, he wants (and thinks it possible) to balance the preservation of selected differences against peaceful amalgamation and progress. But this willingness to respect selected differences is inextricably related to the fact that difference no longer poses a danger.[69] When the Baron regains his estate, it is no longer a feudal barony but an untitled property bought with money. He "has been 'restored' as an antique among antiquities, . . . a 'figurehead.' . . . Bradwardine becomes at the new Tully-Veolan the prisoner of a feudal 'Scotland' he is made to embody."[70] The neutralization of the Baron's eccentricities can also be read as a national allegory: "His absurdities, which had appeared grotesquely ludicrous during his prosperity, seemed, in the sunset of his fortune, to be harmonised and assimilated with the noble features of his character, so as to add peculiarity without exciting ridicule" (450). Again, the sunset imagery also seems to symbolize the decline of an entire sociocultural system. But Edward's example suggests that some of the laudable old values which are endangered by progress can be detached from their original cultural and historical matrix, to be grafted onto representatives of the new order—perhaps especially onto young people who are more open-minded, impressionable, and flexible than their older, more irreconcilable compatriots. The youth of such hybridized mediator figures also symbolizes hope for the future.[71]

Eventually, even extreme instances of otherness like Jacobitism and Gaeldom, previously so harmful that they had to be uprooted, can be partially integrated into the new nation—but only in a form which neutralizes both the threatening aspects of otherness and the gruesomeness of the conquest. One strategy for neutralizing the Jacobite and Gaelic peril lies in the multiple time frames of *Waverley*: the past in which the action is set is not just once, but twice removed from the time when the novel reached its first audiences. This temporal distance strengthens the sense of containment. The novel was published in 1814, while the date of the narration is 1805, and the main action is set in 1745. "From the beginning, then, the reader is conscious that a lost world is being . . . reconstructed and that the gulf dividing him from the period under discussion is bridgeable only in imagination."[72] The intervening years seemed to have shown that history was on the side of the Lowlanders and Hanoverians.[73] The implications of the subtitle "'Tis Sixty Years Since" are ambiguous. On the one hand, it gives immediacy, suggesting that it is *only* sixty years since parts of Scotland were so unsettled and barbarous. On the other hand, the dangerous aspects of this otherness have now disappeared, and only the temporal distance makes it safe to relish them.[74]

Further containment takes place on the level of plot. The circular structure of this novel means that gaelicization and political dissent are only a passing episode in Waverley's life which is overcome before the story ends. Protagonist and readers are only temporarily swept away into Highland romance and a "backward" stage of social development, until both return to a dynamic, modernizing world in which they can function as loyal pro-Hanoverian British subjects. Even the Gaelic characters seem already once removed from their traditions: Flora can be seen as a revivalist of a waning cultural heritage.[75]

The effect of celebrating and commemorating vanishing traditions while firmly containing them in the past is reinforced in the postscript.[76] The postscript also makes clear that remembering the past can contribute to the ideological affirmation of the present. Helping readers of Scott's own time to recall how different and "primitive" their country had recently been underlines the huge development which happened in the meantime, thus nourishing pride in the progress made:

> The effects of the insurrection of 1745—the destruction of the patriarchal power of the Highland chiefs—the abolition of the heritable jurisdictions of the Lowland nobility . . .—the total eradication of the Jacobite party, which, averse to intermingle with the English, or adopt their customs, long continued to pride themselves upon maintaining ancient Scottish manners and customs—commenced this innovation. The . . . influx of wealth, and extension of commerce, have since united to render the present people of Scotland . . . different from their grandfathers. . . . We are not aware of the progress we have made, until we fix our eye on the now distant point from which we have been drifted. (492)

Highlanders are appropriated by the mainstream "as museum pieces for the appreciation and self-comprehension of those who are supposed to have left them behind."[77]

The unionist "museumization" of history also requires that the atrocities committed by the Hanoverian regime to suppress Jacobitism and clanship must be silenced or at least softened. There is no direct description of the Battle of Culloden and the harsh penalty measures inflicted on the Gaidhealtachd during its aftermath. The only glimpse of the effects of penalty measures in rural Scotland is restricted to the Lowlands, which were less seriously affected. We see the Baron expropriated, outlawed, and in hiding, but he does not suffer too badly and is eventually reintegrated into society without serious losses—while in reality such lenience was apparently never shown to people who had participated in both the 1715 and the 1745 rebellion. Scott also softens or rewrites history in the court scene when Evan is offered a pardon in exchange for pleading that he only rebelled on his chief's orders, not of his own accord—an offer he refuses (466). In reality, there were indeed clansmen who tried to achieve a pardon by pleading that they had been coerced into rebellion, but the courts did not accept such pleas. Scott's fictionalization of history presents the clansmen as more loyal to their chiefs, and the laws as more lenient, than they really were. Another silencing occurs when Fergus forbids Waverley to attend his execution—as a result, the reader does not get a direct, detailed impression of the scene either. If such a description had been included, the extremely cruel methods used in the execution of Jacobite leaders—hanging, drawing, and quartering—might have created so much empathy in readers that it might have damaged the novel's project of affirming the Hanoverian order.[78] Historical horrors are largely neutralized and softened into historical or personal romance. One such neutralization occurs after Fergus's execution:

> The impression of horror with which Waverley left Carlisle, softened . . . into melancholy, . . . accelerated by the painful, yet soothing, task of writing to Rose; and, while he could not suppress his own feelings of the calamity, by endeavouring to place it in a light which might grieve her, without shocking her imagination. The picture which he drew for her benefit he gradually familiarized to his own mind, and his next letters were more cheerful, and referred to the . . . peace and happiness which lay before them. (478)[79]

History and tradition can also be neutralized by transforming them into safely contained, decontextualized museum pieces. This happens not only through the time structure and the conception of *Waverley* as a historical novel, but also on the level of plot. Edward museumizes Gaelic culture when he, after leaving the Jacobite army, decides to preserve the Highland dress and arms he wore on campaign. This is partly because he regards them as objects of curiosity (428). During his time as an adopted Gael, he used them as objects of daily wear, but now these things are re-othered by a newly de-gaelicized Waverley who regards them as exotic objects of wonder. His second reason for preserving them lies in their being a souvenir of his friend Fergus (428). Soon after, the re-englishized Waverley is asked by a fellow Englishman who has no firsthand knowledge of Gaelic culture to give some specimen, and manages to "satisfy his curiosity by whistling a pibroch, dancing a strathspey, and singing a Highland song" (428–29). Later, it is reported that the young English onlooker has been "seized with a tartan fit ever since" (490). Now that the Highland army is no longer a danger to England, this Englishman can develop romantic curiosity and enthusiasm for the Highlanders' culture. Elements of that culture are conveyed to him not by full immersion (e.g., by a Highland journey of his own), or even by a real expatriate Highlander, but by Waverley, a non-dangerous Englishman who is no Other himself, but has sufficient knowledge of the Other to act as a cultural mediator by giving harmless snippets of Gaelic culture in a perfectly safe anglophone environment.

Further museumization occurs when the characters celebrate the restoration of Tully-Veolan manor to Rose's father. A shadow of the feudal customs witnessed at previous Glennaquoich scenes is preserved—but no more than a shadow: the fountain is filled with brandy instead of water to give the "lower orders" a share in the festivities. However, this is emphatically "for that night only" (490), in implicit contrast to the more imprudent, because more frequent, entertainment of the lower orders which *Highland* tradition had demanded of feudal elites and about which Fergus had complained. Post-Culloden Scotland preserves a hint of its feudal traditions, but only to a limited extent which does not impede capitalist economizing and modern estate management.

Museumization can also be seen in the decorations which, at the end of the novel, grace the refurbished house at Tully-Veolan. The arms which Edward wore as a soldier are now just a wall ornament. A portrait of Waverley and Fergus in Highland dress, with clansmen and mountain scenery in the background, has been painted by a London artist after a sketch that was made of the two friends while on campaign in Edinburgh (489). Thus, the picture gives some representation of Gaelic tradition and Jacobite history, but it is several times removed from reality: even when the sketch was taken, the wild mountains can not have been there, as the drawing was made in the Lowland capital. The final painting was executed even further from the Highlands, in London. Moreover, the depicted past has in the meantime been contained by the realities of the Hanoverian victory: Fergus and traditional chieftainship are dead, and the clansmen shown in the background will march to rebellion no more. The painting eclipses the unpleasant aspects of both the recent past and the present of Highland experience, such as Fergus's execution and life under the penalty measures. Only by eclipsing these nasty details, and focusing on the picturesque and noble (pretty plaids, handsome young friends), can the portrait be aesthetically enjoyable: though beholders may shed a few tears for the late Fergus, the aesthetics are not marred by overly upsetting details about his execution.[80]

While the novel presents a partisan rewriting of history which silences many problematic aspects, it could also be argued that the way in which such rewritings (e.g., the portrait) are described, and the narratorial ironies which deconstruct romanticizations, at least show a metatextual awareness which draws attention to the fact that such images of the past are not necessarily realistic but may show a significant degree of partiality, artificiality, conjecture, and remoteness from the reality they purportedly represent.[81]

Nonetheless, it seems to have been the containing, unionist, and colonizing aspects of *Waverley* which played an important part in ensuring this novel a favorable reception at the time, and a lasting influence on the depiction of colonized peoples in Britain and overseas. Many readers praised *Waverley* as a remarkably accurate description of culture and history.[82] Several early reviews drew on Enlightenment theories of history and on the "contemporary ancestor" theme, praising Scott's novel for illustrating earlier stages of society which in the Highlands, and partly even the Lowlands, seemed just a few decades away, whereas in the rest of Europe they might have been gone for centuries. The *Edinburgh Review* commented:

> [The 1745 rebellion] brought . . . to light . . . for the last time, the fading image of feudal chivalry in the mountains, and vulgar fanaticism in the plains; and startled the more polished parts of the land with the wild but brilliant picture of the devoted valour, incorruptible fidelity, patriarchal brotherhood, and savage habits, of the Celtic Clans on the one hand,—and the dark, untractable . . . bigotry of the Covenanters on the other. Both forms of society had indeed been prevalent in the other parts of the country,—but had there been so long superseded by more peaceable habits, and milder manners, that their vestiges were almost effaced, and their very memory nearly forgotten. . . . When the . . . central Highlands . . . were opened up to the gaze of the English, it seemed as if they were carried back to the days of the Heptarchy;—when they saw the . . . West-country Whigs, they might imagine themselves transported to the age of Cromwell. The effect, indeed, is almost as startling at the present moment; and one great source of the interest which the [novel] . . . possess[es], is . . . the surprise . . . that in our own country, and almost in our own age, manners and characters existed . . . which we had been accustomed to consider as belonging to remote antiquity, or extravagant romance.[83]

Waverley was praised as an authentic ethnographic document, not only on customs and mentalities of the past, but also—at least to some extent—on those of the present:

> The object of the work . . . was evidently to present a faithful . . . picture of the manners and state of society that prevailed in this northern part of the island, in the earlier part of the last century; . . . and . . . the basis of almost all that was peculiar in the national character. . . . The . . . delineation has been made from actual experience and observation; . . . [though] perhaps only . . . [of] a few surviving relics and specimens of what was familiar a little earlier—but generalized from instances sufficiently numerous and complete, to warrant all that may have been added to the portrait. . . . The great traits of Clannish dependence, pride, and fidelity, may still be detected in many districts of the Highlands, though they do not now adhere to the chieftains when they mingle in general society; and the existing contentions of Burghers and Antiburghers, and Cameronians, though shrunk into comparative insignificance . . . may still be referred to, as complete verifications of all that is here stated. . . . The traits of the Scottish

> national character [as depicted in the novel] can still less be regarded as antiquated.[84]

Concerning the faithfulness of the novel's ethnographic account of Highlanders, the reviewer further singles out the "gradations of the Celtic character, from . . . savage imperturbability of . . . [one] who stalks about with a battle-axe on his shoulder, to . . . lively unprincipled activity . . . coarse unreflecting hardihood and heroism . . . and . . . pride, gallantry, elegance and ambition."[85] Another contemporary reviewer called *Waverley* "a vehicle of curious accurate information upon a subject which must . . . command our attention—the history and manners of a . . . large and renowned portion of the inhabitants of these islands; of a race who, within these few years, have vanished from the face of their native land."[86] Since the Gaels are here claimed as part of the national community, possessing some knowledge about them is considered a duty of every British subject. This might be interpreted as an act of discursive conquest. Like Waverley and the narrator, many readers expressed relief that the upheavals of national hyper-heterogeneity and civil war had been left behind.[87] Katie Trumpener lucidly observes the links between the discursive internal colonization of Scotland and the colonization of other peoples overseas:

> Scott's historical novel, with its stress on historical progress, . . . won out as the paradigmatic novel of empire, appealing to nationalist, imperialist, and colonial readers alike. For Scott insists simultaneously on the self-enclosed character of indigenous societies (living idyllically, if anachronistically, outside of historical time), on the inevitability with which such societies are forcibly brought into history, and on the survival of cultural distinctiveness even after a loss of political autonomy. As he enacts and explains the composition of Britain as an internal empire, Scott underlines the ideological capaciousness of empire . . . and argues for the continued centrality of national identity as a component of imperial identity.
>
> Throughout the nineteenth century, . . . in the . . . British overseas colonies, the Anglo–Celtic model of literary nationalism that arose in response to British internal colonialism . . . helps ensure that cultural nationalism (as long as it separates cultural expression from political sovereignty) can be contained within an imperial framework.[88]

This helps to explain why Scott's Waverley novels were among the most widely circulated books throughout the nineteenth-century British Empire.[89] Macpherson's and Scott's descriptions of Gaels had a strong influence on "dying race" literature in more obviously colonial contexts overseas, for instance on James Fenimore Cooper's *Last of the Mohicans* (1826), one of the first treatments of the "last of the race" motif that used "race" in the modern sense of cultural and physical differences between sections of the human species.[90] Cooper's America and romantic-era Scotland both saw the increasingly successful establishment of a (white or Lowland/anglicized) mainstream, so that it became possible to look on the marginalization of indigenous (Native American or Gaelic) culture with mixed feelings which also included guilt and romanticism. In both cases, the disappearance of native culture was claimed to be inevitable, though somewhat tragic. The mainstreams had no local ancestry to root them in the newly conquered soil, placate occasional pangs of conqueror's guilt, and legitimate their rule. In both countries, selected elements of marginalized indigenous cultures were appropriated and romanticized to partially "nativize" the colonizers and validate their supremacy on those territories.[91] Another white North American author whose portrayal of Native Americans is comparable to Scott's portrait of Gaels is the Canadian Thomas H. Raddall.[92]

However, there are also differences between Scott's portrayal of Gaels and North American authors' portrayals of Native Americans. For Scott, the difference between Gaels and anglophone Britons is linguistic and cultural, but not racial in the modern sense. Moreover, while all these authors show regret *and* relief about the decline of indigenous cultures, the proportions of these feelings seem different: in white American literature, relief seems stronger and regret somewhat weaker than in Scott.[93]

Such differences in nuancing notwithstanding, *Waverley* is another anglophone Scottish text about Highlanders which, despite its relatively positive portrayal of the Other, can be read as part of a colonial discourse tradition which stretches (in time) all the way back to classical antiquity and (in space) all the way to America and other parts of the modern British Empire. However, not all romanticizations of Highlanders through colonial discourse tropes have been constructed by colonizing outsiders: the same tropes have been used by Gaelic-speaking or Highland authors themselves, in ways which could either be regarded as submission and self-colonization or as subtle tactics of adaptation, self-advancement, and subversion.[94]

In romantic thought, "Celts were no longer unwanted aliens . . . to British civic society," but "the picturesque representations of both the heroic bedrock and finer feelings of that society."[95] The very success of the "civilizing" missions had made this possible. However, this was not the last word: in the further course of the nineteenth century, social developments created anxieties about whether the civilizing project had miscarried. These setbacks were not blamed on the new social order, but on the Gaels themselves. Voices which insisted on the lingering otherness and inferiority of the Celt again became louder, and were now often linked to a new branch of social and anthropological science: race theory. These developments are explored in the next chapter.

Chapter 5

Of Celts and Teutons

Racial Biology and Anti-Gaelic Discourse, ca. 1780–1860

Neither the progressivism of the Enlightenment nor romantic Celticism died out during the nineteenth century.[1] But they now were complemented by a third discursive strand, which came to run parallel with (and partly also intermingled) with them: older cultural stereotypes solidified into biologistic racial typology. This is not to imply that these accounts were *only* preoccupied with biological, that is, physical, characteristics, or that biology was already a fully developed "scientific" discipline in the modern sense. For instance, not all nineteenth-century race discourse attempted to substantiate its claims with (quasi-)"scientific" quantitative data, head measurements, and so on; even the anatomist Robert Knox rather relies on philosophical, historical, and cultural reflections. The same applies to many other thinkers on the subject. Moreover, despite the component of physicality and heredity, the question of just how predetermined and static the bodily and mental features of "races" really were—for example in relation to intermixture and evolution—was answered differently by different thinkers.[2] Nonetheless, race theory did assume *some* form of physical basis (hereditary character, coloring, physiognomy, etc.) which could supposedly be connected to sociocultural issues, and this makes notions of cultural difference, development, and hierarchy more inflexible than before. Initially, racialization entailed a more pessimistic view of Celticity. Enlightened progressivism thought the center superior over the "primitive" periphery, but was confident that even the latter had great potential for improvement. Romanticism saw at least some "primitive" features as noble and worthy of conservation, but—somewhat wistfully—shared the belief that development was possible, and already happening. Racism called the feasibility of civilizing missions into question. It shared Enlightenment beliefs in metropolitan preeminence and primitive inferiority, but doubted that "primitive" peoples could ever assimilate to metropolitan standards. Cultural boundaries and hierarchies seemed much more immutable.[3] This justified prevailing social inequalities; for instance, even where colonized populations appeared to have been somewhat "improved" or "domesticated" by empire, it was declared that their underlying "racial inferiority" still made them unfit for parity and rule.

Teutonist History, Economic Change, and Public Opinion

Although race theory often doubts the possibility of civilizing missions, the origins of anti-Celtic racism in Scotland lay in a period when the "civilizability" and integration of the Gaels into the mainstream seemed highly probable and already underway, that is, the late eighteenth century. In fact, sometimes it was these very successes which sparked anti-Celtic sentiments, as several Lowlanders felt that the Ossianic hype, the fame of Highland regiments, and the transformation of Highland iconography into pan-national symbols threatened to marginalize Lowland Scottish traditions and achievements. Several non-Gaelic Scottish intellectuals reacted by reaffirming older notions about the negative traits of Gaelic mentality and its irredeemable otherness. The increasing hybridization of the former Other and its successful entry into the mainstream created anxiety among the mainstream's "older" occupants about a potential loss of their superiority. The "old mainstreamers" from the Lowlands—long used to being the "superior" part of Scotland's population, and also integrated into the pan-British mainstream for slightly longer—reacted by reaffirming the very difference that was in fact disappearing, portraying the Gaels as *incorrigibly* alien.

The Lowland antiquarian and philologist John Jamieson (1759–1838) and the Orcadian historian Malcolm Laing (1762–1818) both seemed anxious to downplay the Gaelic element in Scotland's heritage and emphasize Lowland achievement instead. Jamieson's linguistic analysis of the Scots language minimized the acknowledgment of Gaelic influences. Besides the Gaels, the second major early medieval "founding people" of Scotland were the Picts. Jamieson asserts that the Picts were not Celts, but Goths, that is, a "Teutonic" people like modern Lowlanders. Laing originally admired James Macpherson and Celticism, but later changed sides and developed strong anti-Celtic, pro-Germanic leanings.[4]

The most abusive and most openly racist Scottish intellectual of that period was John Pinkerton. Like Laing, he was a former Macphersonist turned Teutonist, and like Jamieson he rejected the popular claim that the Gaels were Scotland's original inhabitants. Instead, he asserted that the nation's true ancestors were the Picts, whom he considered as Teutonic Goths.[5] For Pinkerton, the Celts were a morally and physically inferior race—savage, lazy, and weak—that once was Europe's aboriginal population, but had been conquered by a superior race of "Scythian" or "Gothic" invaders (he uses these two terms synonymously). He likens the Celts to indigenous populations of modern overseas colonies: "The Celts were so inferior . . . , being to the Scythians as a negro to an European, that . . . to see them, was to conquer them; . . . and . . . they had no arts, nor inventions, of their own."[6] "To see them, was to conquer them" might be an allusion to Caesar's famous bon mot "Veni, vidi, vici," and thus another example of how Roman discourse colored modern British readers' perceptions of the "Celts" of their own time and of colonized peoples overseas, and how Celtic Others provided a discursive bridge across the geographical and temporal chasms between ancient and modern empires. Pinkerton's associative leap from Europe's Celtic margins to overseas colonies becomes explicit in his comparison between Celts and black people, both placed on the lowest step of the ladder of social evolution from savagery via barbarism to civilization. Black people are not the only modern overseas "savages" to whom the Celts are likened. Native Americans and Pacific Islanders also feature in Pinkerton's equations. He asserts that the ancient Celts had been to the Gothic incomers "what the savages of America are to the Europeans."[7] Furthermore, he claims:

> The Celts had no monuments any more than the savage Americans or Samoiedes. . . . The manners of the Celts perfectly resembled those of the present Hottentots. . . . What their . . . mythology was we do not know, but in all probability resembled that of the Hottentots, or others of the rudest savages, as the Celts anciently were, and are little better at present, being incapable of any progress.[8]

This alignment with nonwhite overseas populations underscores the impression that the Celts are an "inferior race," just as primitive and Other as Native Americans, black Africans, or Pacific Islanders allegedly were. According to Pinkerton, the Celts "are savages, have been savages since the world began, and will be for ever savages while a separate people; that is, while themselves, and of unmixt blood."[9] As such, they had always been a millstone round Scotland's neck, delaying the nation's Lowland-propelled journey on the path to progress. Pinkerton claimed that even in his own time they still were

> mere radical savages, not yet advanced even to a state of barbarism; and if any foreigner doubts this, he has only to step into the Celtic part of Wales, Ireland, or Scotland, and look at them, for they are just as they were, incapable of industry or civilization, even after half their blood is Gothic, and remain, as marked by the ancients, fond of lyes, and enemies of truth.[10]

Indicting Celts as liars might imply another parallel between Celts and non-European Others: beyond potential allusions to Macpherson's Ossianic (part-)forgeries, untruthfulness is apparently also considered a general racial characteristic, and as such might place Celts on a par with "Orientals," who have likewise been frequently portrayed as deceitful.

Comparisons between ancient "Celts," modern "Celts," and modern non-European colonized peoples were nothing new. But it had usually been assumed that these Others could be lifted up from their "inferior" stage of civilization. Pinkerton, by contrast, believed otherness and inferiority to be essentially immutable, thus anticipating nineteenth-century racism. For him, Teutons and Celts, like Europeans and Africans, were distinct races classed in an unalterable hierarchy. The weaknesses of the "inferior races" could not be rooted out—either by education or by racial intermixture. In Pinkerton's view it was always the weaker, Celtic inheritance which surfaced in hybrid offspring, so that intermarriage with inferior peoples would lead Teutons to racial degeneration. As an example, Pinkerton cites the aristocracy of early medieval Dál Riata, who in his view were no Gaels, but of Gothic stock—apparently because their considerable achievements would have belied his dogma of Gaelic incapability, so that he had to redefine the Dálriatans as part-Teuton to uphold his prejudiced claims.[11] He argues that this Gothic Dálriatan elite became degenerate in blood and language because they intermixed with Gaels.

Pinkerton's contempt for everything Gaelic extended to the language itself, which he perceived as markedly inferior, a mere gibberish only held together by loanwords from other, superior languages. Further signs of inferiority are identified in Celtic physiognomy and conduct:

> The Lowlanders . . . are as different from the Highlanders, as the English are from the Wel[s]h. The race is so extremely distinct as to strike all at first sight. . . . The Lowlanders are tall and large, with fair complexions, and often with flaxen, yellow, and red hair, and blue eyes; the grand features of the Goths. . . . The lower classes of the Highlanders are . . . diminutive, . . . except some of the Norwegian descent; with brown complexions, and almost always with black curled hair, and dark eyes. In mind and manners the distinction is as marked. The Lowlanders are acute, industrious, sensible, erect, free. The Highlanders indolent, slavish, strangers to industry.[12]

As Fenyö points out, this parallels contemporaneous developments in anthropology, which from the 1780s and 1790s onwards constructed racial hierarchies and presented small bodily stature as an indicator of racial inferiority. In Pinkerton's account, Celts are not only racially but also aesthetically inferior: contemporary ideals of beauty preferred fair skin and hair, as well as blue eyes, so that darker "races," including the allegedly dark-haired Gaels, are supposedly uglier than their light-colored Teutonic superiors. Fenyö plausibly suggests that the alleged darkness of not only Highland hair but also Highland skin, as well as the adjective "slavish," might be intended to emphasize similarities between Gaels and black people. She stresses that African physique and supposed inferiority were much discussed during that period, and often in terms which corresponded to Pinkerton's juxtaposition of Celts and Teutons. Carl von Linné, a pioneer of racial anthropology, portrayed white people in terms of virtues like inventiveness, order, and cleverness, and black people as deceitful, indolent, and incapable of self-rule. At that time, however, such distinctions were usually made only between Europeans and non-Europeans, not among the Europeans themselves.[13] Pinkerton's Celtic-African alignments use widespread public acceptance of black people's inferiority in order to gain support for his own (then much more controversial) thesis of *Gaelic* racial inferiority. Pinkerton is thus one of the first authors to invent racial distinctions among white Europeans, an invention which mainstream opinion only adopted several decades later.[14] In earlier periods, intra-European Others like the "Celts," and traditional ways of textualizing them, had served as a model for descriptions of more recently encountered overseas "savages." Now the flow of influence changed direction: the idea of immutable biological distinctions, first used to denigrate non-European indigenous populations, was gradually imported into intra-European othering. As non-European peoples seemed more obviously "other" and inferior than Europe's "Celtic" fringes, the latter's otherness could be made more plausible by claiming analogies between them and non-European "races."

For commentators like Pinkerton, this need to reaffirm Gaelic otherness and inferiority via hardened, "racial" distinctions was still mainly based on the *success* of contemporary "civilizing missions," whose efficiency caused Lowland anxieties about Gaelic competition and a loss of their own dominance. Anti-Gaelic racism was not yet a dominant viewpoint in the national zeitgeist. This was soon to change: nineteenth-century Highland economic crises seemed to suggest that the mission of civilizing the Gaidhealtachd and transforming it into a prosperous, well-integrated part of the nation was bound to fail after all. Many mainstream commentators were unwilling to blame the region's increasing pauperism on the capitalist system itself, for example, the mutability of the system's markets and the necessary ups and downs in its economic cycles. Instead, they blamed its victims, crediting them with an unreformable racial character whose laziness and other inborn defects doomed even the best development plans to failure. Anti-Gaelic racism became more common, though it never entirely replaced the romantic streak of Highlandism which coexisted with it throughout the nineteenth century—and which survived even beyond, long after anti-Celtic racism had dwindled.

One economic problem was the chieftains' spending habits: those profits which were not swallowed up by debt payments were usually not invested in sustained economic development of the Highland region, but squandered for personal aristocratic consumption elsewhere—a problem also associated with colonial or neocolonial comprador bourgeoisies. The Gaidhealtachd's economy reached crisis point when the growth sectors of the "improvement" era foundered during the early nineteenth century, especially after the Napoleonic Wars. Overcrowding of land was exacerbated by homecoming soldiers. Demand for Highland products had heavily depended on the war economy; in peacetime, demand and prices fell. There were few alternative lines of business to cushion the fall. As James Shaw Grant put it, "the Highlands had only three commodities to offer the world market, all of them vulnerable to colonial exploitation. Agricultural products . . . fisheries . . . people."[15] The kelp industry collapsed in 1825. Pauperism and rent arrears also had psychological effects: despair and resignation often reduced the clan commoners' willingness to make economic efforts—possibilities for which were limited enough in the first place. This affirmed Lowland and English stereotypes about traditional Highland laziness. The only economic fields which now promised profit were sheep farming and the new trend to transform Highland estates into deer-hunting grounds and holiday homes for the wealthy. None of these needed many laborers, so that much of the Highland population became economically superfluous. This resulted in further clearances, evictions, and emigration (now often with landlord and government support) to Lowland cities or the colonies.[16]

Racist ideologies about Celtic inferiority could be used to justify expulsion, extinction, or at best complete assimilation without preserving any aspects of "noble savagery." Gaelic "Celts" were branded as an irredeemably backward, unimprovable race which threatened to corrupt the Saxon Lowlanders as well if kept any longer in proximity to them, and which appeared increasingly obsolete in a scheme of evolution that demanded the survival of the fittest races only.

A relatively early commentator who linked this kind of racial thought to economic crisis in the Highlands was Patrick Sellar, a solicitor from Morayshire with an Edinburgh education who was an estate administrator and sheep farmer in Sutherland during the Clearances.[17] His writings on the subject are often reminiscent of colonial discourse, for instance when he describes the Gaels as a "savage" population living "in a country of sloth and idleness."[18] But his views on how to tackle this "savagery" varied, reflecting shifts in the general zeitgeist. Until about 1810, Sellar seems to have believed in progress through developmental aid, like investment in building, infrastructure, and agricultural improvement. Wholesale clearances or evictions did not yet seem an unavoidable precondition for development. Later, his opinion of the Highlands and its population became more pessimistic. While he still retained some belief in civilizing missions, these could now only be effected through clearances, the introduction of large sheep farms in the fertile inland glens, and the forced resettlement of tenants on the coast as fishermen.[19] Sellar commended these measures as follows: "the proprietors *humanely* ordered this . . . most benevolent action, to put those barbarous hordes into a position, where they could . . . apply to industry, educate their children, and advance in civilization."[20]Again, several motifs are reminiscent of colonial discourse: the "natives" are denigrated as "barbarous hordes," expropriation and coercion into a new social order are deemed a praiseworthy civilizing mission, and this mission also entails education and the extinction of native laziness by teaching the "natives" skills which are economically profitable to the colonizer/landlord.

Another colonial motif, familiar from overseas contexts and romantic British Highlandism, occurs in a note Sellar penned in 1816. Here, the "Celt" is partly romanticized, but only within safe limits. Attempts to defend "Celtic" traditions are only noble when confined to the remote past, that is, antiquity, while the traditionalism displayed by Gaels in Sellar's time inspires nothing but disgust. Modern Gaels are not portrayed as noble savages, but through nineteenth-century concepts of inevitable and contemptible racial decline:

> [They are] the sad remnant of a people who once covered a great part of Europe, and who so long and so bravely withstood the invading . . . Roman Empire. Their obstinate adherence to the barbarous jargon of the times when Europe *was possessed by Savages*, their *rejection* of any of the several languages now used in Europe, and which being sprung or at least improved from those of the greatest nations of antiquity, carry with them the collected wisdom of all ages, and have raised their possessors to the most astonishing pitch of *eminence* and *power*—Their [*sic*] seclusion . . . from this grand fund of knowledge, places them, with relation to the enlightened nations of Europe in a position not very different from that betwixt the American Colonists and the Aborigines of that Country. The one are the Aborigines of Britain shut out from the general stream of knowledge and cultivation, flowing in upon the Commonwealth of Europe from the remotest fountain of antiquity. The other are the Aborigines of America equally shut out from this stream; Both live in turf cabins in common with the brutes; Both are singular for patience, courage, cunning and address. Both are most virtuous where least in contact with men in a civilized State, and both are fast sinking under the baneful effects of ardent spirits [alcohol].[21]

Sellar's increasingly negative view of Gaeldom is also reflected in a passage which asserts that the Highlanders lack "every principle of truth and candour."[22] However, even at that point Sellar apparently still believed that decline was not inevitable, and that it might be redeemed through appropriate policies, such as the eviction of tenants from their old habitat and their removal to new fishing townships.[23] Even then he remained a believer in civilizing missions, at least to a certain extent. But over the years his pessimism seems to have increased further, until overseas emigration was deemed the only viable answer. Already in 1816 he assessed some tenants' migration plans as follows: "It would be a most happy thing if they did [emigrate]. . . .

They are just in that state of society for a savage country . . . , when landed in the woods of America."[24] By 1832, he apparently believed that the emigration of almost all native Highlanders was the best solution.[25]

Economic crisis in the Highlands and anti-Gaelic racism in anglophone popular opinion reached a climax in the 1840s and early 1850s through the potato crop failure caused by a fungus, and through the resulting famine. More famously, the famine also devastated Ireland, where it arrived a year earlier. In Scotland's northwestern Highlands and the Hebrides, many people were on the verge of starvation for several years, but unlike in Ireland there were few actual deaths. Mitigating factors included the better situation of the Scottish economy at large, and a relatively efficient aid machinery. Nonetheless, the situation in the Highlands was severe and received considerable attention in the press and wider public opinion, where Fenyö identifies three kinds of response: first, blaming economic problems on alleged faults in the Gaels' ethnic or racial character; second, sympathy and social criticism; and third, romanticization, for instance of a better Highland past or of the now-emptied landscapes. While these tendencies often existed side by side, ethnic or racial denigration seems to have been the strongest one, at least during the 1840s and early 1850s.[26]

The "Saxon race" was deemed superior: "the contrast . . . between the habits and condition of the . . . two races . . . living side by side, point[s] . . . to the main cause of destitution. . . . The evil is in the character and the inveterate habits of the [Celtic/Gaelic] race."[27] Among the most frequently cited flaws of Gaelic racial character was laziness. This was not only a racial but also a class issue: in Victorian times, poor people in general were often blamed for laziness, no matter which "race" or nation (English or Scottish) they belonged to. It was often thought that all those poor people should best be disposed of—a notion advanced, for instance, by Herbert Spencer's *Social Statistics, or the Conditions Essential to Human Happiness* (1851) and later by social Darwinism. The wish to dispose of unwanted paupers, even English ones, was often linked to race discourse, for example when the poor were portrayed as a degenerate part of the English race which threatened to corrupt the *entire* race.[28] Even non-Celtic paupers were often seen as lazy people who needed lessons in diligence, but Fenyö plausibly argues that such ideas were even stronger with regard to the *Gaelic* poor.[29] Thus, one newspaper article asserted that "the consequences of the late failure in the potato crop a virtuous people would have got over; but here the calamity fell on a degraded and indolent race."[30] For several centuries, various authors had claimed the Highlanders for the Scottish or British nation by stressing their difference from the Irish. Now, the Highlanders were re-othered and placed again in the same category as the Irish. Both kinds of Gaels were deemed lazy and dirty by dint of their racial character.[31] The journalist James Bruce expressly uses ideas of racial inferiority to debunk romantic clichés of Gaelic noble savagery:

> Highlanders tell us of . . . their noble pride, their manly independence, and so on—but . . . what is considered respectable in the Highlands would be called meanness in the Lowlands. . . . What is called working in the Highlands would be called play in the Lowlands. . . . The Highlander['s] . . . pride . . . would be more . . . to his credit, and much more for the good of the society, if it would make him too proud to remain the starving indolent serf of a mighty chief, with centuries of ancestors of unpronounceable names—if it would make him proud enough to remove . . . to a locality where a comfortable livelihood is to be had for hard labour.[32]

> Morally and intellectually they are an inferior race to the Lowland Saxon—and . . . before they can in a civilised age be put in a condition to provide for themselves and not to be throwing themselves on the charity of the hard-working Lowlander, the race must be improved by a Lowland intermixture, their habits, which did well enough in a former stage of society, must be broken up by . . . Lowland example.[33]

Bruce expresses surprise that such a degree of barbarism, which he so far had only known from books about non-Europeans, could be found so close to home.[34]

However, Bruce's hope for the beneficial effects of Lowland intermixture shows that in the 1840s many who believed in the Gaels' racial inferiority still thought that racial flaws could be improved by education or intermixture. Educating the "inferior race" was also important in famine relief measures, which were organized as another civilizing program. One strategy to root out Gaelic indolence involved a particular approach to food rations. These were scant enough in any case: just enough to ensure subsistence, and only half the usual prison ration. But even these scant famine relief rations were only given in exchange for extremely hard labor in specially created employment schemes. Some of these schemes aimed at estate improvement, for instance through drainage, but others were pointless tasks intended solely to promote labor as an end in itself, for instance in building a useless tower in the middle of a loch. At times, another required sign of racial improvement was cleanly housekeeping.

Gradually, the attitudes of landlords, government, and the general public became increasingly skeptical about the Gaels' racial improvement potential. Now, racial discourse often asserted that the Highlanders' plight was a natural consequence of historical evolution and racial destiny:

> The utilitarian march of Lowland enterprise must inevitably settle this question by the imperious laws of political economy, and the function of the philanthropist will not be in attempting to prevent the conversion . . . but in the modification of the process by mercy

> and kindness to the poor Celt. Gradually he was driven from the flat country to the mountain because active energetic people could apply the plain to use. The same people now find in sheep-farming a use for the mountain, and, by the gradual . . . pressure which drives the idle out . . . , the Celts must give up the mountain to the sheep-farmer. He must be "improved out."[35]

This suggests the inevitability and legitimacy of replacing racially inferior Celtic Highland tenants by capitalistically more profitable forms of land use imported mainly by a Teutonic race of Lowlanders and Englishmen. If any solution for the Highland problem still seemed possible, it lay in emigration. While the Gaels' alleged racial character now made them incapable of learning better ways at home, abroad they were suddenly thought improvable.[36]

> Ethnologically the Celtic race is an inferior one . . . destined to give way . . . before the higher capabilities of the Anglo-Saxon. In the meantime, . . . as a part of the natural law which had already pushed the Celt from continental Europe westward, emigration to America is the only available remedy for the miseries of the race, whether squatting listlessly in filth and rags in Ireland, or dreaming in idleness and poverty in the Highlands and Islands of Scotland.[37]

Fenyö aptly comments that "this amounted to nothing less than the theory of race decay."[38] Those who did not even believe in the Gaels' potential for self-improvement abroad at least saw in emigration an improvement for the British mother country which could thus be rid of that un-Saxon, degraded Celtic race. There was even talk of a "final settlement" by deporting the immense number of 30,000 to 40,000 people to Australia—which, however, was not put into practice.[39] Officially, the author of this suggestion masked his plans as philanthropy, but private communications revealed that his main motive was racial cleansing. He hoped that deported Gaels could be replaced by people who were less "other" to the Teutonic British mainstream of Lowlanders and Englishmen: he wanted to resettle the Highlands with Teutonic Germans, "an orderly, moral, industrious and frugal people, less foreign to us than the Irish or Scotch Celt, a congenial element which will readily assimilate with our body politic."[40] This racist resettlement plan eerily foreshadows schemes developed in the 1930s and 1940s to replace an allegedly inferior "Slavonic race" with German colonizers in eastern Europe. In mid-nineteenth-century Scotland, the influence of racist theorizing sometimes appears to have made eviction measures even more brutal than before.

Racist currents also inform nineteenth-century scholarship on Scottish history. Although Pinkerton's wilder flights of fancy (e.g., describing the Picts as Goths) became less acceptable, the *essence* of his Teutonism remained current and attributed anything valuable in Scotland's heritage to the Anglo-Saxon element of the country's post-Pictish history. Several historians, such as John Hill Burton or Thomas Carlyle, either ignored the Gaels entirely or relegated them to the role of lazy, wild barbarians ultimately subjugated by their Teutonic superiors, the united brotherhood of Englishmen and Lowland Scots. Like Jamieson, Burton denied the importance of Gaelic influences on the Scots language, and like Pinkerton he assumed that the Celts were a separate, inferior race destined to give way to a conquering race of Germanic invaders, as the Romano-British had done.[41]

Partly such anti-Celtic biases were reinforced by anxieties about the stability of British rule in Ireland, where a growing anti-imperial nationalist movement often used Gaelic cultural distinctness for political ends. Many Scottish-British patriots took pride in the empire and its sway over Ireland. The Gaelic, and thus part-Irish, element in Scottish history had to be played down.[42] To admit that Scotland had developed from a "Dark Age" Irish colonial movement would have meant an uncanny reversal of these regions' modern roles, where Scotland was not only a globally imperialist junior partner but had also played a key role in colonizing Ulster.

Victorian Anthropology: Anti-Celticism in Robert Knox's *The Races of Men*

The racial typology which informed historical scholarship and public opinion was objectified through Victorian anthropology, which often distinguished not only between a white/European "master race" and the various "inferior" overseas "races" it was allegedly destined to subdue, but also between several white "races," such as Teutonic, Celtic, and Slavonic ones. Intra-European racial distinctions frequently appeared just as clear and insurmountable as the distinction between Europeans and Africans or Native Americans. Typologies of racial character built on older stereotypes about ethnic traits and habits of Self and Other, as when the laziness and irrationality of "barbarian races" were juxtaposed against the diligent work ethic and rationality of "civilized" Saxons. Such juxtapositions had long been in use with regard to both Celtic and non-European (e.g., "Oriental") Others, but previously often implied that civilizing missions were able to improve racial character. However, by the mid-nineteenth century, alleged ethnic character traits were ossified into eternal anthropological fixities.[43]

An early example from Victorian science is the Edinburgh anatomist and physiologist Alexander Walker, whose work in the 1830s employed "principles of physiognomy to delineate the different racial characteristics of Celts and Goths" in England, Scotland, and Ireland.[44] Walker's views also inspired the influential Scottish anatomist Robert Knox, whose interest in comparative anatomy and ethnology already became manifest during the 1820s and 1830s. During the 1840s, Knox gave public lectures on his racialist theories in many British cities. These lectures became the basis of his book *The Races of Men*, which appeared in 1850.[45] He criticized the way in which older usage had employed the term "race" in a looser way as a mere synonym for "nation" or "cultural community":

> The term race . . . is not . . . new . . . , but I use it in a new sense; . . . whilst [previously] the statesman . . . and . . . scholar . . . attached no special meaning to the term . . . ; or refused to follow out the principle to its consequences; or ascribed the moral difference in the races . . . to fanciful causes, such as education, religion, climate, &c. (*Races of Men* 7–8)

The new concept of race which Knox advocates is strictly biologistic: each race has peculiar "physical and mental qualities" (56), and "human character, individual and national, is traceable solely to the nature of that race to which the individual or nation belongs" (v). Intellectual and cultural history, as well as linguistic differences, are mere correlatives of racial biology: "race in human affairs is everything . . . : literature, science, art—in a word, civilization, depends on it."[46] Nation and state are dismissed as artificial constructs (4); he asserts that the only natural and viable source of collectivity and identity is race. The essence of racial character is, according to Knox, unalterable—not even "interbreeding" can produce lasting change because he considers hybrids as ultimately nonreproductive, or bound to revert to one of the constituent pure types after a few generations.[47] Evolution over time *within* the same race is likewise declared impossible: a race's typical "countenances, . . . forms, . . . organization, . . . [and] mental disposition . . . never alter. Modified they may be by time and circumstances, but they alter not" (337). While romantic thought had sometimes assumed a timeless ethnic character only for "primitive" peoples like "Celts" or "Orientals," but considered the occupants of the center (often "Teutonic" cultures) as dynamic and evolving, for Knox even the civilized races have not altered much over the centuries: even Saxons have remained essentially unchanged since Roman times (11).

Within the British Isles, the "Saxon race" has a binary opposite in the "Celtic race." Knox states that many of his contemporaries accept racialist anthropological distinctions between Europeans and non-Europeans, but are still reluctant to apply similar ideas to *intra*-British cultural differences. His own application of race theory to the peoples of the British Isles is seen as an important conceptual innovation.

> As a consequence of . . . misdirection, on the mere mention of the word race, the popular mind flies off to Tasmania, the polar circle, or the land of the Hottentot. Englishmen . . . can scarcely be made to comprehend, that races of men, differing as widely from each other

> as races can possibly do, inhabit, not merely continental Europe, but portions of Great Britain and Ireland. And next to the difficulty of getting this . . . admitted . . . , has been an unwillingness to admit the full importance of *race*, militating as it does against the . . . prejudices of the so-called civilized state of man; opposed as it is to the Utopian views based on education, religion, government. (23–24, Knox's italics)

"Utopian views" alludes to the progressivism and universalism which characterized Enlightenment texts on "primitive" peoples and "civilizing missions," as well as eighteenth-century attempts to forge a unified British nation out of different ethnic components. The application of racial theories to Europe is also advocated in the following passage:

> When the word race . . . is spoken of, the English mind wanders immediately to distant countries; to Negroes and Hottentots, Red Indians and savages. He admits that there are people who differ a good deal from us, but not in Europe; there, mankind are clearly of one family. . . . But the object of this work is to show that the European races . . . differ from each other as widely as the Negro does from the Bushman; the Caffre from the Hottentot, the Red Indian of America from the Esquimaux; the Esquimaux from the Basque. (44, also see 76–78, 80–81)

Knox criticizes generalizing notions of a unified "European civilization," "an abstraction which does not exist": "To me the Caledonian Celt of Scotland appears a race as distinct from the Lowland Saxon . . . as any two races can possibly be: as negro from American; Hottentot from Caffre; Esquimaux from Saxon."[48] Most races in his typology are endowed with negative *and* positive characteristics—even some non-Europeans like Arabs and selected Africans are credited with certain virtues. Nonetheless, there is a clear sense of racial hierarchy, with several European "races" at the top. Among the most superior is the "Saxon" or "Scandinavian" race, although even their character is not without flaws. The position of the "Celts" is more ambiguous: in a global or pan-European context they are usually classed among the most superior races. In an inner-British context, they usually appear as markedly inferior to their Saxon neighbors. This oscillation of Knox's Celts between master and subject race is one more manifestation of the Celts' ambivalent position in the general history of colonial, anti-, and postcolonial discourse as both (or alternately) colonizer and colonized, Same and Other.

The Saxons, who dominate England and Lowland Scotland (138, 318), are credited with many characteristics that are familiar from metropolitan Anglo-British self-descriptions since the seventeenth and eighteenth centuries. These self-portraits are strongly marked by middle-class values, by a capitalist work ethic, and by patriotic pride in Britain's constitutional monarchy, its Protestantism, and its overseas empire. For Knox, support for the Reformation is a Saxon racial characteristic (3–4)—and so is the love of freedom and democracy.[49] The Saxon is also characterized by great self-assurance and self-confidence (e.g., 46, 54), an "abhorrence for theory—that is, for science" (10, also see 58), common sense (169), an "acquisitive and applicative genius" (10), materialism (169), and utilitarianism (412).

> Thoughtful, plodding, industrious beyond all other races, a lover of labour . . . ; he cares not its amount if it be but profitable; large handed, mechanical, a lover of order, of punctuality in business, of neatness and cleanliness. In these qualities no race approaches him. (53–54)

> Accumulative beyond all others, the wealth of the world collects in their hands. (54)

The practical Saxons live only in the present and future, interested neither in the past (58) nor in metaphysical or speculative intellectual pursuits. Their desire for action and exertion is reflected in their preference for sports (54). Athleticism is also manifest in their physical appearance, foreshadowing late nineteenth- and early twentieth-century European Aryanism where fitness and fair coloring go hand in hand: "a tall, powerful, athletic race of men; the strongest, as a race, on the . . . earth. They have fair hair, with blue eyes, and so fine a complexion, . . . almost . . . the only absolutely fair race on the . . . globe" (50).

Nonetheless, even the Saxons possess physical flaws: "Generally speaking, they are not a well . . . proportioned race, . . . the torso being large, vast, and disproportioned" (50). Flaws of intellect and character include their "contempt for art" (10) and a lack of creative genius (58). "[The Saxon's] genius is wholly applicative, for he invents nothing. In the fine arts, and in music, taste cannot go lower. The race in general has no musical ear" (54). The Saxons' coarse art is even lumped with that of non-European peoples, which momentarily blurs the boundary between English "civilized" coloniser and Asian "barbarian" colonized (219). The epitome of art and civilization is located in ancient Greece (396, 407, 446). Even among the modern races, the Saxons are partially surpassed by others, for instance by the Slavonians in intellect (vi, 356).

The Saxons' moral flaws include "hypocrisy and . . . selfishness" which "give . . . to Saxon war a vulgar, . . . mercenary spirit, cold and calculating. . . . The plains of Hindostan have been the grand field for Saxon plunder" (80). This temporary critique of overseas colonialism is offset by other passages which reassert the superiority of the European races and the historical necessity of imperialism, even though the moral legitimations of "civilizing missions" are exposed as a sham masking material self-interest. Apart from hypocrisy and egotism, Knox identifies another moral flaw in the Saxons' overinflated self-esteem (vi, 46, 59). Apparently referring to both confidence and greed for wealth, he warns the Saxons that "good when in excess become[s] . . . vices" (54). He asserts that the Saxon race is "of all others the most outrageously boasting, arrogant, self-sufficient beyond endurance, holding in utter contempt all other races and all other men" (131). His warnings that the Saxons, though admirable, are not as uniquely superior as they might think, refer not only to past and present racial rankings, but also to future developments—he comments "the theory that the Saxon race is the highest development" with the laconic words: "So would have reasoned the saurians" (466). He implies that the future may see the evolution of even more superior races, while the Saxons, despite their virtues and present global eminence, might ultimately be bound to disappear, just as Native American peoples were already disappearing before the encroachment of the "superior" Saxons in the nineteenth century, as Knox observed. Notably, Knox even admits the possibility that his ranking of the Saxons among the most superior races might be due to the fact that he is a Saxon himself and thus potentially biased (57).

Despite his acknowledgments of Saxon flaws and his own potential bias, he retains his belief in the Saxons' overall superiority, if not in all, then at least in many respects—especially as some of their defects can be overcome, or at least sufficiently tempered. This belief in the possibility of education and racial improvement is formulated in his remarks on Saxon attitudes to warfare:

> Soldiering they despise as being unworthy of free men: the difficulty of teaching them military discipline and tactics, arises from the awkwardness of their forms and slowness of movement, and from their inordinate self-esteem. But when disciplined, their infantry, owing to the strength of the men, becomes the first in the world. (59)

Ultimately the Saxons appear as the most superior of the existing white races. This is suggested by a passage which polarizes between the darkest "races" as the lowest ones in the global hierarchy, and the Saxons as the highest (449).

A not-quite-so-dark race which in Knox's account often appears as a binary opposite to Saxondom is the Celtic one, which according to Knox occupies Ireland, Wales, Highland Scotland, the entirety of France, and the formerly French colony of Quebec. As with other races, their character appears unchanged by time, a claim substantiated by parallels between modern specimens and those described by writers from classical antiquity:

> The true Celt: [neither] time nor circumstances have altered him from the remotest period, . . . that character . . . common to all the Celtic

> race. . . . Civilization but modifies, education effects little; . . . his morals, actions, feelings, greatnesses, and littlenesses, flow distinctly and surely from his physical structure; . . . [neither] climate, nor time, affect man, physically . . . [or] morally. Let the history of the Gauls speak for itself. (318–19)

Knox mentions not only Caesar's account of the Gallic Wars, but also earlier Celtic attacks on Rome and Delphi. These episodes from antiquity are presented as evidence of traits which can still be discerned in modern Celts: "War and plunder, bloodshed and violence, [are the things] in which the race delights. . . . I do not blame them: I pretend not to censure any race: I merely state facts. . . . War is the game for which the Celt is made. Herein is the forte of his physical and moral character" (319). Knox praises the Celts' "muscular energy and rapidity of action, surpassing all other European races" (320), and their related preeminence in military glory (26, 320–21, 330). This reflects that the major role allocated to Gaels in British national affairs since the late eighteenth century was soldiering. Like romantic Highlandism, Knox's post-romantic racial assessment identifies the Celts' prowess in war as one of their major assets. Another romantic trope in Knox's racial typology is the notion that the Celts have an impulsive and emotional temper (267, 320) which gives them a special talent for literature, music, and art:

> [The Celt is] an admirer of beauty of colour, and beauty of form, and therefore a liberal patron of the fine arts. Inventive, imaginative, he leads the fashions all over the civilized world. Most new inventions and discoveries in the arts may be traced to him; they are then appropriated by the Saxon race, who apply them to useful purposes. His taste is excellent, though in no way equal to the Italian. . . . The musical ear of the [Celtic] race is tolerably good; in *literature* and *science*, they follow method and order, and go up uniformly to a principle; [though] in the *ordinary* affairs of life, they despise order. (320, italics mine).

Although Knox does not explicitly link artistic and emotional leanings with femininity, the gendering of these traits was widespread enough to allow the assumption that an *implication* of femininity might also be picked up by many of Knox's readers. This would, again, give the Celtic image a gender ambiguity which it already possessed during the romantic age: Knox as well gives the Celts both hypermasculine (warfare) and quasi-feminine attributes (emotion, art).

The Celts' lack of order in everyday life is one of their major character flaws and stands in direct opposition to the Saxon capitalist work ethic. Divergence from Saxon capitalist values marks Celtic society as inferior: pre-1745 Scottish Highland life is denigrated as "a state of barbarism" (375), while elsewhere Knox talks more generally of the "semi-barbarous modern Celt" (74–75). One of the chief Celtic vices is laziness:

> The Saxon, to whom . . . labour is a natural instinct; him they [the Celts] look on as a mean-spirited, low-minded scoundrel, who would work the soul out of himself for a few shillings, instead of acting as they do—I mean . . . the Celt—never doing any labour which they can get another to do for them; thus living a fine, dashing, do-nothing life, like a true-born gentleman. (158–59, also see 18)

This presents Celtic commoners as presumptuously aspiring to the idle lifestyle and self-esteem of a gentlemanly rank to which they are, by Saxon standards, not entitled. This echoes eighteenth-century anglophone discourse on the undue arrogance and aristocratic ego of Highland tacksmen, who prided themselves on their political and social rank as relatives of the chieftain, members of the clan elite, and military commanders, while economically being much worse off than the Lowland or English gentry. More recent anti-Gaelic texts, that is, those relating to famine relief and the labor-for-food program, are echoed in Knox's claim that "rather than labour, they would willingly starve" (158). Diligence is not the only aspect of capitalist work ethics and middle-class value systems which the Celts are supposed to lack: "they despise . . . economy, cleanliness; of to-morrow they take no thought" (320). The Celt is diagnosed as a "despiser of the peaceful arts, of labour, of order, and of the law" (322), having "no accumulative habits" (26), "no self-esteem, no confidence in [his] individual exertions" (330). The unprofitability of Celtic economy is blamed on flaws in their racial character: "you have no individual self-reliance, and so you divide and sub-divide, in the Irish cotter style, the bit patch of land left you by your forefathers, until your condition be scarcely superior to the hog who shares it with you" (330).

Lack of self-reliance is not only responsible for the Celts' economic problems, but also for their political leanings, which are undemocratic, feudal, and absolutist, showing a yearning for strong, autocratic leaders, in binary opposition to Saxon democracy.[50] Celtic undemocratic inclinations are associated with several systems and events which were, or had been, perceived as dangerous to the British mainstream. First, this echoes customary anglophone mainstream critiques of the despotic nature of the old clan system. Second, it reflects the seventeenth- and eighteenth-century association between Gaels and the absolutist leanings of the Stuart monarchs and their supporters. The Jacobite association might also underlie Knox's assertion that the Celtic racial character shows "furious fanaticism; a love of war and disorder" (26). The fanaticism of Scott's Flora Mac-Ivor likewise comes to mind. Apart from bygone Jacobitism, such Knoxian comments might, third, also reflect recent events in late eighteenth- and early nineteenth-century Ireland, whose growing nationalism appeared to Victorian English or anglophile eyes as a major threat. This preoccupation with the threat of Irish rebellion, and its explanation by reference to racial character rather than social factors, becomes more explicit when Knox attempts to substantiate his characterization of the Celts as "restless, treacherous, uncertain" by the remark "look at Ireland" (26, also see 320). A fourth threat to the British status quo which underlies Knox's assessment of the Celtic political mindset is the string of French revolutions which had shaken Europe, most notably in 1789 and 1848: "to revolutionize is Celtic; to reform, Saxon" (329). This reflects widespread British pride in the stability and moderateness of their constitutional monarchy since the earlier revolutions of the seventeenth century, as opposed to the instability and radicalism of recent French politics.

This association of the Celtic "race" with a precapitalist economy and an absolutist social order long superseded by Britain's Saxon mainstream accords with Knox's presentation of the Celts as a backward-looking people more preoccupied with the past than with the present or future: "Children of the mist, even in the clear and broad sunshine of day, they dream of the past: nature's antiquaries" (322, also see 320). This is another romantic trope which now hardens into racial typology. It also ties in with Knox's idea that the Celts are doomed to decline—another parallel to romantic Ossianism: "the Caledonian Celtic race . . . fell at Culloden, never more to rise; the Boyne was the Waterloo of Celtic Ireland" (15). Among the various sub-segments of the Celtic race, the Gaels seem especially liable to Celtic gloom:

> Looking on the *darkening* future, which they cannot, try not, to scan, . . . gaunt famine behind them, no hopes of to-morrow, cast loose from the miserable patch he held from his ancestry, the dreamy Celt, the seer of second sight, still clinging to the past, exclaims at his parting moment from the horrid lands of his birth, "We'll maybe return to Lochaber no more."[51]
>
> And why should you return . . . to the dark and filthy hovel you never sought to purify? to the scanty patch of ground on which you vegetated? Is this civilization? . . . Chroniclers of events blame your religion: it is your race. Why cling to the patch of ground with such pertinacity? I will tell you: you have no self-confidence, no innate courage, to meet the forest or the desert; without a leader, you feel . . . lost. It is not the land you value as land, for you are the worst of agriculturists; but on this spot you think you may rest and have refuge. Now look at the self-confident Saxon. . . . Does he fear to quit the land of his birth? Not in the least; . . . he becomes a real American . . . a native Tasmanian, Australian; . . . he has forgot . . . the land of his forefathers. . . . [Showing] his go-ahead principles . . . he plunges into the forest; boldly ventures on the prairie; *fears no labour*—that is the point; loves that which you most abhor—profitable labour. . . . With him all is order, wealth, comfort; with you reign

> disorder, riot, destruction. (322–24, first italics mine, subsequent ones original)

The Celt looks ever backward, the Saxon ever forward. As binary opposites, these two "races" are claimed to be incapable of intermixing. Hybridization, mutual influence, and change of mentality are deemed impossible and cannot be effected in any imaginable way, whether by education, interbreeding, or migration:

> 700 years of absolute possession has not advanced by a single step the amalgamation of the Irish Celt with the Saxon English: the Cymbri of Wales remain as they were: the Caledonian still lingers in diminished numbers, but unaltered, on the wild shores of his lochs and friths, scraping a miserable subsistence from the narrow patch of soil left him by the stern climate of his native land.[52] Transplant him to another climate, a brighter sky, a greater field, free from the . . . routine of European civilization; carry him to Canada, *he is still the same*. (18, Knox's italics)

> [L]e bas Canadian, is a being of the age of Louis Quatorze. Seignories, monkeries, Jesuits, grand domains; idleness, indolence, slavery; a mental slavery, the most dreadful of all human conditions. See him cling to the banks of rivers, fearing to plunge into the forest; without self-reliance; without self-confidence. If you seek an explanation, go back to France; go back to Ireland, and you will find it there: it is the race. (18)

> Climate has no influence in permanently altering the . . . races . . . it cannot convert them into any other race; nor can this be done even by act of parliament. . . . It has been tried in Wales, in Ireland, in Caledonia—and failed. . . . [Another] gentleman . . . maintained, that we had forced Saxon laws upon the Irish too hurriedly; that we had not given them time enough to become good Saxons, into which they would be metamorphosed at last. In what time . . . do you expect this . . . change? The experiment has been going on already for 700 years; I will concede you seven times 700 more, but this will not alter the Celt: no more will it change the Saxon. (53, also see 68–69, 137–38)

Elsewhere, Knox claims that a durable hybrid race is just as impossible to produce through intermixture between Saxons and Celts as it is through intermixture between Saxons and Africans (88).

However, all these attempts to cast the Celts as a diametrically opposed Other to a frequently superior Saxon norm do not tell the whole story. Even such a master of categorization as Knox finds himself faced with the problem that the Celts are in many ways too obviously "Same," too European, to be easily subsumed under his racial dichotomies. In *The Races of Men*, this ambiguity surfaces in several respects, notably in Knox's account of ancient history and his uneasy attempts to grapple with intra-Celtic heterogeneity, for instance between powerful modern France and destitute insular Gaels, or between Catholics and Protestants.

Knox is another patriot who proudly places his own nation's role as a modern center of world civilization in the illustrious tradition of ancient Greek and Roman precedents. He even claims that those Greek and Roman achievements were largely owed to a temporary admixture of northern European blood (47, 397–404, 407). This racial commonality between ancient and modern civilizational centers can, according to Knox, still be discerned in physical similarities between the modern English population and the people portrayed in classical art (403). While many other texts connect this alignment between modern England and ancient Greece or Rome with a denigration of past and present "Celts" as barbarian Others, Knox's book takes a different turn. The Celts' long-standing in-betweenness as both Other and Same is reflected in the fact that *The Races of Men* positions at least the ancient Celts not among the Greeks' and Romans' barbarian inferiors, but within the classical center, as another superior northern race that, along with the Saxons, temporarily infused the ancient Mediterranean world with blood and perfection:

> To the Scandinavian . . . Greece owed her grandeur of forms, especially in woman; . . . common sense, mechanical genius, large-limbed men, athletae, matchless perseverance. To the admixture of Celtic blood may be traced her warlike disposition, energy, vivacity, wit; and to Slavonian and Gothic we must trace . . . the transcendental qualities of her philosophy and morals; the substratum was an Oriental mind. (404, also see 400–401)

A similar positioning of Celts between barbarism and civilization can be discerned in Knox's struggle with the definitional problems arising from his attempt to claim Celtic racial unity from France to Ireland, while recognizing a striking difference in power, polish, and prestige between the subaltern Celts of the British Isles and their far more elegant, respected, and modern cousins on the Continent: "France; a Celtic race, . . . the most highly civilized people on the earth" (128). France's status is recognized in Knox's allusion to her former power during the Hunnish and Ottoman invasions (321), and more recently in the Napoleonic era when French Celts and "Sarmatian" Russians had been "the two *dominant races* of Europe" (60, Knox's italics). While he recognizes the "disaster of 1815" as a potentially irredeemable reduction of status (15), he considers even the diminished France of his own day as a representative of great civilization and "the dominant race of the earth" (321). Whereas he usually portrays Celts (especially insular ones) as a race in decline, for France he envisions a successful future as a major power both in Europe (321) and in overseas colonialism (e.g., 246, 268). He lists the French among the major colonialists of the future—at least as far as colonialism can, in Knox's view, be successful at all.[53] This runs counter to his portrait of insular Celts as fit for no more than becoming colonized themselves.

The ambivalent position of the Celts as occupying both the lowest and the highest levels of civilization is explicitly acknowledged: "The Celtic race presents the two extremes of what is called civilized man; in Paris we find the one; in Ireland, . . . the other" (324). The great discrepancies in lifestyle and prestige between rural Ireland and urban France make it difficult to subsume both under the same racial denominator. Faced with this quandary, Knox searches for an explanation which will allow him to retain his racialist dogmas. And at least in one field he seems to have found such an explanation—the field of literature. While Celts and their literature are generally considered to be innately primitive, the French are an exception because they have profited from classical Mediterranean influences: "As a race, the Celt has no literature, nor any printed books in his original language. Celtic Wales, Ireland, and Scotland are profoundly ignorant. There never was any Celtic literature, nor science, nor arts: these the modern French Celt has borrowed from the Roman and Greek" (325). Knox seems aware that this maneuvers him into a paradox: suggesting a profound foreign influence in this particular field (literature) contradicts his general dogma of immutable racial traits. The latter, consequently, must be immediately reasserted, but again Knox's formulation reflects his struggle with the contradiction between undeniable polish on the one hand and an assumed sameness of French and Irish people on the other: "French literature . . . is of the highest order, *and, to a certain extent, . . .* deeply influenced by, the race" (325, italics mine). In a way, these internal ambiguities within Knox's book reflect a wider split in nineteenth-century anthropological discourse between those who believed that racial difference might only be valid for certain periods, after which they could change, and those who believed in the permanence of difference.[54]

A second difficulty which France's civilizational eminence poses to Knox's theorizing concerns the hierarchization of Celts and Saxons. He usually asserts Saxon superiority over the Celt in most walks of life. France, however, threatens his Saxon superiority complex: Knox presently finds himself unable to name a society which is more polished than that of Paris (324–25). He might hope that the Saxons will in time rise to the racial challenge to surpass the Celts even there. In the meantime, he seems relieved that Saxon superiority can at least be asserted in some other area of contemporary life: "Paris is the centre of the fashionable, the civilized world; always in advance, in literature, science, and the fine arts. . . . Even in ship building they transcend all other races; but they cannot man them; they are no sailors" (326, also see

472). The Saxons, by contrast, are born to sail the seas: "The proper field for action of the Saxon is the ocean" (472).

Another field where intra-Celtic heterogeneity threatens to destabilize the dogma of unalterable racial distinctness and unity is religion: for Knox, the Celtic character is essentially opposed to the Reformation (3–4), which runs counter to the fact that "the Caledonian Celt is an Evangelical Protestant, and so also is the . . . Welsh" (69). This not only undermines appearances of racial unity, but could also be interpreted as an instance where historical developments have at least partly obliterated the boundaries between religiously reformed Celts and likewise Protestant Saxons. Again, Knox counters such definitional insecurities by tenaciously reasserting that—despite apparent destabilizations of racial identity on the surface—the underlying *essence* of Celticity remains unaltered:

> Is the [Protestant] Caledonian Celt better off than the [Catholic] Hibernian? is he more industrious? more orderly, cleanly, temperate? has he accumulated wealth? does he look forward to to-morrow? Though a seeming Protestant, can you compare his religious formula with the Saxon? It is the race, then, and not the religion; that elastic robe, modern Christianity, adapts itself . . . to all races and nations. It has little or no influence . . . over human affairs. . . . The . . . broad principles of the morality of man have nothing to do with any religion. The races of men still remain distinct. (69)

That is, where the doctrine of racial unity and distinctness seems to be contradicted by facts, Knox asserts the superiority of his dogma through a suitable reinterpretation of these facts: "All over the world the Celtic race is, properly speaking, Catholic, even when not Roman. . . . The reformed Celts have never joined the churches 'as by law established' " (327). The latter refers to the fact that Welsh and Highland Scottish Protestantism had largely taken a form which differed from the national Protestant churches of England and Scotland, both of which were an official part of the state establishment. The nineteenth-century Highlands were dominated by an evangelical movement which in 1843 had seceded from the Church of Scotland to form the Free Church; while Wales was a stronghold of Methodism. For Knox, this intra-Protestant divergence from English or Lowland Scottish norms is enough to justify a classification of the Welsh and the Gaels as essentially Catholic—although in reality the dissenting Protestant churches were arguably much further removed from Catholicism than the national churches of Scotland and England were.

Thus reasserted, the immutability of racial character and the impermeability of racial boundaries pose practical political questions: different races can never coexist peacefully within the same state. Knox considers national and state collectives as artificial constructs:

> Empires, monarchies, nations, are human contrivances; often held together by fraud and violence. (4)

> We call the Celtic Welsh, Irish, and Highland Scotch, Britons; citizens of Britain; and sometimes, which is most amusing, Englishmen! The same legal fiction extends to India, as the . . . Mauritanian inhabitants of Northern Africa were called Roman citizens! (309)

Although it is possible to form multiethnic/multiracial nations and empires, their artificiality means that they cannot survive, as the purity of races will naturally reassert itself (109) and may result in intra-national strife: "Woe to the empire or nation composed . . . of different races . . . ! Let Ireland teach the incredulous" (292). In Knox's eyes, the rebellious tendencies in Ireland are not attributable to the smallness of agricultural holdings or other social factors, but to a biological reason: the untenability of racial coexistence, which sooner or later must end in a "war of race."[55] Similarly, he describes eighteenth-century Jacobitism not as a result of clashing political or economic interests, but as a racial conflict (15). Racial war, he asserts, will always end with the victory of one race over the other; and in confrontations between Celts and Saxons, the Saxons are invariably destined to win. While Knox might not envisage a Saxon invasion of France, for the British spheres of interest in Canada and the British Isles he prophesies a complete Saxon victory and declares the subjugation, displacement, or even extermination of the inferior Celtic race to be justified. One way of justifying such conquests is the assertion that the Celts are incapable of making efficient use of the land they hold: "Ireland, Caledonia, are even yet in the hands of the Celtic race—hence their terrible condition" (390, also see 402). Thus, their expropriation by a stronger, more competent race is required on economic grounds.[56]

> [A] portion of a Celtic race from France seized on a part of Canada; . . . they carried with them the Celtic character . . . their natural indolence . . . ; their habits of clinging to each other and leaving the country desolate; they huddled themselves in villages, seemingly terrified to locate in the open country; they had no self-dependence, no go-ahead notions; and so they all but stood still. . . . Then poured in the Saxon upon them; seized their territory, and advised them to become English. With this seemingly quite reasonable request they refused compliance; hence the revolts—hence the attempts to re-establish Celtic authority in Canada. This struggle can only cease when the Saxon has become the preponderating race in Lower Canada. . . . [We] have the same effect . . . in Ireland: Canada is merely a western Ireland and Wales; the inextinguishable hatred of races is in full play; unite they never will; one must become extinct. Now it is easy to see which goes first to the wall; . . . the Saxon steps in with his

self-dependent, go-ahead principle; then flourish commerce, manufacture, agriculture, and every useful speculation; then will Ireland become Saxon. . . . So will "Le bas Canada," . . . soon, under such circumstances, cease to be Celtic. (265–66))

Culloden decided the fate, not of Scotland, . . . but of the Caledonian Celt: the Lowland Saxon Scotch took part against them: Celtic Ireland fell at the Boyne. . . . Sir Robert Peel's Encumbered Estate Bill aims simply at the quiet and gradual extinction of the Celtic race in Ireland . . . , and it will prove successful. A similar bill . . . for Caledonia . . . may be required shortly: the Celtic race cannot too soon escape from under Saxon rule. As a Saxon, I abhor all dynasties, monarchies and bayonet governments, but this latter seems to be the only one suitable for the Celtic man. (26–27, also see 266–67)

The really momentous question for England, as a *nation*, is the presence of three sections of the Celtic race still on her soil: the Caledonian or Gael; the . . . Welsh; and the Irish . . . ; and how to dispose of them. The Caledonian Celt touches the end of his career: they are reduced to about one hundred and fifty thousand; the Welsh Celts are not troublesome, but may easily become so; the Irish Celt is the most to be dreaded. . . . The race must be forced from the soil; by fair means, if possible; still they must leave. England's safety requires it. I speak not of the justice of the cause; nations must ever act as Machiavelli advised. (378–79, author's italics)

Knox probably does not mean to advocate direct slaughter: his condemnation of genocide in Tasmania as "a cruel, cold-blooded, heartless deed" (145) suggests that he considers open massacre as overly cruel. However, another way of attaining similar results—ridding a desirable territory of an inconvenient native population—would be to let people die by slow starvation and then blame it on their own indolence. Knox's comments on Celtic laziness and land use suggest that he deems the latter strategy more acceptable.[57]

For the future, Knox envisages an Ireland which by the mid-twentieth century will be entirely settled by Saxons (379). This proposed policy of more thoroughly colonizing and exterminating Britain's "Celtic fringe" populations is clearly considered as a parallel to the development of overseas colonies, whose indigenous peoples were already receiving similar treatment.[58] This parallel between domestic and overseas colonization becomes explicit in another formulation of Knox's vision for Ireland:

Sell the island to Saxon men. It is a powerful measure. It has succeeded seemingly against some of the dark races of men, whom it has brought to the verge of destruction. Caffre and Hottentot, Tasmanian

> and American: why not against a fair race—the Celtic natives of Ireland, Wales, and Caledonia . . . ? . . . Placed front to front, antagonistic . . . with a stronger race, our reason . . . might hastily decide in foretelling their extermination. (78)

While the words "seemingly" and "hastily" might indicate skepticism about the feasibility of this vision, the previously quoted passages on Ireland's future do not seem to leave room for such doubts. With regard to indigenous populations of overseas colonies—much more obviously "other" than the Celts, for example in skin color—such a policy of extermination was often much more advanced than on the Celtic fringe. Moreover, European mainstream opinion often deemed such ruthless action more acceptable in an overseas context than in a domestic, Celtic one. Apparently, Knox's strategy of drawing parallels between Celts and overseas colonized peoples of darker "races" aims to defuse the scruples which hindered the application of extermination policies to Celtic areas. One of the dark-skinned "races" invoked for comparison with Celtic subject peoples are the East Indians: "Ireland . . . is no [settler] colony as yet: it is . . . merely a country held by force of arms, like India; a country inhabited by another race" (374–75).[59] *The Races of Men* also contains an illustration showing a "Celtic group" of characters with features that evoke stereotypical portrayals of Africans, such as curly and closely-cropped hair, a flat nose, full lips, and even a dark complexion (52). The darkness of complexion is partly rendered artistically plausible by the faces (or parts of them) being in the shadow, which means a merely temporal darkness. But this portrait also evokes the more permanent darkness of African people's skin, an association reinforced by African-style curls and facial features.[60] Proximity between Celts and "darker races" is also implied in Knox's claim that Celtic French-Canadians are "amalgamating readily with the Red Indian by intermarriage, (for the Celt has not that antipathy to the dark races which . . . characterizes the Saxon)" (74–75).

Not only are some non-European "races" said to be equally flawed as the Celts, but some of them are even deemed superior to the Celts in certain respects. Knox respects the work ethic of Muslim Moors and regrets that southern France no longer has a "Moorish population" because the latter would have been "an active, energetic, industrious body of artizans" "superior in all respects to the lazy, worthless Celt" (337).[61]

At times, comparisons with overseas colonies even suggest that the Celtic "colonies" within the British Isles might be the *only* colonial projects which are really feasible. Knox is very skeptical about the possibility of sustaining overseas colonialism over a longer period, for reasons which partly lie in climate and partly in racial character. In the tropics there can be no proper settler colonialism because white people's bodies cannot adapt to those climes, so that European control can only be maintained through an ever-fresh influx of new, still healthy people from the mother country. Such places can only be held as zones of military occupation, with a minority of whites ruling "as military masters . . . over a slave population" (291), but not as settler colonies.[62] Even military occupation is not universally possible on a long-term basis. Places like India might be occupied with relative ease because Asians seem comparatively unthreatening. But certain black populations in Africa or the Caribbean can at most be brought to a temporary retreat: they will then flee into the jungle, where the Europeans cannot follow them because the white races are not adapted to its conditions. Thus, the jungle provides a refuge for black people in which they can recover before setting out to reconquer the land for their own race.[63]

In the more moderate climes of North America or parts of Australia, settler colonies do seem possible in Knox's eyes, but he thinks that even in these regions British colonies cannot be retained for long because of the nature of the Saxon race, to which most settlers belong: since Saxons love independence, they easily split into small factions, so that the Saxon overseas settlers will ultimately secede from the mother country.[64] Moreover, even in those temperate overseas climes, the Saxon race cannot really flourish:

> No existing race is equal to the colonization of the whole earth. . . . Already the Anglo-Saxon rears with difficulty his offspring in Australia: it is the same in most parts of America. But for the supplies they receive from Europe the race would perish, even in these most healthy climates. (471)

> The Saxon . . . race cannot domineer over the earth—cannot even exist permanently on any continent to which he is not indigenous—cannot ever become native, true-born Americans—cannot hold in permanency any portion of any continent but the one on which he *first* originated. (vi, Knox's italics)

Even the moderate climatic difference of the Mediterranean makes permanent Saxon settlement impossible (47, 131–32). The only territories which might allow enduring Saxon colonization seem to be the Celtic fringes of the British Isles, whose climate is sufficiently similar to the English one. The geographical proximity of the Celtic areas to England, which in some people's eyes has precluded their inclusion in the category "colony" (or "postcolonial"), does in Knox's eyes make the Celtic fringes the only viable colonies that Britain may ever have. And even that is uncertain, at least as regards the retention of the successfully saxonized territories in British possession: "a hundred years hence, . . . a *Saxon population* in Ireland will . . . forget that they ever came from England. . . . Then come the struggle of self; the Saxon against Saxon."[65]

Despite these insecurities, Knox's racial theories about Celts and Saxons allow considerable space for justifying the internally colonial marginalization and expropriation of Celtic populations by dint of biologically ingrained mentalities and hierarchies. Knox provides one of the most important anthropological accounts which apply scientific race theory to intra-British cultural distinctions. Despite precursors like Pinkerton, Walker, and certain journalists, Knox considered his own proposition of intra-European racial divisions as a pioneer project. In subsequent decades, the concept of intra-European racial differences gained increasing acceptance in professional anthropology. While Knox's book had attempted to sort the entire human species into categories, the major work of his younger Welsh-English colleague John Beddoe focused exclusively on *The Races of Britain*.[66]

At times, Lowland Scots even claimed that their own racial inheritance was more purely Teutonic than that of the English.[67] This might reflect anxiety that Scotland's frequent association with Gaelic-based national symbols placed a Celtic taint on the nation that signaled the admixture of inferior racial stock. Such a taint might threaten Lowland Scottish ambitions for parity with hegemonic England, and pull them back toward the barbarism they had struggled so long to escape. As a counterreaction, it might have seemed safer not just to claim parity with, but even superiority to, the English, by claiming ultra-pure hyper-Saxonness.[68]

Anthropology, history, and anti-Celtic popular opinion were not the only fields which became permeated by racialist theories. Depictions of Celts as a separate racial entity can also be found in cultural criticism, creative writing, and even among the works of intellectuals of the Gaelic revival. Even those whose opinions were not anti- but rather pro-Celtic frequently believed in the typologies which anthropologists had done so much to solidify and propagate. Only the evaluation of the Celts' alleged racial characteristics changed, from a largely negative to a largely positive verdict—as the following chapter testifies.

Chapter 6

Racist Reversals

Appropriating Racial Typology in Late Nineteenth-Century Pro-Gaelic Discourse

There were various reasons why, during the second half of the nineteenth century, a more sympathetic outlook on the Celtic Other again appeared more widely tolerable. Several of these reasons resembled the factors which had been responsible for earlier romanticizations of Gaelic noble savagery in the romantic period: capitalism, industrialization, urbanization, rural depopulation, overseas emigration, and mass pauperism not only persisted, but had greatly intensified, and still created longings for actually or supposedly more traditional, rural, slow-paced, socially cohesive, and humane ways of life. Again, this longing often took the form of ideological compensation and temporary escapism rather than practical initiatives for radical social change. Romanticized Celtic noble savagery could still be an attractive focus for compensatory and escapist fantasies, provided that they posed no practical threat to the modern British, anglocentric status quo. What had, since the romantic period, sometimes militated against such idealizations of Celticity was the anxiety that they might still jeopardize the status quo, for example, by becoming so fashionable that they might overshadow Lowland Scots culture, or by proving incapable of long-term economic improvement. Those who did feel such anxieties may have been more inclined to return to older notions of Celtic ignoble savagery, now propped up by modern concepts of immutable racial essences which suggested the fruitlessless of improvement efforts and justified harsh policies through ideas of natural hierarchy and race decline. However, even at the height of anti-Celtic racism, not everyone seemed to feel sufficiently threatened or unsympathetic to subscribe to those notions. Romanticization and sympathy remained alternative options throughout.[1] But they seemed to become more widespread when sociocultural developments of the second half of the nineteenth century proved previous anxieties to be unfounded. For example, after the Great Famine the Highland economy showed a modest degree of recovery which restored some mainstream onlookers' belief in improvement, though this may have been mainly based on landlords' profits, not on the life situations of lower-class Gaels, which often remained dire. Further clearances had moved many more Gaels into "useful occupations," whether in their home districts or—often more likely—in Britain's growing cities and overseas colonies. Formal education, which also spread the English language, was progressing as well. Hence, it may have seemed that the Other was now truly contained, and thus safe to romanticize in non-subversive frameworks.

But there were also more subversive elements. One of these was the land agitation movement, which lasted, with intermissions and varying intensity, from the 1880s to the early twentieth century, and which has been considered the biggest political crisis in the Highlands since the end of Jacobitism.[2] The main demand was for more land, fair rents, and secure tenure. The movement linked grassroots activism in the rural Gaidhealtachd with sympathetic newspapers and journals, the urban Gaelic scene, certain anglophone intellectuals, and a number of politicians. Several, though by no means all, Scottish land rights campaigners declared their solidarity with the Irish land agitators and with Irish Home Rule. Irish nationalist politicians in turn supported Highland crofting demands because they perceived analogies between their respective situations.[3] But there are also important differences between the Scottish land agitation on the one hand and Irish or overseas anticolonial movements on the other. One of these differences lies in the fact that the Scottish Highland agenda aimed mainly for social reform and economic change, without drawing the conclusion that many foreign anticolonial resistance fighters drew, that is, that social and economic change could only be achieved through nationalism. Although Scottish Gaels at times harbored anti-English or anti-Lowland sentiments, they never developed a secessionist nationalism aiming to establish the Highlands and the islands off the west coast as an independent Gaelic nation state. Neither did they develop any notable agitation for an independent re-gaelicized Scotland.[4]

In terms of mainstream opinion, one important effect of the land agitation was that it brought the harshness of Highland "modernization" to the attention of a wider public: "Lowland consciousness of the injustice inflicted for a century on their compatriots was the highest it had ever been."[5] Even among members of the mainstream who were not directly connected with the movement, increased public knowledge of the extent of Highland suffering created a greater readiness to sympathize with the Gaelic Other. Many seemed to think that, although the Gaels' social traditions and language were still doomed to disappear, the tragedy might at least be alleviated by compassion and understanding, easing the culture's death by the palliative medicine of kindness rather than envisioning immediate violent cultural execution. The continued attractiveness of romantic "dying race" tropes also fits into this framework: insisting that Celtic culture was indeed about to die could relieve any remaining anxieties about the subversive potential of the land agitation or cultural revivalism, while the sentimental treatment of this death asserted the mainstream's essential benevolence and alleviated any potential sense of guilt which the internal colonizers might have felt.

These kinds of romantic motivations—fantasy escapes from capitalism, alleviating guilt, and so on—may have been found among both Scottish and English people. Perhaps the most influential of the anglophone mainstream intellectuals who now sported an interest in Celtic culture was the English writer and cultural critic Matthew Arnold. While a detailed analysis of his work lies outside the scotocentric scope of the present study, he must briefly be noted as a major influence on some of the Scottish texts discussed here. His book *On the Study of Celtic Literature* sees the Saxon or Germanic race as practical, good-natured, steady, and reasonable, but also somewhat dull and philistine.[6] The Celtic character is the opposite: emotional, impulsive, spiritual, sensitive to beauty and nature, but also irrational and inefficient. Despite Arnold's belief in racial intermixture, these essentialist attributions are largely unchallenged. A colonizing impetus is also evident in his insistence that Saxons are the superior element in the United Kingdom's national mix: Celts are a feminized, dying race, without autonomous linguistic or political futures, only acceptable as harmless folklore, museum pieces, and ennobling intellectual/artistic trace elements in *anglophone* culture. Conquest is deemed inevitable, but should be made more palatable by benevolence.[7] Arnold had a wide-ranging impact, for instance on anglophone literary criticism, the late nineteenth-century "Celtic Renaissance"/"Celtic Twilight" in anglophone Irish and Scottish literature, and in the development of Celtic studies as an academic discipline.

For Scottish intellectuals, (re-)romanticizing the Celt could also hold another attraction, in addition to the ones already mentioned. This additional motivation lay in Scottish cultural patriotism. As in the romantic period, Victorian Scottish patriotism often remained confined to the cultural sphere, without any significant political aspirations, as unionism still dominated the zeitgeist, partly due to the rewards offered by Britain's overseas empire. Thus, endorsements of Scottish cultural autonomy could again have a merely compensatory function. But to some extent, Victorian Scotland also showed tendencies toward a more political nationalism, especially in the Home Rule movement.[8] Again, this was partly inspired by Irish initiatives. Political nationalism could also be linked to elements of the wider Scottish national resurgence which was evident in the cultural sphere. Examples of this cultural resurgence from the 1880s include important new collections of folk songs, as well as the foundation of significant cultural institutions like the Scottish National Portrait Gallery, the Scottish Text Society, and the Scottish Historical Society. A reassertion of autonomous national values in Scottish historical discourse had become tangible even earlier. This also had an impact on the way in which historians perceived the position of Gaelic tradition within Scotland's national history. As a mark of Scottish distinctness from England, the Gaelic heritage had often been downplayed by unionists. Despite the Teutonists' urge to de-gaelicize Scottish history, other nineteenth-century historians were willing to acknowledge the Gaelic element, although the latter's Irish roots were still frequently played down. Celticist fashions in Scottish literature can likewise be seen as part of a wider, pan-Scottish assertion of cultural autonomy and confidence.

The Celtic Renaissance which appeared on the horizon of the late Victorian anglophone literary scene spanned both Ireland and Scotland. In certain respects the Irish Celtic revival seems to have been an inspiration for the Scottish scene, and several contacts and cross-fertilizations existed between the two. One aspect of this Celtic Renaissance was the Celtic Twilight, a mainly literary movement which displayed a deep interest in dreams and the unreal, as well as nostalgia for an idealized and allegedly more beautiful, brave, and poetic Celtic past. Their image of Celticity reflected the influence of Matthew Arnold and earlier romantic models like James Macpherson's Ossian.[9] Despite such fatalistic, romantic, and escapist tendencies, the Celtic Renaissance in Ireland also had connections to the nationalist movement, as nostalgia for the past could be associated with an indictment of British hegemony as a culprit for the decline of indigenous Celtic culture. In Scotland, the Celtic Renaissance was considerably less radical than its Irish counterpart, both linguistically and politically.[10]

In addition to such appropriations by a non-Gaelic mainstream, there was also a resurgence of interest in Gaelic tradition among Gaelic speakers themselves. Both Scotland and Ireland developed a Gaelic revival movement. Many Scottish Gaelic revivalists were educated middle- or upper-class Highlanders based in the Lowlands or England, or people from non-Gaelic backgrounds who had learned the language out of antiquarian, folkloristic, or political interests. A lot of them lived in an urban environment. Scotland's landed aristocracy also played an important role in the revival, just as it had done earlier in the Highland Societies.[11] New cultural associations were founded to promote the Gaelic language and Gaelic culture, such as the Gaelic Society of Inverness in 1871 and An Comunn Gaidhealach in 1891. There was also an interest in Gaelic cultural festivals; the first National Mòd was held in 1892. These developments were paralleled by a vogue for linguistic scholarship, for collecting and publishing Gaelic folklore, and for the academic study of Gaelic history and literature. Antiquarian interests often reflected a desire to write back against mainstream anti-Celticism and against indigenous cultural cringes by rehabilitating Gaelic culture and enhancing indigenous self-confidence. For instance, the folklorist Alexander Nicolson wrote back to charges of savagery by drawing attention to cultural and moral achievements which, in his view, showed that the Gaels were at least on a par with other "civilized" cultures, if not even superior.[12] Attempts to rehabilitate the Gaelic heritage often entailed a relatively uncritical, idealizing stance toward anything which could be labeled "traditional" or "indigenously

Gaelic." Similar attempts to study, revalidate, and at times idealize indigenous traditions and precolonial histories have been discernible in early anti- and postcolonial nationalism overseas, for instance in Africa. However, glorifications of the past are not exclusively colonial or postcolonial phenomena, as they also occur in other social contexts with a sense of historical disruption or trauma. Urban city-dwellers in industrial Western societies have since the late eighteenth century shown tendencies to romanticize country life. Similarly, capitalist Victorian England often glorified the precapitalist values and social practices of the Middle Ages.

Nineteenth-century Scottish Celtic revivals were largely confined to the cultural sphere; in Ireland they were strongly linked to political objectives. But even in Scotland there were occasional, though less aggressive, political connotations, for example in Alexander Carmichael's hope that the rehabilitation of indigenous culture might move the colonizer to grant political concessions, and that his vast collection of Gaelic folk traditions "might perhaps be the means of conciliating some future politician in favour of our dear Highland people."[13] Similar hopes were entertained by some anticolonial intellectuals in twentieth-century Africa, and were famously criticized by Frantz Fanon: "You do not show proof of your nation from its culture but . . . in the fight . . . against the forces of occupation. . . . You will never make colonialism blush for shame by spreading out little-known cultural treasures under its eyes."[14] Nonetheless, such cultural initiatives can indirectly contribute to current or future political struggles by promoting self-confidence.

Celtic "writing back" also adapted elements of colonial discourse for its own (at least partly subversive) purposes, parallel to similar appropriations in overseas anti- and postcolonialism.[15] For instance, while Arnold's colonizing perspective advocated the extinction of Celtic languages as living speech and only vindicated them as an antiquarian interest, some revivalists built on his foundations to campaign for the future survival of Celtic tongues, "seeking to de-Anglicise and . . . re-Celticize the Celtic countries."[16]

Not all these reassertions of Celtic, Scottish, and Gaelic cultural worth were articulated through concepts of race. There were also continuations of older traditions which merely operated in terms of ethnic or national, that is, sociocultural rather than biological, categories. But now that race discourse was available and widely accepted, it also frequently inflected and modified older concepts of ethnicity and nationhood. So, what may have been romanticized ethnic traits of Gaelic noble savagery in the later eighteenth century often became romanticized racial traits in the late nineteenth. While anti-Celtic authors were inclined to interpret wildness, irrationality, primitiveness, and other alleged Celtic traits as weaknesses, pro-Celtic supporters of race theory might have believed in the same racial traits, but gave them a more neutral or even positive evaluation, for instance as freedom of spirit or proof of the venerable antiquity of Celtic culture.[17] To some extent, this reevaluation of formerly negative anti-Celtic stereotyping in positive terms paralleled earlier shifts from Enlightened to romantic paradigms. It also anticipated positive reevaluations of formerly negative racial stereotypes which occurred in the black diaspora in the early and mid-twentieth century under the name of "negritude."[18] However, while negritude often allied itself to anticolonial projects, nineteenth-century Celtitude reimagined the Celtic "subject race" as a "master race" destined to share global imperial power with the Anglo-Saxons. The following pages offer case studies of racialist thinking in Scottish pro-Celtic anglophone fiction and scholarship.

Racial Typology in Anglophone Celticist Fiction: William Sharp / Fiona Macleod's Novel *Green Fire*

William Sharp (1855–1905) was one of the most prominent representatives of the Celtic Twilight in the Scottish context. His relevance to the present study lies in the particularly lucid way in which he exemplifies how older tropes of romantic Celticism could survive throughout the entire nineteenth century while at the same time acquiring a new quality as they coexisted, and in some cases mingled, with the more recent developments of biologistic racism. Sharp, a scion of the Lowland Scottish middle class, lived mainly in and near London, was well-traveled in Europe and overseas, but also spent considerable time in Argyll and Edinburgh. A friend of William Butler Yeats, Sharp associated Celticity with sensitivity, mysticism, anti-Presbyterian sensuousness, antimaterialism, femininity, childhood, timelessness, an idealized golden age in the past, and a fated decline under the tragically irresistible onslaught of modernity. He had already worked as a journalist, editor, writer, and literary critic under his own name before he adopted an additional authorial identity under the female Gaelic pen name "Fiona Macleod" in 1894. Under this pseudonym, he wrote a number of works which were very popular at the time and included poems, novels, short stories, and drama. All these works were written in English.[19] His perception of Celticity as a tragically fated counter-construct to modernity is illustrated by the following passage:

> In Wales, a great tradition survives; in Ireland, a supreme tradition fades through sunset-hued horizons to the edge o' dark; in Celtic Scotland, a passionate regret, a despairing love and longing narrows yearly before a bastard utilitarianism which is almost as great a curse to our despoiled land as Calvinistic theology has been.[20]

Terence Brown rightly points out that this perspective is reminiscent of Ossianism, for example in its romantic pathos and the nostalgic interpretation of modern Celticity as the declining remains of ancient greatness.[21] The Ossianic connection is also illustrated by the fact that Sharp produced a new edition of *The Poems of Ossian* in 1896. Matthew Arnold's influence is evident in various explicit references in Sharp's literary criticism.[22] Further Arnoldian echoes appear in Sharp's simultaneous racialization and gendering of Celtic Others.[23] It seems no coincidence that Sharp's Celtic pseudonym, whose alleged Highland and Gaelic-speaking identity is embodied in the surname Macleod, is feminine. As a woman, "Fiona" apparently seemed a more appropriate medium for the literary articulation of the spirit of a race whose impractical, dreamy, and irrational character was now commonly seen as feminine.[24] A salient example of how the influences of various strands of eighteenth- and nineteenth-century Celticism translate into "Macleod's" fictional works is afforded by *Green Fire*, which brings out the racist elements of Sharp's Celticism with particular lucidity.[25]

The plot of this novel can be characterized as a romance with Gothic elements, embedded in the wider history of a pan-Celtic family. The initial scenes are set at a manor house in Brittany which is inhabited by the family of the Breton Marquis Tristran de Kerival and his estranged Gaelic-speaking wife Lois, who is originally a member of the Scottish Hebridean aristocracy. They have two grown-up daughters, the gentle and dreamy Ynys and the much wilder Annaik who spends much time outside in the forest and appears less good-natured, more violent-tempered, more hysterical, and more "barbaric" (*Green Fire* 264) than her sister (e.g., 31–33, 266). A fifth important family member is Alan, a young man who is the son of Lois's dead sister Silis but has been adopted and raised by Lois and Tristran. At the beginning of the story, the identity of Alan's father is still unknown to him. Alan and Ynys, who are deeply in love with each other, share a strongly Celtic consciousness and identity, manifest in their love for poetry, nature, romance, dreams, and gaelophone conversation. The first major turning point appears when Alan discloses his love for Ynys to her parents, who refuse their consent to the couple's marriage. On the same day, Alan learns about the identity of his father—an impoverished minor Gaelic aristocrat called Alexander Carmichael—shortly after the latter has been killed by Tristran in a duel. Lois dies soon afterwards. Carmichael's death and the marriage issue deepen the hatred between Tristran and Alan and prompt the latter to depart for his ancestral Scotland. Ynys accompanies him and becomes his wife. They set up house in a small castle, "not much more than a keep" (132), on the Isle of Rona which Alan has inherited from his Scottish forebears. The newlyweds hope to enjoy life in a Gaelic world which strongly appeals to their romantic sensibilities. But superstitious prophecies and mysterious happenings cast a shadow on their bliss: the islanders are suspicious of the couple because Alan or a mysterious doppelgänger of his has appeared to them in ominous visions, and several characters, including the two protagonists, encounter this doppelgänger in person. For a long time, they are unsure whether Alan's double is a supernatural apparition or a living man. Sometimes this enigmatic stranger is associated with a more positive omen, that is, the notion that Ynys might give birth to a child who will be the savior of the much-oppressed Gaelic race. Insecurities about the identity of the doppelgänger and about the question whether these contradictory portents bode well or not make the couple increasingly uneasy. Eventually, a natural explanation is found: Alan's double is a long-lost cousin who once committed a murder that has condemned him to the life of an outcast hidden in the islands' caves. Only his accidental death and the discovery of his corpse make it possible to solve the mysteries of most of the "visionary" sightings. The other mystery, the prophecy regarding Ynys's child, turns out to be a hallucination caused by her overwrought nerves. The babe is stillborn, and eventually the couple returns to the happier shores of Brittany. As Tristran and Annaik have died in the meantime, Alan and Ynys inherit the family seat where they finally enjoy a happy life and have a new baby.

The racism which characterizes Sharp's text is far less anti-Celtic than Knox's—instead, it is ostensibly sympathetic, just as Arnold's account had been.[26] Another factor which distinguishes Sharp and Arnold from anthropologists like Knox is that the former are more exclusively preoccupied with spiritual markers of racial distinctness, while physical features such as skin and hair color appear less important. In *Green Fire* this becomes obvious in the considerable physical differences between the book's various Celtic characters—while all of them are tall and graceful, their coloring varies: Ynys is dark-haired and suntanned, with greyish-green eyes (18–19); Annaik is pale, with reddish hair and "amber-brown eyes" (20); Alan has fair skin, "wavy brown hair," and "grey-blue eyes" (50, also see 265). Racial unity is conveyed not so much through physical similarities as through shared intellectual and emotional preoccupations. Several of these allegedly typical Celtic preoccupations are familiar from Macpherson, other romantic authors, and Arnold. One of these is the supposed Celtic ability to unite sensuality with a more spiritual strain, as exemplified by Ynys: "a child of nature, a beautiful pagan, a daughter of the sun, . . . at once this and a soul alive with the spiritual life, intent upon the deep meanings lurking everywhere, wrought to wonder even by the common habitudes of life, to mystery even by the familiar and the explicable" (57–58).[27]

Another feature of romantic and Arnoldian Celticism which resurfaces in Sharp's novel as an inherited racial characteristic is the Celts' alleged intimacy with nature.[28] Ynys is associated with what the narrator calls the "sun-life," which seems to mean a love of nature and the open air. The wording suggests that it is not a mere personal preference, but a racial inheritance:

> She was of that small clan, the true daughters of the sun. . . . She loved the open air. . . . The sun-life was even in that shadowy hair of hers, which had a sheen of living light wrought into its . . . dusk: it was in her large, deep, translucent eyes, of a soft, dewy twilight-grey often filled with green light, as of the forest-aisles or as the heart of a

> sea-wave . . . : it was in the heart and in the brain of this daughter of an ancient race—and the nostalgia of the green world was hers. For in her veins ran the blood not only of her Armorican ancestors, but of another Celtic strain— . . . the Gael of the Isles. (19)

Although "clan" might here be just a metaphor for "a group of humans," without any specific reference to the Gaelic world in which the term was coined, this Gaelic context is present in the associative background of the metaphor, suggesting that "the sun-life" and a love for nature are found most often in people with Gaelic family connections. The biological factor becomes even clearer in the statement that "it was in the heart and in the brain of this daughter of an ancient race," which implies that genetic racial inheritance determines a person's thoughts and feelings. Celtic closeness to nature is further highlighted by the metaphors describing Ynys's physique—metaphors which are all taken from the natural world: sunlight, sky, forest, sea. Similarly, the sound of Annaik singing Breton folk ballads is compared to "the strange . . . music of the forest-wind" (26). As "nature" often connotes the absence of restrictions associated with civilized human society, the closeness of the Celtic temperament to nature also implies particularly strong passions. The passionate Celtic temperament is again portrayed through nature imagery. Annaik's eyes are described as "aflame with stormy light" (20), both fire and storm being powerful natural forces which are difficult or even impossible to control. Annaik's uninhibited temperament is also expressed in the assertion that she possesses "an even wilder grace than Ynys" (20)—throughout the novel she appears even more passionate and Celtically hysterical than her sister, but the extremity of her wildness makes her more sinister and ultimately self-destructive.

Apart from closeness to nature, another romantic and Arnoldian feature of Sharp's image of the Celtic race is the latter's delight in poetry, romance, and history.[29] Alan is described as follows: "His soul must have lived a thousand years ago. In him, at least, the old Celtic brain was reborn with a vivid intensity" (37). This suggests a continuity of intellect over a period of a thousand years, which can only be based on genetic inheritance.

However, the addition "at least" might imply that this racial inheritance does not surface with equal prominence in *all* Celts. This is confirmed through Tristran, whose disillusioned and dismissive comments about love, women, and marriage (62–63) make him much less romantic than his "racial" inheritance might lead one to expect. Another instance in Sharp's novel which demonstrates that the call of racial inheritance can be overruled by individual emotion and personal choice is the reaction of Alan's Hebridean servant to his master's intention to elope with Ynys. At first, the servant argues that marrying the daughter of someone who has killed one's father does not behove a Gael (151). Soon afterwards, however, he acquiesces out of personal sympathy: "It was against the tradition of his people; but he loved Ynys as well as

Alan, and secretly he was glad" (154). This decision to ignore racial tradition is apparently also approved by the narrator.

Alan and various other characters are, however, very strongly determined by racial inheritance. Alan is "ever occupied by that wonderful past of his race which was to him a living reality. . . . He turned . . . insatiably to the past with its deathless charm, its haunting appeal" (22). A teacher of his says that Alan "was born a thousand years too late" (22) and that his circle of friends consists of long-dead Celtic heroes and poets like "Taliésin, Merlin, and Oisin" (22). These associations are elaborated as follows:

> Alan's mind was . . . irresistibly drawn to the Celtic world of the past. . . . In a word, he was not only a poet, but a Celtic poet; and . . . a dreamer of the Celtic dream.
>
> Perhaps this was because of the double strain in his veins. Doubtless, too, it was . . . enhanced by his intimate knowledge of two . . . Celtic languages, that of the Breton and that of the Gael. . . . Language . . . is the surest stimulus to the remembering nerves. We have a memory within memory, as layers of skin underlie the epidermis. With most of us this anterior remembrance remains dormant throughout life; but to some are given swift ancestral recollections. Alan . . . was one of these few. (23)

"The double strain in his veins" presumably refers to his doubly Celtic inheritance of Breton and Gaelic elements. Of course, later it is revealed that the heritage in his veins, that is, his "blood" and genes, is not really double, as both his parents were Gaels. Strictly speaking, the doubleness is not in his veins but in his mind: the Breton element is based on a Breton upbringing, that is, socialization instead of biology. A conflict between biological and social explanations for cultural and territorial allegiances can also be discerned in Alan's shifting notions of home: just before he leaves for Scotland, Alan calls Brittany "an alien land" (150). At first this seems odd, considering that he grew up there. The implication must be that the land feels alien to him because his genetic origin is entirely Gaelic. Interestingly, he feels the alienness of Brittany only after somebody has informed him of his father's Scottishness. Thus, it is his intellect which dictates the instinct for home, which makes it no longer an instinct but a biologistic fiction. At the end of the book, Alan ceases to consider Brittany as alien and adopts it as his truest "home," a term which is applied to Brittany three times on page 268 alone, and again on page 274. Thus, at least in some instances, *Green Fire* seems to acknowledge the superior importance of socialization over biology. But elsewhere in this novel, the predominance of biology remains unchallenged. The intensity of Alan's "racial" memory, and the way it is described, clearly suggest a biological dimension—certain character traits and cultural knowledges seem hard-wired into his system by racial inheritance. For instance, we are told:

> With this double [linguistic] key, Alan unlocked many doors. All the wonderful romance of old Armorica and of ancient Wales was familiar to him, and he was deeply versed in the still more wonderful and magical lore of the Gaelic race. In his brain ran ever that Ossianic tide which has borne so many marvellous argosies through the troubled waters of the modern mind. Old ballads of his native isles, with their haunting Gaelic rhythms and idioms, and their frequent reminiscences of the . . . viking . . . , were often in his ears. He had lived with . . . Cuchullin . . . and . . . Oisin. . . . He had watched the *crann-tara* flare from glen to glen, and at the bidding of that fiery cross he had seen the whirling of swords. . . . He had followed Nial of the Nine Hostages, and . . . heard Merlin and Taliesin speak of the secret things of the ancient wisdom. . . .
>
> . . . All this marvellous life of old . . . wrought upon Alan de Kerival's life as by a spell. Often he recalled . . . words of . . . Gaelic . . . which made a light shoreward eddy of the present, and were solemn with the deep-sea sound of the past that is with us even as we speak. (24–26)

The notion that Ossianic literature bears "marvellous argosies" through troubled modern waters suggests that those remnants from the past are an enrichment of the modern world, although the latter continually besieges these traditions: the waters are "troubled," which implies danger to the richly laden ships of Celtic heritage that travel these seas. Alan, and by extension his entire "race," are portrayed as a repository of premodern historical and literary traditions, as living archives which preserve humanity's past as a supplementary benefit for a modern world whose mainstream has long turned away from that heritage in favor of a more prosaic course. This does not mean that Alan is *entirely* backward-looking: he also enjoys the present and has hopes for the future, for instance regarding his love for Ynys (22). His poetic and romantic leanings are complemented by an interest and competence in science, although the latter is not as dear to him as poetry (36–37). However, the particular field of science he has chosen—astronomy—is a branch of rational inquiry which seems more congenial to the Celtic penchant for history and romance than other sciences: astronomy is described as "the science of the innumerous concourse of dead, dying, and flaming adolescent worlds" (37). In astronomy, this refers to the death and birth of stars, but it also has an earthly equivalent in Alan's interest in dead or dying cultural or racial (Celtic) worlds. New stars born in the heavens are equivalent to new, progressive cultures or races that have gained ascendancy over the older, Celtic ones. Alan's nocturnal sky- and stargazing as well as his Celtic propensity for dreams, mysteries, and "other worlds" are paralleled in Annaik and Ynys's proneness to somnambulism. Annaik's Celtic temper again takes a more uncontrolled and pathological form than her sister's: while Ynys seems to have been cured of her somnambulism, Annaik is not (83–84). Nonetheless, even Ynys's Celtic sensibilities sometimes run out of control:

> Sometimes, when she had sat in the twilight at Kerival . . . listening to tales of that remote North [Gaelic Scotland] to which her heart had ever yearned, she had suddenly lost all consciousness of the speaker, or of the things said, and had let her mind be taken captive by her uncontrolled imagination, till in spirit she was far away, and sojourned in strange places, hearing a language that she did not know, and yet which she understood, and dwelt in a past or a present which she had never seen and which yet was familiar. (210–11)

The unknown language heard in these visions can not be Gaelic, since that is a tongue she knows. It might be inferred that the voices belong to an even older insular culture, and that the racial memory or the racial imagination indeed reaches very far back.[30] Another passage which suggests a particular connection between Celticity, dreaminess, unreality, and the past is a general narratorial comment on dreams: "What are dreams but the *dust* of wayfaring thoughts? Or whence are they, and what air is upon their *shadowy* wings? Do they come out of the *twilight* of man's mind: are they *ghosts* of *exiles* from *vanished palaces* of the brain . . . ?" (238, italics mine). On the surface this appears to be a general contemplation that is not limited to ethnic or racial particularities of the Celts. On a deeper level, however, it does suggest Celtic connections because the metaphors which here describe dreams are frequently applied to the Celtic spirit, both in this novel and elsewhere. Images of shadow and twilight often appear in the Celtic world of *Green Fire*. The image of exile recalls the real historical experience of Gaelic emigration which features more directly in other parts of this novel. The "vanished palaces" subtly reflect the historical decline of the Lordship of the Isles and Highland chieftainly feudalism, a decline which elsewhere in the book is more openly acknowledged. "Dust" evokes death, as corpses are commonly pictured as crumbling into dust, while "ghosts" are an even more direct reference to mortality. Such images of death echo the "dying race" trope which had so frequently been associated with Celticity ever since Macpherson's Ossian.

Elsewhere, Sharp's belief that the Celts are a dying race becomes even more explicit. His nonfictional works label the Celts as a "doomed and passing race," for instance in the essay "Iona."[31] The label "passing race" reoccurs in the prefatory material to the novel *Pharais* and in his introduction to the anthology *Lyra Celtica*.[32] Sharp's assertion that, as "the Celt fades, . . . his spirit rises in the . . . Anglo-Celtic peoples, with whom are the destinies of the generation to come," is again reminiscent of Matthew Arnold.[33]

In *Green Fire*, the association between Celticity, gloom, death, and twilight—a twilight so characteristic that it gave its name to an entire literary movement—is also reflected in the description of Annaik's eyes as "shadowy" (20), as well as of Ynys's hair color as "dusk" and of her eyes as "twilight-grey" (19). Apart from reflecting the destiny of a dying race, the twilight metaphor also functions on an individual level, expressing a personal mood which appears especially preponderant in members of this race: a mood of gloom, metaphorically associated with the gloom of a dying day. Moreover, twilight imagery connotes a nocturnal darkness which threatens to obscure visual perception, and this impaired vision can be interpreted metaphorically as a general Celtic lack of conceptual clarity, as Celts had long been considered irrational. Further, the metaphor of impaired vision can be connected to a racial penchant for mystery. Another "typically Celtic" trait is passion, which is likewise associated with gloom, both in human moods and in the landscape. This becomes clear in the description of a journey made by an excited and worried Alan through stormy scenery: "Deep passion instinctively moves towards the shadow rather than towards the golden noons of light. . . . Deep passion is always in love with death" (38). This is not the only passage where the gloominess of the Celtic soul and of Celtic racial destiny is mirrored in the gloominess of the Celtic landscape. The protagonists' native part of Brittany is described as "an ancient land, with ever upon it the light of olden dreams, the gloom of indefatigable tragedy, the mystery of a destiny long ago begun and never fulfilled" (41). An equally significant feature of the Celtic landscape are the caves of Rona, described as an "obscure place" (250–51), "dim arcades" holding "secrets" (165), full of "deep gloom, . . . even on . . . [a] day of golden light and beauty . . . heavy with shadow . . . [and] a deathly chill" (245). Elsewhere, these caves are characterized as follows: "a pale green gloom, . . . dusky green obscurity, and some are at all times dark with a darkness that has seen neither sun, nor moon, nor star for unknown ages. . . . Day and night, . . . from year to year, from age to age, that awful . . . darkness prevails unbroken" (165). This part of the Hebridean landscape is crucial to the plot: it is here that most of the apparitions and mysteries occur and are eventually solved. The gloom, timelessness, and mysteriousness of this central location mirror the gloom, timelessness, and mysteriousness of the Celtic racial soul.

Sharp's racial typology is essentially pan-Celtic, as can be seen from Lois's comments about her loveless marriage: "My husband and I had at least this to unite us: that we were both Celtic, and had all our racial sympathies in common" (136). However, there are important sub-distinctions: while in Knox's and Arnold's works the conflict between dreaminess and rationality, or tradition and modernity, is acted out between Celts and Teutons, in Sharp's novel the Teutons do not feature at all, so that the contest between romance and reality is fought out on an intra-Celtic level. Sharp distinguishes between different kinds of Celts, suggesting that in some subvarieties the general Celtic tendencies for melancholy and mysticism come out even more prominently than in other subvarieties. There is a difference between p- and q-Celts: Brittany appears tendentially milder and more light-hearted than the gloomy

Gaidhealtachd, the latter being the region where Celtic racial traditions are preserved in the purest form. This distinction is suggested by a narratorial comment on Alan and Ynys which states that "the mysticism which was part of the spiritual inheritance come with . . . [their] northern strain was one of the deep bonds which united them" (58). The notion that mysticism and other "typical" Celtic traits are particularly strong in the Gaidhealtachd is also reflected in the following passage about Ynys:

> Through her mother, Lois Macdonald, of the . . . Outer Hebrides, the daughter of a line as ancient as that of Tristran de Kerival, she inherited even more than her share of the gloom, the mystery, the sea-passion, the vivid oneness with nature which have disclosed to so many of her fellow-Celts secret sources of peace. (19)

While a basic love for nature and mystery might be common to all Celts, some Celts feel it more intensely than others, as the Gaelic line seems to bring out this tendency more strongly than the Breton one. This distinction, and the position of the Gaels as the most Celtic of Celts, is even clearer in the narrator's assertion that Gaelic lore is "still more wonderful and magical" than that of Brittany and Wales (24).[34]

Another important intra-Celtic distinction in Sharp's novel is based on gender: Celtic women are even more susceptible to gloom, romance, and hysteria than Celtic men, which accords with Ernest Renan's and Matthew Arnold's tenet that Celticity and femininity share several mental characteristics, and that the Celts are thus a more feminine race than the rational and masculine Teutons. Sharp draws the logical conclusion that, while a general irrational strain is shared by all Celts, Celtic women must be doubly irrational and doubly dreamy: "If Alan were a dreamer, Ynys was even more so" (31). The importance of gender difference and the distinction between p- and q-Celts is also reflected in the fact that Ynys's tendency for mysticism and brooding—strong from the outset even while she still dwells in Brittany—increases further during her stay in the Hebrides: "All that dreaming mysticism which had wrought so much of beauty and wonder into her girlhood in Brittany had expanded into a strange flower of the imagination . . . whose subtle fragrance affected her inward life" (234–35; also see 179, 210). One reason given for this intensification is her pregnancy (179, 211, 238, 241), that is, a specifically female state, which reinforces the impression that general Celtic traits of gloom and irrationality are even stronger in the female part of the Celtic population. A second reason for the increase in her gloominess and wild imaginings lies in the landscape: "the melancholy of the isles" (179). This again implies that the Gaidhealtachd is the most Celtic of all Celtic regions and brings out general racial tendencies even more strongly. These tendencies include not only a penchant for lonely brooding and flights of fancy, but also a love for nature:

> Ever since she had come to the Hebrid Isles, her love of the sea had deepened, and had grown into a passion for its mystery and beauty. Of late, too, something impelled to a more frequent isolation: a deep longing to be where no eye could see and no ear hearken. Those strange dreams which in a confused way had haunted her mind in her far Breton home, came oftener now and more clear. (210)

> Long ago had Lois . . . spoken of the danger that lay for Ynys, . . . the inheritor of a strange brooding spirit which belonged to her people. Now, in this remote place, the life of dream and the life of reality had become one; and Ynys was as a drifted ship among unknown seas and mists. (248)

Alan displays some un-Celtic masculine traits by growing ever more rational. This is exemplified by an inner monologue in which he ponders on the supernatural visions which he and his wife seem to have seen:

> Was the island haunted, he wondered. . . . Or had he been startled into some wild fantasy, and imagined a likeness where none had been? Perhaps, even, he had not really seen any one. He had read of similar strange delusions. The nerves can soon chase the mind into the dark zone wherein it loses itself.
>
> Or was Ynys the vain dreamer? That, indeed, might well be, and she with child, and ever a visionary. Mayhap she had heard some fantastic tale from Morag MacNeill or from old Marsail Macrae. (218)

While Ynys is convinced that the visions are indeed supernatural, Alan seeks for a rational explanation. Significantly, the two islanders whom he surmises to have contributed to Ynys's superstitions are women, too: Morag and Marsail (also see 239), whose superstitions are also highlighted by other passages. Alan's male rationalism increases as time goes by: "at last he came to the conviction that what he had seen was an apparition, projected by the fantasy of overwrought nerves" (223), and "the belief that he had been duped by his imagination deepened almost to conviction" (224). At the same time, his wife becomes ever more dreamy and irrational:

> Day after day soft veils of dream obscured the bare realities of life. (224)

> Ynys no longer doubted . . . that . . . a special message had come to her, a special revelation. On the other hand, he [Alan] had himself swung back to his former conviction: that the vision he had seen . . . was in truth . . . a living man. (238–39)

The contrast between husband and wife also becomes clear in several conversations where Ynys reasserts her belief in the supernatural character of her visions, while Alan contradicts because he "knew [them] to be a madness"—a formulation which also implies the narrator's assent to this interpretation (244). Alan even fears that Ynys might become permanently insane (also see 246–49). Due to these dangers, Alan and the narrator see the eerie, superstition-ridden Hebrides in an increasingly negative light. Superstitions are called "unfortunate" (241) and are compared to "a poisonous weed" (225). The entire island world becomes associated with an unwholesome unreality—a "strange and dream-like life" (235), "a life of dream" (238), apparently incompatible with youth and happiness. Thus, Alan concludes that it would be best for himself and his wife to leave Rona again, exchanging the irredeemably oppressive gloom of the Gaidhealtachd for the more light-hearted and life-inducing Celticity of Brittany:

> It is a mistake to be here, on Rona, now. . . . You and I are young, and we love: let us leave . . . these melancholy isles, and go back into the green sunny world wherein we had such joy . . . even . . . to Kerival, anywhere where we may live . . . with joy and glad content—but not here, not in these melancholy haunted isles, where our dreams become more real than our life, and life itself, for us at least, the mere shadow of being. (246)

His conviction that Gaelic dreaminess and superstition pose a danger to happiness, sanity, and life also inflects what he says after having found the outcast's corpse, a discovery which proves that the visions were amenable to rational explanation: "Out of this all our new happiness may come. For now we know what is this mysterious shadow that has darkened our lives ever since we came to Rona. . . . Come, we will go now and never come here again" (252–53). As the Gaelic world is doomed, those who have the possibility of leaving should seek their individual happiness elsewhere, abandoning the Hebrides and the stay-behinds to their dark racial destiny. Belief in the omnipotence of the gloomy Gaelic strain is ultimately maintained, even in the face of such exceptions as the merry winter ceilidhs (social gatherings featuring conversation, storytelling, poetry, music, and dance): "It was a new delight to . . . Alan and Ynys to find that the islanders could be so genial and almost gay, with a love of laughter and music and grotesque humour which even in the blithe little fishing haven of Ploumaliou [in Brittany] they had never seen surpassed" (260). But the significance of such gaiety for the interpretation of Gaelic mentality and racial destiny is denied:

> Laughter and tears, ordinary hopes and pleasures, and even joy itself and bright gaiety, and the swift spontaneous imagination of

> susceptible natures—all this, of course, is to be found with the island Gael as with his fellows elsewhere. But, every here and there are some who have in their minds the inheritance from the dim past of their race, and are oppressed as no other people are oppressed, by the gloom of a strife between spiritual emotion and material facts. It is the trains of dreamers such as these which clear the mental life of the community; and . . . in these brains are the mysterious looms which weave the tragic and sorrowful tapestries of Celtic thought. It were a madness to suppose that life in the isles consists of nothing but . . . melancholy. It is not so, or need not be so, for the Gael is a creature of shadow and shine. But whatever the people is, the brain of the Gael hears a music that is sadder than any music there is, and has for its cloudy sky a gloom that shall not go, for the end is near, and upon the westernmost shores of these remote isles, . . . the Voice of Celtic Sorrow may be heard crying *Cha till, cha till, cha till mi tuille*—I will . . . return no more. (235–36)

Like Arnold, Sharp occasionally admits that the gloom thesis does not tell the whole story of Celtic or Gaelic life.[35] But—again similarly to Arnold—Sharp dismisses these exceptions to his gloomy rule as irrelevant to the general picture, by claiming that the truest Celtic spirits are the gloomy ones. His phrase "the end is near" alludes to the imminent death of the Gaelic race and its culture, while the Gaelic words quoted at the end of this passage hint at one of the causes for this cultural decline, that is, emigration: they echo a Gaelic song which is often thought to have been sung by emigrants going overseas. Sharp's vision of the Gaels' racial future might go further than emigration, dispersal, and a resultant loss of cultural distinctness, to encompass the biological death of the race. This is suggested by Ynys's failure to bear living offspring on the island, which symbolizes a general sterility and a failure of the community to replicate itself. The symbolic function of children as tokens of cultural rebirth is also reflected in the narrator's remark that "the perpetuation of life is the unconscious protest of humanity against the destiny of mortality" (179).[36] Apart from referring to human mortality in general, this might also allude specifically to racial mortality. The association of childbirth with the general survival of Hebridean culture becomes explicit in the hopes which Ynys harbors for her firstborn during her pregnancy: unwilling to accept the decline of Scottish Celticity as inevitable, she dreams of a Celtic messiah who will be born to save his race. Already before her arrival in Scotland, "no legend fascinated her more than that . . . of how Arthur the Celtic hero would come again . . . and redeem his lost receding peoples" (31). The Hebrideans are shown to harbor similar hopes (e.g., 233–34). Ynys comes to believe that her first baby will be that savior, and that the mysterious man from everybody's visions is a prophet of this coming:

> His . . . presence there upon Rona seemed a pre-ordained thing for her. . . . She felt . . . assured that some hidden destiny had controlled all this . . . mischance, had led her and Alan there to that lonely island.
>
> She knew that the wild imaginings of the islanders had woven the legend of the Prophet, . . . out of . . . the longing and the deep nostalgia whereon is woven that larger tapestry, the shadow-ridden life of the island Gael. . . .
>
> Ynys . . . too dreamed her Celtic dream—that, even yet, there might be redemption for the people. She did not share the wild hope which some of the older islanders held, that Christ Himself shall come again to redeem an oppressed race; but might not another Saviour come . . . ? And . . . might not that child of joy be born . . . of her? (234–37)

> Has not the prophet said that one shall be born upon this island who will redeem his oppressed people? He has said . . . that . . . the child I shall bear will be he of whom men have dreamed in the isles for ages. (247)

This hope for a Gaelic savior and the regeneration of the Hebridean community is disappointed: her child is stillborn (254, 257), which signifies that the decline and death of the Gaelic race are unavoidable. The image of sterility is reinforced by the comparison of the baby to a "snowdrop" (257), a token of winter, the season in which little seems to grow. While the general future of Hebridean Gaeldom appears hopeless indeed, the personal future of the cosmopolitan, educated, and part-Breton upper-class couple Alan and Ynys seems much brighter. Once her hopes for a messiah have been shattered, Ynys recovers from her brooding and madness (257–58, 260), which again implies that Celtic dreaming is an impediment to life. Only if the inevitable realities of racial decline are accepted can some lucky few of the Celts survive and escape into a happier, though perhaps less racially pure, future elsewhere—Alan and Ynys escape to Brittany, which is still Celtic but not quite as purely or typically Celtic as the Gaidhealtachd. Although there is a brief period after the couple's recovery when they toy with the idea of staying on Rona after all (260), they are relieved when the death of other family members calls them home to Brittany:

> With light hearts they realised . . . that they were free at last of a life for which they were now unfitted. (269)

> Ynys . . . was . . . glad to leave Rona and return to Brittany. . . .
>
> . . . Ynys clearly realised the deep gladness with which she left the lonely Isle. . . . That it would have been impossible for her to live there long she was now well assured; and for Alan, too, the life was

> not suitable. For the north, and for the islands, they would ever have a deep feeling almost sacred in its intensity; but all that had happened made living there . . . difficult and painful for them; and, moreover, each . . . missed that green woodland . . . which made . . . Kerival so fragrant. (267–68)

The feelings of the protagonists for the Hebrides reflect what many representatives of the Celtic Renaissance felt: a duality between deep affection for an idealized rural Gaidhealtachd and a sense that this affection often thrives best at a distance, from a safe base in more densely populated and less savage places. The latter, more "civilized" locations were ultimately the preferred homes for authors like Sharp, who cherished the remote Isles as a temporary escape and spiritual reference point rather than as a real focus of one's life. This is also reflected when the narrator likens Alan and Ynys's return to Brittany to the journey of "pilgrims returning homeward from a shrine sacred to them by profound and intimate associations" (268). The Gaidhealtachd is a spiritual shrine which can be worshipped on the spot only on a part-time basis; for the rest of the time it is best worshipped from a distance.

For the protagonists of *Green Fire*, a happy life and a new, living baby (282) are only possible outside Gaelic Scotland. The Gaels who stay in the Isles, mostly lower-class characters, are left behind without a savior. The few members of the Hebridean upper classes who feature in this novel (mainly indirectly through reports given by other characters) also tend to die premature and sometimes violent deaths. This applies not only to those who remain in Scotland but also to those who migrate to France, such as Lois or Alan's father. Even for the Celts of Brittany, a successful and happy life seems extraordinarily difficult to attain: the only characters who enjoy a happy ending are Alan and Ynys, while most of the other characters from both upper and lower classes experience a more tragic outcome—Annaik and Tristran lead essentially unhappy lives and, later in the story, die, while Annaik's lover Judik is a gloomy pauper who dwells in the woods. The Celtic mentality always threatens to pose an obstacle to life and happiness. The novel's two protagonists—as well as, presumably, many mainstream Celtic Revivalists like Sharp and his readers—can only enjoy the hyper-Celtic Hebrides on a part-time basis, as a site for brief escapades and holidays before they get on with their real lives elsewhere. The merely temporary validity of Gaelic landscapes and Gaelic culture as a playground where fantasies can be acted out for a finite period of escapism which ultimately must be abandoned for the serious pragmatics of real life is also reflected in the association of Celtic romance with adolescence. The same association appears in Walter Scott's *Waverley* and Robert Louis Stevenson's *Kidnapped* (1886).[37] In Sharp's *Green Fire*, Alan and Ynys's Gaelic dabblings are similarly connected to a growing-up phase, their first months of married life and adult responsibility. Their total immersion in Hebridean life is just a passing phase before adult disillusionment and increased social responsibilities as manor-house owners lead the protagonists elsewhere. The theme of growing up is highlighted when their return to Brittany after less than two years in Scotland is described as a return to a place where "they had been young" (274)—as if they had lost their youth entirely in those brief months. The implication is that they have grown up, and that the Hebrides and Celtic dreaming are unfit for adults, although they have made an important contribution to the protagonists' emotional and intellectual development.

Both Sharp and Arnold suggest that the Celtic or Gaelic world, while unable to sustain a viable social community and future of its own in an inevitably hostile modern world, can nonetheless play a praiseworthy role as a romantic and poetic counterweight to a modern metropolitan culture, offering a valuable complement to the latter by providing spiritual escapism. The same logic underlies Sharp's dual authorial identity as the Lowland male intellectual William Sharp on the one hand, and the romantic female Highland writer Fiona Macleod with interests in the supernatural on the other. His female alter ego offered Sharp a temporary escape into an alternative Celtic and romantic self, although in essence he remained a male Lowlander. A similar duality can be discerned in the novel's treatment of the supernatural: Celtic folklore, romance, and superstitions are exploited for thrill and effect, but readers and protagonists are ultimately provided with rational explanations. Thus, even within the book there is a return from otherworldly escapism to a more realistic mode.[38] The escapist potential of Highland romance presumably also appealed to "Macleod's" readers. Escapism tends towards a strong romanticization and idealization of the Celtic world, despite the shortcomings which the novel identifies. Concrete historical experiences and unpleasant details of present-day social life are obscured.

One consequence of this logic is the exaggeration of Celtic cultural purity: if the Celtic world is to function as a temporary escape from readers' ordinary modern lives, it must be presented as a site where modernity truly cannot reach (at least not yet), a site which is *completely* Other. To a certain extent, such a portrait is also presented in *Green Fire*: although the references to the "dying race" trope imply the powerful encroachment of a non-Celtic modernity, other aspects of the novel construct a Celtic world which is unrealistically pure. Non-Celtic people, cultures, or places hardly feature at all; and little cultural hybridization between the Celts and the respective British "Teutonic" or French "Latin" mainstreams is shown to take place. All the principal characters are either Bretons or Gaels, who intermarry with each other and even learn each other's languages rather than taking the more realistic course of intermixing with anglophone British or francophone French people. Encroaching non-Celtic mainstreams are almost entirely blocked from view, along with the existence of hybridized Celtic elites—Breton and Hebridean landlords all seem to be happily and naturally Celtic-speaking:

> The Marquise, true Gael of the Hebrid Isles . . . loved the language of her people, and spoke it, as she spoke English, even better than French. (23)

> Armorican was exclusively used throughout the whole Kerival region, was the common tongue in the manor itself, and was habitually affected even by the Marquis. (23–24)

> Latterly, . . . Ynys had become as familiar with the one Celtic tongue as the other. (24)

These idealized elites are also interested in other Celtic traditions, in whose proliferation they take an active part. Annaik sings Breton folk ballads by heart (24). Alan "loved to tell anew, in Breton, to the peasants of Kerival, some of the wild north-tales, or to relate in Gaelic to his aunt and to Ynys the beautiful folk-ballads of Brittany" (26). Similar cultural purity is claimed for Gaelic Scotland. Clanship and the Gaidhealtachd's elites are idealized, and no cultural breach between tenants and landlords is discernible when Lois tells Alan about the Hebridean islands of Rona, Mingulay, and Borosay: "these . . . were once populous, and it was there that for hundreds of years your father's clan, of which he was hereditary chief, lived and prospered" (133). The generation of Alan's father is portrayed as if they were old-fashioned chieftains although the novel is set in the second half of the nineteenth century. The supreme chief of the Rona region is even referred to by the unusual epithet "the Lord of the South Isles" (228)—capitalization suggests that this is an official title, while such a title in fact never existed. The closest approximation is the medieval Lord of the Isles, to which the narrator probably means to allude. The application of such a title in a nineteenth-century context elides several centuries of Hebridean political history and Scottish centralization, in the course of which the quasi-autonomy that the medieval Gaidhealtachd had possessed under the Lords of the Isles had crumbled, and during which local elites had been progressively anglicized or even replaced by English and Lowland incomers altogether. The only historical breach admitted in this context is the post-1745 depopulation which Lois alludes to on page 133—but even here she seems to lay the blame entirely on central government policies without acknowledging the complicity of modernizing local elites.

Two important traumas of modern Highland history are indeed mentioned, but only in strongly softened or even romanticized terms. One of these traumas is the Jacobite rebellion of 1745 and its aftermath, notably the post-Culloden flight of "Bonnie Prince Charlie" from his pro-Hanoverian persecutors through the Gaidhealtachd before he escaped on a ship to France. *Green Fire* romanticizes these events, focusing not on the intricacies of Jacobite politics but on individual adventures and moral bravery: "the evil days, when the young king was hunted in the west . . . , and when our brave kinswoman, Flora Macdonald, proved that women as well as men could dare all for a good cause" (133). The precise identity of that "cause" is not specified and discussed. Lois's reference to Charles Edward Stuart as "king" does suggest Jacobite sympathies, as it implies a belief in the continued legitimacy of that family's claim to the throne. However, her main emphasis lies elsewhere, on romance and individual gallantry. Lois is not the only voice that, from the safe distance of a long-pacified nineteenth-century world, expresses romantic sympathies with Jacobitism: the narrator does the same, again by applying the epithet "king" to the Stuart prince, when he talks of "the time when the last Scottish king took shelter in the west" (165). Other allusions to Jacobitism can be found in Lois's assertions that her own, Alan's, and Alasdair's fathers had all been officers in the French Army (134, 136), which was a common career path for exiled Jacobites. The most explicit reference to 1745 and its outcome is the narrator's still rather oblique mention of "the evil time after Culloden" (184).

The second concrete event of Highland history which the novel refers to, again with a softening brevity which obscures the details of suffering and thus renders the margin's traumatic experiences palatable to an escapist and romantic metropolitan readership, is the mid-nineteenth-century potato blight which resulted in famine and depopulation: "the year of the great blight, when the potatoes and the corn came to nought, and when the fish . . . swam away from the isles. In the autumn of that year there was not a soul left on Rona except Silis Macdonald and . . . her father" (229). Unlike Jacobitism, the famine is hardly idealized in this text. Nonetheless, a romantic element can be discerned even here, as the mood in which the famine is remembered is elegiac and vague, lacking realistic detail which might convey the full implications of suffering and oppression, and failing to draw any pragmatic conclusions for present or future resistance. Highland history is presented as a tragedy without remedy—although this novel came out at a time when the realities of Gaelic life were dominated by a very practical land agitation movement which had been active for over a decade. The critical potential of the novel's reference to the famine is further blunted by the fact that the disaster is only blamed on natural causes which are beyond social control (and thus also beyond resistance): potato blight and scarcity of fish. The role of clearances and landlordism are left out of the picture: the few members of the Highland elites who are mentioned appear to be benevolent traditional chieftains, with the exception of the even more benevolent, democratically minded Alan who occasionally helps the commoners with the fishing, laboring like the others (209), and who generously leaves his small castle to these islanders as their new communal home when he returns to Brittany (267).

This escapist outlook implies that a Celtic Renaissance is only possible in literature, but not on the level of social reality and economic or political reform. Literature functions as a substitute for social regeneration. The same logic underlies the following comment about Alan:

> In heart and brain that old world lived anew. Himself a poet, all that was fair and tragically beautiful was for ever undergoing in his mind a . . . magical resurrection . . . wherein what was remote and bygone, and crowned with oblivious dust, became alive again . . . intense and beautiful. (37–38)

This passage, like *Green Fire* as a whole, implies that the resurrection of the old Celtic world is only possible "in heart and brain" and in the literary imagination, a project which reflects not only Alan's interests but also the preoccupations informing the entire literary work of "Fiona Macleod." Moreover, "her" oeuvre suggests that even in the realm of literature Celtic culture can only be preserved in mediated, that is, anglicized, form: "she" writes in English, although "her" work often includes snippets of Gaelic or Breton text such as proverbs, incantations, names, or poetry, usually in both the original language and English translation. Some of these represent authentic fragments taken, for instance, from Alexander Carmichael's collection *Carmina Gadelica* (in *Green Fire,* e.g., 181–82). This real-life folklorist also seems to have inspired the naming of the fictional character of Alan's father in *Green Fire*. Like Macpherson and Arnold, Sharp suggests that Celtic literature cannot survive in its "pure" form and in its own language, but only as an inspiration for, or a local branch of, anglophone mainstream literature:

> Proud as I might be to be Highland, or Scottish, or Irish, or Welsh, or English, I would be more proud to be British—for, there . . . we have a bond to unite us all. . . .
>
> As for literature, there is, for us all, only English literature. All else is provincial or dialectic.
>
> But gladly I . . . am willing to be designated Celtic, if the word is to signify no more than that one is an English writer who . . . has an outlook not distinctly English, . . . with a racial instinct that informs what one writes, and, for the rest, a common heritage.
>
> The Celtic element in our national life has a . . . great part to play . . . , not to perpetuate feuds, not to try to win back what is gone away . . . but . . . to achieve, that . . . what is left of the Celtic races, of the Celtic genius, may permeate the greater race of which we are a vital part, so that with this . . . Celtic emotion, . . . love of beauty, and . . . spirituality . . . a nation may issue, . . . refined and strengthened by the . . . Celt and Saxon, united in a common fatherland.[39]

Sharp's work shows that even those Victorian literary texts which remain strongly indebted to earlier romantic models—that is, which idealize rather than denigrate the Gaelic Other—are not entirely free from the influence of more recent developments in nineteenth-century race theory. Although Sharp sympathizes with the Celtic margins, his defense of the Other employs several tropes from race theory. Like Arnold, he reiterates romantic stereotypes about the Celtic mentality which predated the Victorian era, but hardens them into a racial typology. *Green Fire* dramatizes the often destructive intrusions of a dark, atavistic Celtic racial character into nineteenth-century lives. The Victorian fascination with this subject is also reflected in a contemporary review which discerned in "Macleod's" work a "strange, barbaric element, which sometimes breaks up even the thick crust of an elaborate civilisation."[40] This review throws additional light on the connections between overseas and intra-Scottish colonial discourse, as the theme of ancient barbaric strata breaking through the crust of civilization also occurs in texts which are concerned with overseas "barbarian" or "savage" "races," such as Joseph Conrad's *Heart of Darkness*.

Anthropology and the Intellectuals of the Gaelic Revival

Sometimes racial theories were even internalized by members of the Gaelic intelligentsia. The Scottish Celtic scholar John Stuart Blackie shared the belief in racial differences, but instead of denigrating the Celts, he hoped that they would have a civilizing influence on their (part-)Saxon conquerors. He thought that Celtic literature was also worth preserving for the Celts' own purposes and in their own languages. Celtic languages were not merely appreciated on antiquarian terms, but as living tongues.[41] Further intellectuals who squared Gaelic revivalism with race theory can at times be encountered in the scholarly journal *Transactions of the Gaelic Society of Inverness*, containing papers presented at the Gaelic Society's meetings. The following pages consider two papers in detail: Rev. J. Macgregor's "Celts and Teutons: A Study in Anthropology" and L. Macbean's "The Mission of the Celt."[42]

Macgregor charts the history of Celts and Teutons from biblical to modern times. He shares various mainstream notions about racial character. For example, he describes the Celts—here meaning mainly Gauls and Gaels ("Celts and Teutons" 30)—as "quick, lively, courageous, and eager for change," and the Teutons as "patient, methodical, and persevering" (31). For anti-Celtic authors like Knox, these attributes often implied that the Celts' rashness, fickleness, and blind (though gallant) daring-do made them inferior to the more efficient Teutons. Macgregor, however, regards both groups as equally meritorious master races in joint superiority over all others (e.g., 27, 31–32). Their supposed ability for international leadership and colonizing prowess is presented as eternal racial destiny. This becomes clear when he compares the prehistoric settlement of Europe by German and Celtic incomers to modern British colonialism overseas:

> History repeats itself. The leading families of mankind, in the very early ages of the world, had to move . . . west . . . to find new openings for their energies, just as their descendants at the present day have to flock . . . to America, there to settle, and lay the foundations . . . of many new nations. (31)

This analogy between prehistoric Indo-European migrations and modern overseas colonialism is continued when Macgregor speculates about the "feelings . . . of the first travellers when they drew near the Hellespont, and saw, across the waves, what was to them . . . a new world" (31). In both historical scenarios, Celtic and Germanic migrants must cross an ocean before a continent can be settled. Even the wording ("new world") evokes American parallels.

> It was the destiny of both Celts and Teutons to leave their first homes far behind, and seek their fortune in an unknown land. . . . They made their way across [the Hellespont], and proceeded to take possession. A new inheritance lay before them, and . . . they were prepared to make a vigorous effort to secure themselves in it. The original inhabitants must have thought it rather hard to . . . give place to the invaders, but they were overpowered, and driven into remote corners. (31–32)

"Inheritance" suggests legitimacy, presumably bestowed by the laws of racial destiny. The image of chasing Europe's earlier populations to geographical peripheries again suggests modern American parallels, that is, the westward push of the frontier and the creation of "Indian" reservations. Macgregor recounts how the victorious "Japhetic" incomers—Celts, Teutons, Greeks, and Slavs—settled in Europe, and concludes:

> Celts and Teutons . . . have become the most famous of them all, and . . . united, they bid fair to possess the world. . . . Liberty and order are two of the greatest blessings which a nation can enjoy. . . . The two races . . . have been distinguished . . . for their attachment to these two great foundations upon which power rests. With the Celts the love of freedom seems to have always been the ruling passion. Witness the untiring zeal with which our forefathers resisted, against such tremendous odds, the power of Saxon England, when it was *unrighteously* exercised to crush them, in the middle ages. . . . The inherent principle . . . in their hearts . . . still abides, to keep down every unjust attempt to bear the sway over them. No doubt this . . . disposition . . . may be carried too far, and the Highlanders have on more than one occasion marred their fortunes by a too eager desire to have their own way. This was conspicuously the case in the history of the Highland clans. (32, italics mine)

Macgregor's typology echoes earlier anti-Celtic discourse which juxtaposed Celtic unruliness against Saxon order. To illustrate his point, he uses historical examples of English-Scottish or Hanoverian-Stuart conflicts: Scotland's medieval "Wars of Independence," the time after the 1603 Union, the Battle of Killiecrankie, and the Jacobite rising of 1745. However, the familiar theme of Scottish or Gaelic threats to an English-dominated British status quo is immediately neutralized. First, these threats are contained in the past; the most recent one happened over 100 years before Macgregor's time of writing. Second, the author at least partially redeems the image of Gaelic history by pointing out that in 1745 there were also many Highlanders who supported the Hanoverians (32–33). Third, he emphasizes that those individual rebellions should not be used as a basis for adverse *generalizations* about the Gaelic racial character:

> It may be supposed that this [the 1745 rebellion, etc.] says very little for the capacity of the Celtic races to take a share in ruling the world. We shall see . . . how this overgrowth of an independent spirit has been tempered into manageable proportions.
>
> With the Teutons . . . love of freedom has been no less strong than with the Celts, but it has been accompanied by an equally strong desire for order and settled government. We are accustomed to regard the Germans as a thoughtful, cautious race, whose delight is in philosophy, music, and . . . all that pertains to civilisation. And upon the whole this estimate is correct. The natural disposition of the people is towards the arts of peace. . . . Germany has for many centuries been the chief civiliser of the world. Let it not be supposed that this throws any discredit on our own country, for . . . the English are really a people of Teutonic descent, and . . . by their union with Scotland they have secured for our nation the two chief elements of national greatness.
>
> . . . The relations . . . between the two principal branches of the Japhetic races have, for the most part, been . . . hostile. . . . Only in modern times . . . any kind of union between them has taken place. That union has been chiefly confined to English-speaking nations, and, even within these limits, Ireland forms a partial exception. The Irish difficulty, though closely connected with the subject of the present enquiry, must be left out of account, as it is a political problem that causes an unpleasant difference of opinion. We need not, however, hesitate to remark that the troubles of Ireland have arisen almost wholly from the ancient, and not yet quite extinct, feud between Celt and Teuton. (33–34)

Macgregor's vision of an amicable Celtic-Teuton partnership of master races is again disturbed by memories of intra-British cultural, national—or, as he might put it, "racial"—conflict. Again, he counters this threat of ideological destabilization by trying to contain the conflicts in the past, in pre-Union history. The greatest source of unease is Ireland, whose threats of insurrection preoccupied many Victorian minds. However, Macgregor downplays this problem, too, proclaiming that the ancient feud is almost over.

Macgregor believes in the potential of racial amalgamation and even declares that this was the foundation of modern France and Britain's superpower status. French success, he claims, was based on a Germanic (Frankish) conquest of a Celtic people and on subsequent amalgamation of the former enemies and their respective assets, that is, the two major ingredients of national greatness, liberty, and order. In Britain, the burying of Teuton-Celtic animosities was likewise "for the most part to our advantage" (35):

> We have a . . . habit of thinking of our own nation as the greatest in the world. . . . We have good grounds for our belief. But we are also apt to think that this pre-eminence has been ours for an indefinite period, . . . which is an error. . . . When England and Scotland were two separate nations . . . almost constantly at war with each other . . . , it was not possible for either of them to exercise much influence [at] the councils of Europe. (36)

> The fusion of races was a work of time, and till it was carried out there was little but violence and disorder. (36)

This fusion was finally achieved with the Union of 1707, "the birth of a new nation, the greatest that the world has ever seen" (37). The merger was facilitated by geography: on the European Continent, post-conquest amalgamations had often failed "because . . . there was always plenty of elbow room," so that "vanquished people could simply move . . . away" (37). But Britain is an island on the edge of Europe, where the vanquished could flee no further, so that amalgamation was the only option for survival. The role of Britain as Europe's land's end in intra-European colonial encounters is a very old theme in Scottish ideological history, for example, featuring in the Declaration of Arbroath (1320) and even in Tacitus's *Agricola*. There, too, Scotland's native inhabitants were portrayed as "the last of the free," an isolated, still unconquered people facing an expanding empire, in a place where they could flee no further. In those older texts, this motif entailed a desperate wish to remain separate. But for Macgregor, land's end has positive associations—joy about the eventual benefits of conquest and forced assimilation. Macgregor's awareness of the Roman connotations is clear from his sketch of "the days of Queen Anne" (37), when Celtic-Teutonic fusion became tangible and "Britain first became the ruling power of the world" (37):

> The British empire was not much longer to be confined to the old world. . . . Regions that Caesar never knew, and where his eagles

> had never flown, were to be possessed by the descendants of the rude tribes of the North, whom he tried so hard to subdue. The valour of the one [the Celts], with the steady perseverance of the other [the Teutons], made the united nation so irresistible, and her people are now dominant in every quarter of the globe. (38)[43]

Britain, which in Roman times had been barbarian territory, has now risen to imperial glory itself. The same potential of emancipation and a rise from colonized rags to world-power riches is ungrudgingly granted to Britain's own colonies:

> [A] violent rupture took place last century between the North American colonies and the mother country. Nor is it . . . unlikely that in the process of time other colonies, both in the New World and at the Antipodes, may spring up into new nations. All this is part of the general law of nature, . . . children grown to manhood cease to depend upon the parent. This should be no cause for serious regret, and it is certainly no cause for thinking that the Anglo-Saxon, or rather the Anglo-Celtic race, has begun to decline. . . . The right view to take is, that new nations springing from the old stock . . . carry the vigour and the enterprise of the races from which they have sprung, in a chain of increasing strength around the world. (38)

His readiness to concede "grown-up" colonial "children" a right to independence resembles Robert Knox's attitudes. For both, however, this is limited to white settler societies largely sprung from British stock. Other colonies, where white minorities ruled over a numerically superior indigenous population as in Africa or India, are apparently excluded from Macgregor's vision of emancipation, just as they are from Knox's. This is suggested by Macgregor's assertion that in future "the extension of the Anglo-Celtic race must go on till the language of Britain becomes the universal language, and British civilisation rules mankind" (39). That he speaks of "the language of Britain" in the singular is noteworthy—although this text is linked to the Gaelic revival, the preeminence of the English language and the linguistic assimilation of the Celtic fringe is not openly questioned.

Many themes of Macgregor's essay reappear in Macbean's, which is likewise concerned with racial destiny and the Celts' position in the world at large (e.g., "Mission of the Celt" 56–57). Macbean explicitly writes back to earlier anti-Celtic stereotypes, but in a way which still stands on the shoulders of anglocentric writers—especially Arnold's, it seems. But, like Macgregor, Macbean goes further than Arnold in several respects, as well as turning the defense of the Celtic internal colonized into a vision of Celtic glory in the role of overseas colonizer.

Macbean's desire to write back to anti-Celticism is obvious in the following passage:

> For more than a century there have been two views regarding the future of the Gaelic-speaking Highlander—the one held by supercilious Englishmen and echoed by feeble Highlanders, the other held by a small but patriotic set of Highlanders. The first view is that the Celt . . . is a relic of barbarism, a nuisance in the way of civilisation that must be speedily swept out of the way, with the exception that Celts who can transform themselves into imitations of Englishmen, be allowed to live on in subordinate positions suitable to their capabilities. . . . The second view . . . has been that of . . . patriots who protested against the invasion of the English tongue and English ideas, and declared that extinction was preferable to submission.
>
> . . . Both views have been wrong. The Highlander is . . . in a better position than either . . . dreamed of. Our fate as a race is neither to die out nor to be Anglicised. On the contrary, it is important even for the future of Saxon civilisation that certain qualities of the Celtic nature should be preserved. (62)

For Macbean, every race has a valid contribution to make—or at least every white race, as the only ones he names in this context are Saxons, Jews, Slavs, Greeks, and Celts (56–57): "every race must add its own endowment to the common heritage of man, and the Celt must take care that the Celtic contribution is not . . . withheld" (57); "the Gaelic race must give its own contribution to the progress of humanity" (62). He argues that one task of the "Gaelic Renaissance" is to ensure that this Gaelic contribution is made and recognized (56, also see 57–61), both in the cultural and the socioeconomic realm. The particular contributions he assigns to each race are congruous with the racial typologies familiar from elsewhere. The Teutons, for instance, contribute "the fruits of plodding industry" (62), echoing Knox's contention that Saxons are diligent and persevering. The Celts are said to cherish "ideals of freedom" (64), which resembles Macgregor's text and romantic accounts of noble savagery. Macbean's reference to Celtic "sentiments of humanity and lofty principle" (64) has precedents in various texts about the moral rigor of noble savages from Tacitus onwards, in Macpherson's Ossianic sentimentality, and in Arnold's theories. The Arnoldian streak is especially clear in the following passage:

> The Gael has the very qualities in which the Saxon is most deficient. It is ideality, . . . sentiment, . . . enthusiasm, . . . *èlan* [*sic*], . . . intensity, . . . imagination, delicacy of fancy, humour, love of colour, love of nature . . . , in a word, all that is spirituelle and opposed to the sordid and the worldly. These are the very qualities which the Teutonic race

> and modern utilitarian civilisation lack most, and the mission of the Celt is to supply them. (62–63, Macbean's italics)

The first hint of Arnoldian connections might be discerned in Macbean's use of the French adjective in the feminine spelling "spirituelle," while a similar construction in a French text would use the masculine form. Perhaps this is a mere spelling error, like "*èlan*" for *élan*. But there may be a deeper significance: perhaps Macbean, whether purposefully or unconsciously, used the feminine form because he considered the Celts to be a feminine race—an idea also propagated by Arnold, to whom Macbean's account owes so much and who is explicitly mentioned in the paragraph below the "spirituelle" passage (63). In the passage quoted here, the second hint of Arnoldian connections is the notion that the Celtic character perfectly complements the Teutonic one, supplying what the latter lacks, and for the latter's benefit. This is also a major tenet of Arnold's. Macbean probably has Arnold in mind when he remarks that his own views had previously been advanced by English writers (63). Macbean presents these parallels in English discourse as an argument in favor of his own thesis—which again reflects how much his "writing back" still defers to English discursive authority.[44] Likewise in Arnoldian fashion, he asserts:

> Of course an educated Englishman is smarter than an ignorant Highlander; but taking both races on the lowest level, . . . a lecturer or vocalist would be more likely to find an intelligent and responsive audience among the crofters of a Highland clachan than among the heavy, clod-hopping, honest hinds [farm laborers] of an English rural district. The . . . Gael (like all Celts) is nervous, sensitive to the influences from the unseen, much impressed by . . . death . . . , keenly sensitive to the lash of conscience. He is by nature an idealist and enthusiast. (63)

However, Macbean is uneasily aware of the impossibility of neat categorization. He acknowledges exceptions to his racial typology—not all Englishmen are dull, and not all Gaels are temperamental. But, like Knox, he evades the unsettling implications of hybridity by immediately reiterating and reaffirming racialist dogma: "we British are a mixed people, and there is in these islands no such thing as purity of race. . . . But still we must hold to the broad facts" (63).

Despite such assertions of purity, Macbean—like Arnold—advocates greater intermixture and cross-fertilization between Celt and Saxon, and identifies instances where this has already happened, for example, Celtic influence on anglophone British literature, mainstream music, and theology (64–65). He also draws the Arnoldian conclusion that this represents a spiritual triumph of the Celtic colonized over their Saxon colonizers: "modern British life is becoming Celticised. The Celtic population had to recede before the aggressive Saxon, but the Celtic spirit conquers in the end" (65).[45]

Celticization also extends to Britain's genetic makeup, for example because "city life is so enfeebling that few families are able to stand it for more than two generations" (65–66), so that dead town-dwellers must always be replaced by a fresh influx of country-folk from the Highlands who thus reinvigorate the British racial stock—both physically and morally. In support, Macbean quotes a royal commission on the crofter question which asserted:

> The . . . population of the Highlands . . . is a nursery of good workers and citizens for the whole empire. . . . The stock is exceptionally valuable. By sound physical constitution, native intelligence, and good moral training, it is particularly fitted to recruit the people of our industrial centres.[46]

Macbean summarizes the Celts' function for the nation as follows: "by infusion of ideas and transfusion of blood to leaven modern civilisation with its own awakening spirit. It is to . . . transform by nobler sentiments the results of art and science and culture as these have been evolved by the sturdy Anglo-Saxon race" (66). But Macbean, unlike Arnold, thinks that the Celtic race can only fulfill this function if it retains the Celtic languages as living forms of expression—only then can their racial identity (with its many merits) be preserved (58). That Macbean's support for Celtic distinctness goes further than Arnold's is also clear in the following passage, especially its opening sentences which directly seem to write back to *On the Study of Celtic Literature*:

> Are we Gaels to be simply lost in the great ocean of Saxon civilisation? Must we become extinct as a race, our only immortality being a slightly more spirituelle aroma about English literature, and a slightly less German cast of the features of the English people? . . . But to the real question—Whether the Gaelic race as a race is to survive and take a recognised part in the . . . civilisation of the future. . . . If the Gael is to be a real and acknowledged factor . . . he must preserve his heritage of Celtic ideals, and . . . endeavour to rid his character of its historic weaknesses. (66–67)

These weaknesses are "fatalism and pessimism" (68), "instability" (67), and "pride" (67–68). Moreover, Macbean implores his fellow Celts:

> We must learn . . . humility and brotherliness towards other races. If . . . the Celts are the oldest Aryan race in Europe, they ought to act the part of an elder brother. The Gael ought especially to make himself master of English literature and science and art. . . . For the perfecting of his own nature, as well as for the serving of the empire and the world, he must cast away his traditional pride, and assimilate the best that modern civilisation can produce. (67–68)

> We shall be better Celts when we rid ourselves of these weaknesses, but if we are to remain Celts . . . , not to speak of Celticising the British nation, we must keep in touch with the spirit of the race as embodied in our literature and traditions, for any real progress must bear some relation to the past. While appropriating the civilised institutions, the industrial arts, the literature, and even the language of the Saxon, we must remain Gaels. It is only thus that we can have any real power. (68–69)

This desire for "real power" distinguishes Macbean from Arnold. For the latter, the Celts' importance was largely confined to the past, apart from limited influences on present and future anglophone literature. For Macbean, the Celtic contribution extends more strongly into the present and future, as well as into the practical, material spheres of politics (64) and overseas imperialism. The latter is expressly recommended to the Gaels as a compensation for their history of victimization by British internal colonialism: "We should like to see our . . . Gaelic nation playing a high and noble role even yet on the stage of history. . . . All that is best in the empire is already ours for the taking, and . . . the opportunity of serving the empire is open to us all" (66–67). To illustrate this, he stresses the Celtic element among colonial governors (64), religious missionaries, and imperial soldiers (64–65). For Macbean, Celtic participation in British overseas imperialism is clearly a matter of pride. And the particular qualities of the Celtic character are recommended as invaluable assets for colonizers and a morally redeeming force for Britain's global civilizing mission:

> Civilisation has terrible problems that await solution. Side by side with its enormous increase of intellectual and material wealth there is an increase of degradation and vice. It needs the touch of some Celtic fairy to change it into some semblance of her own ideals. The British Empire . . . is founded on brute force, and it needs to be inspired with Celtic sentiment and sympathy, and lofty idealism, and the generous chivalry of Ossian and Fionn. . . . On some such lines . . . Providence intends the Gael to accomplish his mission. (69)

Macbean's wish to inspire the brutal materialism of an empire built by Saxons with the spirituality and moral vision of the Celts again echoes Arnold's gendered racial typology: Victorian concepts of gender portrayed women as guardians of morality, spirituality, and idealism which counterbalanced and ennobled the gritty, practical, materialist male spheres of politics and business. The Celts as a feminine race play a similar role in Macbean's vision of the Celtic-Saxon imperialist partnership. The morally redeeming function of the feminine touch in an otherwise over-harsh male-dominated imperialism is also apparent in Kurtz's "Intended" in Conrad's *Heart of Darkness*. Macbean criticizes the "Gaelic gloom" cliché not primarily because it supports Anglo-British internal colonialism on the Celtic fringe, but because it might prevent the Celts from becoming successful colonizers themselves:

> Until quite lately, we seem to have been a race under some evil enchantment. We were ashamed of our Gaelic, ashamed of being Highlanders, and, like a people in dotage, living only in the past. Our music was only in the minor key. . . . But all this is changed. . . . The Gael feels the current of youth coursing through his veins. He knows that a high destiny awaits him. (69)

Much of this "high destiny" lies in overseas colonialism: the Gaelic revival as perceived by Macbean helps to transform Britain's Celts from colonized to colonizer.

Both Macbean and Macgregor transplant racialist theories from an originally anglophone Teutonist background to an intellectual coterie speaking for, and partly even from, the Gaelic margin. Their reinterpretation of Celticist racial typology transformed the alleged weaknesses of a subject people into the strengths of a global master race whose fate and merits were equally glorious as that of their erstwhile Saxon conquerors, so that both could now proceed hand in hand to subdue the rest of the globe. The perpetual dialectic of the Celtic margin's predicament as both Other and Same could hardly be illustrated more clearly.

CONCLUSION

Appropriations of racist discourse in order to defend the Gaels and other "Celts" against quasi-colonial representations were not the only responses to the continued marginality of the Gaidhealtachd, or of Scotland as a whole, during the nineteenth century. There were also other—and at times much more radical—forms of resistance, both ideological and practical. In the press, the racist responses discussed in chapter 5 were complemented by more sympathetic voices which were informed in varying proportions by continued affirmations of progressivism, romanticizations of the Highland predicament, and radical social criticism. Several journalists resisted the widespread racialization of Highland-related reporting, deconstructed racist representations, stressed the importance of local "inside" perspectives, highlighted social rather than racial factors as the causes of the Highland problem, and at times also campaigned for radical social change.[1]

Later, the land agitation movement also linked Highland social criticism to robust grassroots activism and practical resistance. Although it was not linked to the political secessionism more typical of Irish and overseas anticolonial politics, Scottish Gaelic land rights activism attained important results, such as security of tenure as well as low and stable rents, which might be celebrated as the success of an anti-imperial resistance movement. A more skeptical perspective could argue that, even in its successes, the land rights movement still relied on assumptions more reminiscent of colonial than anticolonial thought. Malcolm Chapman argues that the extraordinary social security now granted to crofters often exceeded that of other capitalist subjects and "defined [the Highlands] out of the sphere of modern economics" and of modernity itself. He further argues:

> Whatever we might think of the morality of the economic system within which we find ourselves, it can be argued that isolation from it, while it might confer immunity of a kind, also represents a confirmation . . . of a wider economic impotence. . . . The crofting laws have . . . operated to keep the crofter in . . . [an] idealist half-world . . . , economically and politically irrelevant. The crofting legislation . . . was predicated upon the desirability of keeping the stout Highland stock working the land.[2]

Chapman thus suggests that the (arguably colonizing) romantic idealization of the Gaels as rural noble savages was partly responsible for the Lowland- or English-based establishment's assent to some of the crofters' demands.

Another reaction to internal colonialism was the linguistic and cultural revivalism of the Gaelic intelligentsia, though they partly aimed to achieve their own culture's rehabilitation by placing it at the service of Britain's external colonialism in the overseas empire.

Further Scottish voices of resistance which became slightly louder toward the end of the nineteenth century came from the aforementioned resurgence of Scottish cultural and political nationalism. Although the latter was still dominated by unionism and a desire for limited regional autonomy rather than radical secessionism, the nineteenth-century Home Rule movement might be seen to anticipate elements of a Scottish decolonizing nationalism which built up stronger momentum in the twentieth century. Endorsements of Celticity by Scotland's anglophone mainstream can be seen as part of a wider context of *cultural* patriotism, even where these endorsements seem *politically* rather disabling, as in Celtic Twilight fictions like Sharp's which seem to effect Lowland Scottish cultural gains at the price of racializing and discursively colonizing the Celtic fringe. The backward-looking and feminizing elements in Sharp's work also point toward a colonizing rather than a decolonizing effect. Nonetheless, there were also authors and artists who tried to put images of feminized Celticity to more modern, forward-looking uses, such as Margaret Oliphant or Margaret and Frances MacDonald.[3] This in turn can be seen to build a bridge to the way in which "Celtic" or Gaelic elements are treated by the modernist writers of the twentieth-century Scottish Renaissance, such as Hugh MacDiarmid: here as well, there is an attempt to fuse "Celtic tradition" with "modernity" to create an image of Scottish culture which is rooted, distinctive, *and* progressive.[4] While nineteenth-century appropriations of Celticity were supposed to energize not only the Scottish, but also—and especially—the British nation (given the dominance of unionism), twentieth-century appropriations laid their national focus on energizing the *Scottish* nation, often allied to a more pronounced political nationalism. The twentieth century also saw a greater readiness by mainstream anglophone celtophiles to not just reimagine "the Celtic perspective," or arrogate the right to speak for it, but also let "Celtic" voices speak for themselves and engage in more genuine dialogue with Gaelic culture, for instance through anthologies and other literary projects which brought together both anglophone and gaelophone authors.

In addition to nationalist appropriations, late nineteenth- and early twentieth-century discourse also invoked Gaelic experiences as precedents and indigenous reference points for modern radical politics. The radical movement after 1885 interpreted the Highland Clearances "not just as highland history but as a symbol for the exploitation of the Scottish people."[5]

Traditional "Celtic" precapitalist communal landholding patterns could be interpreted as a sort of Celtic communism. This might be seen to parallel similar concepts developed in overseas (post-)colonies, such as ideas of "African socialism," which likewise reinterpreted selected aspects of precolonial and precapitalist indigenous social structures as valuable reference points in the search for anticolonial, anticapitalist alternatives in present and future liberation struggles. However, in Scotland the fusion of "Celtic" culture with nationalist politics could not be achieved as easily as in Wales and Ireland, because in Scotland the proportion of the population that spoke the Celtic language was numerically much more marginal.[6]

Those "anticolonial" voices which could be heard in nineteenth-century Scotland were often mainly directed against intra-British marginalization, while overseas imperialism was often condoned. A prominent exception was the anglophone Scottish writer and politician R. B. Cunninghame Graham, who not only supported Scottish and Irish Home Rule, but also leveled fairly radical critiques at British overseas colonialism, for instance in his sarcastic ironicization of colonial discourse in his essay "'Bloody Niggers'" (1897).[7] This essay satirizes "Celto-Saxon" pretensions to being the global master race and stresses that race is a social construct, not a biological reality.[8] The author also criticizes the Roman Empire which modern Britons invoked as their model, and compares overseas colonialism to "Aryan" European mainstream attitudes toward Finns and Basques, thus suggesting a notion of internal colonialism within Europe.[9]

In the twentieth century, the decolonizing dynamic of Scottish identity discourse became even more pronounced, and transperipheral solidarity with overseas (post-)colonies became more frequent. Twentieth- and twenty-first-century Scottish society and culture have often critically engaged with older colonial patterns of textualizing Scotland and/or Gaeldom, as well as continuing and radicalizing earlier "anticolonial" discursive traditions. Decolonizing trends can be discerned in many fields, including politics, economics, education, history, literature, and the media. Prominent themes and strategies include the critique of cultural cringes, the reclaiming of discursive authority, the rewriting of history, a direct nationalist politicization of literature, the indigenization of educational and cultural standards, and the subversion of linguistic hierarchies. While some "writing back" merely seems to stand colonial patterns on their head, other Scottish texts transcend colonial dichotomies more fully, for instance by recognizing or even embracing the inevitability of hybridity and transculturality. All these features have also occurred in overseas anti- and postcolonial or transcultural writing. Many modern Scottish texts explicitly recognize these transperipheral parallels, although some of them also acknowledge the complications arising from Scotland's ambiguous historical position as both intra-British colonized and overseas colonizer. Whereas in some overseas contexts postcolonialism is already considered to be on the way out, in the "Celtic fringe" its heyday seems far from over, perhaps especially so because full independence has so far not been achieved, except in the Irish Republic.

This study has shown that anglophone texts have often constructed Scottish Gaelic identity in ways which show considerable similarities with strategies of colonial or postcolonial writing. Such strategies include the legitimation of political, legal, administrative, and economic domination of the margins by hegemonic outsiders; negotiations of religious, linguistic, and other cultural differences; discursive power imbalances; civilizational hierarchies and "civilizing missions"; the hegemony of metropolitan cultural norms on the periphery; both negative and positive stereotypes of othering (i.e., both ignoble and noble savagery); and even biologistic racism. Many features which are stereotypically ascribed to Gaels also appear in overseas colonial othering, such as barbarism, backwardness, provincialism, disorder, illogicality, indolence, filth, femininity, and childishness. There have also been signs of cultural cringes, the imitation of metropolitan standards in anglophone Highland literature, various kinds of writing back, ambivalence, and hybridity.

On the basis of these similarities, a postcolonial "school" within Scottish studies has already been evolving for some time, although this has been much more delayed than corresponding developments in Irish studies, and although the international mainstream of postcolonial studies has largely ignored these developments so far, despite a few important exceptions. The present study aims to encourage further dialogue in this area.

It is also noteworthy that many constructions of Scottish and/or Gaelic identity in colonial terms refer back to Celticist writings from antiquity. Greek and Roman texts about civilization and barbarism often functioned as models for colonial images of modern "Celts"; moreover, images of both ancient and modern Celts furnished models for the representation of overseas colonial populations. Images of Scottish Gaels, as part of a wider Celticist discourse, act as a bridge between ancient and modern colonial discourse, thus occupying a central function in the development of the British global colonial imagination.

Naturally, there are also important specificities. For instance, concentric circles of intra-British marginalization and othering are complemented by concentric circles of same-ing and concentric national *loyalties*. Scots, including the Gaels, have often been less thoroughly othered than, say, colonized indigenous peoples overseas. But the existence of concentric loyalties in Scotland is not necessarily an argument against "(post)colonial" comparability, since similar phenomena have been identified in overseas colonial settler societies.[10]

Concentric, inclusive concepts of British national identity also help to account for the fact that local elites and a certain degree of political choice played an important part in this "internal colonial" project. In Scotland, the degree of "native" collaboration was arguably much greater than it was in

Ireland or various overseas territories. The deep involvement of many Scots in transoceanic colonizing ventures is another important site of ambivalence. However, it should be borne in mind that such complicity in imperialism has also been displayed by certain overseas colonized people. For instance, black African slave traders were members of a colonized region who participated in the colonization of their own region. Examples of colonized subjects who participated in the colonization of other regions and peoples of the globe include white settler societies colonizing the indigenous peoples of "their" country, and both white and nonwhite scions of the colonies that propped up the empire by fighting in the British Army. Thus, the difference between overseas colonized peoples and the Scots might be regarded as being of degree rather than kind. Moreover, such instances of hybridity, which transgress simplistic binarisms between (ex-)colonizer and (ex-)colonized, have already been an important focus of interest in postcolonial scholarship for years, so that the inclusion of Scotland as yet another highly ambivalent field in the discipline might be considered a valuable addition.

Interdisciplinary dialogue also offers important benefits to Scottish studies. International postcolonial and transcultural scholarship has developed a wealth of tools for the analysis of multi- or transcultural societies, of correlations between social and cultural power imbalances, and of (re)constructions of national identities. All these issues are also highly important concerns in contemporary Scottish culture and academia, which might profit from a more sustained engagement with international theoretical developments and comparative studies.

It is thus hoped that this volume has been able to give an introduction to the Scottish postcolonial question which will help to promote an interdisciplinary rapprochement and dialogue between Scottish studies on the one hand and international postcolonial studies and critical ethnic studies on the other.

ABBREVIATIONS

The following abbreviations are used throughout the notes and works cited:

ASLS	Association for Scottish Literary Studies
MS(S)	manuscript(s)
OED	*Oxford English Dictionary*
SGS	*Scottish Gaelic Studies*
SHR	*Scottish Historical Review*
SRO	Scottish Record Office, Edinburgh
TGSI	*Transactions of the Gaelic Society of Inverness*

NOTES

Introduction

1. The concept of internal colonialism was first applied to "Celtic" contexts by Michael Hechter's sociological study *Internal Colonialism: The Celtic Fringe in British National Development 1536–1966* (London: Routledge and Kegan Paul, 1975). Despite its controversial reception, it is still a canonical source on the subject.

2. There is a continuum between the language of England and the language of Lowland Scotland (Scots). Scots is customarily seen as either a regional variety or a closely related sister tongue of English. Scots and (English) English have evolved in parallel from a common root, that is, the language spoken by post-Roman/early medieval Anglo-Saxon incomers who settled in Britain. Anglo-Saxon dialects existed in southern Scotland since the beginning of this settlement. By late medieval times, Scots and English seemed on the way to becoming two separate national languages, though closely related, like Dutch and German or Swedish and Norwegian. That divergence was curtailed after the Unions of 1603 and 1707: Hegemonic (Standard) English gradually replaced Scots as a high-register language for official and intellectual purposes. Remaining usages and forms of Scots were also affected by anglicizing influences, for example, in grammar and vocabulary. Thus, modern Scots today seems more like a regional variety on an international English dialect continuum than a fully separate language. Nonetheless, some nationalists have claimed separate linguistic status for Scots, and partly attempted to (re-)increase its distance from Standard English through language planning and language development. For further information, see the first chapters of J. Derrick McClure, *Scots and Its Literature* (Amsterdam: John Benjamins, 1995) or Michael Gardiner, *Modern Scottish Culture* (Edinburgh: Edinburgh University Press, 2005), 121–28, 130. The present study uses the term "anglophone" for both Scots and (Standard) English, often in contradistinction to "Gaelic," the other indigenous language still spoken in Scotland, which is not part of the Scots-English continuum as it belongs to a different Indo-European language family, that is, the "Celtic" languages, whereas Scots and English are "Germanic" tongues.

3. Edward W. Said, *Orientalism* (1978, repr. with new afterword, New York: Penguin, 1995).

4. Frantz Fanon, *Black Skin, White Masks*, trans. Charles Lam Markmann (New York: Grove, 1967).

5. See the texts discussed in Robert Young's critical study *Colonial Desire: Hybridity in Theory, Culture and Race* (New York: Routledge, 1995).

6. Examples of texts which essentialize "East" and "West" as two distinct clashing civilizations can not only be found in colonial discourse as discussed by

Said and others, but also in contemporary post-9/11 Western right-wing media discourse and popular stereotypes about "Western" vs. "Islamic" culture. For a lucid critique of such Western discourse, see Thomas Bauer, "The Islamization of Islam," in *Ideological Battlegrounds—Constructions of Us and Them before and after 9/11*, vol. 1: *Perspectives in Literatures and Cultures*, ed. Joanna Witkowska and Uwe Zagratzki (Newcastle, Eng.: Cambridge Scholars, 2014).

7. For foundational postcolonial studies of ambivalence, mimicry, and hybridity, see Homi K. Bhabha, "Of Mimicry and Man: The Ambivalence of Colonial Discourse" (1984), "Signs Taken for Wonders: Questions of Ambivalence and Authority under a Tree Outside Delhi, May 1817" (1985), and "The Commitment to Theory" (1989), all repr. (partially rev.) in Bhabha, *The Location of Culture* (New York: Routledge, 1994); and R. J. C. Young, *Colonial Desire*.

8. For foundational works that focus on colonial contexts, see the earlier studies by H. Bhabha and R. J. C. Young quoted above. For a more recent example of postcolonial scholarship on hybridity which focuses on primary texts from the post-colonial period, see Jahan Ramazani, *The Hybrid Muse: Postcolonial Poetry in English* (Chicago: University of Chicago Press, 2001).

9. See, for example, Ranajit Guha and Gayatri Chakravorty Spivak, eds., *Selected Subaltern Studies* (New York: Oxford University Press, 1988); and Spivak, "Can the Subaltern Speak?" (1985), in *Marxism and the Interpretation of Culture*, ed. Larry Grossberg and Cary Nelson (Urbana: University of Illinois Press, 1988).

10. See, for example, Kirsten Holst Petersen and Anna Rutherford, eds., *A Double Colonization: Colonial and Post-colonial Women's Writing* (Mundelstrup, Denmark: Dangaroo, 1986).

11. See, for example, Michelle Keown, David Murphy, and James Procter, eds., *Comparing Postcolonial Diasporas* (New York: Palgrave Macmillan, 2009); and Cristina Şandru, Sarah Lawson Welsh, and Janet Wilson, eds., *Rerouting the Postcolonial: New Directions for the New Millennium* (New York: Routledge, 2010), for example, the editors' "General Introduction," 2–3.

12. See, for example, Frank Schulze-Engler, "Theoretical Perspectives: From Postcolonial to Transcultural World Literature," in *English Literatures across the Globe: A Companion*, ed. Lars Eckstein (Paderborn: Wilhelm Fink, 2007), 20–32, and "Introduction," in *Transcultural English Studies: Theories, Fictions, Realities*, ed. Sissy Helff and F. Schulze-Engler (Atlanta: Rodopi, 2009), especially xi–xiii, xvi; as well as John McLeod, "Sounding Silence: Transculturation and Its Thresholds," *Transnational Literature* 4, no. 1 (2011), http://fhrc.flinders.edu.au/transnational/vol4_issue1.html.

13. See, for example, Ines Detmers, Nancy Grimm, Katrin Thomson, and Laurenz Volkmann, eds., *Local Natures, Global Responsibilities: Ecocritical Perspectives on the New English Literatures* (New York: Rodopi, 2010); Graham Huggan and Helen Tiffin, *Postcolonial Ecocriticism: Literature, Animals, Environment* (New York: Routledge, 2010); Elizabeth DeLoughrey and George B. Handley, eds., *Postcolonial Ecologies: Literatures of the Environment* (Oxford: Oxford University Press, 2011).

14. See. for example, Gert Buelens and Stef Craps, eds., "Postcolonial Trauma Novels," special issue, *Studies in the Novel* 40, nos. 1–2 (2008); Irene Visser, "Trauma Theory and Postcolonial Literary Studies," *Journal of Postcolonial*

Writing 47, no. 3 (2011); Norman Saadi Nikro, ed., "Postcolonial Trauma Studies," special issue, *Postcolonial Text*, 9, no. 2 (2014), www.postcolonial.org.

15. The postcolonial road map given here places special emphasis on classical concepts and thinkers of the field since this might be the best starting point for exploring fundamental interfaces with Scottish studies. Moreover, even recent postcolonialists habitually refer back to principal concepts developed by earlier scholars, even where they do so critically. Focusing on those foundations keeps references in this introductory survey to a manageable size while pointing to issues that remain central to many contemporary discussions. However, I have tried to give at least a few pointers to more recent innovations as well, such as postcolonial ecocriticism or trauma studies. More thorough introductions to postcolonial studies can, for instance, be found in John McLeod, *Beginning Postcolonialism,* 2nd ed. (2000; New York: Manchester University Press, 2010); Bill Ashcroft, Gareth Griffiths, and Helen Tiffin, *The Empire Writes Back: Theory and Practice in Post-Colonial Literatures,* 2nd ed. (1989; New York: Routledge, 2002); and Laura Chrisman and Patrick Williams, eds., *Colonial Discourse and Post-Colonial Theory: A Reader* (New York: Columbia University Press, 1994).

16. While the term "settler colonies" has been retained here for pragmatic reasons, as an established shorthand to describe colonies with a large proportion of British immigrants, it should be noted that the term is problematic because it can be misunderstood to imply that the colonies were not settled (properly inhabited and owned) before the arrival of the Europeans, although in reality the land was, of course, already settled previously, by Native Americans, Maori, Aboriginal Australians, and so on.

17. For example, see the early discussion in Stephen Slemon, "Unsettling the Empire: Resistance Theory for the Second World," *World Literature Written in English* 30, no. 2 (1990).

18. For instance, *The Arnold Anthology of Post-Colonial Literatures in English*, ed. John Thieme (New York: Arnold, 1996), has regional sections on Africa, Australia, Canada, the Caribbean, South Asia, Southeast Asia, and New Zealand and the South Pacific. The latter also features texts like Katherine Mansfield's "The Garden Party" or Frank Sargeson's "I've Lost My Pal" which do not deal with specifically colonial or postcolonial themes and whose only connection to the postcolonial seems to be that they are from a former colony, that is, New Zealand. A regional rather than thematic understanding of postcolonialism is also evident when Thieme's "Introduction" states that the anthology aims to give a "cross-section of . . . the 'new' anglophone literatures" from "countries other than Britain and the United States" (1). This is at odds with the fact that he elsewhere does suggest a focus on specific themes like migration, hybridity, and cultural change (e.g., 3). On the regional versus thematic understandings of postcolonial studies, also see Frank Schulze-Engler, "Exceptionalist Temptations—Disciplinary Constraints: Postcolonial Theory and Criticism," in "Current Critical Theories in Europe," ed. Catherine Bernard, Claire Connolly, and Ansgar Nünning, special issue, *European Journal of English Studies* 6, no. 3 (2002): 290–92.

19. For example, Moritz Csáky, Johannes Feichtinger, and Ursula Prutsch, eds., *Habsburg Postcolonial: Machtstrukturen und kollektives Gedächtnis* (Innsbruck: Studienverlag, 2003); Violeta Kelertas, ed., *Baltic Postcolonialism* (Amsterdam: Rodopi, 2006).

20. For example, Sylvia Tomasch, "Postcolonial Chaucer and the Virtual Jew," in *The Postcolonial Middle Ages*, ed. Jeffrey Jerome Cohen (New York: St. Martin's, 2000); Jamie S. Scott, "Postcolonial Cultures and the Jewish Imaginary" (paper presented at the conference "Transcultural English Studies" hosted by the Association for the Study of the New Literatures in English (ASNEL), Frankfurt a.M., May 20, 2004), and the debate about disciplinary extension which ensued at the same conference during a plenary discussion on "Transculturality and the Future of Postcolonial Studies" (May 23).

Other studies portray contemporary Jews as colonizers rather than (post)colonized, namely concerning the treatment of Palestinians in Jewish-dominated Israel: see, for example, Elia T. Zureik, *The Palestinians in Israel: A Study in Internal Colonialism* (Boston: Routledge and Kegan Paul, 1979); and Anna Ball, *Palestinian Literature and Film in Postcolonial Feminist Perspective* (New York: Routledge, 2012).

21. For a discussion of the varying implications of the term "Celtic fringe," see Murray G. H. Pittock, *Celtic Identity and the British Image* (New York: Manchester University Press, 1999), 1.

22. Today, the term "Western Isles" is often understood to mean only the Outer Hebrides. Historically, however, it has also been used (for instance by Donald Monro and Martin Martin) in a more inclusive sense that also extended to other islands off Scotland's west coast, such as the Inner Hebrides and the Clyde Islands. The present study follows this historical, more inclusive usage—not only in order to mirror some of its key sources, but also in order to reflect the fact that all those islands were historically a part of the Gaelic cultural sphere, so that an umbrella category seems useful. Another term which is here used in an inclusive sense is "Highlander." In Scottish identity constructions, the geographical margins represented by the Highlands and the Western Isles have often been collapsed into one; moreover, they have also been conflated with a linguistic and sociocultural margin (Gaelic speakers with their distinct forms of social organization and cultural life). Thus, in the present study the term "Highlander" also often includes people from those islands, and is also often used synonymously with "Gael." This is, however, merely a pragmatic decision dictated by the source material. As a diplomatic alternative to these two English terms, I also use the Gaelic loanword "Gaidhealtachd" to express both—similar to Malcolm Chapman's usage in *The Gaelic Vision in Scottish Culture* (Montreal: McGill-Queen's University Press, 1978), 233.

23. On the concept of Celticity and its long-standing relation to othering and marginality, see, for example, Malcolm Chapman, *The Celts: The Construction of a Myth* (New York: St. Martin's, 1992); Simon James, *The Atlantic Celts: Ancient People or Modern Invention?* (London: British Museum, 1999); Pittock, *Celtic Identity*; John Collis, *The Celts: Origins, Myths & Inventions* (Stroud, Eng.: Tempus, 2003); Michael Newton, *Warriors of the Word: The World of the Scottish Highlanders* (Edinburgh: Birlinn, 2009), 48–49.

24. An early example of postcolonial ecocriticism in Scottish studies is Mark Toogood, "Decolonizing Highland Conservation," in *Decolonizing Nature: Strategies for Conservation in a Post-Colonial Era*, ed. William M. Adams and Martin Mulligan (Sterling, Va.: Earthscan, 2003).

25. The terms "Celticism" and "Highlandism" are, for instance, used in Charles Withers, "The Historical Creation of the Scottish Highlands," in *The*

Manufacture of Scottish History, ed. Ian Donnachie and Christopher Whatley (Edinburgh: Polygon, 1992); T. M. Devine, *Clanship to Crofters' War: The Social Transformation of the Scottish Highlands* (Manchester: Manchester University Press, 1994), 84–99; Terence Brown, ed., *Celticism* (Atlanta: Rodopi, 1996); and Toogood, "Decolonizing Highland Conservation," 154.

26. The direct quotations are from Newton, *Warriors of the Word*, 64. When I speak of English, or more generally anglophone, British culture as a center which supposedly represented civilized sophistication, this refers mainly to the status of this culture within the British Isles, in relation to internal margins like the Gaelic world. Second, I sometimes refer to the ambition to give anglophone culture *international* eminence, for instance through the emerging overseas empire. However, as Alok Yadav has shown, international ambitions were not immediately achieved. In the seventeenth and early eighteenth centuries, British writers, even from the intra-British metropolis of London, still felt marginalized by more prestigious European cultures, like ancient Greece and Rome or modern France, so that Anglo-British cultural self-assertions must be read against a background of "provincial anxieties." Even in the late eighteenth century, there was anxiety, for instance about whether the empire was already declining (*Before the Empire of English: Literature, Provinciality, and Nationalism in Eighteenth-Century Britain* [New York: Palgrave Macmillan, 2004], 1, also see, for example, 2–5, 10–12, 16–21). But in intra-British cultural relations, the focus of the present study, anglophone and especially English culture had already achieved a firm sense of hegemony and metropolitan centrality. In English struggles for international respectability among Europe's metropoles, English denigrations of (Lowland and Highland) Scottish culture fulfilled similar functions to Scottish Lowland denigrations of Highland culture: distancing from an intra-national "uncouth" provincial culture aided self-alignment with the "higher" cultural level of an external center. Hence, *complete* elimination of provincial otherness was not *always* desired; instead, some wanted to retain vestiges of rusticity on the margins, so that anglophone elite culture would shine more brightly by comparison (Yadav, *Before the Empire of English*, 45–47).

27. A different postcolonially inflected application of subaltern studies to Scottish contexts can be found in Stefanie Lehner, *Subaltern Ethics in Contemporary Scottish and Irish Literature: Tracing Counter-Histories* (Basingstoke, Eng.: Palgrave Macmillan, 2011). Rather than linking subaltern studies to the Gaelic ethnic minority, as I do here, Lehner links them to anglophone victims of intra-Scottish class and gender oppression.

28. See, for example, Billy Kay, *Scottish World: A Journey into the Scottish Diaspora* (Edinburgh: Mainstream, 2006); Angela McCarthy, ed., *A Global Clan: Scottish Migrant Networks and Identities since the Eighteenth Century* (London: I. B. Tauris, 2006); Tanja Bültmann, Andrew Hinson, and Graeme Morton, *Ties of Bluid, Kin and Countrie: Scottish Associational Culture in the Diaspora* (Guelph, Ontario: Centre for Scottish Studies, 2009) and *The Scottish Diaspora* (Edinburgh: Edinburgh University Press, 2013); and T. M. Devine, ed., *To the Ends of the Earth: Scotland's Global Diaspora, 1750–2010* (London: Allen Lane, 2011).

29. For instance, I have repeatedly encountered such positions during discussions at academic conferences. Also see Thieme's aforementioned *Anthology of*

Post-Colonial Literatures, which has numerous regional sections on areas which were once formally colonized, but none on Scotland.

30. On Irish postcolonialism, see, for example, Seamus Deane, *Celtic Revivals: Essays in Modern Irish Literature, 1880–1980* (London: Faber and Faber, 1985); David Cairns and Shaun Richards, *Writing Ireland: Colonialism, Nationalism and Culture* (Manchester: Manchester University Press, 1988); David Lloyd, *Anomalous States: Irish Writing and the Post-Colonial Moment* (Dublin: Lilliput, 1993); Declan Kiberd, *Inventing Ireland* (London: Jonathan Cape, 1995); Luke Gibbons, *Transformations in Irish Culture* (Cork: Cork University Press, 1996); Gerry Smyth, *Decolonisation and Criticism: The Construction of Irish Literature* (London: Pluto, 1998); Claire Connolly, ed., "Postcolonial Ireland?" special issue, *European Journal of English Studies* 3, no. 3 (1999); Colin Graham and Willy Maley, eds., "Irish Studies and Postcolonial Theory," special issue, *Irish Studies Review* 7, no. 2 (1999); Colin Graham and Glen Hooper, eds., *Irish and Postcolonial Writing: History, Theory, Practice* (Basingstoke, Eng.: Palgrave Macmillan, 2002); Eóin Flannery, *Ireland and Postcolonial Studies: Theory, Discourse, Utopia* (Basingstoke, Eng.: Palgrave Macmillan, 2009). On Welsh postcolonialism, see Kirsti Bohata, *Postcolonialism Revisited* (Cardiff: University of Wales Press, 2004); Stephen Knight, *A Hundred Years of Fiction: Writing Wales in English* (Cardiff: University of Wales Press, 2004); Jane Aaron and Chris Williams, eds., *Postcolonial Wales* (Cardiff: University of Wales Press, 2005).

31. For example, "Scotland and the Colonial Experience," special issue, *Scotlands* 2, no. 1 (1995); Berthold Schoene-Harwood, "Emerging as the Others of Ourselves: Scottish Multiculturalism and the Challenge of the Body in Postcolonial Representation," *Scottish Literary Journal* 25, no. 1 (1998); Roderick Watson, "Postcolonial Subjects? Language, Narrative Authority and Class in Contemporary Scottish Culture," *The European English Messenger* 7, no. 1 (1998). An excellent 1990s monograph which applies postcolonial perspectives is Leith Davis, *Acts of Union: Scotland and the Literary Negotiation of the British Nation, 1707–1832* (Stanford, Calif.: Stanford University Press, 1998). Important post-millennial books which likewise connect Scotland with the position of the (post)colonized, although this does not become unmistakably clear from their titles, include Janet Sorensen, *The Grammar of Empire in Eighteenth-Century British Writing* (New York: Cambridge University Press, 2000); Ray Ryan, *Ireland and Scotland: Literature and Culture, State and Nation, 1966–2000* (Oxford: Clarendon, 2002); Douglas S. Mack, *Scottish Fiction and the British Empire* (Edinburgh: Edinburgh University Press, 2006); and Lehner, *Subaltern Ethics.*

32. An attempt to lay *some* systematic groundwork, but mainly with regard to Gaelic-language literature, is made in Silke Stroh, *Uneasy Subjects: Postcolonialism and Scottish Gaelic Poetry* (Amsterdam: Rodopi, 2011), but there is still need for postcolonial introductions to anglophone Scottish writing, and for studies addressing a wider range of genres, both fictional and nonfictional.

33. These two collections were published by Edinburgh University Press (Edinburgh) and Cambridge Scholars (Newcastle, Eng.) respectively.

34. For notable exceptions, see C. L. Innes, *The Devil's Own Mirror: The Irish and the African in Modern Literature* (Washington, D.C.: Three Continents Press, 1990), and "Postcolonial Studies and Ireland," in *Comparing Postcolonial*

Literatures: Dislocations, ed. Ashok Bery and Patricia Murray (New York: St. Martin's, 2000); Murray and Riach, "Celtic Nationalism and Postcoloniality"; Robert J. C. Young, *Postcolonialism: An Historical Introduction* (Oxford: Blackwell, 2001), for example, 96–98, 166, 299–307, and Young, "Scots' Goal Must Be Postcolonial Nationhood," *The Scotsman*, August 15, 2010, www.scotsman.com/news/robert-jc-young-scots-goal-must-be-postcolonial-nationhood-1–821303.

35. Indispensable foundations for any future investigation of these issues were laid by Davis, *Acts of Union*.

36. Peter Hulme, "Including America," in "Postcolonialism and Its Discontents," special issue, *Ariel* 26, no. 1 (1995): 120. Also see Stuart Hall, "When Was 'the Post-Colonial'?: Thinking at the Limit," in *The Post-Colonial Question: Common Skies, Divided Horizons*, ed. Iain Chambers and Lidia Curti (New York: Routledge, 1996), 246.

37. The concept of transperipherality also features in Katie Trumpener's analysis of literary connections between the "Celtic fringe" and the overseas colonies (*Bardic Nationalism: The Romantic Novel and the British Empire* [Princeton, N.J.: Princeton University Press, 1997], viii, 289).

38. While subaltern studies is clearly relevant to the postcolonial study of Scottish Gaeldom in general, it is less of a focus in the present book because the latter concentrates on anglophone texts, whereas subaltern studies concentrate on the subaltern's own perspective, so that any reading of Gaeldom in subaltern terms should focus on Gaelic-language texts. Where this book considers anglophone texts by authors from Gaelic backgrounds (such as Martin Martin or, more briefly, James Macpherson), these authors have already transcended the status of the subaltern to a considerable degree, not only through a high level of formal education which gave them access to the English language and privileged metropolitan channels of written expression, but also through their class position. Both writers came from the Gaelic middle class and, because of their education, mode of writing, lifestyle, and professional achievement, gained admission to the anglophone middle class as well. To the extent that the term "subaltern" connotes an even greater degree of "muting" and exclusion than the terms "internally, doubly, or multiply colonized," the latter occupy a more prominent position in this volume.

39. The standard reference point for postcolonial engagements with "the native intellectual" is still Frantz Fanon, for example, "On National Culture" (1959), in *The Wretched of the Earth*, trans. Constance Farrington (New York: Grove, 1963), 206–48.

40. Examples from recent postcolonial scholarship include Keown, Murphy, and Procter, *Comparing Postcolonial Diasporas*; Graham Huggan, *The Postcolonial Exotic: Marketing the Margins* (New York: Routledge, 2001), for example, 19, 25–27, 85; Sarah Brouillette, *Postcolonial Writers in the Global Marketplace* (New York: Palgrave Macmillan, 2007), for example, 61, 70–71, 79–83; and Sandra Ponzanesi, *The Postcolonial Cultural Industry: Icons, Markets, Mythologies* (New York: Palgrave Macmillan, 2014), for example, 72–78, 87–89.

Chapter 1

1. Also see, for example, Withers, "Historical Creation," 144–45; Jane Dawson, "The Gaidhealtachd and the Emergence of the Scottish Highlands," in *British*

Consciousness and Identity: The Making of Britain, 1533–1707, ed. Brendan Bradshaw and Peter Roberts (Cambridge: Cambridge University Press, 1998), 268–95, 300; Michael Lynch, "A Nation Born Again? Scottish Identity in the Sixteenth and Seventeenth Centuries," in *Image and Identity: The Making and Remaking of Scotland through the Ages*, ed. Dauvit Broun, R. J. Finlay, and M. Lynch (Edinburgh: John Donald, 1998), 93; Jane H. Ohlmeyer, "'Civilisinge of Those Rude Partes': Colonization within Britain and Ireland, 1580s–1640s," in *The Oxford History of the British Empire*, ed. Roger Louis, vol. 1, *The Origins of Empire: British Overseas Enterprise to the Close of the Seventeenth Century*, ed. Nicholas Canny (New York: Oxford University Press, 1998), 124–31; Newton, *Warriors of the Word*, 64.

2. Sorensen, *Grammar of Empire*, 34.

3. For more details on these historical and discursive developments, see, for example, Michael Lynch, *Scotland: A New History* (1991; rev. and repr. London: Pimlico, 1992), for example, 236–38, 291–92; Allan I. Macinnes, "Crown, Clans and Fine: The 'Civilizing' of Scottish Gaeldom, 1587–1638," *Northern Scotland* 13 (1993); Colm Ó Baoill, "Introduction," in *Gàir nan clàrsach / The Harps' Cry: An Anthology of 17th Century Gaelic Poetry*, ed. C. Ó Baoill, trans. Meg Bateman (Edinburgh: Birlinn, 1994), 2–8; Ohlmeyer, "'Civilisinge of Those Rude Partes,'" for example, 132–35, 141–46.

4. A. I. Macinnes, "Crown, Clans and Fine," 32–33.

5. A. I. Macinnes, "Crown, Clans and Fine," 31. It is, however, important to note that the extent of feuding varied between different Highland regions and over time; for instance, Allan Kennedy stresses that it was exceptional in the northern Highlands during the mid-seventeenth century ("'A Heavy Yock Uppon Their Necks': Covenanting Government in the Northern Highlands, 1638–1651," *Journal of Scottish Historical Studies* 30, no. 2 [2010]: 99–100). Moreover, he stresses that feuding not only used direct violence, but also employed juridical and arbitration strategies which respected the structures of central state authority (*Governing Gaeldom: The Scottish Highlands and the Restoration State, 1660–1688* [Boston: Brill, 2014], 105–8).

6. Chapman, *Celts*, 187.

7. Dawson, "Gaidhealtachd," 286.

8. Peter Womack, *Improvement and Romance: Constructing the Myth of the Highlands* (Basingstoke, Eng.: Macmillan, 1989), 6.

9. See R. A. Dodgshon's discussion of blackmail, raiding, and feuding in those terms ("'Pretense of Blude' and 'Place of Thair Duelling': The Nature of Scottish Clans, 1500–1745," in *Scottish Society, 1500–1800*, ed. R. A. Houston and I. D. Whyte [New York: Cambridge University Press, 1989], 195–97).

10. Womack, *Improvement and Romance*, 12, also see 6. W. H. Murray presents blackmail somewhat differently, as "irregular in law rather than illegal, for it was sanctioned by government" (*Rob Roy MacGregor: His Life and Times* [1982; repr. Edinburgh: Canongate, 1995], 60).

11. Lynch, *Scotland: A New History*, 332, 334; T. M. Devine, *The Scottish Nation: 1700–2000* (1999; repr. Harmondsworth, Eng.: Penguin, 2000), 170. Also see the remarks on seventeenth-century cattle raiding in Allan Kennedy, "The Highlands and the Restoration Regime," *History Scotland* 15, no. 1 (2015) and 15, no. 2 (2015): 35.

12. James VI, *Basilicon Doron,* repr., ed. James Craigie, 2 vols. [1599; Edinburgh: William Blackwood, 1944 and 1950], 1:71. Also see Newton, *Warriors of the Word*, 66.

13. "Instructions Concerning the Isles," February 1609, Register of the Privy Council of Scotland, quoted from Edward J. Cowan, "James VI, King of Scots, and the Destruction of the Gàidhealtachd," in *Écosse des Highlands: Mythes et réalité: Actes du Colloque international, Brest, 22–23 Mars 2002*, ed. Bernard Sellin (Brest: Centre de Recherche Bretonne et Celtique, Université de Bretagne Occidentale, 2003), 160; Act of Parliament, "Anent the Lewis Adventurers" (1598), quoted from W. C. MacKenzie, *History of the Outer Hebrides* (Paisley, Scot.: Alexander Gardner, 1903), 178; Act of Parliament, December 14, 1599, ratified 1600, quoted from MacKenzie, *History of the Outer Hebrides*, 196; James VI, letter dated 1608, quoted from Maurice Lee, Jr., *Government by Pen: Scotland under James VI and I* (Urbana: University of Illinois Press, 1980), 77. Also see Newton, *Warriors of the Word*, 65. "Humanity" here can mean either "belonging to the human race," "polite manners," "kindness," "compassion," or "learning."

14. MacKenzie, *History of the Outer Hebrides*, 180. However, MacKenzie's critique is mainly constructive, denouncing metropolitan economic motivations but endorsing a "better" colonial ideal of genuinely philanthropic civilizing missions spreading religion and learning (179–80).

15. James Hunter, *Glencoe and the Indians* (Edinburgh: Mainstream, 1996), 52. Also see E. J. Cowan, "James VI, King of Scots, and the Destruction of the Gàidhealtachd," 163.

16. For example, William Ferguson, *The Identity of the Scottish Nation: An Historic Quest* (Edinburgh: Edinburgh University Press, 1998), 151–54.

17. Wendy Davies, "The Myth of the Celtic Church," in *The Early Church in Wales and the West: Recent Work in Early Christian Archaeology, History and Place Names*, ed. Nancy Edwards and Alan Lane (Oxford: Oxbow, 1992), 12–13.

18. English, Scottish, and Welsh public opinion, London government policies, and Irish self-images tended to treat Ireland as fundamentally different from Britain, often with a "colonial" sense of hierarchy and rigor. Ireland frequently appeared more colonial than Scotland—the latter was, after all, part of the "main" (and Protestant) British island, and often complicit in the colonization of Ireland (also see Linda Colley, *Britons: Forging the Nation, 1707–1837* [1992; repr. London: Pimlico, 1994], 8; Davis, *Acts of Union*, 17).

19. Ferguson, *Identity of the Scottish Nation*, especially 110–16. The Spottiswoode text which Ferguson refers to is *History of the Church of Scotland Beginning the Year of our Lord 203, and Continued to the End of the Reign of King James VI*, ed. Rt. Rev. M. Russell, 3 vols. (Edinburgh: Spottiswoode Society, 1851).

20. Also see Newton, *Warriors of the Word*, 75.

21. T. M. Devine, *Scotland's Empire, 1600–1815* (London: Allen Lane, 2003), 3.

22. Ferguson, *Identity of the Scottish Nation*, 122–23.

23. In other cases, elites raised rents to compensate for their loss of income, leading to the first evictions of tenants unable to pay. On these various developments, see, for example, A. I. Macinnes, "Crown, Clans and Fine," 33–35, 40–41; Dawson, "Gaidhealtachd," 266.

24. Michael J. Enright, "King James and His Island: An Archaic Kingship Belief?" *SHR* 55 (1976).

25. William Ferguson, *Scotland's Relations with England: A Survey to 1707* (Edinburgh: John Donald, 1977), 20, and *Identity of the Scottish Nation*, 122, 151–52.

26. For more details, see "The National Covenant" (1638), in *A Source Book of Scottish History*, ed. William Croft Dickinson, Gordon Donaldson, and Isabel A. Milne, 3 vols. (1952–54; repr. London: Thomas Nelson 1958–61); Lynch, *Scotland: A New History*, especially 248–53, 270–86, 294–95, and "A Nation Born Again?," 91–92, 97; I. B. Cowan, "Covenanters," in *The New Companion to Scottish Culture*, ed. David Daiches (Edinburgh: Polygon, 1993); Ó Baoill, "Introduction," in *The Harps' Cry*, 10–14; John R. Young, "The Scottish Parliament and National Identity from the Union of the Crowns to the Union of Parliaments, 1603–1707," in Broun, Finlay, and Lynch, *Image and Identity*, especially 107–19, 122–24; Allan Kennedy, "The Covenanters of the Northern Highlands," *History Scotland*, 10, no. 1 (2010) and 10, no. 2 (2010).

27. Ferguson, *Identity of the Scottish Nation*, 151–58, 165–67.

28. Signed "A Citizen of Edinburgh," cited from 2nd ed. (London: W. Nicoll, 1765), 14. Nonetheless, the pamphlet's ultimate plea is not for independence, but for an improved Union which is more amicable and equitable (20–21).

29. Basil William Hamilton, Lord Daer, letter to Charles Grey, January 17, 1793, publ. in Edward Hughes, "The Scottish Reform Movement and Charles Grey 1792–94: Some Fresh Correspondence," *SHR* 35 (1956): 34.

30. In addition to ventures initiated by Scottish state authorities or Scottish companies, many Scots embarked on careers in the service of foreign colonial projects, such as English and Dutch ones. On these issues, see, for example, Lynch; *Scotland: A New History*, 307–8; Michael Fry, *The Scottish Empire* (Edinburgh: Birlinn, 2001), xxi, 19–40, 84; Devine, *Scotland's Empire*, 1–7, 26–48, 227.

31. For discussions of the benefits and disadvantages of Union and Empire, see, for example, Hamilton, Lord Daer, letter to Grey, in Hughes, "Scottish Reform Movement," 34–36; Hechter, *Internal Colonialism*, 71–72, 83–84; 93–95, 256; Lynch, *Scotland: A New History*, for example, 309–26, 386–88; Colley, *Britons: Forging the Nation*, for example, 55–71, 117–32; Paul Henderson Scott, "'A Severed and Withered Branch': The Rise and Fall of Britishness," in *Scotland to Slovenia: European Identities and Transcultural Communication*, ed. Horst W. Drescher and Susanne Hagemann (Frankfurt a.M.: Peter Lang, 1996); Scott, ed., *Scotland: An Unwon Cause: An Anthology with a Commentary* (Edinburgh: Canongate, 1997), 38–68; and Scott, "An English Invasion Would Have Been Worse: Why the Scottish Parliament Accepted the Union," *Scottish Studies Review* 4, no. 2 (2003); J. R. Young, "Scottish Parliament," 124–29; Devine, *Scottish Nation*, for example, 3–30, 49–63, 200–1, 213, and Devine, *Scotland's Empire*.

32. For example, see Murray G. H. Pittock, *Poetry and Jacobite Politics in Eighteenth-Century Britain and Ireland* (Cambridge: Cambridge University Press, 1994), 3, 133–86; Newton, *Warriors of the Word*, 34.

33. For instance, Sir John MacLean of Duart (1670–1716), wanting to regain ancestral lands which had fallen to the Campbells, supported the Stuarts in the hope that, after a Jacobite victory, the Hanoverian Campbells would be punished

and their possessions redistributed. See Ronald Black, ed. and trans., *An lasair: Anthology of 18th Century Scottish Gaelic Verse* (Edinburgh: Birlinn, 2001), 390.

34. "Jacobitism," in *The Companion to Gaelic Scotland*, ed. Derick S. Thomson (Oxford: Basil D. Blackwell, 1983), 140. On the history of the Jacobite movement, also see Lynch, *Scotland: A New History*, 319–38; P. H. Scott, *Scotland: An Unwon Cause*, 69–72; Devine, *Scottish Nation*, 32–48; James Hunter, *Last of the Free: A Millennial History of the Highlands and Islands of Scotland* (1999; repr. Edinburgh: Mainstream, 2000), 190–99, 210. On notions of divine right, see David Findlay, "Divine Right and Early Modern Gaelic Society," in *Rannsachadh na Gàidhlig 2000: Papers Read at the Conference "Scottish Gaelic Studies 2000" Held at the University of Aberdeen 2–4 August 2000*, ed. Nancy R. McGuire and Colm Ó Baoill (Aberdeen: An Clò Gaidhealach, 2002). It is also important to remember that not all Gaels supported the Royalist side—for instance, see the examples discussed in A. Kennedy, "Heavy Yock," and A. Kennedy, "Covenanters of the Northern Highlands." But mainstream stereotypes about Gaeldom nonetheless seized more on the Royalist side of Highland history, which could also lead to hostile othering by Lowlanders who sympathized with the anti-Stuart revolutions.

35. For example, see Colley, *Britons: Forging the Nation*, 5–8; Devine, *Scottish Nation*, 47, 58, and *Scotland's Empire*, 74.

36. Lynch, *Scotland: A New History*, 343; Colley, *Britons: Forging the Nation*, 6, 373–74; Richard J. Finlay, "Caledonia or North Britain? Scottish Identity in the Eighteenth Century," in Broun, Finlay, and Lynch, *Image and Identity*; Graeme Morton, "What If? The Significance of Scotland's Missing Nationalism in the Nineteenth Century," in Broun, Finlay, and Lynch, *Image and Identity*, 160; Devine, *Scottish Nation*, 29–30.

37. Ironically, many Gaels likewise seem to have felt concentric loyalties to clan, Gaidhealtachd, Scotland, and Britain, but did not always regard the Hanoverian monarchy as the right guardian of Scottish or British national interests (see Stroh, *Uneasy Subjects*, 85–93). Anglophone anti-Gaelic discourse interpreted this not as *alternative* Scottish/British patriotism, but as a sign that Gaels were totally unpatriotic.

38. Devine, *Scottish Nation*, 26.

39. Lynch, *Scotland: A New History*, 386, 388; Colley, *Britons: Forging the Nation*, 8, 140, 373, and Linda Colley, *Acts of Union and Disunion: What Has Held the UK Together—and What Is Dividing It?* (London: Profile, 2014), 99, 120; James Hunter, *A Dance Called America: The Scottish Highlands, the United States and Canada* (Edinburgh: Mainstream, 1994), and Hunter, *Glencoe and the Indians*; Devine, *Scottish Nation*, 26, 60–61, 115, and *Scotland's Empire*; Fry, *Scottish Empire*.

40. Similar things happened in Ulster, but not in southern Ireland.

41. James Hunter, *The Making of the Crofting Community* (1976; rev. ed. Edinburgh: John Donald, 2000), 44. Usually, the term "neocolonial" is used for "Third World" countries which were once formally colonial, then gained independence, but remain under more informal imperialist influence (e.g., via the International Monetary Fund) of foreign imperialist powers—sometimes their former colonizers like the United Kingdom or France, sometimes more recent world powers like the United States or China. In this strict sense, the label "neocolonial" is

inapplicable in Scotland because a post-British independence phase has not been reached. Hunter evidently applies the term in a looser sense in order to imply that the Highlands were not officially a colony but nominally an equal, fully integrated part of Britain, that is, "neocolonial" here means "nominal parity with the imperialists, but de-facto inferiorization nonetheless." While I would not personally endorse this loose usage of the term "neocolonial," Hunter's implication of inferiorization despite nominal parity is correct. Moreover, his use of the term is worth citing because it is an example of how modern Scottish historians with an interest in national or regional emancipation use several kinds of colonial labels to draw analogies with overseas experiences.

42. Devine, *Scottish Nation*, 57–59. On the Scottish and Irish economy, also see ibid., 107–14, 152–95, 214; Tom Nairn, *The Break-Up of Britain: Crisis and Neo-Nationalism*, exp. 2nd ed. (1977; London: Verso, 1981), for example, 11–12, 72, 138–48, 176; James Shaw Grant, "Highland History—A British Asset," *TGSI* 52 (1980–1982): 463–75; Lynch, *Scotland: A New History*, 381; Robert [D.] Clyde, *From Rebel to Hero: The Image of the Highlander, 1745–1830* (East Linton, Scot.: Tuckwell, 1995), 25, 36; Luke Gibbons, "'Some Hysterical Hatred': History, Hysteria and the Literary Revival," *Irish University Review* 27, no. 1 (1997): 9–11.

43. Beattie, letter to Sylvester Douglas, Lord Glenbervie, January 5, 1778, publ. in Sir William Forbes, *An Account of the Life and Writings of James Beattie*, 2 vols. (Edinburgh: Archibald Constable, 1806), 2:16–17, also see 18.

44. David Hewitt, "Scoticisms and Cultural Conflict," in *The Literature of Region and Nation*, ed. R[onald] P. Draper (Basingstoke, Eng.: Macmillan, 1989), 126–28, 131–33; Lynch, *Scotland: A New History*, 343–44; Franklin E. Court, *Institutionalizing English Literature: The Culture and Politics of Literary Study, 1760–1900* (Stanford, Calif.: Stanford University Press, 1992), 17–20, 37; Devine, *Scottish Nation*, 29; Robert R. Crawford, *Devolving English Literature,* 2nd ed. with new afterword (1992; Edinburgh: Edinburgh University Press, 2000), for example, 16–44, and Crawford, ed., *The Scottish Invention of English Literature* (Cambridge: Cambridge University Press, 1998).

45. Evan Gottlieb, *Feeling British: Sympathy and National Identity in Scottish and English Writing, 1707–1832* (Lewisburg, Pa.: Bucknell University Press, 2007), for example, 46–49, 108, 208. Similar arguments appear in Juliet Shields, *Sentimental Literature and Anglo-Scottish Identity, 1745–1820* (Cambridge: Cambridge University Press, 2010), for example, 2, 8, 85–86.

46. John Home's work, however—despite its popularity in Edinburgh—was only successful in London theaters until the Londoners found out that the author was Scottish. On Scoto-British careers and the unease they inspired in England, see Richard B. Sher, "Percy, Shaw, and the Ferguson 'Cheat': National Prejudice in the Ossian Wars," in *Ossian Revisited*, ed. Howard Gaskill (Edinburgh: Edinburgh University Press, 1991), 212–15, 234–35; Colley, *Britons: Forging the Nation*, 105–16, 120–21; Leith Davis, "'Origins of the Specious': James Macpherson's Ossian and the Forging of the British Empire," *The Eighteenth Century: Theory and Interpretation* 34, no. 2 (1993): 140; Trumpener, *Bardic Nationalism*, 312; Pittock, *Celtic Identity*, 31–33.

47. J. Derrick McClure, "Lowland Scots: An Ambivalent National Tongue" (1984), rev. and repr. in McClure, *Scots and Its Literature*, 9–11; Hewitt,

"Scoticisms," 131–32; Robert Crawford, "Introduction," in R. Crawford, *Scottish Invention*, 4–5; Fiona Stafford, "Hugh Blair's Ossian, Romanticism and the Teaching of Literature," in R. Crawford, *Scottish Invention*, 69–70; Finlay, "Caledonia or North Britain?" 148–51; Devine, *Scottish Nation*, 29–30.

48. See, for example, Edward Lhuyd, *Archaeologia Britannica, Giving Some Account Additional to What Has Been Hitherto Publish'd, of the Languages, Histories and Customs of the Original Inhabitants of Great Britain: From Collections and Observations in Travels through Wales, Cornwal, Bas-Bretagne, Ireland and Scotland, Vol. I: Glossography* (1707), repr. in *Celtic Linguistics, 1700–1850*, vol. 2 (London: Routledge, 2000); "Fear Chanaidh" (J. L. Campbell), "Eideard Lhuyd agus Archaeologia Britannica," *Gairm* 21 (1957): 37–41; Ian Grimble, "The Rev. Alexander Pope's Letter to James Hogg, 1774," *SGS* 11, no. 1 (1966); Fiona Stafford, *The Sublime Savage: A Study of James Macpherson and the Poems of Ossian* (Edinburgh: Edinburgh University Press, 1988), 63; Ferguson, *Identity of the Scottish Nation*; James, *Atlantic Celts*, 44–47; Collis, *Celts*, 47–53. The best modern edition of Macpherson's Ossianic writings is *The Poems of Ossian and Related Works*, ed. Howard Gaskill (Edinburgh: Edinburgh University Press, 1996).

49. "When Was Gaelic Scottish? The Origins, Emergence and Development of Scottish Gaelic Identity, 1400–1750," in McGuire and Ó Baoill, *Rannsachadh na Gàidhlig 2000*, 239.

50. For example, this seems to be implied by Devine, *Scottish Nation*, 29–30.

51. See, for example, Samuel Johnson, *A Journey to the Western Islands of Scotland* (1775), repr. together with James Boswell's *The Journal of a Tour to the Hebrides with Samuel Johnson* (1785), ed. Peter Levi (Harmondsworth, Eng.: Penguin, 1984), 51; Andrew Sanders, *The Short Oxford History of English Literature,* rev. 2nd ed. (1994; Oxford: Clarendon, 1996), 256–57, 276; Mack, *Scottish Fiction*, 95–97; Newton, *Warriors of the Word*, 48–49. However, classicism was not only a vehicle for the British mainstream's internal or external imperialism—it could also express Jacobite or peripheral/regional-nationalist dissent (Pittock, *Poetry and Jacobite Politics*, for example, 7, 81–82, 149–62).

52. Martin Price, "The Restoration and the Eighteenth Century," in *The Oxford Anthology of English Literature*, gen. eds. John Hollander and Frank Kermode, 2 vols. (Oxford: Oxford University Press, 1973), 1:1555.

53. For example, the phrase "Athens of Britain" was used by the eighteenth-century painter Allan Ramsay; quoted from Nicholas Phillipson, "The Scottish Enlightenment," in *The Enlightenment in National Context*, ed. Roy Porter and Mikuláš Teich (Cambridge: Cambridge University Press, 1981), 19. The phrase "Athens of the North" was apparently first used by James Stuart in Nicholas Revett and J. Stuart, *The Antiquities of Athens*, vol. 1 (London: John Haberkorn, 1762)—see Trevor Royle, *The Mainstream Companion to Scottish Literature* (Edinburgh: Mainstream, 1993), 13.

54. Editorial, "On the Proposed National Monument at Edinburgh," *Blackwood's Edinburgh Magazine* 5, no. 28 (1819): 385.

55. Chapman, *Celts*, for example, 201–5; Ferguson, *Identity of the Scottish Nation*, 202–6; James, *Atlantic Celts*, 44–47, 51–53; Collis, *Celts*, 36–52, 71–73.

56. Edward J. Cowan suggests that this three-way connection already existed in the sixteenth century ("The Discovery of the Gàidhealtachd in Sixteenth

Century Scotland," *TGSI* 60 [1997–98]: 280; and "James VI, King of Scots, and the Destruction of the Gàidhealtachd," 155).

57. On universalist concepts of progress—and the perception of cultural and spatial difference as temporal difference—in Renaissance texts, also see Walter Mignolo's discussion of Europe's Central and South American Others in *The Darker Side of the Renaissance: Literacy, Territoriality, and Colonization,* 2nd ed. (1995; Ann Arbor: University of Michigan Press, 2003), for example, 256–57, 327–30, 454. The connection to ancient Greece and Rome is also noted by E. J. Cowan, "Discovery of the Gàidhealtachd," 278, and studied at length in Ronald L. Meek's *Social Science and the Ignoble Savage* (Cambridge: Cambridge University Press, 1976). Although Meek focuses on Enlightenment Scotland and France, both of which possessed "Celtic fringes," neither ancient nor modern "Celtic" barbarians play a prominent role in his study, despite a few passing references. His prime examples of "ignoble savagery" are ancient Germans and modern Native Americans. However, the comparative perspective can be extended to "Celtic" contexts—also see the example cited in Newton, *Warriors of the Word*, 49.

58. James Chandler, *England in 1819: The Politics of Literary Culture and the Case of Romantic Historicism* (Chicago: University of Chicago Press, 1998): for example, 36, 127–31, 166–67.

59. The romantic age later used the same binarism, only with reversed evaluations: the center's traits now appeared as (over-)formality, slavish adherence to inhibiting conventions, sterility, emotionless calculation or materialism, and would seem boring and artifical. The noble and exotic savages/barbarians/Others would be considered as refreshingly and endearingly informal, unconventional, creative, free, fertile, spontaneous, imaginative, modest, passionate, interesting, and natural. These alleged character traits and their binary structures are also noted by Womack, *Improvement and Romance*, 168–69; Chapman, *Celts*, 129; Withers, "Historical Creation," 148; and Newton, *Warriors of the Word*, 49. For nineteenth- and twentieth-century examples of the binarism, see Patrick Sims-Williams, "The Visionary Celt: The Construction of an Ethnic Preconception," *Cambridge Medieval Celtic Studies* 11 (1986).

60. James, *Atlantic Celts*, for example, 47, 138. Similarly, one reason why non-Celtic-speaking Galicia has claimed a Celtic identity was a desire for supranational affiliations to counterbalance marginalization by a Castilian-dominated Spanish state. See Dietrich Briesemeister, "Keltentum und Nationalismus in Galicien," in *Nationalism in Literature—Literarischer Nationalismus: Literature, Language and National Identity: Third International Scottish Studies Symposium—Proceedings*, ed. Horst W. Drescher and Hermann Völkel (Frankfurt a.M.: Peter Lang).

61. On the sixteenth century, see E. J. Cowan, "Discovery of the Gàidhealtachd," 278–79.

62. Anon., "Preface," *Edinburgh Review* 1 (1755), repr. in *The Edinburgh Review for the Year 1755* (London: Longman, Hurst, Rees, Orme and Brown, 1818), iii. Also see Lynch, *Scotland: A New History*, 343–44.

63. For example, see the overseas examples discussed in Nicholas Thomas, *Colonialism's Culture: Anthropology, Travel and Government* (Princeton, N.J.: Princeton University Press, 1994), 98, 132–36, 140–42.

64. However, the disdain of Enlightened intellectuals for Scottish history little diminished the glory of national heroes like Wallace, Bruce, or the Covenanters in popular opinion.

65. Ferguson, *Identity of the Scottish Nation*, 206–7; Devine, *Scottish Nation*, 29.

66. Quoted from R. L. Meek, *Ignoble Savage*, 161.

67. Sermon, quoted from R. L. Meek, *Ignoble Savage*, 137.

68. Adam Smith, *An Inquiry into the Nature and Causes of the Wealth of Nations* (1776), repr. ed. R. H. Campbell and A. S. Skinner, 2 vols. (Oxford: Clarendon, 1976): 344, 689–93, 776. On other sources which compare Gaels and Native Americans, see Michael Newton, "Celtic Cousins or White Settlers? Scottish Highlanders and First Nations," in *Rannsachadh na Gàidhlig 5 / Fifth Scottish Gaelic Research Conference*, ed. Kenneth E. Nilsen (Sydney, Nova Scotia: Cape Breton University Press, 2010), 225–32.

69. Chapman, *Gaelic Vision*, 19–20. Also see Devine, *Scottish Nation*, 241.

70. Womack, *Improvement and Romance*, 20–25. Also see Fiona J. Stafford, *The Last of the Race: The Growth of a Myth from Milton to Darwin* (Oxford: Clarendon, 1994), 91.

71. Chandler, *England in 1819*, 130–32.

72. The colonial implications of Enlightened universalism and monogenism, as well as the gradual transition to the more static notions of polygenism and racism which became prevalent in the nineteenth century, are lucidly mapped by R. J. C. Young, *Colonial Desire*, for example, 6–13, 31–49, 65–67.

73. *Smith, Wealth of Nations,* 133, 179, 237–41, 413, 944.

74. Errors he sees in previous and contemporary imperial policies include mercantilism, harsh treatment of colonized populations, and the hypocrisy of hiding economic exploitation behind a rhetoric of sacred Christianizing missions. He even wonders whether decolonization, followed by free alliances and exchange, might not be the best solution, though he thinks it unlikely that the colonizers (misled by national pride) would voluntarily accept this. Hence, a reform rather than the abolition of empire is deemed a more likely—and still very promising—solution. Necessary reforms include free trade, representative government, and accelerated "improvement" (Smith, *Wealth of Nations*, for example, 561–69, 581–635, 944–47).

75. Ferguson, *Identity of the Scottish Nation*, 215–17.

76. See Ferguson, *Identity of the Scottish Nation*, 209–10.

77. Jürgen Osterhammel, *Die Entzauberung Asiens: Europa und die asiatischen Reiche im 18. Jahrhundert* (Munich: Beck, 1998).

78. For example, see Osterhammel, *Entzauberung*, 400.

79. Later this piece of news turned out to be false: their attempt to kill him had been unsuccessful.

80. In *Scotish Elegiac Verses. M.DC.XXIX–M.DCC.XXIX*, ed. James Maidment (Edinburgh: Thomas G. Stevenson, 1842), xxxix–xlix. The editor does not give a precise date, but a statement that it was written during Rob Roy's old age (p. xl) points to the 1720s or 1730s.

81. Brougham, letter to Lord Robertson, August 14, 1799, publ. in *The Life and Times of Henry Lord Brougham, Written by Himself*, 3 vols. (Edinburgh: William Blackwood, 1871), 1:105, Brougham's italics. Further references to St.

Kildans as "savages" appear in the same letter, 100–101, 103, 106. An earlier letter to the same addressee (dated "August 1799," day unspecified, publ. ibid., 92–99) describes the Hebrides in general as "remote and barbarous" (97).

82. Brougham, same letter, 107–8. Despite these denigrations, there are also elements of noble savagery: he calls the Hebrideans "a very simple and worthy set of men" (letter to Lord Robertson, August 1799, 98).

83. Hunter, *Last of the Free*, 197–98.

84. Similarly, Womack notes desires of conquest underlying the first climbs of Highland summits by non-Highland geographers, botanists, and geologists in the eighteenth century (*Improvement and Romance*, 71–72).

85. On modern European forms of geographical knowledge, their links to overseas colonial expansion, and their roots in Roman imperial traditions, also see Mignolo, *Darker Side*, for example, 243, 281, 283.

86. A. Kennedy, "Heavy Yock"; and Kennedy, *Governing Gaeldom*, 6–9, 29–31, 64, 251–55.

87. A. Kennedy, *Governing Gaeldom*, 9, 251–52.

88. To some extent, this is also noted by Allan Kennedy, who acknowledges discursive othering (e.g., "Reducing That Barbarous Country: Center, Periphery, and Highland Policy in Restoration Britain," *Journal of British Studies* 52, no. 3 [2013]; and Kennedy, *Governing Gaeldom*, 17–29, 64, 252–55). But even here he downplays comparability to colonial contexts, at least for the Restoration period. That Highlanders were regarded as "barbarous" is, in his view, not enough to make them a colonial-style Other because the label could sometimes "merely" mean "lawless" or "disorderly" and was even applied to censure such behavior among people who were unambiguously seen as members of the mainstream's Self (*Governing Gaeldom*, 29–31). I would argue, however, that the latter does not necessarily invalidate the association with colonial discourse—arguably, the very force of "barbarian" as a term of censure for misbehaving mainstreamers comes from such colonial associations: one implies that such behavior might have a place among "savage" societies somewhere else, but surely not in "a civilised society such as ours." Non-Europeans who have regarded the label "barbarian" as a colonial insult to their cultures surely have not considered the label any less colonial just because their European colonizers also used it within their own in-groups to insult each other.

89. Pittock, *Celtic Identity*, 29.

90. James VI, *Basilicon Doron*, 1:71.

91. Statement made apparently by King James VI, ca. 1607/1608; quoted from Isabel Frances Grant, *The Macleods: The History of a Clan 1200–1956* (London: Faber and Faber, 1959), 208. Also see MacKenzie, *History of the Outer Hebrides*, 188–89.

92. For example, see MacKenzie, *History of the Outer Hebrides*, 171–235; David Harris Willson, *King James VI and I* (1956, repr. London: Jonathan Cape, 1959), 119; I. F. Grant, *Macleods*, 188–207; Ó Baoill, "Introduction," *The Harps' Cry*, 3; Angus Martin, *Kintyre: The Hidden Past* (Edinburgh: John Donald, 1999), 2.

93. Lynch, *Scotland: A New History*, 242. This does not mean that their relations with the government were entirely free from tension: for example, the government attempted to curb "overmighty," all-too-independent powers, interests, and

policies of the Campbells of Argyll (Lynch, *Scotland: A New History*, 291–97). Also see A. Kennedy, "Heavy Yock," and "Reducing That Barbarous Country."

94. For example, see Allan I. Macinnes, "Seventeenth-Century Scotland: The Undervalued Gaelic Perspective," in *Celtic Languages and Celtic Peoples: Proceedings of the Second North American Congress of Celtic Studies*, ed. Cecil J. Byrne, Margaret Harry, and Pádraig Ó Siadhail (Halifax, Nova Scotia: D'Arcy McGee Chair of Irish Studies, St. Mary's University, 1992), 536, and "Crown, Clans and Fine"; Dawson, "Gaidhealtachd," 266, 297; A. Kennedy, "Heavy Yock" and *Governing Gaeldom*.

95. Both quotations from Dawson, "Gaidhealtachd," 297.

96. Lynch, *Scotland: A New History*, 284, 299, and "A Nation Born Again?" 90.

97. For example, see "Jacobitism," in Thomson, *Companion*, 140; Lynch, *Scotland: A New History*, 331–32; Devine, *Scottish Nation*, 39–43.

98. Lynch, *Scotland: A New History*, 319–20.

99. Hunter, *Making of the Crofting Community*, 40.

100. For example, Clyde, *From Rebel to Hero*, 3–5, 181.

101. *Scots Magazine* (1745), 518; quoted from Chapman, *Gaelic Vision*, 21.

102. Womack, *Improvement and Romance*, 14.

103. National Library of Scotland, Adv. MS. 16.1.14, 6–7; quoted from Clyde, *From Rebel to Hero*, 10–11.

104. National Library of Scotland, Adv. MS. 16.1.14, 1–3; quoted from Clyde, *From Rebel to Hero*, 10–11.

105. James Chevalier de Johnstone, *Memoirs of the Rebellion in 1745 and 1746*, trans. from French ms. (London: Longman, Hurst, Rees, Orme and Brown, 1820), 76–77.

106. Colley, *Britons: Forging the Nation*, 85–88.

107. Duncan Forbes, "Some Thoughts Concerning the State of the Highlands of Scotland" (1746?), in *Culloden Papers*, ed. H. R. Duff (London: T. Cadell and W. Davies, 1815), 298–99.

108. Forbes, "Some Thoughts," 300–301.

109. George, 3rd Lord Reay, letter to an unknown addressee, probably a government official, September. 2, 1746; publ. in Angus Mackay, *The Book of Mackay* (Edinburgh: Norman MacLeod, 1906), 456. Also see Ian Grimble, *The World of Rob Donn* (Edinburgh: Edina, 1979), 70–71.

110. William Mackay, "Instructions by Cumberland after Culloden; Instructions by General Wolfe before Quebec," *TGSI* 32 (1924–25): 306; "Jacobitism," in Thomson, *Companion*, 140; Hunter, *Last of the Free*, 200–202; Devine, *Scottish Nation*, 45–47. Hunter and Devine also give examples of local resistance.

111. Lynch, *Scotland: A New History*, 339.

112. Hunter, *Last of the Free*, 211; also see Newton, *Warriors of the Word*, 71.

113. *The Highlands of Scotland in 1750: From Manuscript 104 in the King's Library, British Museum*, ed. Andrew Lang (Edinburgh: Blackwood, 1898), 144–45; also see 159–60.

114. Ibid., 31.

115. Z. S. Strother, "Display of the Body Hottentot," in *Africans on Stage: Studies in Ethnological Show Business*, ed. Bernth Lindfors (Bloomington: Indiana University Press, 1999), 13; also see 2–4, 49.

116. *OED.*

117. On the Khoikhoi side of the equation, see Strother, "Display of the Body Hottentot," 2–3, 11–12, 16.

118. For example, Voltaire, *Essai sur les moeurs et l'esprit des nations* (1756); repr., ed. Rene Pomeau, 2 vols. (Paris: Garnier, 1963), 308.

119. Strother, "Display of the Body Hottentot," 13.

120. *Highlands of Scotland*, 160.

121. Grant, "Highland History," 462.

122. On religious and educational missions in the Highlands, also see, for example, Hunter, *Making of the Crofting Community*, 143; Victor Edward Durkacz, *The Decline of the Celtic Languages: A Study of Linguistic and Cultural Conflict in Scotland, Wales and Ireland from the Reformation to the Twentieth Century* (Edinburgh: John Donald, 1983); Lynch, *Scotland: A New History*, 364–66; A. I. Macinnes, "Crown, Clans and Fine," 37–39, 47; Ó Baoill, "Introduction," in *The Harps' Cry*, 5–6; Clyde, *From Rebel to Hero*, 49–67; Devine, *Scottish Nation*, 93–97.

123. Quoted from Gordon Donaldson, ed., *Scottish Historical Documents* (1970; rev. and repr. Edinburgh: Scottish Academic Press, 1974), 178.

124. Letter publ. in Sir William Fraser, ed., *The Sutherland Book*, 3 vols. (Edinburgh, 1892), vol. 2, *Correspondence*, 359. Also see Newton, *Warriors of the Word*, 67.

125. Charles I, letter to the archbishops and bishops, August 25, 1626, publ. in *Miscellany of the Maitland Club, Consisting of Original Papers and Other Documents Illustrative of the History and Literature of Scotland*, ed. James Dennistoun and Alexander Macdonald, vol. 2, ed. A. Macdonald and Joseph Robertson (Edinburgh, 1840).

126. Ó Baoill, "Introduction," in *The Harps' Cry*, 8.

127. Stafford, *Sublime Savage*, 17.

128. SSPCK, *State of the Society in Scotland, for Propagating Christian Knowledge, Giving a Brief Account of the Condition of the Highlands and Islands of Scotland. . . . Together with Some Account of the Society's Missionaries for Converting the Native Indians of America* (Edinburgh: R. Fleming, 1741). Also see Sorensen, *Grammar of Empire*, 236; Newton, *Warriors of the Word*, 219.

129. SSPCK minutes of Directors of the Society, March 20, 1755, Scottish Record Office (SRO), Edinburgh, GD.95/2/7; quoted from Clyde, *From Rebel to Hero*, 58.

130. Walker, Report to the General Assembly on the state of the Highlands and Islands, SRO, CH.1/1/55, 596; quoted from Clyde, *From Rebel to Hero*, 61.

131. MS, SRO, E. 783/55 nos. 2(1) and 5; quoted from Ronald Black, "Mac Mhaighstir Alasdair in Rannoch: A Reconstruction," *TGSI 59* (1994–96): 363.

132. For examples from the South Pacific, see Thomas, *Colonialism's Culture.*

133. MS CH1/2/24/1 pt.1 fo.7, Papers and Letters of the General Assembly of the Church of Scotland, 1703–1727, SRO; quoted from Durkacz, *Decline of the Celtic Languages*, 49. "Interest" and "danger" probably refer to Jacobitism.

134. MS CH1/2/24/1 pt.1 fo.7, Papers and Letters of the General Assembly of the Church of Scotland, 1703–1727, SRO; quoted from Durkacz, *Decline of the Celtic Languages*, 49.

135. SSPCK document, 7 June 1716, MS, SRO, GD.95 1 1, 294; quoted from Charles W. J. Withers, *Gaelic in Scotland 1698–1981: The Geographical History of a Language* (Edinburgh: John Donald, 1984), 122.

136. An exception to the Church of Scotland's generally weak support for Gaelic literacy were the considerable efforts undertaken in this direction by the synod of Argyll in the seventeenth century (Durkacz, *Decline of the Celtic Languages*, 15–17, 22).

137. Grant, "Highland History," 462.

138. Sorensen, *Grammar of Empire*, 224, also see 4, 37, 39.

139. Moreover, the Catholic Highland mission foundered in the first decades of the nineteenth century—due to internal problems rather than outward pressure. Lynch, *Scotland: A New History*, 366–67; Clyde, *From Rebel to Hero*, 57, 67–68.

140. MS, CH 8/212/1, Miscellaneous Papers Relating to Church Matters, 89 f, SRO. Quoted from Durkacz, *Decline of the Celtic Languages*, 70, italics mine.

141. Anon., *A Short Account of the Society in Scotland for Propagating Christian Knowledge in the Highlands and Islands* (London, 1809), 1, 5–6; quoted from Clyde, *From Rebel to Hero*, 62–63.

142. Hunter, *Making of the Crofting Community*, 142, also see 143.

143. Hunter, *Making of the Crofting Community*, 142–57, 217, 291; Durkacz, *Decline of the Celtic Languages*, 126–29; Lynch, *Scotland: A New History*, 364–65, 375; Clyde, *From Rebel to Hero*, 68–73. On intricacies and local differences, see Ewen A. Cameron, "Embracing the Past: The Highlands in Nineteenth Century Scotland," in Broun, Finlay, and Lynch, *Image and Identity*, 197–200.

144. Clyde, *From Rebel to Hero*, 49, 80–81, 90.

145. Durkacz, *Decline of the Celtic Languages*, 5.

146. Durkacz, *Decline of the Celtic Languages*, 23.

147. Durkacz, *Decline of the Celtic Languages*, 45–52, 61–68; Devine, *Scottish Nation*, 96–97.

148. Grant, "Highland History," 462. Exceptions to the ban on Highland dress were the army, the stage, and posing for paintings—for example, see Ian Brown, "Introduction: Tartan, Tartanry and Hybridity," in *From Tartan to Tartanry: Scottish Culture, History and Myth*, ed. Brown (Edinburgh: Edinburgh University Press, 2010), 5; Michael Newton, "Paying for the Plaid: Scottish Gaelic Identity Politics in Nineteenth-Century North America," in *From Tartan to Tartanry*, 63.

149. See, for example, Devine, *Scottish Nation*, 233. For strategies to resist and evade the Disclothing Act, see Black, *Lasair*, 456.

150. See Hunter, *Making of the Crofting Community*, 38–46, and Hunter, *Last of the Free*, 207–26; Durkacz, *Decline of the Celtic Languages*, 70–72; Lynch, *Scotland: A New History*, 363, 368–70; Colley, *Britons: Forging the Nation*, 119–20; Devine, *Scottish Nation*, 171–72, 185–86.

151. Grant, "Highland History," 462.

152. John Walker, *Report on the Hebrides of 1764 and 1771*, ed. Margaret M. McKay (Edinburgh: John Donald, 1980), 33; quoted from Clyde, *From Rebel to Hero*, 33.

153. Walker, *Report*, 35; quoted from Clyde, *From Rebel to Hero*, 33.

154. Walker, *Report*, quoted from Clyde, *From Rebel to Hero*, 33–34.

155. Robert Anstruther, "Memorial in Relation to the Roads of Communication Made at the Public Expence through the Highlands of Scotland," MS, National Library of Scotland, Adv.Ms.33.4.19, 1–2; quoted from Clyde, *From Rebel to Hero*, 24.

156. James Small, "Report & Answers by Ensign James Small, Factor on the Estate of Strowan, to the Instructions given him by the Commissioners for Managing the Forfeited Estates in Scotland Anexed to the Crown" (1755), quoted from Black, "Rannoch," 361.

157. Cornelius Tacitus, *Agricola* (ca. 98 AD), in Tacitus, *Agricola and Germany*, trans. Anthony R. Birley (Oxford: Oxford University Press, 1999), chap. 21.

158. Kelp is a certain type of seaweed. It is also the name for an alkaline substance which is produced by the burning of such seaweed. In the eighteenth and nineteenth centuries it was used in several industries such as soap- or glassmaking.

159. Board of Trustees for Manufactures and Fisheries, report to the Lord's Commissioners of the Treasury, January 21, 1763; MS, SRO, NG.1/1/17/76; quoted from Clyde, *From Rebel to Hero*, 24.

160. James Hall, *Travels in Scotland, by an Unusual Route: With a Trip to the Orkneys and Hebrides*, 2 vols. (London: J. Johnson, 1807), 2:547–49. Hall was a Lowland Scottish clergyman living in England (see Briain Ó Dálaigh, ed., *The Strangers Gaze: Travels in County Clare, 1534–1950* [Ennis, Ireland: Clasp, 1998], 158).

161. Quoted from William Matheson, ed. and trans., *The Songs of John MacCodrum* (Edinburgh: Oliver and Boyd, 1938), 241.

162. There was also Highland migration to the towns. Until the late nineteenth century, Highlanders' migrations within Scotland were mostly seasonal. But more permanent urban migration also took place from at least the seventeenth century onwards. Hence, after the mid-eighteenth century, substantial Gaelic communities existed in many Scottish towns.

163. For example, see Hunter, *Making of the Crofting Community*, 44–45; and Hunter, *Last of the Free*, 219. On exceptions, see Hunter, *Last of the Free*, 213–16.

164. Hunter, *Making of the Crofting Community*, 70.

165. See Stroh, *Uneasy Subjects*, 113–21.

166. James MacDonald, *General View of the Agriculture of the Hebrides, or Western Isles of Scotland* (Edinburgh, 1811), 5, also see 119–20.

167. Such a transformation from colonized to colonizer could also lead to an embrace of colonial ideologies about the supposed inferiority of other marginalized peoples, such as indigenous populations overseas. However, there are also cases where diasporic Gaels have developed transperipheral solidarities with overseas colonized populations, despite their ambiguous role as co-colonizer. For instance, see some of the case studies in Michael Newton's works on North American Gaels, such as "'Did You Hear about the Gaelic-Speaking African?': Scottish Gaelic Folklore about Identity in North America," in "The Celtic Nations and the African Americans," special issue, *Comparative American Studies* 8, no. 2 (2010), and "Cò a dhìthich clann Ghàidheal? Cnuasachd air ìmpireachd, fèin-aithne is ceartas sòisealta ann am fuadach nan Gàidheal / Bury My Heart at Culloden: Reflections on Empire, Identity and Social Justice in the Gaelic Diaspora," in

Struileag: Shore to Shore / Cladach gu cladach, ed. Kevin MacNeill / Caoimhin MacNèill (Edinburgh: Polygon, 2015).

168. Hunter, *A Dance Called America*; Michael Kennedy, "'Lochaber No More': A Critical Examination of Highland Emigration Mythology," in *Myth, Migration and the Making of Memory: Scotia and Nova Scotia c. 1700–1990*, ed. Marjory Harper and Michael E. Vance (Edinburgh: John Donald, 1999), for example, 279, 293; Devine, *Scotland's Empire*.

Chapter 2

1. I have used the following modern editions: Martin Martin, *"A Description of the Western Islands of Scotland" by Martin Martin, Including "A Voyage to St. Kilda" by the Same Author and "A Description of the Western Isles of Scotland" by Sir Donald Monro*, ed. Donald J. MacLeod (1934; repr. Edinburgh: Birlinn, 1994); Martin, *"A Description of the Western Islands of Scotland" ca 1695 and "A Late Voyage to St Kilda" [by] Martin Martin with "A Description of the Occidental i.e. Western Islands of Scotland" [by] Donald Monro*, with new introductions by Charles W. J. Withers and R. W. Munro (Edinburgh: Birlinn, 1999); and Martin, *Curiosities of Art and Nature: The New Annotated and Illustrated Edition of Martin Martin's Classic "A Description of the Western Isles of Scotland,"* ed. Michael Robson (Port of Ness, Scot.: Islands Book Trust, 2003). Since the Birlinn editions are more widely available than Robson's, my page references refer to the 1994 Birlinn edition, unless otherwise stated. Readers might also find the Birlinn editions more user-friendly. Wherever possible, subsequent references to the 1994 edition appear in parentheses in the main text, *Description of the Western Islands* being abbreviated as "*WI*" and *Voyage to Saint Kilda* as "*SK*." Occasionally, the 1999 and 2003 editions are cited as supplementary references, mainly for their valuable introductions and annotations. In those cases, references are in endnotes, marked with the abbreviation "*WI* (1999)" or "*WI* (2003)."

2. On European geography, see Charles W. J. Withers, *Geography, Science and National Identity: Scotland since 1520* (New York: Cambridge University Press, 2001), for example, 243. For Mignolo, see *Darker Side*, 194–99, 283–84, 291.

3. Donald J. MacLeod, "Editorial Note," *WI* 9, 14; Charles W. J. Withers, "Introduction" to Martin's works in the 1999 edition, 1–2; Johnson, *Journey to the Western Islands*; Boswell, *Journal of a Tour*. Johnson's and Boswell's texts also perform important negotiations of the relationship between Highland Scotland, Lowland Scotland, and England, competing and concentric patriotisms in post-Union Britain, "barbarism" and progress, and Enlightenment and Romanticism. See Davis, *Acts of Union*, for example, 76–77, 89–106.

4. MacLeod, "Editorial Note," *WI* 14.

5. The ambivalence of Martin's speaking position and his role as a cultural mediator are also discussed in Withers, "Introduction" to Martin's works (1999), 2–3, 7–8, 11; and the "Introduction" (presumably by the editor Michael Robson) to *WI* (2003), xxv–xxvi.

6. Mary Louise Pratt, "Arts of the Contact Zone," *Profession* 91 (1991), 35; and Pratt, *Imperial Eyes: Travel Writing and Transculturation* (New York: Routledge, 1992; rev. 2nd ed. 2008), 9.

7. The biographical summary given here is based on D. J. MacLeod, "Editorial Note," *WI* 10–13; Thomson's entry on Martin in his *Companion*, 197;

Withers, "Introduction" to Martin's works; and Withers, *Geography, Science and National Identity,* 85, 87–96, 243; John N. Moore, "John Adair's Contribution to the Charting of the Scottish Coasts: A Re-assessment," *Imago Mundi* 52 (2000), 43–44, 56–57; "Introduction" to *WI* (2003); Domhnall Uilleam Stiùbhart, "Martin, Martin," in *Oxford Dictionary of National Biography* (Oxford: Oxford University Press, 2004, online ed. 2008).

8. Withers, *Geography, Science and National Identity*, 88.

9. Martin Martin, "Several Observations in the North Islands of Scotland," and "A Relation of a Deaf and Dumb Person, who Recovered His Speech and Hearing after a Violent Fever: with Some Other Medicinal and Chirurgical Observations," published in the Royal Society's *Philosophical Transactions*, vol. 19 (1695–1697), no. 233 (October 1697), 727–29, and vol. 25 (1706–1707), 2469–70, respectively.

10. Scottish Parliament, "Act in Favors of John Adair Geographer for Surveying the Kingdome of Scotland and Navigating the Coasts and Isles thereof," quoted from Moore, "John Adair's Contribution," 56, 61.

11. Scottish Parliament, "Act in Favours of John Adair Geographer and Captain John Slezer," quoted from Moore, "John Adair's Contribution," 56–57, 61.

12. See Stroh, *Uneasy Subjects*, 113–21, 130–46.

13. *WI* 61. Similarly, the first chapter of *SK* (403) complains that all previous descriptions of St. Kilda had been secondhand.

14. The "Preface" to *SK* (398–99), by contrast, highlights Martin's hybridity. The author is presented as uniting the best of both worlds: a native Hebridean informant's authenticity, inside knowledge, and local acquaintances to give him privileged access to information, combined with a university education, foreign travel, and contact with the Royal Society, to whose president *SK* is dedicated. As a Hebridean, Martin is supposed to have access to interesting special experiences, while his learning enables him to make sense of these experiences and present them in good mainstream form. This hybridity allegedly enables him to describe the Western Isles "more exactly than any other."

15. For example, *WI* 125, 265–66, 274, 280, 285, 296–97, 301, 312; *SK* 447.

16. This can be inferred because he apparently refers primarily to pleasure visits rather than business, military, or exploratory journeys. Moreover, Martin mentions foreign libraries, arts, and fashion, whereas the new colonies hardly offered anything in this vein that, by the norms of his time and class, was worth mentioning.

17. Facsimile of 1703 title page of *WI*, D. J. MacLeod's edition, 5.

18. A similar shift between outside and inside perspectives, exoticizing the periphery to pander to metropolitan readers' views while also claiming superior insider knowledge, has been identified in the francophone writings of the nineteenth-century Breton author Auguste Brizeux (Heather Williams, "Writing to Paris: Poets, Nobles, and Savages in Nineteenth-Century Brittany," *French Studies* 57, no. 4 [2003]: 481–83).

19. But elsewhere, when on their own territory, islanders are expressly described as *not* stupid. Moreover, at times the center's normative gaze is exposed as limited, and is even returned by the "natives" themselves—see below.

20. Huggan, *Postcolonial Exotic*; Brouillette, *Postcolonial Writers*; Ponzanesi, *Postcolonial Cultural Industry*.

21. For example, Huggan, *Postcolonial Exotic*, ix–xi, 19–20, 164–66; Brouillette, *Postcolonial Writers*, 26–27, 39–43, 80–81; Ponzanesi, *Postcolonial Cultural Industry*, 1, 3, 78, 89.

22. It is only in recent years that the Ordnance Survey has fundamentally changed its approach, re-gaelicizing maps and providing background information on Gaelic place-names on its website. See, for example, www.ordnancesurvey.co.uk/about/news/2000/gaelic.html, and www.ordnancesurvey.co.uk/about/news/2004/gaelicplacenames.html; and anon., "Getting the Name Right," *West Highland Free Press*, October 8, 2004, www.whfp.com.

23. This concerns mostly place-names (*WI* 97, 286, 301, 304–5; *SK* 409), but there are also instances relating to names for agricultural techniques (*WI* 86), alcoholic drinks (*WI* 86–87), food (*WI* 93), earlier human populations (*WI* 99), animals (*WI* 130, 141, 210), surnames (*WI* 138), and measurements (*WI* 163). The use of local names and its connection to respect for local knowledge is also briefly noted in Withers, "Introduction" to Martin's works, 8.

24. In this passage, "Lewis" and "Long Island" are used as synonyms for the entire island chain of the Outer Hebrides. Elsewhere, Martin uses "Lewis" in the narrower sense ("Lewis, properly and strictly," *WI* 85, also see 94–95) which would be more familiar today, that is, as the name of the northernmost island in this chain. One hundred miles is roughly the length of all the Outer Hebrides together in old Scottish miles as given on Martin's own map (the best facsimile is in *WI* [2003], 17). Also see the "Introduction" in *WI* (2003), xiv.

25. Pratt, *Imperial Eyes*, 9.

26. This is not exclusive to Martin: other producers and collectors of geographical knowledge at that time affirmed the importance of local knowledges, whether Highland or not (e.g., see Withers, *Geography, Science and National Identity*, 86–87). But in Martin's work, general respect for the geographical research conventions of his time does not seem to be the only reason for the emphatic vindication of local viewpoints. There is also a significant dimension of writing back to non-geographical discourse which regarded Gaels as disrespectable barbarians. This desire to write back is evident in his explicit critique of the label "barbarous," quoted above, in his vindication of the second sight (the psychic faculty of having prophetic visions or seeing physically remote people and objects), and in other instances discussed below.

27. For similar phrases, see *WI* 104–5, 111–12, 116, 134–35, 140–42, 156, 196, 204, 209, 216, 287; *SK* 433, 465–66.

28. Also noted by Withers, for example, "Introduction" to Martin's works (1999), 10–11; and the editor's "Introduction," *WI* (2003), xxvi.

29. For instance, Sibbald's own geographical research seems to have privileged elite informers (Withers, *Geography, Science and National Identity*, 86, 242).

30. *WI* 330–31. The third location is "parts of Holland" (ibid.), but he does not specify which. Thus, it cannot be ascertained whether these are likewise rural backwaters.

31. Cairns Craig's *Out of History: Narrative Paradigms in Scottish and English Culture* (Edinburgh: Polygon, 1996) analyzes the same paradigm with reference to Scotland as a whole in relation to England.

32. Other folk traditions, both mythological and historical, appear, for example, on p. 131 of *WI*. Such efforts to seek out local sources are not always free

from skepticism: Martin's remark that "Macneil, being the thirty-fourth of that name by lineal descent that has possessed this island, if the present genealogers can be credited" (*WI* 164) might imply caution in assessing indigenous claims.

33. For example, *WI* 96, 100, 146, 174, 209, 229, 290, 325, 332–33, 337, 340, 343–47.

34. For example, *WI* 145, 174, 209, 229, 231, 321, 331, 336–37, 341–42, 344, 346–48.

35. This common feature of culture contact is lucidly discussed by Chapman, *Celts*, 159–79.

36. Here, "tribe" does not necessarily carry the associations of primitiveness which characterize its use in many other texts, for instance in colonial discourse. Martin might use the term in a non-derogatory sense, as a category for social group identity on a sub-national level, often connected to notions of kinship and common ancestry.

37. *SK* 447–48. Martin gives two examples of undue rigidity on pp. 448–49.

38. Modern scholars tend to assume that, despite such remoteness, early modern Gaels would have understood a Classical Gaelic poem when they heard one.

39. Richard Holland, *The Buke of the Howlat,* in *Longer Scottish Poems*, vol. 1, *1375–1650*, ed. Priscilla Bawcutt and Felicity Riddy (Edinburgh: Scottish Academic Press, 1987).

40. *WI* 76, 240–41. Also see 81, 309, and *SK* 438.

41. This resembles the widespread colonial strategy of describing the colonized as contemporary ancestors who represent an earlier stage of development which the metropolis has long left behind. Martin's use of this strategy was unquestioningly echoed by his 1930s editor (D. J. Macleod, "Introduction," 20–22).

42. *WI* 172; also see 171, 174–75, 177.

43. The parallels between Martin's portrait of St. Kilda and classical concepts of Arcadia and the Golden Age (as well as the works produced by James Macpherson in the second half of the eighteenth century) are also noted by Stafford, *Sublime Savage*, 9–10.

44. The phrase "this place" at the beginning of this quote apparently refers not only to the fort but to St. Kilda as a whole, as the preceding paragraphs discuss its inaccessibility due to perilous sea and weather.

45. On the islanders' comeliness, also see *WI* 80, 93, 146, 260, 272, 275, 280, 303, 308, 314, and *SK* 436–38. Health and physical fitness also fit this pattern, and form another parallel to Roman praises of noble savages. However, even in St. Kilda some degeneration is observable: "the present generation comes short of the last in strength and longevity" (*SK* 437)—perhaps due to increased contact with "civilization," though Martin does not make the reason explicit.

46. Phrases like "the credulous natives" (e.g., *WI* 290) should be read in the same light: while such formulations seem to imply that *all* the locals are credulous, they might only mean "the more credulous among the natives." This accords with Martin's repeated emphasis on the unevenness with which folk beliefs were preserved. Moreover, his defense of second sight explicitly asserts that local credulity does not reach any exceptional level (*WI* 328).

47. *WI* 107. For another instance of anti-Catholic irony, see 108.

48. His concern with improvement is also briefly noted in Withers, "Introduction" to Martin's works, 8–9.

49. On non-populated landscape descriptions in colonial discourse, see, for example, Mary Louise Pratt, "Scratches on the Face of the Country; or, What Mr. Barrow Saw in the Land of the Bushmen," in "Race, Writing, and Difference," ed. Henry Louis Gates, Jr., special issue, *Critical Inquiry* 12, no. 1 (1985).

50. The wide-ranging landscape transformation envisaged here can also be connected to postcolonial ecocritical readings of Scottish "improvement" discourse.

51. Quoted from a discussion with Newton at the first World Congress of Scottish Literatures, University of Glasgow, July 3, 2014.

52. The following passage, by contrast, almost sounds like an imperialist offensive: "The settling a fishery [*sic*] in those parts would prove of great advantage to the Government, and be an effectual means to advance the revenue, by the customs. . . . It would also be a nursery of stout and able seamen . . . to serve the Government on all occasions" (*WI* 353). Either Martin's stance on overseas colonialism is ambivalent, or his reference to seamen only pertains to intra-European trade and power struggles—but even then his attitude can hardly be classed as anti-imperialist.

53. Later, the same argument was echoed in Tobias Smollett's novel *The Expedition of Humphrey Clinker* (1771): travelling in Argyllshire, one of the protagonists, Matthew Bramble, argues that "a company of merchants might . . . turn to good account a fishery . . . in this part of Scotland—Our people have a strange itch to colonize America, when the uncultivated parts of our own island might be settled to greater advantage" (repr. Athens: University of Georgia Press, 1990, 248). Similarly, in 1785 the economist and agriculturalist James Anderson complained that "the most distant parts of the globe have been attentively explored . . . to discover new sources of trade, and to give encouragement for the manufactures of Britain," while the Scottish Highlands, "so peculiarly our own, and . . . much better calculated to encrease the trade, to encourage the manufactures, and to augment the revenues of this nation, than any others . . . on the globe, . . . remain . . . unexplored," "neglected and unknown" (Anderson, *An Account of the Present State of the Hebrides and Western Coasts of Scotland* [Edinburgh: G. Robinson and C. Elliot, 1785], xii).

54. Dedication, *WI*, in Mcleod's ed. p. 59. Martin also argues in terms of government interest when he suggests free-port status for Skye to "add strength and reputation to the Government. Since these isles are capable of . . . improvements . . . it is a great loss to the nation they should be . . . neglected" (*WI* 358). On "native worth," also see several quotes given above, as well as *WI* 146, 311 and *SK* 444–45. Where serious moral defects are found, they are apparently again blamed on Catholicism: "hospitable, well-meaning people, but the misfortune of their education disposes them to uncharitableness, and rigid thoughts of their Protestant neighbours" (*WI* 154). Interestingly, Martin does not explicitly record, let alone criticize, any discrimination vice versa, by Protestants against Catholics, though it is likely that misgivings were mutual. Martin's own anti-Catholic bias makes it appear very probable that some fellow Protestants in the Isles shared his arrogance, and perhaps also translated this self-righteousness into practical discrimination.

55. In the Northern Isles, cultural otherness based on Scandinavian heritage was still an issue in Martin's own time. For instance, the Norn language highlighted the region's difference from the Scottish mainstream.

56. *WI* 126, 196, 198–201, 213–15, 219, 350, 354–55.

57. However, this may not be his only motivation. His preface also relates his interest in climate, soil, flora, and fauna to a general contemporary interest in natural science as such (61), which accords with the progressive and scientific spirit of the Royal Society.

58. Facsimiles in MacLeod's ed., 2–3, 396.

59. On the general relationship between geography, national identity, and the early modern state, see Withers, *Geography, Science and National Identity*, 30–111. On the relationship between the extension of geographical knowledge, literary engagements with this knowledge, and the consolidation—but also problematization—of British national identity at a later stage, in the romantic period, see Penny Fielding, *Scotland and the Fictions of Geography* (Cambridge: Cambridge University Press, 2008). She also strongly engages with the postcolonially pertinent concepts of center and periphery, though *explicit* references to a Scottish (post)colonized condition are much rarer, and at times skeptical (113, 138, 140, 162, 186).

60. In the north, Martin likewise highlights rough climatic and topographic conditions which make people, horses, and sheep sturdy (*WI* 377, 380–81), comely, healthy (*WI* 373, 377), and virtuous (*WI* 374, 385). He recognizes locally specific terms (e.g., *WI* 376), voices (*WI* 372–73), laws, and rules (e.g., *WI* 384), though respect for local discursive authority is tempered by condescension toward folk beliefs related to Catholicism. He relates incidents from local history (e.g., *WI* 374–75), though most of them (perhaps more so than in the Western Isles) concern the locality's relations to hegemonic centers (*WI* 367–70, 377, 381, 388). He notes instances of mismanagement, potential for economic improvement (*WI* 384, 390), and already extant signs of hybridization such as trilingual Shetlanders speaking English, Norn, and Dutch, the latter for communication with incoming traders (*WI* 385).

61. Although this is a general remark, it also alludes specifically to the people of the Western Isles, whose medical knowledge is praised in the surrounding sentences and whose illiteracy Martin repeatedly mentions throughout his work. While an interest in local medicine was also shown by other geographers like Sibbald (Withers, *Geography, Science and National Identity*, 75), Martin's vindication of *Gaelic* medicine, and even that of the lower classes of Gaelic society, arguably goes beyond this because he saw Gaelic folk knowledge to be in need of *special* vindication, in view of the fact that many outsiders denigrated this culture as barbarian (see above).

62. However, another passage uses the same metaphor of soil cultivation in a more typically colonial sense, assigning cultivation to outsiders alone: "the improvement of the isles in general . . . depends upon the Government of Scotland to give encouragement . . . to . . . public-spirited persons or societies . . . to lay out their endeavours that way; and *how large a field they have to work upon* will appear by taking a survey" (*WI* 65, italics mine). It is also noteworthy that "public-spirited" implies that investments are acts of unselfish philanthropism rather than a matter of profit, though Martin elsewhere admits profit to be "another" important motivation.

63. Joseph Conrad, *Heart of Darkness* (1899), repr. in Hollander and Kermode, *Anthology of English Literature*.

64. Also see Martin's assurance that there are no cases of madness on Jura (*WI* 267), and his remarks on sanity in the Isles in general (*WI* 327).

65. That is, an answer.

66. See Stroh, *Uneasy Subjects*, 69–152.

Chapter 3

1. Edward Gibbon, *The History of the Decline and Fall of the Roman Empire*, 6 vols. (London: W. Strahan and T. Cadell, 1776–88).

2. E. W. Montagu Jr., *Reflections on the Rise and Fall of the Antient Republicks: Adapted to the Present State of Great Britain* (London: A. Millar, 1759), 373.

3. For example, see William Duncan, "A Discourse Concerning the Roman Art of War," in *The Commentaries of Caesar*, trans. Duncan, 2 vols. (1753; London: J. R. Tonson, 1755), 1: cvii; James Macpherson, "Preface" to *Fingal* (1763; repr. in *Poems of Ossian*, ed. Gaskill), 36; Stafford, *Sublime Savage*, 33–35, 154, and Stafford, *Last of the Race*, 86–87; Carla Sassi, *"Imagined Scotlands": Saggi sulla letteratura scozzese* (Trieste: Edizioni Parnaso, 2002), 50.

4. For details, see, for example, Womack, *Improvement and Romance*, 27–39; Hunter, *A Dance Called America*, 51–72, and Hunter, *Last of the Free*, 244–46; Clyde, *From Rebel to Hero*, 150–77; and Devine, *Scottish Nation*, 239.

5. The connection between a general romantic penchant for the rural and a more specific romanticization of rural Celts, in this case Bretons, is also discussed by H. Williams, "Writing to Paris," 480.

6. Also see Stafford, *Sublime Savage*, 12, 62, 171, and Stafford, *Last of the Race*, 109, 235; Womack, *Improvement and Romance*, 80–82, 150–65; James, *Atlantic Celts*, 48–49; Pittock, *Celtic Identity*, 36. On later examples of romanticized Celts as binary opposites of modern materialistic life, see Patrick Sims-Williams, "The Invention of Celtic Nature Poetry," in T. Brown, *Celticism*.

7. For example, Hugh Blair, "A Critical Dissertation on the Poems of Ossian, the Son of Fingal" (1763), repr. in Macpherson, *Poems of Ossian*, ed. Gaskill, 345–46, 357. Societies where eighteenth-century literary critics identified primitive genius included Homer's Greece, Old Testament Hebrews, ancient Scandinavian poetry, and the Gaidhealtachd. Also see Chapman, *Gaelic Vision*, 44; Anthony Pagden, "The Savage Critic: Some European Images of the Primitive," in "Colonial and Imperial Themes," ed. G. K. Hunter and C. J. Rawson, special issue, *Yearbook of English Studies* 13 (1983): 40; Stafford, *Sublime Savage*, 32–33, 86–93, 100; Sanders, *Short Oxford History of English Literature*, 322–23.

8. Stafford, *Sublime Savage*, 98–101; Ferguson, *Identity of the Scottish Nation*, 206–8.

9. Also see Pittock, *Celtic Identity*, 36.

10. Also see Womack, *Improvement and Romance*, 80–81; Chapman, *Celts*, 125–30, 138–39; Luke Gibbons, "Race against Time: Racial Discourse and Irish History" (1991), rev. and repr. in Gibbons, *Transformations*, 158.

11. Ian Duncan, "The Study of Scottish Literature," *ScotLit* 28 (2003): 2.

12. "Philosophic Light and Gothic Gloom: Landscape and History in Eighteenth-Century Scotland," in *Aberdeen and the Enlightenment*, ed. Jennifer J. Carter and Joan H. Pittock (Aberdeen: Aberdeen University Press, 1987). Yadav likewise problematizes the period distinction between "Classicist/Enlightened" and "Romantic" (*Before the Empire of English*, 6, 165–66, 171–74).

13. On this, see Ian Duncan, "The Pathos of Abstraction: Adam Smith, Ossian and Samuel Johnson," in *Scotland and the Borders of Romanticism,* ed. Leith Davis, I. Duncan, and Janet Sorensen (Cambridge: Cambridge University Press, 2004), for example, 39–41; and Matthew Wickman, *The Ruins of Experience: Scotland's "Romantick" Highlands and the Birth of the Modern Witness* (Philadelphia: University of Pennsylvania Press, 2007).

14. Chapman, *Celts*, 132, author's italics. Also see ibid., 130–31; Ferguson, *Identity of the Scottish Nation*, 231.

15. Sims-Williams, "Invention of Celtic Nature Poetry," 103, also see 104.

16. Sims-Williams, "Invention of Celtic Nature Poetry," 103–4, 108, 110.

17. John Ogilvie, *Rona, a Poem, in Seven Books* (London: J. Murray, 1777), 58.

18. William Donaldson, "Bonny Highland Laddie: The Making of a Myth," *Scottish Literary Journal* 3, no. 2 (1976); Chapman, *Celts*, 142–43, 216–17; Pittock, *Poetry and Jacobite Politics*, 141–42, 164. A further complication of the masculine/feminine dichotomy is that even non-Gaelic British masculinities in the eighteenth century increasingly incorporated qualities which were traditionally rather associated with femininity, such as sentimentalism, sensibility, and empathy. Only the *combination* of "masculine" strength, assertiveness, and rationality with "feminine"(?) sentiment made a truly rounded modern civilized male, without causing effeminacy or emasculation (see, e.g., Shields, *Sentimental Literature*, 5, 9). The mainstream's embrace of supposedly Gaelic "primitive" virtues, which likewise combined "feminine" sentiment and "masculine" vigor, could thus be seen as part of a wider quest for a more emotive British modern masculinity. For an account which traces early roots of the romantic and eroticized "Bonnie Highland Laddie" in late seventeenth- and early eighteenth-century orature and literature, both anglophone and Gaelic, see Dòmhnall Uilleam Stiùbhart, "Highland Rogues and the Roots of Highland Romanticism," in *Crossing the Highland Line: Cross-Currents in Eighteenth-Century Scottish Writing. Selected Papers from the 2005 ASLS Annual Conference*, ed. Christopher MacLachlan (Glasgow: ASLS, 2009).

19. For example, see Thomas, *Colonialism's Culture*, 133; Hans Ritz, *Die Sehnsucht nach der Südsee: Bericht über einen europäischen Mythos* (Göttingen: Muriverlag, 1983), 20, 88.

20. Fanon, *Black Skin, White Masks*, 46.

21. W. Donaldson, "Bonny Highland Laddie." Despite such parallels, it should be borne in mind that ascribing sexual potency and libertinage to Others is not *exclusively* a colonial trope. Similar stereotypes exist in mutual otherings by members of European mainstream cultures, for instance in English clichés about the French.

22. For relatively recent examples from settler (post-)colonies, see Thomas, *Colonialism's Culture*, 28–31, 171–72, 182–86. For examples from eighteenth- and nineteenth-century Ireland, see Liz Bellamy, "Regionalism and Nationalism: Maria Edgeworth, Walter Scott and the Definition of Britishness," in *The Regional Novel in Britain and Ireland, 1800–1990*, ed. K. D. M. Snell (Cambridge: Cambridge University Press, 1998), 57–58.

23. James, *Atlantic Celts*, 128.

24. For a comparative discussion of pan-Celticism and pan-Africanism, see Daniel G. Williams, "Is the 'Pan-' in Pan-Celticism the 'Pan-' in Pan-Africanism?

Language, Race and Diaspora," in *Celts in the Americas*, ed. Michael Newton (Sydney, Nova Scotia: Cape Breton University Press, 2013).

25. For example, Briesemeister, "Keltentum," 347, 349–54.

26. For example, see Womack, *Improvement and Romance*, 144–48; Lynch, *Scotland: A New History*, 344–45; Finlay, "Caledonia," 148–51.

27. See, for example, Pittock, *Poetry and Jacobite Politics*, 180; Colin Kidd, "Teutonist Ethnology and Scottish Nationalist Inhibition," *SHR* 74 (1995): 45–47; Ferguson, *Identity of the Scottish Nation*, 181.

28. Devine, *Clanship to Crofters' War*, 84–98. Similar appropriations of a Celtic margin as a pan-national marker of distinctness and authenticity have been observed in relation to Brittany and France after 1789 (H. Williams, "Writing to Paris," 478–79).

29. On the authenticity question and the relationship between Gaelic and mainstream elements, see, for example, Derick S. Thomson, *The Gaelic Sources of Macpherson's "Ossian"* (Edinburgh: Oliver and Boyd, n.d. [1951]), and Thomson, "'Ossian' Macpherson and the Gaelic World of the Eighteenth Century," *Aberdeen University Review* 40 (1963); Stafford, *Sublime Savage*; Donald E. Meek, "The Gaelic Ballads of Scotland: Creativity and Adaptation," in Gaskill, *Ossian Revisited*; Davis, "Origins of the Specious"; Howard D. Weinbrot, *Britannia's Issue: The Rise of British Literature from Dryden to Ossian* (Cambridge: Cambridge University Press, 1993); Luke Gibbons, "This Sympathetic Bond: Ossian, Celticism and Colonialism," in T. Brown, *Celticism*; Peter Mackay, "Negotiations of Barbarity, Authenticity and Purity in Eighteenth and Nineteenth Century Gaelic Literature," in Sassi and van Heijnsbergen, *Within and without Empire*, 37–39.

30. On noble savagery, also see Thomson, *Gaelic Sources*, 1–2; Leah Leneman, "Ossian and the Enlightenment," *Scotia: American–Canadian Journal of Scottish Studies* 11 (1987): 21; Stafford, *Sublime Savage*, 35, 158–59; Sassi, "*Imagined Scotlands*," 50. For endorsements of Macpherson's Ossian among anglophone literati, see, for example, Tobias Smollett's favorable reviews of *Fingal* and *Temora* in *Critical Review, or, Annals of Literature* 12 (1761), 13 (1762) and 15 (1763); as well as Blair, "Critical Dissertation."

31. On Macpherson's influence, see, for example, Arthur E. McGuinness, "Lord Kames on the Ossian Poems: Anthropology and Criticism," *Texas Studies in Literature and Language* 10 (1968): 69–71; Stafford, *Sublime Savage*, for example, 177–178; Chapman, *Celts*, 123–24; Christopher Harvie, "Anglo-Saxons into Celts: The Scottish Intellectuals 1760–1930," in T. Brown, *Celticism*, 234–35.

32. However, Macpherson also inspired some attempts to preserve gaelophone traditions, such as improved archiving of literary manuscripts or romantic revivals of the office of the clan bard maintained by the chieftain.

33. Thomas, *Colonialism's Culture*, 186.

34. Huggan, *Postcolonial Exotic*, 174–76.

35. See, for example, Susan Manning, "Ossian, Scott and Nineteenth-Century Scottish Literary Nationalism," *Studies in Scottish Literature* 17 (1982); Durkacz, *Decline of the Celtic Languages*, 193–95; Stafford, *Sublime Savage*, 166–71; Sher, "Percy"; Ferguson, *Identity of the Scottish Nation*, 233–34, 240–43; Philippe Laplace, "L'Institution du corpus imaginaire gaélique dans la littérature écossaise: Macpherson et Scott, entre idéologie et synecdoque culturelle," *Études*

Écossaises 6 (1999–2000): 133–35, 138–39; Donald E. Meek, "The Sublime Gael: The Impact of Macpherson's *Ossian* on Literary Creativity and Cultural Perception in Gaelic Scotland," in *The Reception of Ossian in Europe*, ed. Howard Gaskill (New York: Thoemmes, 2004).

36. Roderick Watson, *The Literature of Scotland* (Basingstoke, Eng.: Macmillan, 1984), 221; Fiona Stafford, "Primitivism and the 'Primitive' Poet: A Cultural Context for MacPherson's Ossian," in T. Brown, *Celticism*, 86–89; Ferguson, *Identity of the Scottish Nation*, 181; Sorensen, *Grammar of Empire*, 154–55. However, the Scots vernacular was not *always* associated with romanticism's noble savagery—it also featured in literary texts which were more Enlightened in spirit, and could mark an alternative "high culture" (e.g., see Hewitt, "Scoticisms"; Pittock, *Poetry and Jacobite Politics*, 152).

37. Walter Scott, ed., *Minstrelsy of the Scottish Border: Consisting of Historical and Romantic Ballads, Collected in the Southern Counties of Scotland; with a Few of Modern Date Founded upon Local Tradition* (1802; repr. ed. T. F. Henderson, 4 vols. [New York: Charles Scribner's Sons, 1902]).

38. "Introduction," *Minstrelsy of the Scottish Border*, ed. W. Scott, 1:175.

39. See, for example, Womack, *Improvement and Romance*, 144–48; Craig, *Out of History*, 116–17.

40. Repr. in *Scotlands: Poets and the Nation*, ed. Douglas Gifford and Alan Riach (Manchester: Carcanet, 2004).

41. For Smollett's *The Adventures of Roderick Random*, see, for example, repr. Athens: University of Georgia Press, 2012, 68–69, 72, 86, 94, 139. For Smollett's *Humphrey Clinker*, see below. A helpful analysis of *Roderick Random*'s representation of Scottish-English inequalities in relation to its treatment of overseas imperialism can be found in Suvir Kaul, *Eighteenth-Century British Literature and Postcolonial Studies* (Edinburgh: Edinburgh University Press, 2009), 95–108, 116–18.

42. For example, Smollett, *Humphrey Clinker*, 192–93, 198, 206–8, 213–14, 216, 225–28, 230–33, 238, 245, 248, 265–68.

43. For postcolonially relevant readings of Smollett, see also Davis, *Acts of Union*, 63–73, 190; R. Crawford, *Devolving English Literature*, 54–75; Sorensen, *Grammar of Empire*, 104–37, 254–59. For other pertinent readings, see Gottlieb, *Feeling British*, especially 63–77, 80–98, and Shields, *Sentimental Literature*, 59–69, 87–95, 185–91, though these are ambivalent about the applicability of postcolonial approaches to Scotland. Both argue that Smollett's use of affect and sympathy to bridge cultural differences, transcend Scottish–English animosities, and promote British nation-building is part of a wider trend in Enlightenment and romantic writing, though the limitations of this strategy were also reflected.

44. Smollett, *Humphrey Clinker*, 233.

45. Womack, *Improvement and Romance*, 38; Devine, *Scotland's Empire*, 312. Juliet Shields argues against distinctions between earlier (political/practical) and later (romantic/sentimental) Jacobitism, pointing out that earlier, political Jacobitism had already invoked sentiment and nostalgia (*Sentimental Literature*, 4–5). However, I would argue that the distinction is helpful because earlier Jacobitism used sentiment as ideological support for practical political resistance, whereas romantic Jacobitism used sentiment as mere compensation for past defeat and

present political submission. The same applies to sentimental compassion with clearance victims, which is often compensatory rather than a call for practical resistance, as Shields notes herself (138).

46. For example, Chapman, *Celts*, 106.

47. Ferguson, *Identity of the Scottish Nation*, 176, 181. Nonetheless, such scholarly interest can also be found among Highland literati, often native Gaelic speakers who had obtained a mainstream education and returned to the Gaidhealtachd as clergymen.

48. Womack, *Improvement and Romance*, 116.

49. Lynch, *Scotland: A New History*, 369.

50. Quote from Womack, *Improvement and Romance*, 117.

51. See, for example, Hunter, *Last of the Free*, 262; Womack, *Improvement and Romance*, 115–18, 124. In this context, Womack explicitly refers to Michael Hechter's concept of internal colonialism, though he stresses that his results are different.

52. Chapman, *Celts*, 143. A recent reassessment of the complexities of tartan's role in Scottish culture through the ages, including more subversive functions, can be found in I. Brown, *From Tartan to Tartanry*.

53. Newton, "Paying for the Plaid," 65, 75–77; quote from 77.

54. Chapman, *Celts*, 117–18.

55. Durkacz, *Decline of the Celtic Languages*, 191–97; Ronald A. Black, "The Gaelic Academy: The Cultural Commitment of the Highland Society of Scotland," *SGS* 14, no. 2 (1986) and 15, no. 1 (1988); Withers, "Historical Creation," 150–51; Clyde, *From Rebel to Hero*, 34–35; Laplace, "L'Institution," 141–42; Newton, *Warriors of the Word*, 76; Janice Fairney, "The Branch Societies of the Highland Society of London," in Nilsen, *Rannsachadh na Gàidhlig 5*.

56. *The Scotsman*, June 9, 1821; quoted from Laplace, "L'Institution," 142.

57. Trevor Royle, "From David Stewart to Andy Stewart: The Invention and Re-invention of the Scottish Soldier," in I. Brown, *From Tartan to Tartanry*, 59–60.

58. This refers to key foreign battles of the British army. The connection between military service as atonement for Jacobite transgressions and a way to rehabilitate Gaeldom in the eyes of the British mainstream can be found in Gaelic poetry from the time of the Seven Years War (Michael Newton, "Jacobite Past, Loyalist Present," *e-Keltoi: Journal of Interdisciplinary Celtic Studies* 5 [2003], www4.uwm.edu/celtic/ekeltoi/volumes/vol5/5_2/newton_5_2.pdf, pp. 40–42).

59. Craig, *Out of History*, 110. Also see John Prebble, *The King's Jaunt: George IV in Scotland, August 1822: "One and Twenty Daft Days"* (London: Collins, 1988).

60. For example, anon. ("A Londoner, but No Cockney"), "The King's Visit to Edinburgh," *Blackwood's Edinburgh Magazine* 12 (September–October 1822): 493. Also see Caroline McCracken-Flesher, *Possible Scotlands: Walter Scott and the Story of Tomorrow* (Oxford: Oxford University Press, 2005), 74, 85, 87.

61. Clyde, *From Rebel to Hero*, 128. Also see Pittock, *Celtic Identity*, 39–40.

62. McCracken-Flesher, *Possible Scotlands*, 73–113.

63. Lynch, *Scotland: A New History*, 357; Clyde, *From Rebel to Hero*, 128–29; Devine, *Scottish Nation*, 235; Laplace, "L'Institution," 143; McCracken-Flesher, *Possible Scotlands*, 87, 109.

64. Nairn, *Break-Up of Britain*, 167–68; Gibbons, "Some Hysterical Hatred," 7–12; Leerssen, "Celticism," in T. Brown, *Celticism*, 12; Pittock, *Celtic Identity*, 25, 63–64.

65. For example, see the texts about the South Pacific analyzed in Ritz, *Sehnsucht*.

66. Chapman, *Gaelic Vision*, 19–20; Osterhammel, *Entzauberung*, 37. A similar point about the Gaels' intermediate position between domestic(ated) Same and exotic Other had already been made by Martin Martin (*SK* 397). The same notion continues to influence today's tourism: for British travelers who cannot afford or do not wish to go abroad, Wales or the Scottish Highlands are an attractive alternative. The existence of a different language makes these places feel foreign and interesting. The Highland tourism industry actively promotes Gaelic in this way, for example by putting up *Fàilte* signs (the Gaelic word for "welcome") at tourist informations, hotels, and village entrances. But linguistic difference is safely contained so that it cannot cause inconvenience: abroad, foreign languages are used all the time and not everybody speaks English, which might cause communication problems to tourists. In the Gaidhealtachd, everybody can speak English, nobody expects tourists to acquire even a smattering of Gaelic, and neither does this occur to most tourists themselves, whereas in France or Italy they might at least learn the local expressions for "good morning" or "thank you." While the tourism industry markets Gaelic as an exotic asset, the highly threatened status of the language—and the role which tourism arguably plays in language decline—is discreetly pasted over.

67. Womack, *Improvement and Romance*, 130.

68. Chapman, *Celts*, 142–43.

69. Womack, *Improvement and Romance*, 62–82; Withers, "Historical Creation," 146–47.

70. Cited from the reprint of the obituary in D. S. Thomson, "Unpublished Letters by the Poet Ewen MacLachlan," *SGS* 11, no. 2 (1968): 226.

71. Ibid., 227.

72. Ibid., 228.

73. Ibid., 227.

74. Ibid.

75. Ibid.

76. Ibid., 228.

77. Similarly, big cities today are often felt to look similar the world over, for instance concerning prestige architecture like television towers or office skyscrapers; and the most obvious national differences can supposedly be encountered in older cultural expressions and more rural places.

78. These notions are, for instance, reflected in eighteenth- and nineteenth-century Scottish and Irish Ossianism, works of nineteenth-century Highland folklorists like Alexander Carmichael's *Carmina Gadelica* (compiled 1855–99; vols. I and II publ. Edinburgh: T. and A. Constable, 1900; 2nd ed. in 6 vols., ed. Elizabeth C. C. Watson, James Carmichael Watson, and Angus Matheson, Edinburgh: Oliver and Boyd, 1928–71) or J. F. Campbell, ed., *Popular Tales of the West Highlands* (1860–62; repr., 2 vols., Edinburgh: Birlinn, 1994), the Grimm brothers' collection of German fairy tales, and nineteenth-century Galician cultural nationalists like the poet Eduardo Pondal (see Briesemeister, "Keltentum," 349–50, 353–54).

79. Lynch, *Scotland: A New History*, 355.

80. Shields, *Sentimental Literature*, 128–29, 135–36. For her, this is not exclusively a sign of disempowerment, but also a potential site of reempowerment by stressing the Highlanders' importance to the nation (136). However, I would argue that this importance is still couched in terms of disempowerment because it is based on colonial-style external projections of "noble savagery." Moreover, the governing interests are those of the center which uses Highlanders as exploitable raw materials, rather than the Highland periphery's own needs, as Shields notes herself (138).

81. Pittock points out that there was also a more radical strand linking Jacobitism with Jacobinism and republicanism or left-wing social criticism, for instance concerning the Clearances. Scottish sympathizers with the French Revolution also sympathized with Irish nationalism, contrary to the anti-Irish and procolonial sentiments which Anglo-Scottish mainstream discourse had displayed for about two centuries. A few Scots even favored the establishment of separate Scottish, Irish, and English republics. The establishment was aware that some strands of Jacobitism retained antiestablishment potential: the last arrest based on suspicions of Jacobitism was made in 1817; and despite the romantic fashion for Jacobite songs, not all of those songs were deemed acceptable (Pittock, *Poetry and Jacobite Politics,* for example, 177, 208–29, 235).

82. James Hogg, "Donald MacDonald," ca. 1803; repr. in *The Poetry of Scotland: Gaelic, Scots and English 1380–1980*, ed. Roderick Watson (Edinburgh: Edinburgh University Press, 1995), 422–23. On the date, see Peter Garside, "The Origins and History of James Hogg's 'Donald MacDonald,'" *Scottish Studies* 7, no. 2 (2006).

83. For an excellent discussion of deer-stalking in relation to national identity, see Maureen M. Martin, *The Mighty Scot: Nation, Gender, and the Nineteenth-Century Mystique of Scottish Masculinity* (Albany: State University of New York Press, 2009), 39–79.

84. On these matters, see Womack, *Improvement and Romance*, 49–53, 138; Lynch, *Scotland: A New History*, 355, 357; Withers, "Historical Creation," 153–54; Devine, *Scottish Nation*, 237–40, and Devine, *Scotland's Empire*, 340; Mack, *Scottish Fiction*, 10–11.

85. Womack, *Improvement and Romance*, 28, also see 27.

86. See, for example, Womack, *Improvement and Romance*, 27–39; Clyde, *From Rebel to Hero*.

87. Anglophone Jacobites described themselves and their cause alternately in Roman and barbarian (Highland) terms. Another, partly related antiestablishment cause whose non-Gaelic supporters had already idealized and appropriated Gaelic icons like tartan before 1745 was anti-unionism. Murray G. H. Pittock, *Poetry and Jacobite Politics*, 41–42, 81–82, and Pittock, "Plaiding the Invention of Scotland," in I. Brown, *From Tartan to Tartanry*, 35–39; Hugh Cheape, "Gheibhte breacain charnaid ('Scarlet Tartans Would Be Got . . .'): The Re-Invention of Tradition," in I. Brown, *From Tartan to Tartanry*, 27–28.

88. Robert Chambers' Jacobite Papers, 1623–1869, National Library of Scotland, MS 1696.f.90; quoted from W. Donaldson, "Bonny Highland Laddie," 30–31. All brackets except the last were added by Donaldson to indicate editorial uncertainties.

89. Pittock, *Poetry and Jacobite Politics*, 141–42.

90. See, for example, Devine, *Scotland's Empire*, 304–6, 314. An overview of the image and practical role of Highlanders in the British Army can be found in T. M. Devine, "Soldiers of Empire, 1750–1914," in *Scotland and the British Empire*, ed. T. M. Devine and John M. MacKenzie (Oxford: Oxford University Press, 2011).

91. Anon., *A Short History of the Highland Regiment: Interspersed with Some Occasional Observations as to the Present State of the Country, Inhabitants and Government of Scotland* (London: Jacob Robinson, 1743), 1; quoted from W. Donaldson, "Bonny Highland Laddie," 44.

92. W. Donaldson, "Bonny Highland Laddie," 44.

93. See, for example, Womack, *Improvement and Romance*, 27–39; Hunter, *A Dance Called America*, 50–72; Clyde, *From Rebel to Hero*, 150–77; Devine, *Scottish Nation*, 239–40, and Devine, *Scotland's Empire*, 293–319, 339–40.

94. Matthew Dziennik, "Whig Tartan: Material Culture and Its Use in the Scottish Highlands, 1746–1815," *Past and Present* 217 (2012), 122, also see 119, 145. Interestingly, not all this marketing relied on primitivism—Dziennik foregrounds an opposite dimension which posited Highland dress as a symbol of modernity, for instance as part of a general militarization of British eighteenth-century dress codes that signified an individual's commitment to the modern state. In this context, it is also interesting that the tartans for the first uniforms of the Breadalbane Fencibles were made not in the Highlands (as might have befitted a "primitivist" image), but through mass manufacture in England (120, 124, 135–36).

95. Pittock, *Celtic Identity*, 108.

96. Harvie, "Anglo-Saxons," 246.

97. Devine, *Scotland's Empire*, 294–301, 309–113, 358. However, already in the 1790s many Highland regiments had to enlist significant numbers of Lowlanders and even Englishmen. Despite proportionally huge subscription rates, the Highlands did not have enough population to fill all the regiments, partly also due to previous over-recruitment. The myth of the Highland soldier was so attractive that restocking the regiments with fake Highlanders seemed preferable to discarding the concept of Highland regiments altogether—as long as the fakes did not get too obviously numerous: in 1809, several mixed regiments lost the status and uniforms of Highland troops because the proportion of Lowlanders that was necessary to fill the ranks had become too large to sustain the Highland label (Devine, *Scotland's Empire*, 298–99, 308; and Devine, "Soldiers of Empire"). In 1881, by contrast, army reforms decreed that even Lowland Scottish regiments should wear tartan, thus ratifying the transformation of Highland dress into a pan-Scottish symbol. For further examples of Highlandism and pan-Scottish identity constructs in a military context, see Cameron Pulsifer, "A Highland Regiment in Halifax: The 78th Highland Regiment of Foot and the Scottish National/Cultural Factor in Nova Scotia's Capital, 1869–1871," in Harper and Vance, *Myth, Migration and the Making of Memory*, for example, 144–46.

98. W. Donaldson, "Bonny Highland Laddie," 45.

99. The phrase "the garb of old Gaul" recurred in the next century when the Caledonian Society of London proclaimed the preservation of the "garb of old Gaul" as one of its main objectives and drank to the welfare of the thus-labeled costume (1837; cited from Graeme Morton, "Ethnic Identity in the Civic World

of Scottish Associational Culture," in Bültmann, Hinson, and Morton, *Ties of Bluid*, 39, 48; who in turn cites from D. Hepburn and J. Douglas, *The Chronicles of the Caledonian Society of London, 1837–1905* [London: Waterlow, 1890], direct quote from 2, reference to the toast apparently from 3–4, 8 or 12).

100. Quoted from *Ancient and Modern Scottish Songs, Heroic Ballads, etc.*, ed. David Herd, 2 vols. (Edinburgh: printed by John Wotherspoon for James Dickson and Charles Elliot, 1776), 1:116–17. Also see the comments in Thomas Crawford, "Political and Protest Songs in Eighteenth-Century Scotland," *Scottish Studies* 14 (1970): 30–31.

101. Smollett, *Humphrey Clinker*, 245–47; Smith, *Wealth of Nations,* 415–21, 690–93, 700–706, 786–87. Another familiar feature of Gaelic noble savagery endorsed by Smith is a paternal, convivial chieftain–tenant relationship in peacetime, manifest in large numbers of retainers, munificence, and communal feasting. This seems morally superior to greedy modern landowners who spend all their income on frivolous luxuries for themselves. But again, Smith's approval of "primitiveness" is limited. He does not want to return to precapitalist patterns. In general, modern capitalism is still deemed the best system: despite individual selfishness, it can—if properly administered—organize selfish individuals in a way which also benefits society as a whole (412–22, 706, 908–9).

102. See, for example, Chapman, *Celts,* 118.

103. Col. David Stewart of Garth, *Sketches of the Character, Manners, and Present State of the Highlanders of Scotland: With Details of the Military Service of the Highland Regiments*, 2 vols. (Edinburgh: Archibald Constable; and London: Longman, Hurst, Rees, Orme and Brown, 1822); quoted from Clyde, *From Rebel to Hero*, 175.

104. Womack, *Improvement and Romance*, 46.

105. Trumpener, *Bardic Nationalism*, 361; also see Murray G. H. Pittock, *The Invention of Scotland: The Stuart Myth and the Scottish Identity, 1638 to the Present* (New York: Routledge, 1991), 62.

106. Clyde, *From Rebel to Hero*, 176; Hunter, *Last of the Free*, 244–46; Devine, *Scotland's Empire*, 318.

107. For example, Devine, *Scotland's Empire*, 130–35, 218–19.

108. Clyde, *From Rebel to Hero*, 177. We might also add Mohawks to this list.

Chapter 4

1. Walter Scott, *Waverley; or, 'Tis Sixty Years Since* (1814; repr. Harmondsworth, Eng.: Penguin, 1985). Wherever possible, subsequent references appear in the main text.

2. For example, James Kerr, *Fiction against History: Scott as Story-Teller* (Cambridge: Cambridge University Press, 1989), 3, 21; Claire Lamont, "One Good Reason for Reading Scott: The Highland Works," *Scott Newsletter* 23/24 (1993/1994): 8, and Lamont, "Scott and Eighteenth-Century Imperialism: India and the Scottish Highlands," in *Configuring Romanticism: Essays Offered to C. C. Barfoot*, ed. Theo D'Haen, Colin Ewen, Peter Liebregts, and Wim Tigges (Amsterdam: Rodopi, 2003), 41, 48–50; Chris Ferns, "Regions of the Empire: Scott, Raddall, Farrell and the Voices of the Colonized," *Swansea Review* (1994), and Ferns, "Look Who's Talking: Walter Scott, Thomas Raddall, and the Voices of the Colonized," *Ariel* 26, no. 4 (1995); Virgil Nemoianu, "Absorbing

Modernization: The Dilemmas of Progress in the Novels of Walter Scott and in *Faust II*," in *Interpreting Goethe's "Faust" Today*, ed. Jane K. Brown, Meredith Lee, and Thomas P. Saine (Columbia, S.C.: Camden House, 1994), especially 2; James Buzard, "Translation and Tourism: Scott's *Waverley* and the Rendering of Culture," *The Yale Journal of Criticism: Interpretation in the Humanities* 8, no. 2 (1995): 36–38, 44, 58; Saree Makdisi, "Colonial Space and the Colonization of Time in Scott's *Waverley*," *Studies in Romanticism* 34, no. 2 (1995), though his reading is often oversimplistic; Ina Ferris, "Translation from the Borders: Encounter and Recalcitrance in *Waverley* and *Clan-Albin*," *Eighteenth-Century Fiction* 9, no. 2 (1997); Bellamy, "Regionalism and Nationalism," 55, 66 (but compare 58, 77); Ian Duncan, "Introduction" to Walter Scott, *Rob Roy*, ed. Duncan (Oxford: Oxford University Press, 1998), x, xvii, xxvi–xxvii; McCracken-Flesher, *Possible Scotlands*; Carla Sassi, *Why Scottish Literature Matters* (Edinburgh: Saltire Society, 2005), 64, 92–93; Mack, *Scottish Fiction*, 8–11, 33, 53–55, 98–100. Further analyses of aspects that are pertinent to a postcolonial approach, though they do not explicitly call themselves postcolonial, are cited below. A more skeptical view on (post)colonial readings of *Waverley* can be found in David Richards, "'Injured by Time and Defeated by Violence': Prospects of Loch Tay," in Sassi and van Heijnsbergen, *Within and without Empire*. Richards's critique is, however, often based on problematic premises (see below).

3. On Scott's anthologizing and ethnographic propensities, also see Louise Z. Smith, "Dialectic, Rhetoric, and Anthropology in Scott's *Waverley*," *Studies in Scottish Literature* 21 (1986): 43–47; and R. Crawford, *Devolving English Literature*, 113–33.

4. Also see Clyde, *From Rebel to Hero*, 122. For example, the explanation that Dundee is "a seaport on the eastern coast of Angusshire" (71) would hardly be necessary to a Scottish audience; it seems mainly for the benefit of English and overseas readers.

5. Murray Pittock argues that such emphases on Highland-Lowland differences in Scott's early work are, in his later works from the 1820s and 1830s, often replaced by a tendency to celticize the whole of Scotland (*Celtic Identity*, 37).

6. Chandler, *England in 1819*, for example, 208–12, 242–43, 250–251, 507.

7. Chandler contends that this anticipates post-structuralist ideas about the constructedness of history (e.g., *England in 1819*, 34–35, 507, 512). Ian Duncan's case study of Walter Scott's *Rob Roy* also stresses the relativity of cultural values, and at times even the victory of "primitive" ones ("Introduction," xxii–xxiv). Alok Yadav argues that even earlier writers, in a phase usually labeled as "pre-romantic," "Enlightened," or "classicist," already show elements of cultural relativism. Even ideas of a "universal republic of letters" did not always assume universal standards of cultural value. For instance, insistence on a plurality of cultural standards could help to assert the value of one's own—for example, British—culture, despite its marginalization by other cultures like those of France or Italy. Thus, even this supposed age of universalism had a particularist, cultural-nationalist dimension (Yadav, *Before the Empire of English*, for example, 96–114, 135, 150–56).

8. Skepticism towards absolute hierarchies can be seen as one element where *Waverley* exhibits a self-critical stance towards progressivist Enlightenment

rationality. Such self-criticism is also stressed by Matthew Wickman, *Ruins of Experience* (13); however, my own reading deems the critical dimension to be more limited.

9. Gottlieb, *Feeling British*, 187.

10. Scott's interest in prejudice, cultural differences, and mediation is also highlighted by Brian Hollingworth, "Completing the Union: Edgeworth's *The Absentee* and Scott the Novelist," in *Scott in Carnival: Selected Papers from the Fourth International Scott Conference, Edinburgh, 1991*, ed. J. H. Alexander and David Hewitt (Aberdeen: ASLS, 1993), 509, 511; R. Crawford, *Devolving English Literature*, 114–33; Buzard, "Translation and Tourism," 38–39; and Ferris, "Translation from the Borders," for example, 208–9, 218–19.

11. D. Richards, "Injured by Time," 19–20.

12. For example, see Benedict Anderson, *Imagined Communities: Reflections on the Origin and Spread of Nationalism*, new ed. (1983; New York: Verso, 2006), 163–64, 170–78; Homi K. Bhabha, "Introduction: Narrating the Nation," in *Nation and Narration*, ed. Bhabha (New York: Routledge, 1990): 7, and Bhabha, "DissemiNation: Time, Narrative, and the Margins of the Modern Nation," in *Nation and Narration*.

13. The importance of cultural and linguistic boundary-crossing in *Waverley* is also stressed by R. Crawford, *Devolving English Literature*, 123–30; Makdisi, "Colonial Space," 156–57; and Ferris, "Translation from the Borders."

14. D. Richards, "Injured by Time," 14–16, 19, 21–22.

15. On Scott's rootedness in Enlightenment discourse on progress and on the differences between "primitive" and "civilized" societies, also see, for example, Michel Maillard, "Le Traitement littéraire du Jacobitisme dans *Waverley*," in *Regards sur l'Écosse au XVIIIe siècle*, ed. Michele S. Plaisant (Lille: Université de Lille, 1977), 222–23; and R. Crawford, *Devolving English Literature*, 111–16.

16. However, not all the Lowlands are considered to be in such a bad state—the area between Stirling and Edinburgh is called "cultivated country" (Scott, *Waverley* 291).

17. Also see Kerr, *Fiction against History*, 22–24.

18. See Joni Buchanan, Christopher Carrell, and Malcolm Maclean's annotations to the pictures in *As an fhearann / From the Land: Clearance, Conflict and Crofting: A Century of Images of the Scottish Highlands*, ed. Christopher Carrell and Malcolm Maclean (Edinburgh: Mainstream, 1986), 72; the reproduction of one such postcard, in *From the Land*, 77; and John Murray, "Whistlers in the Dark: The Hielan Picture Postcard," in *From the Land*, 87.

19. This difference is also pointed out by Makdisi, "Colonial Space," 157–59.

20. See Murray G. H. Pittock, "Scott as Historiographer: The Case of *Waverley*," in Alexander and Hewitt, *Scott in Carnival*, 148; and Pittock, *Poetry and Jacobite Politics*, 233–34.

21. Pittock, "Scott as Historiographer," 147–48, and Pittock, *Poetry and Jacobite Politics*, 233. The novel's suggestion that Jacobitism was already dated before 1745 and was bound to be superseded is also discussed by Craig, *Out of History*, 222–23.

22. On the symbolism of youth, see Pittock, "Scott as Historiographer," 147–48, and *Poetry and Jacobite Politics*, 232–33; as well as Makdisi, "Colonial Space," 172.

23. On multivocality and the cattle raid, also see Frank Palmeri, "The Capacity of Narrative: Scott and Macaulay on Scottish Highlanders," *CLIO: A Journal of Literature, History and the Philosophy of History* 22, no. 1 (1992): 42–43.

24. On the multiple names for Fergus and the prince, also see R. Crawford, *Devolving English Literature*, 128–30.

25. Also see Buzard, "Translation and Tourism," 38–39; R. Crawford, *Devolving English Literature*, 128–31.

26. Also see Kerr, *Fiction against History*, 21, Palmeri, "Capacity of Narrative," 39; Buzard, "Translation and Tourism," 36; Makdisi, "Colonial Space," 156–57, 160–62, 164; Craig, *Out of History*, 44, 70–71; Manfred Malzahn, "Exorcising the Past: Scottish Gentlemen and Gentleman Savages," *Scott Newsletter* 29–30 (1996): 8; G. J. Watson, "Celticism," 211; Trumpener, *Bardic Nationalism*, 148. However, one brief passage in *Waverley* even applies the epithet "primitive state of society" to a part of England's populace (northern country folk, 415), which slightly complicates the "boundaries of civilization."

27. W. Scott, "General Preface" appended to Penguin ed. of *Waverley*, 522.

28. Also see Makdisi, "Colonial Space," 157–59; Alison Lumsden, "'Beyond the Dusky Barrier: Perceptions of the Highlands in the Waverley Novels," in *Mìorun Mòr nan Gall, "The Great Ill-Will of the Lowlander"? Lowland Perceptions of the Highlands, Medieval and Modern*, ed. Dauvit Broun and Martin MacGregor (2007; republ. Glasgow: Centre for Scottish and Celtic Studies, University of Glasgow, 2009), 172; Carla Sassi, "Acts of (Un)willed Amnesia: Dis/appearing Figurations of the Caribbean in Post-Union Scottish Literature," in *Caribbean–Scottish Relations: Colonial and Contemporary Inscriptions in History, Language and Literature*, ed. Joan Anim-Addo, Giovanna Covi, Velma Pollard, and C. Sassi (London: Mango, 2007), 164–65.

29. The comparisons to Native Americans are also noted by Palmeri, "Capacity of Narrative," 40–41; and Liam Connell, "Kailyard Money: Nation, Empire and Speculation in Walter Scott's *Letters from Malachi Malagrowther*," in Sassi and van Heijnsbergen, *Within and without Empire*, 101. Scott's connections between the different "primitives" of the Gaidhealtachd, antiquity, the "Orient," and the overseas colonies are also briefly noted by Malzahn, "Exorcising the Past," 5, 7. *Waverley* is not the only work by Scott which uses the term "wigwam" to liken Gaels to Native Americans: the same happens in his "Essay on Imitations of the Ancient Ballad," included in the 1833 edition of *Minstrelsy of the Scottish Border* (vol. 4:45). Further comparisons of this kind in Scott's works are noted by Sassi, *Why Scottish Literature Matters*, 88, 92–93.

30. See Kerr, *Fiction against History*, 11.

31. The repulsion provoked by Donald's hybridity is also noted by Malzahn, "Exorcising the Past," 4.

32. Conrad, *Heart of Darkness*, 1645–46.

33. For example, W. Scott, *Waverley*, 134, 140, 160–61, 187–88, 192, 227, 293, 305–6, 312, 321, 334, 339, 349.

34. Stafford, *Last of the Race*, 166. On de-romanticizing elements, also see L. Z. Smith, "Dialectic, Rhetoric, and Anthropology," 44; Kerr, *Fiction against History*, 11; and R. Crawford, *Devolving English Literature*, 131.

35. See Claire Lamont, "A Note on Gaelic Proverbs in *Waverley*," *Notes and Queries* 220 / 22, no. 2 (1975).

36. Also see Ferns, for example, "Look Who's Talking," 57–64; Ferris, "Translation from the Borders," for example, 208–16; Bellamy, "Regionalism and Nationalism," 73.

37. See Kerr, *Fiction against History*, 7.

38. See Kerr, *Fiction against History*, 7.

39. See Mack, *Scottish Fiction*, 10.

40. This passage is also discussed by Kerr, *Fiction against History*, 29–35; and Lumsden, "Beyond the Dusky Barrier," 174. Also see W. Scott, *Waverley*, 313.

41. Kerr, *Fiction against History*, 32.

42. James Macpherson, *The Poems of Ossian, in the Original Gaelic, with a Literal Translation into Latin, by Robert MacFarlan* (London: W. Bulmer, 1807).

43. Modern scholars have also debated whether he relied on hacks to compile these Gaelic versions—see Thomson, *Gaelic Sources*, 85–89; Thomson, "Gaelic World," 13–14; and Gaskill's annotations to Macpherson's anglophone Ossianic works, 541.

44. This refers to the Waverleys' English family seat.

45. See Maillard, "Le Traitement," 216–19; Kerr, *Fiction against History*, 11–12; R. Crawford, *Devolving English Literature*, 128–31; Palmeri, "Capacity of Narrative," 43; Trumpener, *Bardic Nationalism*, 139–40.

46. Also noted in Andrew Hook's "Introduction" to the Penguin ed. of *Waverley*, 22–23.

47. See Pittock, "Scott as Historiographer," 147, and Pittock, *Poetry and Jacobite Politics*, 232, 234.

48. W. Scott, letter to Anna Seward, ca. September 1806, in *The Letters of Sir Walter Scott*, ed. H. J. C. Grierson, vol. 1 (London: Constable, 1932), 320.

49. Also see Pittock, *Poetry and Jacobite Politics*, 232–33; Makdisi, "Colonial Space," 171–72; Craig, *Out of History*, 70–72.

50. This is also noted by Bellamy, "Regionalism and Nationalism," 68–69.

51. Also see Kerr, *Fiction against History*, 11–12; Hollingworth, "Completing the Union," 508; Bellamy, "Regionalism and Nationalism," 70; Lamont, "Scott and Eighteenth-Century Imperialism," 48; Mack, *Scottish Fiction*, 54.

52. Pittock, *Poetry and Jacobite Politics*, 233, author's italics, also see 232.

53. Craig, *Out of History*, 44, 70–71.

54. Craig, *Out of History*, 222–23.

55. Buzard, "Translation and Tourism," 40.

56. Womack, *Improvement and Romance*, 106.

57. For examples from Macpherson, see his *Poems of Ossian*, 91, 128. 130.

58. For examples from Macpherson, see his *Poems of Ossian*, 101, 120, 152, 164–65, 231.

59. Stafford, *Last of the Race*, 166; also see Elaine Jordan, "The Management of Scott's Novels," in *Europe and Its Others: Procceedings of the Essex Conference on the Sociology of Literature, July 1984*, ed. Francis Barker et al., 2 vols. (Colchester: University of Essex Press, 1985), 2:154.

60. "Ah, Beaujeu, my dear friend, how boring my profession as prince errant sometimes is." (trans. mine)

61. Nonetheless, the respect for women which allegedly marks a higher civilization is not universal among the Lowlanders: later, the Baron displays patriarchal and feudal attitudes to marriage which are very similar to those of Fergus: both

think that a woman's feelings need not be consulted about a match which her male guardians think suitable (W. Scott, *Waverley*, 460).

62. This nonpolitical, erotic dimension of female Jacobitism in *Waverley* is also noted by Claire Lamont, "Jacobite Songs as Intertexts in *Waverley* and *The Highland Widow*," in Alexander and Hewitt, *Scott in Carnival*, 113.

63. Pittock, *Poetry and Jacobite Politics*, 232–33.

64. Also see Edwin Muir, *Scott and Scotland: The Predicament of the Scottish Writer* (1936; repr. Edinburgh: Polygon, 1982), 87, 90–91, 100; Hook, "Introduction," 14–15; Christopher Harvie, "Scott and the Image of Scotland" (1983), in *Patriotism: The Making and Unmaking of British National Identity*, ed. Raphael Samuel, vol. 2, *Minorities and Outsiders* (New York: Routledge, 1989), 190–91; Buzard, "Translation and Tourism," 39–40; Palmeri, "Capacity of Narrative," 39–42, 407–48, 52; Nemoianu, "Absorbing Modernization," 3; Ferns, "Look Who's Talking," 62, 64.

65. Kerr, *Fiction against History*, 13, 21; Bellamy, "Regionalism and Nationalism," 69. However, various critics have argued that Scott's later works show a more complex, skeptical, or downright pessimistic attitude to historical objectivity, progressivism, integration, assimilation, and/or unionism (Harvie, "Scott and the Image of Scotland"; I. Duncan, "Introduction," x, xvi–xvii, xxi–xxviii; Sassi, *Why Scottish Literature Matters*, 65–67, 72; Gottlieb, *Feeling British*, 201–9, 212–13; Shields, *Sentimental Literature*, e.g., 143, 149–51, 166–69). For instance, Duncan asserts that Scott—already in an essay from 1816 and in his 1817 novel *Rob Roy*—questions assumptions about neat successions of sociohistorical stages by stressing that "primitiveness" (exemplified by, though not exclusive to, the Highlands) and modern commercial society can coevally coexist and even complement or constitute each other. Moreover, in contrast to the vanquished, vanishing Gaels in *Waverley*, Duncan reads *Rob Roy* as a narrative of Highland resilience, survival, and partly also ongoing Highland resistance to appropriation and containment. Also see Wickman's reading of *Rob Roy* (*Ruins of Experience*, 47–55).

66. Geoffrey of Monmouth, *The History of the Kings of Britain* (1136), trans. Lewis Thorpe (London: Penguin, 1966), 75.

67. Kerr, *Fiction against History*, 11–12; Pittock, *Poetry and Jacobite Politics*, 233–34.

68. R. Crawford, *Devolving English Literature*, 131.

69. Muir, *Scott and Scotland*, 87, 90, 100; Harvie, "Scott and the Image of Scotland," 190–91; Kerr, *Fiction against History*, 79; Buzard, "Translation and Tourism," 36–37; R. Crawford, *Devolving English Literature*, 114–15, 130–32; Palmeri, "Capacity of Narrative," 47.

70. Buzard, "Translation and Tourism," 44.

71. Nemoianu, "Absorbing Modernization," 3.

72. Stafford, *Last of the Race*, 165, also see 164; Muir, *Scott and Scotland*, 87; Kerr, *Fiction against History*, 38–40; Makdisi, "Colonial Space," 161–62; Bellamy, "Regionalism and Nationalism," 73.

73. See Muir, *Scott and Scotland*, 91, 105–6; Kerr, *Fiction against History*, 14; Makdisi, "Colonial Space," 161–62.

74. The double function of the subtitle, conveying both proximity and remoteness, is noted by R. Crawford, *Devolving English Literature*, 117–18.

75. See Muir, *Scott and Scotland*, 91, 105–6; and Buzard, "Translation and Tourism," 52.

76. Also noted by Stafford, *Last of the Race*, 165; and Makdisi, "Colonial Space," 176–77.

77. Makdisi, "Colonial Space," 177, also see 176, 178.

78. Jordan, "Management of Scott's Novels," 153; Kerr, *Fiction against History*, 20–21, 38, 40; Pittock, "Scott as Historiographer," 150–51; Clyde, *From Rebel to Hero*, 123; Makdisi, "Colonial Space," 173–74; Malzahn, "Exorcising the Past," 10. For different readings which argue that the harshness of post-Culloden realities is not *completely* silenced, see Claire Lamont, "*Waverley* and the Battle of Culloden," *Essays and Studies* 44 (1991): 18–19; and Stafford, *Last of the Race*, 166.

79. This passage is aptly discussed in Lamont, "*Waverley* and the Battle of Culloden," 22–23.

80. Kerr, *Fiction against History*, 19–21, 40; Lamont, "*Waverley* and the Battle of Culloden," 16–17; Buzard, "Translation and Tourism," 48; Makdisi, "Colonial Space," 174–75.

81. See Hook, "Introduction," 15–16; Kerr, *Fiction against History*, for example, 19, 32–33; Buzard, "Translation and Tourism," 48; Makdisi, "Colonial Space," 174.

82. This is, for example, noted by Watson, *Literature of Scotland*, 257; and Ina Ferris, *The Achievement of Literary Authority: Gender, History, and the Waverley Novels* (Ithaca, N.Y.: Cornell University Press, 1991), 80–86.

83. Anon. (apparently by Francis Jeffrey), review of *Waverley*, in *Edinburgh Review* 47 (1814), 209. Also see Ferris, *Achievement of Literary Authority*, 84, 87.

84. Anon. (Jeffrey?), review of *Waverley*, 209–10.

85. Ibid., 210.

86. Anon., in *The British Critic*, August 1814, vol. II, 189–211; quoted from Bellamy, "Regionalism and Nationalism," 72.

87. Watson, *Literature of Scotland*, 257.

88. Trumpener, *Bardic Nationalism*, xiii; also see 246–47.

89. Trumpener, *Bardic Nationalism*, 246–47.

90. For example, Manning, "Ossian, Scott," 51; R. Crawford, *Devolving English Literature*, 182–94; Stafford, *Last of the Race*, 232–33, 259.

91. On these processes in Cooper's America, see Stafford, *Last of the Race*, 238–43, 253–56.

92. See Ferns, "Regions of the Empire," and Ferns, "Look Who's Talking."

93. See the discussions in R. Crawford, *Devolving English Literature*, 187; Stafford, *Last of the Race*, 233; and Ferns, for example, "Look Who's Talking," 50–51, 64. Lamont identifies a similar distinction between Gaelic and non-European "barbarians" within Scott's own work, although here the non-European colonized population is not American but (East) Indian ("Scott and Eighteenth-Century Imperialism," e.g., 44, 48–49).

94. Examples of such anglophone Highland writers include Martin and Macpherson. On gaelophone examples, see Stroh, *Uneasy Subjects*, 159–88.

95. Pittock, *Celtic Identity*, 37.

Chapter 5

1. For instance, see Maureen Martin's case studies of how romantic notions of highlandized kilt-wearing Scots as images of hypermasculinity influenced Victorian negotiations of national and gender identities (Maureen Martin, *Mighty Scot*). She also acknowledges the uses (and limitations) of the "internal colonial" model (3–4, 41, 84, 92, 95, 108). Despite many lucid observations, her study contains some problematic passages where she employs elements of colonial discourse herself: she assumes that Scotland's real national history and "cultivated" life took place exclusively in the Lowlands, implicitly colluding with colonial discourse which locates the Highlands outside culture, history, and the national community (2–3, 9, 24–25, 81). Other points, like her critique of enforced Highland depopulation, suggest an anticolonial stance, but these seem based on purely humanitarian sympathy with a supposedly benighted, primitive people, unaccompanied by a critique of how their "benightedness" and otherness were socially constructed to obscure the centrality of Gaeldom to medieval Scottish national identity and politics, and the fact that the Highlands have been just as "cultivated" as the Lowlands, though differently cultivated, for example, possessing a long tradition of sophisticated literature and learning, both oral and literate, albeit with conventions that partly diverged from Lowland ones.

2. See Robert J. C. Young, *The Idea of English Ethnicity* (Malden, Mass.: Blackwell, 2008), for example, 47–49, 71–81, 124.

3. This difference between eighteenth-century Enlightened and nineteenth-century racist thought is also pointed out by Krisztina Fenyö, *Contempt, Sympathy and Romance: Lowland Perceptions of the Highlands and the Clearances during the Famine Years, 1845–1855* (Edinburgh: Tuckwell, 2000), 17–18, 25.

4. On Jamieson and Laing, see Ferguson, *Identity of the Scottish Nation*, 259–63; and Colin Kidd, "Race, Theology and Revival: Scots Philology and Its Contexts in the Age of Pinkerton and Jamieson," *Scottish Studies Review* 3, no. 2 (2002). On Scottish Teutonism in general, see Kidd, "Teutonist Ethnology."

5. For example, see John Pinkerton, *A Dissertation on the Origin and Progress of the Scythians or Goths: Being an Introduction to the Ancient and Modern History of Europe* (London: George Nicol, 1787), 23–24, 177. On Pinkerton, also see Kidd, "Teutonist Ethnology," 51–54, and Kidd, "Race, Theology and Revival"; Ferguson, *Identity of the Scottish Nation*, 250–56; Fenyö, *Contempt, Sympathy and Romance*, 29–32; R. J. C. Young, *Idea of English Ethnicity*, 81–82.

6. Pinkerton, *Dissertation*, 223.

7. Pinkerton, *Dissertation*, 45.

8. Pinkerton, *Dissertation*, 68.

9. Pinkerton, *Dissertation*, 92.

10. Pinkerton, *Dissertation*, 69.

11. For example, Pinkerton, *Dissertation*, 222.

12. John Pinkerton, *An Enquiry into the History of Scotland, Preceding the Reign of Malcolm III, or the Year 1056*, 2 vols. (1790, repr. Edinburgh: Bell and Bradfute, 1814), 1:339.

13. Fenyö, *Contempt, Sympathy and Romance*, 30–32. On racist dimensions of Scottish Teutonism, also see Kidd, "Teutonist Ethnology," 52–64, and Kidd,

"Race, Empire, and the Limits of Nineteenth-Century Scottish Nationhood," *The Historical Journal* 46, no. 4 (2003): 873–92.

14. Fenyö, *Contempt, Sympathy and Romance*, 31–32.

15. Grant, "Highland History," 472.

16. On all these developments, see Hunter, *Making of the Crofting Community*, 71–135, and Hunter, *Last of the Free*, 262–90; Womack, *Improvement and Romance*, 118; Devine, *Scottish Nation*, 194–95.

17. For more details, see Eric Richards, *A History of the Highland Clearances*, 2 vols. (London: Croom Helm, 1982 and 1985), 2:373–408.

18. For example, in Sellar, note concerning Sutherland, May 1816; publ. in *Papers on Sutherland Estate Management, 1802–1816*, ed. R. J. Adam, 2 vols. (Edinburgh: T. and A. Constable, 1972), 1:184–85, 187.

19. E. Richards, *History of the Highland Clearances*, 2:395.

20. Sellar, letter to Lord Advocate Colquhoun, May 24, 1815; publ. in Adam, *Papers*, 1:156, Sellar's italics.

21. Sellar, note, 175–76, Sellar's italics.

22. Sellar, note, 175.

23. Sellar, note, 177–87.

24. Sellar, unpubl. letter to James Loch, 1816; quoted from E. Richards, *History of the Highland Clearances*, 2:401.

25. E. Richards, *History of the Highland Clearances*, 2:398–402.

26. Fenyö, *Contempt, Sympathy and Romance*, for example, 1–6, 165–68. My information on the famine and contemporary public opinion is mainly based on Fenyö; Hunter, *Making of the Crofting Community*, 91–135, 156, and Hunter, *Last of the Free*, 278–79; and Devine, *Scottish Nation*, 413–21.

27. "Highland Destitution—Skye," *The Scotsman*, July 21, 1847; quoted from Fenyö, *Contempt, Sympathy and Romance*, 69.

28. This link between class and race discourse is also highlighted by R. J. C. Young, *Colonial Desire*, 59, and Young, *Idea of English Ethnicity*, 81; Gustav Jahoda, *Images of Savages: Ancient Roots of Modern Prejudice in Western Culture* (New York: Routledge, 1999), xv; and Fenyö, *Contempt, Sympathy and Romance*, 37–38.

29. Fenyö, *Contempt, Sympathy and Romance*, 58.

30. Quoted from Fenyö, *Contempt, Sympathy and Romance*, 64, which apparently cites from anon., "Notes of a Winter Tour," *Fifeshire Journal*, February 11, 1847.

31. "*The Times* Commissioner," "The Condition of the People in the Highlands of Scotland," *The Times*, October 1, 1846, 5; and another article publ. under the same pseudonym and title, *The Times*, October 7, 1846, 4.

32. Article series "Inquiry into the Distress in the Highlands and Islands," *The Scotsman*, January 30–March 10, 1847, quoted from Fenyö, *Contempt, Sympathy and Romance*, 61.

33. Article series "Inquiry into the Distress in the Highlands and Islands," *The Scotsman*, January 30–March 10, 1847, quoted from Fenyö, *Contempt, Sympathy and Romance*, 61.

34. *The Scotsman*, February 10, 1847; quoted from Fenyö, *Contempt, Sympathy and Romance*, 62.

35. Editorial, *The Scotsman*, September 3, 1851; quoted from Fenyö, *Contempt, Sympathy and Romance*, 85.

36. This contradiction was already noted by Thomas Mulock, "Macleod of Macleod's Attempted Refutation of Mr Mulock's Statements," *Northern Ensign*, January 16, 1851; quoted from Fenyö, *Contempt, Sympathy and Romance*, 141.

37. "New Light on the Highlands," *Fifeshire Journal*, September 11, 1851; quoted from Fenyö, *Contempt, Sympathy and Romance*, 85–86.

38. Fenyö, *Contempt, Sympathy and Romance*, 86.

39. The suggestion was made by Sir Charles Trevelyan in a letter to Thomas Murdoch, March 31, 1852; quoted from T. M. Devine, *The Great Highland Famine: Hunger, Emigration and the Scottish Highlands in the Nineteenth Century* (Edinburgh: John Donald, 1988), 251.

40. Sir Charles Trevelyan, letter to Commissary-General Miller, June 30, 1852, quoted from Devine, *Great Highland Famine*, 251.

41. Ferguson, *Identity of the Scottish Nation*, 286–88, 314; also see Kidd, "Race, Empire," 884–86.

42. Ferguson, *Identity of the Scottish Nation*, 293–95.

43. For a general outline of the hardening of older ethno-cultural typologies into biologically fixed "racial" boundaries, see R. J. C. Young, *Colonial Desire*, 65–67. A specialized study of Irish-related nineteenth-century race discourse can be found in L. P. Curtis, Jr., *Anglo-Saxons and Celts: A Study of Anti-Irish Prejudice in Victorian England* (Bridgeport, Conn.: Conference on British Studies, University of Bridgeport, 1968).

44. R. J. C. Young, *Idea of English Ethnicity*, 60–61.

45. Robert Knox, *The Races of Men: A Fragment* (1850); here quoted from the 2nd ed. (with new subtitle, added illustrations, and a "Supplement" of extra chapters), *The Races of Men: A Philosophical Enquiry into the Influence of Race over the Destinies of Nations* (London: Henry Renshaw, 1862). Wherever possible, page references appear in the main text. On Knox, also see *Dictionary of National Biography* (London: Smith, Elder, 1908–20), vol. 11, ed. Sidney Lee (1909), 330–34; George L. Mosse, *Toward the Final Solution: A History of European Racism* (New York: Howard Fertig, 1978), 57; Fenyö, *Contempt, Sympathy and Romance*, 40; R. J. C. Young, *Colonial Desire*, 72–76, 78–79, and Young, *Idea of English Ethnicity*.

46. Knox, *Races of Men*, v; also see 12, 37.

47. Knox, *Races of Men*, 64–75, 87–93, 97–98, 109–11, 142, 163–64, 242–43, 261–63, 349–50, 382, 389, 400, 407.

48. Knox, *Races of Men*, 56–57 and 14, also see 78–79, 147–48.

49. Knox, *Races of Men*, 5, 11, 46, 193, 359, 374, 469.

50. Knox, *Races of Men*, 5, 18–19, 25, 61, 266–67, 328, 375.

51. This alludes to a famous song which was originally about a soldier's fear of not returning home from war, but by at least the 1840s also became associated with emigration. The mentioning of Lochaber, together with the place-names Knox mentions in the rest of this paragraph, suggests that the passage refers particularly to the *Gaelic* Celts.

52. Knox ascribes the smallness of agricultural holdings in the Highlands merely to soil and climate, without acknowledging that it was mainly a result of social factors, that is, Clearances and crofting.

53. Knox seems undecided about whether the complete extermination of certain races is possible or not. Passages where he does seem to think it possible, for instance regarding Native Americans and South African Caffres, include *Races of Men*, 87, 111–13, 138–39, 184–85, 217–18, 229–30, 234–35, 243, 254, 446, 449–51. At least sometimes, he calls extermination desirable, for example concerning the "gypsies" (157, 159). Elsewhere, Knox suggests that total extermination of a race is impossible (e.g., 67, 71–75, 109, 113, 115–17, 125–28, 139–42). He admits his insecurity in this matter, which he attributes to a lack of conclusive information on the laws of racial development (219, also see 218).

54. See, for example, Heather Winlow, "Anthropometric Cartography: Constructing Scottish Racial Identity in the Early Twentieth Century," *Journal of Historical Geography* 27, no. 4 (2001): 509, 521; R. J. C. Young, *Idea of English Ethnicity*, 47–48, 76, 89–90.

55. Knox, *Races of Men*, 3–4. On racial war, also see 7, 213–14, 265–66, 348 ("war of race . . . must continue whilst race exists").

56. The same strategy of portraying indigenous populations as unable to use their natural resources efficiently, thus justifying colonial takeover on economic or social Darwinist grounds, is identified in an overseas colonial context by Alan Lawson and Chris Tiffin, "The Textuality of Empire," in *De-Scribing Empire: Post-Colonialism and Textuality*, ed. Lawson and Tiffin (New York: Routledge, 1994), 5.

57. Murray Pittock points out that the branding of Celts as an unfit race destined to give way before a fitter race of Saxons gained considerable currency in the second half of the nineteenth century as a strategy to justify marginalization. Most of this discourse referred to Ireland, the most troublesome of the "Celtic" regions. He also quotes examples from the works of Thomas Carlyle and D. H. Lawrence which liken Irish people to Africans (*Celtic Identity*, 70–71).

58. Also see R. J. C. Young, *Idea of English Ethnicity*, 85–86.

59. Usually, Knox applies the term "colony" only to settler colonies.

60. The africanizing elements in this illustration are also discussed in R. J. C. Young, *Idea of English Ethnicity*, 79.

61. However, there are also passages where the Celts are claimed to be superior to nonwhite peoples, for example, Knox, *Races of Men*, 226, 235–36, 281.

62. Also see Knox, *Races of Men*, 51, 53, 62, 70–75, 107–11, 122–23, 125, 129–31, 142–43, 156, 245, 264, 464, 471.

63. Knox, *Races of Men*, 67, 71–75, 109, 113, 115–17, 125–28, 139–42, 218–19, 225–26, 242, 246, 268, 456, 464.

64. Knox, *Races of Men*, for example, 11, 49, 113–14, 222, 264, 279–80, 374, 377, 469. Also see R. J. C. Young, *Idea of English Ethnicity*, 86.

65. Knox, *Races of Men*, 379, italics original. Also see R. J. C. Young, *Idea of English Ethnicity*, 86.

66. John Beddoe, *The Races of Britain: A Contribution to the Anthropology of Western Europe* (1885; facsimile repr. with new introduction, London: Hutchinson, 1971). Also see R. J. C. Young, *Colonial Desire*, 72, 76–77, 81, 192; and Young, *Idea of English Ethnicity*, 131–39.

67. Kidd, "Race, Empire," 886–89.

68. Kidd notes that a Celtic taint was not ascribed to Lowland Scotland in English racial nationalism ("Race, Empire," 875). But anxieties about such a taint

may well have been excited by other discourse fields, for instance earlier uses of Gaelic icons as pan-Scottish national symbols, not only by Scottish patriots, but also by English anti-Scottish discourse (for instance in the eighteenth century), as well as in nineteenth-century English and Scottish popular culture.

Chapter 6

1. As, for instance, illustrated by certain strands of famine journalism (see Fenyö, *Contempt, Sympathy and Romance*).

2. Assessment by Hunter, *Making of the Crofting Community*, 223. For general information on the land reform movement, see Hunter, *Making of the Crofting Community*, 180–279, and Hunter, *Last of the Free*, 304–30; Devine, *Scottish Nation*, 425–47, 496.

3. However, not all Scottish–Irish relations in the nineteenth century were amicable and based on transperipheral solidarity. There was considerable anti-Irish prejudice and discrimination against Irish immigrants (e.g., see Devine, *Scottish Nation*, 488–89, 491, 502; Fry, *Scottish Empire*, 357, 370). Even Scottish *Gaels*, both in the United Kingdom and in the North American diaspora, sometimes tried to distinguish themselves from the Irish Gaels in order to claim a greater affinity with the Anglo-Saxon "master race" that dominated Britain's anglocentric racial hierarchy. Such claims were made to improve the Scottish Gaels' own position in this hierarchy (e.g., see Michael Newton, "How Scottish Highlanders Became White: The Introduction of Racialism to Gaelic Literature and Culture," in Newton, *Celts in the Americas*, 286–87, 295, and Newton, "Bury My Heart at Culloden").

4. Konstanze Glaser, "Essentialism and Relativism in Gaelic and Sorbian Language Revival Discourses," paper presented on January 30, 2002, apparently at the Department of Celtic and Scottish Studies, University of Edinburgh, www.arts.ed.ac.uk/celtic/poileasaidh/seminarwebversion2.html, p. 5.

5. Maureen Martin, *Mighty Scot*, 104, also see 142.

6. Matthew Arnold, *On the Study of Celtic Literature*, serialized 1866; 1st book form 1867; repr. in *The Complete Prose Works of Matthew Arnold*, ed. R. H. Super, vol. 3, *Lectures and Essays in Criticism* (Ann Arbor: University of Michigan Press, 1962).

7. On Arnold, race, ethnicity, and (post)colonialism, also see Innes, *Devil's Own Mirror*, 12–13, and Innes, "Orientalism and Celticism," in Graham and Hooper, *Irish and Postcolonial Writing*, 146–49; Gibbons, "Race against Time," 150, 156, and Gibbons, *Transformations*, 9; R. J. C. Young, *Colonial Desire*, 62–69, 71, 74–87, and Young, *Idea of English Ethnicity*, 140–76; Pittock, *Celtic Identity*, 70; Sassi, *Why Scottish Literature Matters*, 76.

8. For general information, see, for example, Lynch, *Scotland: A New History*, 359–61, 417; P. H. Scott, *Scotland: An Unwon Cause*, 110–24; Devine, *Scottish Nation*, 287, 307–8; Fry, *Scottish Empire*, 354–64, 370, 374.

9. For Arnold, see, for example, *Study of Celtic Literature*, 296–97, 346–47, 351, 361, 375, 390.

10. For example, see Flavia Alaya, *William Sharp—"Fiona Macleod," 1855–1905* (Cambridge, Mass.: Harvard University Press, 1970), 150–51, 168–71; Watson, *Literature of Scotland*, 312–13; Gibbons, "Race against Time," 155–56; Colin Milton, "Cultural and Political Nationalism in the Irish Literary Revival

and the Scottish Renaissance," in *English Studies 4: Proceedings of the Third Conference on the Literature of Region and Nation, Echternach, 10–14 September 1990*, ed. J. J. Simon and Alain Sinner (Luxembourg: Publications du Centre Universitaire de Luxembourg, Département des Lettres et de Sciences Humaines, Section de Lettres Anglaises, 1992); Daniel Williams, "Pan-Celticism and the Limits of Post-Colonialism: W. B. Yeats, Ernest Rhys and William Sharp in the 1890s," in *Nations and Relations: Writing across the British Isles*, ed. Tony Brown and Russell Stephens (Cardiff: New Welsh Review, 2000), 1–29; Tania Scott, "The Fantasy of the Celtic Revival: Lord Dunsany, Fiona Macleod and W. B. Yeats," in *Border Crossings: Narration, Nation and Imagination in Scots and Irish Literature and Culture*, ed. Colin Younger (Newcastle, Eng.: Cambridge Scholars, 2013).

11. This sets the Scottish Celtic revival apart from its Irish and Welsh counterparts (Harvie, "Anglo-Saxons," 247–48). On Scotland, also see I. M. M. MacPhail, "Prelude to the Crofters' War," *TGSI* 49 (1974–76): 167, 169–70; Milton, "Cultural and Political Nationalism," especially 111–12; Newton, *Warriors of the Word*, 42. For a particularly useful discussion of Gaelic revivalism in the late nineteenth and early twentieth centuries, see Michael Newton, "'Becoming Cold-Hearted like the Gentiles around Them': Scottish Gaelic in the United States 1872–1912," *e-Keltoi: Journal of Interdisciplinary Celtic Studies* 2 (2003), www4.uwm.edu/celtic/ekeltoi/volumes/vol2/2_3/newton_2_3.pdf. Though focused on the United States, Newton also discusses numerous international connections, thus giving insight into the Scottish scene.

12. Alexander Nicolson, "Preface" in *A Collection of Gaelic Proverbs and Familiar Phrases*, ed. Nicolson (1881; 3rd ed. abr. repr. Edinburgh: Birlinn, 1996), xxiv–xvii, xxx.

13. Letter to Father Allan MacDonald; quoted from Cameron, "Embracing the Past," 208.

14. Fanon, *Wretched of the Earth*, 223.

15. As discussed in Ashcroft, Griffiths, and Tiffin, *Empire Writes Back* (1989), for example, 78.

16. Sims-Williams, "Visionary Celt," 72–73. Also see "Visionary Celt," 77; and Arnold, *Study of Celtic Literature*, 296–97.

17. Sims-Williams, "Visionary Celt," 74, 76; James, *Atlantic Celts*, 55–56.

18. Also noted by R. J. C. Young, *Idea of English Ethnicity*, 111–12.

19. For general information on Sharp, see Alaya, *William Sharp*; Christine Lahey-Dolega, "Some Brief Observations on the Life and Work of William Sharp (Fiona Macleod)," *Ball State University Forum* 21, no. 4 (1980); Thomas L[ynch] Cooksey, "William Sharp (Fiona Macleod)," in *British Short Fiction Writers, 1880–1914: The Romantic Tradition*, ed. William F. Naufftus (Detroit: Gale, 1996); William F. Halloran, ed., *The William Sharp "Fiona Macleod" Archive*, Institute of English Studies, University of London, www.ies.sas.ac.uk/research/current-projects/william-sharp-fiona-macleod-archive/william-sharp-fiona-macleod-archive.

20. Sharp (as "Fiona Macleod"), open letter to George Meredith, publ. as preface to a collection of Celtic tales by "Fiona Macleod," 1895; quoted from Terence Brown, "Preface," in T. Brown, *Celticism*, vii.

21. T. Brown, "Preface," in Brown, *Celticism*, viii.

22. For instance, William Sharp, "Introduction" to the anthology *Lyra Celtica: An Anthology of Representative Celtic Poetry*, ed. Elizabeth A. Sharp (Edinburgh: Patrick Geddes, 1896), xx, xxiii, xliv; also see xliii, xlviii. On Sharp's debt to Arnold, also see Alaya, *William Sharp*, 156; D. Williams, "Pan-Celticism and the Limits of Post-Colonialism," e.g., 19–20, 28; T. Scott, "The Fantasy of the Celtic Revival," 129–30, 133–34.

23. For example, Arnold, *Study of Celtic Literature*, 335–36, 347, 374.

24. This is also noted by Roderick Watson, "Visions of Alba: The Constructions of Celtic Roots in Modern Scottish Literature," in "Actes du Congrès international d'études écossaises, Grenoble, 1991," special issue, *Études Écossaises* 1 (1992): 254; Sassi, *"Imagined Scotlands,"* 57; and D. Williams, "Pan-Celticism and the Limits of Post-Colonialism," 28. However, "Fiona Macleod" was not the only pseudonym used by Sharp: another was the much less Celtic-sounding "Anne Montgomerie." His further pen names also included male and Continental European ones. See Alaya, *William Sharp*, 103; Lahey-Dolega, "Some Brief Observations," 21; Terry L. Meyers, *The Sexual Tensions of William Sharp: A Study of the Birth of Fiona Macleod, Incorporating Two Lost Works, "Ariadne in Naxos" and "Beatrice"* (New York: Peter Lang, 1996), 15. An additional complication is that, while common, the association of Celticity with femininity and of Saxondom with masculinity was not ubiquitous. As already noted, various Victorian representations continued romantic associations of Celticity with hypermasculinity; and Maureen Martin demonstrates that the other side of this coin was English and Lowland Teutons' anxiety that their own masculinity might be comparatively deficient, thus needing constant reassertion (*Mighty Scot*). For readings which explain Sharp's choice of the pseudonym "Fiona Macleod" through primarily non-Celticist factors, such as a critique of Victorian gender conventions, bisexual leanings, and a heterosexual extramarital romantic attachment, see Meyers, *Sexual Tensions*; and William F. Halloran, "W. B. Yeats, William Sharp, and Fiona Macleod: A Celtic Drama, 1897," in "Yeats and the Nineties," ed. Warwick Gould, special issue, *Yeats Annual* 14 (2001).

25. William Sharp (as "Fiona Macleod"), *Green Fire* (Westminster, Eng.: Archibald Constable, 1896). Subsequent references are based on this edition, with page numbers in brackets in the main text.

26. For example, Arnold, *Study of Celtic Literature*, 296–98.

27. For a relevant passage from Arnold, see his *Study of Celtic Literature*, 246, 347, 351, 355.

28. Arnold, *Study of Celtic Literature*, 347.

29. For Arnold, see *Study of Celtic Literature*, 247, 275, 296.

30. The general importance of "racial memory" in Sharp's work is also noted by Alaya, *William Sharp*, 37–38.

31. In William Sharp (as "Fiona Macleod"), *The Divine Adventure / Iona / By Sundown Shores* (1900; repr. London: William Heinemann, 1927), 245.

32. William Sharp, "Introduction" to *Lyra Celtica*, li, and (as "Fiona Macleod"), *Pharais* (Derby, Eng.: Harpur and Murray, 1894), ix.

33. Sharp, "Iona," 246; also see Sharp, "Introduction " to *Lyra Celtica*, li, and Arnold, *Study of Celtic Literature*, 298, 358, 361, 370, 373, 390.

34. Intra-Celtic distinctions had already been made by Arnold, although for him the main intra-Celtic opposite of hyper-barbarian Gaeldom lay not in the

p-Celtic world in general or in Brittany alone, but in the entirety of France, including the latter's non-Celtic-speaking parts (*Study of Celtic Literature*, 246, 292–93, 338, 349).

35. For Arnold, see his *Study of Celtic Literature*, 343.

36. The association of children with cultural rebirth also occurs in other colonized cultures. A Kenyan example where the (here successful) birth of a child symbolizes hope for a brighter postcolonial future appears in Ngũgĩ's novel *A Grain of Wheat* (1967; rev. and repr. Oxford: Heinemann, 1987).

37. Robert Louis Stevenson, *Kidnapped*, repr., together with Stevenson's *Catriona*, ed. Emma Letley (New York: Oxford University Press, 1986).

38. While *Green Fire* insists on rational explanations for seemingly supernatural events, many of "Fiona Macleod's" short stories revel in supernatural themes without any apparent urge to provide rationalizations. See, for instance, the collections *Wind and Wave* and *The Sunset of Old Tales* (Leipzig: Bernhard Tauchnitz, 1902 and 1905 respectively).

39. Sharp (as "Fiona Macleod"), "For the Beauty of an Idea," in *The Winged Destiny: Studies in the Spiritual History of the Gael* (1904; repr. London: William Heinemann, 1927), 195–96. Also see Alaya, *William Sharp*, 151, 170. Whereas the present reading focuses on the non-subversive side of Sharp's work, a more subversive dimension is identified by Michael Shaw, "William Sharp's Neo-Paganism: Queer Identity and the National Family," in *Queer Victorian Families: Curious Relations in Literature*, ed. Duc Dau and Shale Preston (New York: Routledge, 2015), which reads Sharp's blurring of gender and cultural boundaries as a plea for equality. However, at times he might overrate the subversive side: Sharp's use of biological racism and ideas of inevitable racial decline, foregrounded by my own analysis, reasserts essential differences and hierarchies between Celts and Teutons, and chances for hybridization are couched in strongly unequal terms, for instance when the future of the Celtic literary tradition is reduced to a spiritual influence on anglophone writing.

40. James Ashcroft Noble in *The New Age*; quoted from a brief appendix citing "Opinions of the Press on the Writings of Fiona Macleod" in Sharp/Macleod, *Green Fire*, 286.

41. Durkacz, *Decline of the Celtic Languages*, 201–2.

42. In *TGSI* 16 (1889–90) and 21 (1896–97) respectively. Subsequent references appear in the text.

43. Which races are meant by "the one" and "the other" becomes clear from pp. 27–29.

44. Another vindication of Gaelic culture by citing more prestigious English analogies can be found in Nicolson's work: "We have as yet no absolute standard of Gaelic orthography, and it is no disgrace, considering that William Shakespeare spelled his . . . name in several ways, and that even Samuel Johnson's English spellings are not all followed now" ("Preface," xix).

45. The long-lasting influence of Victorian race theory is evident from the Lowland poet Maurice Lindsay's introduction to *Modern Scottish Poetry: An Anthology of the Scottish Renaissance* (London: Faber and Faber, 1946), where he describes Highland-Lowland relations in terms which strongly resemble Macbean's description of pan-British Celtic-Teuton relations. Lindsay writes, "Two racial strains have gradually intermingled to form the Scottish character. The

sturdy, tough-headed Lowlander has sprung mainly from Teuton stock, while the more romantic Western Highlander is Celtic in his origin. . . . Curiously enough, the gentler strain has predominated, and, for all his wiry practicality, the Lowland Scot carries the mournful blood of the Celt, which . . . distinguishes him from his Northern English neighbour" (15).

46. Macbean does not specify his exact source. In his essay the quote is on p. 66.

Conclusion

1. See Fenyö, *Contempt, Sympathy and Romance*.

2. Chapman, *Gaelic Vision*, 230.

3. See Maureen Martin's discussion of these three women's works in *Mighty Scot*, 129–63. Nonetheless, there are still limitations, for instance elements of racial typology in Oliphant's work (also noted by Martin).

4. For a general reassessment of the ways in which nineteenth-century Scottish literature anticipated the modernism of the twentieth-century Scottish Renaissance, see Douglas Gifford, "Preparing for Renaissance: Revaluing Nineteenth-Century Scottish Literature," in *Scotland and the 19th-Century World*, ed. Gerard Carruthers, David Goldie, and Alastair Renfrew (New York: Rodopi, 2012).

5. Harvie, "Anglo-Saxons," 250, also see 249.

6. See, for example, F. G. Thompson, "Gaelic in Politics," *TGSI* 47 (1971–72): 83–86; Pittock, *Celtic Identity*, 75, 83–84, 125.

7. R. B. Cunninghame Graham, "'Bloody Niggers,'" repr. in Cunninghame Graham, *Selected Writings*, ed. Cedric Watts (Rutherford, N.J.: Fairleigh Dickinson University Press, 1981). On his support for Home Rule, see, for example, Anne Taylor, *The People's Laird: A Life of Robert Bontine Cunninghame Graham* (York, Eng.: Tobias 2005), 163, 180, 197, 317.

8. Cunninghame Graham, "'Bloody,'" direct quote from 64, also see 61–67.

9. Cunninghame Graham, "'Bloody,'" 63–64. However, despite its radical anticolonial stance, the essay still seems partly influenced by elements of colonial discourse: it seems to imply that Native Americans are comparable to prehistoric Europeans, thus reiterating the "contemporary ancestor" trope; and there is also a hint of antisemitism (62).

10. For example, Philippa Mein Smith, *A Concise History of New Zealand* (Cambridge: Cambridge University Press, 2005), 92.

WORKS CITED

Aaron, Jane, and Chris Williams, eds. *Postcolonial Wales*. Cardiff: University of Wales Press, 2005.

Adam, R. J., ed. *Papers on Sutherland Estate Management, 1802–1816*. 2 vols. Edinburgh: T. and A. Constable, 1972.

Alaya, Flavia. *William Sharp—"Fiona Macleod," 1855–1905*. Cambridge, Mass.: Harvard University Press, 1970.

Alexander, J. H., and David Hewitt, eds. *Scott in Carnival: Selected Papers from the Fourth International Scott Conference, Edinburgh, 1991*. Aberdeen, Scot.: ASLS, 1993.

Anderson, Benedict. *Imagined Communities: Reflections on the Origin and Spread of Nationalism*. 1983. New ed. New York: Verso, 2006.

Anderson, James. *An Account of the Present State of the Hebrides and Western Coasts of Scotland*. Edinburgh: G. Robinson and C. Elliot, 1785.

Anonymous (generally ascribed to David Bruce). *The Highlands of Scotland in 1750: From Manuscript 104 in the King's Library, British Museum*. Ed. Andrew Lang. Edinburgh: Blackwood, 1898.

———. "Preface." *Edinburgh Review* 1 (1755), repr. in *The Edinburgh Review for the Year 1755*, i–v. London: Longman, Hurst, Rees, Orme and Brown, 1818.

———(signed "A Citizen of Edinburgh," sometimes ascribed to Tobias Smollett). *A North Briton Extraordinary*. 1765. 2nd ed. London: W. Nicoll, 1765.

———(apparently by Francis Jeffrey). Review of *Waverley* by Walter Scott. *Edinburgh Review* 47 (1814): 208–43.

———. Editorial, "On the Proposed National Monument at Edinburgh." *Blackwood's Edinburgh Magazine* 5, no. 28 (1819): 385.

———("A Londoner, but No Cockney"). "The King's Visit to Edinburgh." *Blackwood's Edinburgh Magazine* 12 (September–October 1822): 268–84 and 492–97.

———(presumably by Michael Robson). "Introduction." In *Curiosities of Art and Nature: The New Annotated and Illustrated Edition of Martin Martin's Classic "A Description of the Western Isles of Scotland,"* ed. Michael Robson, ix–xxxii. Port of Ness, Scot.: Islands Book Trust, 2003.

———. "Getting the Name Right." *West Highland Free Press*, October 8, 2004, www.whfp.com.

Arnold, Matthew. *On the Study of Celtic Literature*. Serialized 1866. 1st publ. in book form 1867. Repr. in *The Complete Prose Works of Matthew Arnold*, ed. R. H. Super, vol. 3, *Lectures and Essays in Criticism*, 291–395. Ann Arbor: University of Michigan Press, 1962.

Ashcroft, Bill, Gareth Griffiths, and Helen Tiffin. *The Empire Writes Back: Theory and Practice in Post-Colonial Literatures*. New York: Routledge, 1989. 2nd ed. 2002.

Ball, Anna. *Palestinian Literature and Film in Postcolonial Feminist Perspective*. New York: Routledge, 2012.

Baridon, Michael. "Philosophic Light and Gothic Gloom: Landscape and History in Eighteenth-Century Scotland." In *Aberdeen and the Enlightenment*, ed. Jennifer J. Carter and Joan H. Pittock, 218–37. Aberdeen: Aberdeen University Press, 1987.

Bauer, Thomas. "The Islamization of Islam." In *Ideological Battlegrounds—Constructions of Us and Them before and after 9/11*, vol. 1: *Perspectives in Literatures and Cultures*, ed. Joanna Witkowska and Uwe Zagratzki, 1–15. Newcastle, Eng.: Cambridge Scholars, 2014.

Beddoe, John. *The Races of Britain: A Contribution to the Anthropology of Western Europe*. 1885. Facsimile repr. with new introduction. London: Hutchinson, 1971.

Bellamy, Liz. "Regionalism and Nationalism: Maria Edgeworth, Walter Scott and the Definition of Britishness." In *The Regional Novel in Britain and Ireland, 1800–1990*, ed. K. D. M. Snell, 54–77. Cambridge: Cambridge University Press, 1998.

Bhabha, Homi K. "The Commitment to Theory." 1989. Rev. and repr. in Bhabha, *Location of Culture*, 19–39.

———. "DissemiNation: Time, Narrative, and the Margins of the Modern Nation." In Bhabha, *Nation and Narration*, 291–322.

———. "Introduction: Narrating the Nation." In Bhabha, *Nation and Narration*, 1–7.

———. *The Location of Culture*. New York: Routledge, 1994.

———, ed. *Nation and Narration*. New York: Routledge, 1990.

———. "Of Mimicry and Man: The Ambivalence of Colonial Discourse" (1984). Repr. in Bhabha, *Location of Culture*, 85–92.

———. "Signs Taken for Wonders: Questions of Ambivalence and Authority under a Tree Outside Delhi, May 1817." 1985. Rev. and repr. in Bhabha, *Location of Culture*, 102–22.

Black, Ronald A. "The Gaelic Academy: The Cultural Commitment of the Highland Society of Scotland." *SGS* 14, no. 2 (1986): 1–38; and 15, no. 1 (1988): 103–21.

———, ed. and trans. *An lasair: Anthology of 18th Century Scottish Gaelic Verse*. Edinburgh: Birlinn, 2001.

———. "Mac Mhaighstir Alasdair in Rannoch: A Reconstruction." *TGSI* 59 (1994–96): 341–425.

Blair, Hugh. "A Critical Dissertation on the Poems of Ossian, the Son of Fingal." 1763. Repr. in Macpherson, *Poems of Ossian*, ed. Gaskill, 345–46, 357.

Bohata, Kirsti. *Postcolonialism Revisited*. Cardiff: University of Wales Press, 2004.

Boswell, James. *The Journal of a Tour to the Hebrides with Samuel Johnson*. 1773. 1st publ. 1785. Repr. together with Samuel Johnson's *A Journey to the Western Islands of Scotland*, ed. Peter Levi, 153–411. Harmondsworth, Eng.: Penguin, 1984.

Bradshaw, Brendan, and Peter Roberts, eds. *British Consciousness and Identity: The Making of Britain, 1533–1707*. Cambridge: Cambridge University Press, 1998.

Briesemeister, Dietrich. "Keltentum und Nationalismus in Galicien." In *Nationalism in Literature—Literarischer Nationalismus: Literature, Language and National Identity. Third International Scottish Studies Symposium—Proceedings*, ed. Horst W. Drescher and Hermann Völkel, 347–58. Frankfurt a.M.: Peter Lang, 1989.

Brougham, Henry Peter. *The Life and Times of Henry Lord Brougham, Written by Himself*. 3 vols. Edinburgh: William Blackwood, 1871.

Brouillette, Sarah. *Postcolonial Writers in the Global Marketplace*. New York: Palgrave Macmillan, 2007.

Broun, Dauvit, R. J. Finlay, and Michael Lynch, eds. *Image and Identity: The Making and Remaking of Scotland through the Ages*. Edinburgh: John Donald, 1998.

Brown, Ian, ed. *From Tartan to Tartanry: Scottish Culture, History and Myth*. Edinburgh: Edinburgh University Press, 2010.

———. "Introduction: Tartan, Tartanry and Hybridity." In *From Tartan to Tartanry*, 1–12.

Brown, Terence, ed. *Celticism*. Amsterdam: Rodopi, 1996.

———. "Preface." In *Celticism*, vii–viii.

Buelens, Gert, and Stef Craps, eds. "Postcolonial Trauma Novels." Special issue, *Studies in the Novel*, 40, nos. 1–2 (2008).

Bültmann, Tanja, Andrew Hinson, and Graeme Morton. *Ties of Bluid, Kin and Countrie: Scottish Associational Culture in the Diaspora*. Guelph, Ontario: Centre for Scottish Studies, 2009.

———. *The Scottish Diaspora*. Edinburgh: Edinburgh University Press, 2013.

Buzard, James. "Translation and Tourism: Scott's *Waverley* and the Rendering of Culture." *The Yale Journal of Criticism: Interpretation in the Humanities* 8, no. 2 (1995): 31–59.

Cairns, David, and Shaun Richards. *Writing Ireland: Colonialism, Nationalism and Culture*. Manchester: Manchester University Press, 1988.

Cameron, Ewen A. "Embracing the Past: The Highlands in Nineteenth Century Scotland." In Broun, Finlay, and Lynch, *Image and Identity*, 195–219.

Campbell, J[ohn] F[rancis], ed. *Popular Tales of the West Highlands*. 1860–62. Repr., 2 vols. Edinburgh: Birlinn, 1994.

Campbell, John Lorne (alias "Fear Chanaidh," "The Man from Canna"). "Eideard Lhuyd agus Archaeologia Britannica." *Gairm* 21 (1957): 37–41.

Carmichael, Alexander. *Carmina Gadelica*. Vols. 1 and 2 publ. Edinburgh: T. & A. Constable, 1900. 2nd ed. in 6 vols., ed. Elizabeth C. C. Watson, James Carmichael Watson, and Angus Matheson. Edinburgh: Oliver and Boyd, 1928–71.

Carrell, Christopher, and Malcolm Maclean, eds. *As an fhearann / From the Land: Clearance, Conflict and Crofting: A Century of Images of the Scottish Highlands*. Edinburgh: Mainstream, 1986.

Chandler, James. *England in 1819: The Politics of Literary Culture and the Case of Romantic Historicism*. Chicago: University of Chicago Press, 1998.

Chapman, Malcolm. *The Celts: The Construction of a Myth*. New York: St. Martin's, 1992.

———. *The Gaelic Vision in Scottish Culture*. Montreal: McGill–Queen's University Press, 1978.

Charles I. Letter to the archbishops and bishops, August 25, 1626. Publ. in *Miscellany of the Maitland Club, Consisting of Original Papers and Other Documents Illustrative of the History and Literature of Scotland*, ed. James Dennistoun and Alexander Macdonald, vol. 2, ed. A. Macdonald and Joseph Robertson, 25. Edinburgh, 1840.

Cheape, Hugh. "Gheibhte breacain charnaid ('Scarlet Tartans Would Be Got . . .'): The Re-invention of Tradition." In I. Brown, *From Tartan to Tartanry*, 13–31.

Chrisman, Laura, and Patrick Williams, eds. *Colonial Discourse and Post-Colonial Theory: A Reader*. New York: Columbia University Press, 1994.

Clyde, Robert [D.]. *From Rebel to Hero: The Image of the Highlander, 1745–1830*. East Linton, Scot.: Tuckwell, 1995.

Colley, Linda. *Acts of Union and Disunion: What Has Held the UK Together—and What Is Dividing It?* London: Profile, 2014.

———. *Britons: Forging the Nation, 1707–1837*. 1992. Repr. London: Pimlico, 1994.

Collis, John. *The Celts: Origins, Myths & Inventions*. Stroud, Eng.: Tempus, 2003.

Connell, Liam. "Kailyard Money: Nation, Empire and Speculation in Walter Scott's *Letters from Malachi Malagrowther*." In Sassi and van Heijnsbergen, *Within and without Empire*, 94–107.

Connolly, Claire, ed. "Postcolonial Ireland?" Special issue, *European Journal of English Studies* 3, no. 3 (1999).

Conrad, Joseph. *Heart of Darkness*. 1899. Repr. in Hollander and Kermode, *Oxford Anthology of English Literature*, 1:1618–79.

Cooksey, Thomas L[ynch]. "William Sharp (Fiona Macleod)." In *British Short Fiction Writers, 1880–1914: The Romantic Tradition*, ed. William F. Naufftus, 312–20. Detroit: Gale, 1996.

Court, Franklin E. *Institutionalizing English Literature: The Culture and Politics of Literary Study, 1760–1900*. Stanford, Calif.: Stanford University Press, 1992.

Cowan, Edward J. "The Discovery of the Gàidhealtachd in Sixteenth Century Scotland." *TGSI* 60 (1997–98): 259–84.

———. "James VI, King of Scots, and the Destruction of the Gàidhealtachd." In *Écosse des Highlands: Mythes et réalité. Actes du Colloque international, Brest, 22–23 Mars 2002*, ed. Bernard Sellin, 149–66. Brest: Centre de Recherche Bretonne et Celtique, Université de Bretagne Occidentale, 2003.

Cowan, I. B. "Covenanters." In *The New Companion to Scottish Culture*, ed. David Daiches, 66–67. Edinburgh: Polygon, 1993.

Craig, Cairns. *Out of History: Narrative Paradigms in Scottish and English Culture*. Edinburgh: Polygon, 1996.

Crawford, Robert. *Devolving English Literature*. 1992. 2nd ed. (with new afterword). Edinburgh: Edinburgh University Press, 2000.

———. "Introduction." In *The Scottish Invention of English Literature*, 1–21.

———, ed. *The Scottish Invention of English Literature*. Cambridge: Cambridge University Press, 1998.

Crawford, Thomas. "Political and Protest Songs in Eighteenth-Century Scotland." *Scottish Studies* 14 (1970): 1–33, 105–31.

Csáky, Moritz, Johannes Feichtinger, and Ursula Prutsch, eds. *Habsburg Postcolonial: Machtstrukturen und kollektives Gedächtnis*. Innsbruck: Studienverlag, 2003.

Cunninghame Graham, R[obert] B[ontine]. "'Bloody Niggers.'" 1897. Repr. in Cunninghame Graham, *Selected Writings*, ed. Cedric Watts, 58–67. Rutherford, N.J.: Fairleigh Dickinson University Press, 1981.

Curtis, L. P., Jr. *Anglo-Saxons and Celts: A Study of Anti-Irish Prejudice in Victorian England*. Bridgeport, Conn.: Conference on British Studies, University of Bridgeport, 1968.

Daer, Lord: *see* Hamilton, Basil William.

Davies, Wendy. "The Myth of the Celtic Church." In *The Early Church in Wales and the West: Recent Work in Early Christian Archaeology, History and Place Names*, ed. Nancy Edwards and Alan Lane, 12–21. Oxford: Oxbow, 1992.

Davis, Leith. *Acts of Union: Scotland and the Literary Negotiation of the British Nation, 1707–1832*. Stanford, Calif.: Stanford University Press, 1998.

———. "'Origins of the Specious': James Macpherson's Ossian and the Forging of the British Empire." *The Eighteenth Century: Theory and Interpretation* 34, no. 2 (1993): 132–50.

Dawson, Jane. "The Gaidhealtachd and the Emergence of the Scottish Highlands." In *British Consciousness and Identity: The Making of Britain, 1533–1707*, ed. Brendan Bradshaw and Peter Roberts, 259–300. Cambridge: Cambridge University Press, 1998.

Deane, Seamus. *Celtic Revivals: Essays in Modern Irish Literature, 1880–1980*. London: Faber and Faber, 1985.

DeLoughrey, Elizabeth, and George B. Handley, eds. *Postcolonial Ecologies: Literatures of the Environment*. Oxford: Oxford University Press, 2011.

Detmers, Ines, Nancy Grimm, Katrin Thomson, and Laurenz Volkmann, eds. *Local Natures, Global Responsibilities: Ecocritical Perspectives on the New English Literatures*. New York: Rodopi, 2010.

Devine, T. M. *Clanship to Crofters' War: The Social Transformation of the Scottish Highlands*. Manchester: Manchester University Press, 1994.

———. *The Great Highland Famine: Hunger, Emigration and the Scottish Highlands in the Nineteenth Century*. Edinburgh: John Donald, 1988.

———. *Scotland's Empire, 1600–1815*. London: Allen Lane, 2003.

———. *The Scottish Nation: 1700–2000*. 1999. Repr. Harmondsworth, Eng.: Penguin, 2000.

———. "Soldiers of Empire, 1750–1914." In *Scotland and the British Empire*, ed. T. M. Devine and John M. MacKenzie, 176–95. Oxford: Oxford University Press, 2011.

———, ed. *To the Ends of the Earth: Scotland's Global Diaspora, 1750–2010*. London: Allen Lane, 2011.

Dictionary of National Biography, vol. 11, ed. Sidney Lee. London: Smith, Elder, 1909.

Dodgshon, R. A. "'Pretense of Blude' and 'Place of Thair Duelling': The Nature of Scottish Clans, 1500–1745." In *Scottish Society, 1500–1800*, ed. R. A. Houston and I. D. Whyte, 169–98. New York: Cambridge University Press, 1989.

Donaldson, Gordon, ed. *Scottish Historical Documents*. 1970. Rev. and repr. Edinburgh: Scottish Academic Press, 1974.

Donaldson, William. "Bonny Highland Laddie: The Making of a Myth." *Scottish Literary Journal* 3, no. 2 (1976): 30–50.

Draper, R[onald] P., ed. *The Literature of Region and Nation*. Basingstoke, Eng.: Macmillan, 1989.

Duncan, Ian. "Introduction." In Walter Scott, *Rob Roy*, ed. Duncan, vii–xxviii. Oxford: Oxford University Press, 1998.

———. "The Pathos of Abstraction: Adam Smith, Ossian and Samuel Johnson." In *Scotland and the Borders of Romanticism*, ed. Leith Davis, Ian Duncan, and Janet Sorensen, 38–56. Cambridge: Cambridge University Press, 2004.

———. "The Study of Scottish Literature." *ScotLit* 28 (2003): 1–4.

Duncan, William. "A Discourse Concerning the Roman Art of War." In *The Commentaries of Caesar*, trans. Duncan (1753), 2 vols., 1: i–cclxviii. London: J. R. Tonson, 1755.

Durkacz, Victor Edward. *The Decline of the Celtic Languages: A Study of Linguistic and Cultural Conflict in Scotland, Wales and Ireland from the Reformation to the Twentieth Century*. Edinburgh: John Donald, 1983.

Dziennik, Matthew. "Whig Tartan: Material Culture and Its Use in the Scottish Highlands, 1746–1815." *Past and Present* 217 (2012): 117–47.

Enright, Michael J. "King James and His Island: An Archaic Kingship Belief?" *SHR* 55 (1976): 29–40.

Fairney, Janice. "The Branch Societies of the Highland Society of London." In Nilsen, *Rannsachadh na Gàidhlig 5*, 67–77.

Fanon, Frantz. *Black Skin, White Masks*. Trans. Charles Lam Markmann. New York: Grove, 1967. [*Peau noire, masques blancs*. 1952.]

———. *The Wretched of the Earth*. Trans. Constance Farrington. New York: Grove, 1963. [*Les Damnés de la terre*. 1961.]

Fenyö, Krisztina. *Contempt, Sympathy and Romance: Lowland Perceptions of the Highlands and the Clearances during the Famine Years, 1845–1855*. Edinburgh: Tuckwell, 2000.

Ferguson, William. *The Identity of the Scottish Nation: An Historic Quest*. Edinburgh: Edinburgh University Press, 1998.

———. *Scotland's Relations with England: A Survey to 1707*. Edinburgh: John Donald, 1977.

Ferns, Chris. "Look Who's Talking: Walter Scott, Thomas Raddall, and the Voices of the Colonized." *Ariel* 26, no. 4 (1995): 49–67.

———. "Regions of the Empire: Scott, Raddall, Farrell and the Voices of the Colonized." *Swansea Review* (1994): 208–20.

Ferris, Ina. *The Achievement of Literary Authority: Gender, History, and the Waverley Novels*. Ithaca, N.Y.: Cornell University Press, 1991.

———. "Translation from the Borders: Encounter and Recalcitrance in *Waverley* and *Clan-Albin*." *Eighteenth-Century Fiction* 9, no. 2 (1997): 203–22.

Fielding, Penny. *Scotland and the Fictions of Geography*. Cambridge: Cambridge University Press, 2008.

Findlay, David. "Divine Right and Early Modern Gaelic Society." In McGuire and Ó Baoill, *Rannsachadh na Gàidhlig 2000*, 243–55.

Finlay, Richard J. "Caledonia or North Britain? Scottish Identity in the Eighteenth Century." In Broun, Finlay, and Lynch, *Image and Identity*, 143–56.

Flannery, Eóin. *Ireland and Postcolonial Studies: Theory, Discourse, Utopia*. Basingstoke, Eng.: Palgrave Macmillan, 2009.

Forbes, Duncan. "Some Thoughts Concerning the State of the Highlands of Scotland." 1746? In *Culloden Papers*, ed. H. R. Duff, 297–301. London: T. Cadell and W. Davies, 1815.

Forbes, Sir William. *An Account of the Life and Writings of James Beattie*. 2 vols. Edinburgh: Archibald Constable, 1806.

Fry, Michael. *The Scottish Empire*. Edinburgh: Birlinn, 2001.

Gardiner, Michael. *Modern Scottish Culture*. Edinburgh: Edinburgh University Press, 2005.

Gardiner, Michael, Graeme Macdonald, and Niall O'Gallagher, eds. *Scottish Literature and Postcolonial Literature*. Edinburgh: Edinburgh University Press, 2011.

Garside, Peter. "The Origins and History of James Hogg's 'Donald MacDonald.'" *Scottish Studies* 7, no. 2 (2006): 24–39.

Gaskill, Howard, ed. *Ossian Revisited*. Edinburgh: Edinburgh University Press, 1991.

Gates, Henry Louis, Jr., ed. "Race, Writing, and Difference." Special issue, *Critical Inquiry* 12, no. 1 (1985).

Geoffrey of Monmouth. *The History of the Kings of Britain*. Trans. Lewis Thorpe. London: Penguin, 1966. [*Historia Regum Britanniae*. 1136.]

Gibbon, Edward. *The History of the Decline and Fall of the Roman Empire*. 6 vols. London: W. Strahan and T. Cadell, 1776–88.

Gibbons, Luke. "Race against Time: Racial Discourse and Irish History." 1991. Rev. and repr. in Gibbons, *Transformations in Irish Culture*, 149–60, 202–6.

———. "'Some Hysterical Hatred': History, Hysteria and the Literary Revival." *Irish University Review* 27, no. 1 (1997): 7–23.

———. "This Sympathetic Bond: Ossian, Celticism and Colonialism." In T. Brown, *Celticism*, 273–91.

———. *Transformations in Irish Culture*. Cork, Ireland: Cork University Press, 1996.

Gifford, Douglas. "Preparing for Renaissance: Revaluing Nineteenth-Century Scottish Literature." In *Scotland and the 19th-Century World*, ed. Gerard Carruthers, David Goldie, and Alastair Renfrew, 21–35. New York: Rodopi, 2012.

Gifford, Douglas, and Alan Riach, eds. *Scotlands: Poets and the Nation*. Manchester: Carcanet, 2004.

Glaser, Konstanze. "Essentialism and Relativism in Gaelic and Sorbian Language Revival Discourses." Paper presented on January 30, 2002, apparently at the Department of Celtic and Scottish Studies, University of Edinburgh, www.arts.ed.ac.uk/celtic/poileasaidh/seminarwebversion2.html.

Gordon, Sir Robert. Letter to his nephew John, 13th Earl of Sutherland. Ca. 1620. Publ. in *The Sutherland Book*, ed. Sir William Fraser, 3 vols., vol. 2, *Correspondence*, 337–68. Edinburgh, 1892.

Gottlieb, Evan. *Feeling British: Sympathy and National Identity in Scottish and English Writing, 1707–1832*. Lewisburg, Pa.: Bucknell University Press, 2007.

Graham, Colin, and Glen Hooper, eds. *Irish and Postcolonial Writing: History, Theory, Practice*. Basingstoke, Eng.: Palgrave Macmillan, 2002.

Graham, Colin, and Willy Maley, eds. "Irish Studies and Postcolonial Theory." Special issue, *Irish Studies Review* 7, no. 2 (1999).

Grant, Isabel Frances. *The Macleods: The History of a Clan 1200–1956*. London: Faber and Faber, 1959.

Grant, James Shaw. "Highland History—A British Asset." *TGSI* 52 (1980–82): 460–79.

Grimble, Ian. "The Rev. Alexander Pope's Letter to James Hogg, 1774." *SGS* 11, no. 1 (1966): 100–113.

———. *The World of Rob Donn*. Edinburgh: Edina, 1979.

Guha, Ranajit, and Gayatri Chakravorty Spivak, eds. *Selected Subaltern Studies*. New York: Oxford University Press, 1988.

Hall, James. *Travels in Scotland, by an Unusual Route: With a Trip to the Orkneys and Hebrides*. 2 vols. London: J. Johnson, 1807.

Hall, Stuart. "When Was 'the Post-Colonial'?: Thinking at the Limit." In *The Post-Colonial Question: Common Skies, Divided Horizons*, ed. Iain Chambers and Lidia Curti, 242–60. New York: Routledge, 1996.

Halloran, William F. "W. B. Yeats, William Sharp, and Fiona Macleod: A Celtic Drama, 1897." In "Yeats and the Nineties," ed. Warwick Gould. Special issue, *Yeats Annual* 14 (2001): 159–208.

———, ed. *The William Sharp "Fiona Macleod" Archive*. Institute of English Studies, University of London, www.ies.sas.ac.uk/research/current-projects/william-sharp-fiona-macleod-archive/william-sharp-fiona-macleod-archive.

Hamilton, Basil William (Lord Daer). Letter to Charles Grey, January 17, 1793. Publ. in Edward Hughes, "The Scottish Reform Movement and Charles Grey 1792–94: Some Fresh Correspondence," *SHR* 35 (1956): 26–41, here 33–37.

Harper, Marjory, and Michael E. Vance, eds. *Myth, Migration and the Making of Memory: Scotia and Nova Scotia c. 1700–1990*. Edinburgh: John Donald, 1999.

Harvie, Christopher. "Anglo-Saxons into Celts: The Scottish Intellectuals 1760–1930." In T. Brown, *Celticism*, 231–56.

———. "Scott and the Image of Scotland." 1983. Repr. in *Patriotism: The Making and Unmaking of British National Identity*, ed. Raphael Samuel, vol. 2: *Minorities and Outsiders*, 173–92. New York: Routledge 1989.

Hechter, Michael. *Internal Colonialism: The Celtic Fringe in British National Development 1536–1966*. London: Routledge and Kegan Paul, 1975.

Helff, Sissy, and Frank Schulze-Engler, eds. *Transcultural English Studies: Theories, Fictions, Realities*. New York: Rodopi, 2009.

Herd, David, ed. *Ancient and Modern Scottish Songs, Heroic Ballads, etc.* 2 vols. Edinburgh: printed by John Wotherspoon for James Dickson and Charles Elliot, 1776.

Hewitt, David. "Scoticisms and Cultural Conflict." In Draper, *The Literature of Region and Nation*, 125–35.

Holland, Richard. *The Buke of the Howlat*. In *Longer Scottish Poems*, vol. 1, *1375–1650*, ed. Priscilla Bawcutt and Felicity Riddy, 46–84. Edinburgh: Scottish Academic Press, 1987.

Hollander, John, and Frank Kermode, gen. eds. *The Oxford Anthology of English Literature*. 2 vols. Oxford: Oxford University Press, 1973.

Hollingworth, Brian. "Completing the Union: Edgeworth's *The Absentee* and Scott the Novelist." In Alexander and Hewitt, *Scott in Carnival*, 502–11.

Hook, Andrew. "Introduction" (1972) to Walter Scott, *Waverley*, 9–27. Repr. Harmondsworth, Eng.: Penguin, 1985.

Horsbroch, Dauvit. "When Was Gaelic Scottish? The Origins, Emergence and Development of Scottish Gaelic Identity, 1400–1750." In McGuire and Ó Baoill, *Rannsachadh na Gàidhlig 2000*, 231–42.

Huggan, Graham. *The Postcolonial Exotic: Marketing the Margins*. New York: Routledge, 2001.

Huggan, Graham, and Helen Tiffin. *Postcolonial Ecocriticism: Literature, Animals, Environment*. New York: Routledge, 2010.

Hughes, Edward. "The Scottish Reform Movement and Charles Grey 1792–94: Some Fresh Correspondence." *SHR* 35 (1956): 26–41.

Hunter, James. *A Dance Called America: The Scottish Highlands, the United States and Canada*. Edinburgh: Mainstream, 1994.

———. *Glencoe and the Indians*. Edinburgh: Mainstream, 1996.

———. *Last of the Free: A Millennial History of the Highlands and Islands of Scotland*. 1999. Edinburgh: Mainstream, 2000.

———. *The Making of the Crofting Community*. 1976. Rev. ed. Edinburgh: John Donald, 2000.

Innes, C. L. *The Devil's Own Mirror: The Irish and the African in Modern Literature*.Washington, D.C.: Three Continents, 1990.

———. "Orientalism and Celticism." In Graham and Hooper, *Irish and Postcolonial Writing*, 142–56.

———. "Postcolonial Studies and Ireland." In *Comparing Postcolonial Literatures: Dislocations*, ed. Ashok Bery and Patricia Murray, 21–30 and 253–54. New York: St. Martin's, 2000.

Jahoda, Gustav. *Images of Savages: Ancient Roots of Modern Prejudice in Western Culture*. New York: Routledge, 1999.

James VI. *Basilicon Doron*. 1599. Repr., ed. James Craigie, 2 vols. Edinburgh: William Blackwood, 1944 and 1950.

James, Simon. *The Atlantic Celts: Ancient People or Modern Invention?* London: British Museum, 1999.

Johnson, Samuel. *A Journey to the Western Islands of Scotland* (1775). Repr. together with James Boswell's *The Journal of a Tour to the Hebrides with Samuel Johnson*, ed. Peter Levi, 33–152. Harmondsworth, Eng.: Penguin, 1984.

Johnstone, James Chevalier de. *Memoirs of the Rebellion in 1745 and 1746*. Trans. from French ms. London: Longman, Hurst, Rees, Orme and Brown, 1820.

Jordan, Elaine. "The Management of Scott's Novels." *Europe and Its Others: Proceedings of the Essex Conference on the Sociology of Literature, July 1984*, ed. Francis Barker et al., 2:146–61. Colchester, Eng.: University of Essex Press, 1985.

Kaul, Suvir. *Eighteenth-Century British Literature and Postcolonial Studies*. Edinburgh: Edinburgh University Press, 2009.

Kay, Billy. *Scottish World: A Journey into the Scottish Diaspora*. Edinburgh: Mainstream, 2006.

Kelertas, Violeta, ed. *Baltic Postcolonialism*. Amsterdam: Rodopi, 2006.

Kennedy, Allan. "The Covenanters of the Northern Highlands." *History Scotland* 10, no. 1 (2010): 22–29, and 10, no. 2 (2010): 15–22.

———. *Governing Gaeldom: The Scottish Highlands and the Restoration State, 1660–1688*. Boston: Brill, 2014.

———. "'A Heavy Yock Uppon Their Necks': Covenanting Government in the Northern Highlands, 1638–1651." *Journal of Scottish Historical Studies* 30, no. 2 (2010): 93–112.

———. "The Highlands and the Restoration Regime." *History Scotland* 15, no. 1 (2015): 34–39, and 15, no. 2 (2015): 44–49.

———. "Reducing That Barbarous Country: Center, Periphery, and Highland Policy in Restoration Britain." *Journal of British Studies* 52, no. 3 (2013): 597–614.

Kennedy, Michael. "'Lochaber No More': A Critical Examination of Highland Emigration Mythology." In Harper and Vance, *Myth, Migration and the Making of Memory*, 267–97.

Keown, Michelle, David Murphy, and James Procter, eds. *Comparing Postcolonial Diasporas*. New York: Palgrave Macmillan, 2009.

Kerr, James. *Fiction against History: Scott as Story-Teller*. Cambridge: Cambridge University Press, 1989.

Kiberd, Declan. *Inventing Ireland*. London: Jonathan Cape, 1995.

Kidd, Colin "Race, Empire, and the Limits of Nineteenth-Century Scottish Nationhood." *The Historical Journal* 46, no. 4 (2003): 873–92.

———. "Race, Theology and Revival: Scots Philology and Its Contexts in the Age of Pinkerton and Jamieson." *Scottish Studies Review* 3, no. 2 (2002): 20–33.

———. "Teutonist Ethnology and Scottish Nationalist Inhibition." *SHR* 74 (1995): 45–68.

Knight, Stephen. *A Hundred Years of Fiction: Writing Wales in English*. Cardiff: University of Wales Press, 2004.

Knox, Robert. *The Races of Men: A Fragment*. 1850. 2nd ed. with new subtitle, different pagination, added illustrations, and a "Supplement" of extra chapters, publ. as *The Races of Men: A Philosophical Enquiry into the Influence of Race over the Destinies of Nations*. London: Henry Renshaw, 1862.

Lahey-Dolega, Christine. "Some Brief Observations on the Life and Work of William Sharp (Fiona Macleod)." *Ball State University Forum* 21, no. 4 (1980): 18–26.

Lamont, Claire. "Jacobite Songs as Intertexts in *Waverley* and *The Highland Widow*." In Alexander and Hewitt, *Scott in Carnival*, 110–21.

———. "A Note on Gaelic Proverbs in *Waverley*." *Notes and Queries* 220 / 22, no. 2 (1975): 64–66.

———. "One Good Reason for Reading Scott: The Highland Works." *Scott Newsletter* 23/24 (1993/1994): 2–8.

———. "Scott and Eighteenth-Century Imperialism: India and the Scottish Highlands." In *Configuring Romanticism: Essays Offered to C. C. Barfoot*, ed. Theo D'Haen, Colin Ewen, Peter Liebregts, and Wim Tigges, 35–50. Amsterdam: Rodopi, 2003.

———. "*Waverley* and the Battle of Culloden." *Essays and Studies* 44 (1991): 14–26.

Laplace, Philippe. "L'Institution du corpus imaginaire gaélique dans la littérature écossaise: Macpherson et Scott, entre idéologie et synecdoque culturelle." *Études Écossaises* 6 (1999–2000): 129–45.

Lawson, Alan, and Chris Tiffin, eds. *De-Scribing Empire: Post-Colonialism and Textuality*. New York: Routledge, 1994.

———. "The Textuality of Empire." In Lawson and Tiffin, *De-Scribing Empire*, 1–11.

Lee, Maurice, Jr. *Government by Pen: Scotland under James VI and I*. Urbana: University of Illinois Press, 1980.

Leerssen, Joep. "Celticism." In T. Brown, *Celticism*, 1–20.

Lehner, Stefanie. *Subaltern Ethics in Contemporary Scottish and Irish Literature: Tracing Counter-Histories*. Basingstoke, Eng.: Palgrave Macmillan, 2011.

Leneman, Leah. "Ossian and the Enlightenment." *Scotia: American-Canadian Journal of Scottish Studies* 11 (1987): 13–29.

Lhuyd, Edward. *Archaeologia Britannica: Giving Some Account Additional to What Has Been Hitherto Publish'd, of the Languages, Histories and Customs of the Original Inhabitants of Great Britain: From Collections and Observations in Travels through Wales, Cornwal* [sic], *Bas-Bretagne, Ireland and Scotland*. Vol. I: *Glossography* (1707). The 1st vol. was to be the only one ever to materialize. Facsimile repr. in *Celtic Linguistics, 1700–1850*, vol. 2. London: Routledge, 2000.

Lindsay, Maurice. "Introduction." In *Modern Scottish Poetry: An Anthology of the Scottish Renaissance*, ed. Lindsay, 15–20. London: Faber and Faber, 1946.

Lloyd, David. *Anomalous States: Irish Writing and the Post-Colonial Moment*. Dublin: Lilliput, 1993.

Louis, Roger, ed. *The Oxford History of the British Empire*. 5 vols. New York: Oxford University Press, 1998–99.

Lumsden, Alison. "'Beyond the Dusky Barrier: Perceptions of the Highlands in the Waverley Novels." 2007. Republ. in *Mìorun Mòr nan Gall, 'The Great Ill-Will of the Lowlander'? Lowland Perceptions of the Highlands, Medieval and Modern*, ed. Dauvit Broun and Martin MacGregor, 158–86. Glasgow: Centre for Scottish and Celtic Studies, University of Glasgow, 2009.

Lynch, Michael. "A Nation Born Again? Scottish Identity in the Sixteenth and Seventeenth Centuries." In Broun, Finlay, and Lynch, *Image and Identity*, 82–104.

———. *Scotland: A New History*. 1991. Rev. and repr. London: Pimlico, 1992.

Mac an t-Saoir, Donnchadh Bàn. *The Songs of Duncan Ban Macintyre*. Ed. and trans. Angus MacLeod. Edinburgh: Oliver and Boyd, 1952.

Macbean, L. "The Mission of the Celt." *TGSI* 21 (1896–97): 56–69.

MacCodrum, Iain (Iain mac Fhearchair / John MacCodrum). *The Songs of John MacCodrum*. Ed. and trans. William Matheson. Edinburgh: Oliver and Boyd, 1938.

MacDonald, James. *General View of the Agriculture of the Hebrides, or Western Isles of Scotland*. Edinburgh, 1811.

Macgregor, Rev. J. "Celts and Teutons: A Study in Anthropology." *TGSI* 16 (1889–90): 27–39.

Macinnes, Allan I. "Crown, Clans and Fine: The 'Civilizing' of Scottish Gaeldom, 1587–1638." *Northern Scotland* 13 (1993): 31–55.

———. "Seventeenth-Century Scotland: The Undervalued Gaelic Perspective." In *Celtic Languages and Celtic Peoples: Proceedings of the Second North American Congress of Celtic Studies*, ed. Cecil J. Byrne, Margaret Harry, and Pádraig Ó Siadhail, 535–54. Halifax, Nova Scotia: D'Arcy McGee Chair of Irish Studies, St. Mary's University, 1992.

Mack, Douglas S. *Scottish Fiction and the British Empire*. Edinburgh: Edinburgh University Press, 2006.

Mackay, Angus. *The Book of Mackay*. Edinburgh: Norman MacLeod, 1906.

Mackay, Peter. "Negotiations of Barbarity, Authenticity and Purity in Eighteenth and Nineteenth Century Gaelic Literature." In Sassi and van Heijnsbergen, *Within and without Empire*, 30–45.

Mackay, William. "Instructions by Cumberland after Culloden; Instructions by General Wolfe before Quebec." *TGSI* 32 (1924–25): 301–10.

MacKenzie, W. C. *History of the Outer Hebrides*. Paisley, Scot.: Alexander Gardner, 1903.

MacLeod, Donald J., ed. *"A Description of the Western Islands of Scotland" by Martin Martin, Including "A Voyage to St. Kilda" by the Same Author and "A Description of the Western Isles of Scotland" by Sir Donald Monro*. 1934. Repr. Edinburgh: Birlinn, 1994.

———. "Editorial Note." Ibid., 9–18.

———. "Introduction." Ibid., 19–58.

MacPhail, I. M. M. "Prelude to the Crofters' War." *TGSI* 49 (1974–76): 158–88.

Macpherson, James. *The Poems of Ossian and Related Works*. Ed. Howard Gaskill. Edinburgh: Edinburgh University Press, 1996.

———. *The Poems of Ossian, in the Original Gaelic, with a Literal Translation into Latin, by Robert MacFarlan*. London: W. Bulmer, 1807.

Maidment, James, ed. *Scotish Elegiac Verses: M.DC.XXIX–M.DCC.XXIX*. Edinburgh: Thomas G. Stevenson, 1842.

Maillard, Michel. "Le Traitement littéraire du Jacobitisme dans *Waverley*." In *Regards sur l'Écosse au XVIIIe siècle*, ed. Michele S. Plaisant, 207–30. Lille: Université de Lille, 1977.

Makdisi, Saree. "Colonial Space and the Colonization of Time in Scott's *Waverley*." *Studies in Romanticism* 34, no. 2 (1995): 155–87.

Malzahn, Manfred. "Exorcising the Past: Scottish Gentlemen and Gentleman Savages." *Scott Newsletter* 29/30 (1996): 1–13.

Manning, Susan. "Ossian, Scott and Nineteenth-Century Scottish Literary Nationalism." *Studies in Scottish Literature* 17 (1982): 39–54.

Martin, Angus. *Kintyre: The Hidden Past*. Edinburgh: John Donald, 1999.

Martin, Martin. *Curiosities of Art and Nature: The New Annotated and Illustrated Edition of Martin Martin's Classic "A Description of the Western Isles of Scotland."* Ed. Michael Robson. Port of Ness, Scot.: Islands Book Trust, 2003.

———. *A Description of the Western Islands of Scotland*. 1703. Repr. in *A Description of the Western Islands of Scotland" by Martin Martin, Including "A Voyage to St. Kilda" by the Same Author and "A Description of the Western Isles of Scotland" by Sir Donald Monro*, ed. Donald J. MacLeod, 2–3, 5, 59–391. Also in *"A Description of the Western Islands of Scotland" ca 1695 and "A Late Voyage to St Kilda" [by] Martin Martin with "A Description of the Occidental i.e. Western Islands of Scotland" [by] Donald Monro*, with new introductions by Charles W. J. Withers and R. W. Munro, 13–231. Edinburgh: Birlinn, 1999.

———. *A Late Voyage to Saint Kilda*. 1698. Repr. in *"A Description of the Western Islands of Scotland" by Martin Martin, Including "A Voyage to St. Kilda" by the Same Author and "A Description of The Western Isles of Scotland" by Sir Donald Monro*, ed. Donald J. MacLeod, 393–476. Also in *"A Description of the Western Islands of Scotland" ca 1695 and "A Late Voyage to St Kilda" [by] Martin Martin with "A Description of the Occidental i.e. Western Islands of Scotland" [by] Donald Monro*, with new introductions by Charles W. J. Withers and R. W. Munro, 233–88. Edinburgh: Birlinn, 1999.

———. "A Relation of a Deaf and Dumb Person, Who Recovered His Speech and Hearing after a Violent Fever: with Some Other Medicinal and Chirurgical Observations." *Philosophical Transactions* [of the Royal Society], vol. 25 (1706–1707), 2469–70.

———. "Several Observations in the North Islands of Scotland." *Philosophical Transactions* [of the Royal Society], vol. 19 (1695–97), no. 233 (October 1697): 727–29.

Martin, Maureen M. *The Mighty Scot: Nation, Gender, and the Nineteenth-Century Mystique of Scottish Masculinity*. Albany: State University of New York Press, 2009.

McCarthy, Angela, ed. *A Global Clan: Scottish Migrant Networks and Identities since the Eighteenth Century*. London: I. B. Tauris, 2006.

McClure, J. Derrick. "Lowland Scots: An Ambivalent National Tongue." 1984. Rev. and repr. in McClure, *Scots and Its Literature*, 5–19.

———. *Scots and Its Literature*. Amsterdam: John Benjamins, 1995.

McCracken-Flesher, Caroline. *Possible Scotlands: Walter Scott and the Story of Tomorrow*. Oxford: Oxford University Press, 2005.

McGuinness. Arthur E. "Lord Kames on the Ossian Poems: Anthropology and Criticism." *Texas Studies in Literature and Language* 10 (1968): 65–75.

McGuire, Nancy R., and Colm Ó Baoill, ed. *Rannsachadh na Gàidhlig 2000: Papers Read at the Conference "Scottish Gaelic Studies 2000" Held at the University of Aberdeen 2–4 August* 2000. Aberdeen, Scot.: An Clò Gaidhealach, 2002.

McLeod, John. *Beginning Postcolonialism*. 2000. 2nd ed. New York: Manchester University Press, 2010.

———. "Sounding Silence: Transculturation and Its Thresholds." *Transnational Literature* 4, no. 1 (2011), http://fhrc.flinders.edu.au/transnational/vol4_issue1.html.

Meek, Donald E. "The Gaelic Ballads of Scotland: Creativity and Adaptation." In Gaskill, *Ossian Revisited*, 19–48.

———. "The Sublime Gael: The Impact of Macpherson's *Ossian* on Literary Creativity and Cultural Perception in Gaelic Scotland." In *The Reception of Ossian in Europe*, ed. Howard Gaskill, 40–66. New York: Thoemmes, 2004.

Meek, Ronald L. *Social Science and the Ignoble Savage*. Cambridge: Cambridge University Press, 1976.

Meyers, Terry L. *The Sexual Tensions of William Sharp: A Study of the Birth of Fiona Macleod, Incorporating Two Lost Works, "Ariadne in Naxos" and "Beatrice."* New York: Peter Lang, 1996.

Mignolo, Walter. *The Darker Side of the Renaissance: Literacy, Territoriality, and Colonization*. 1995. 2nd ed. Ann Arbor: University of Michigan Press, 2003.

Milton, Colin. "Cultural and Political Nationalism in the Irish Literary Revival and the Scottish Renaissance." In *English Studies 4: Proceedings of the Third Conference on the Literature of Region and Nation, Echternach, 10–14 September 1990*, ed. J. J. Simon and Alain Sinner, 103–20. Luxembourg: Publications du Centre Universitaire de Luxembourg, Département des Lettres et de Sciences Humaines, Section de Lettres Anglaises, 1992.

Montagu, Edward Wortley, Jr. *Reflections on the Rise and Fall of the Antient Republicks: Adapted to the Present State of Great Britain*. London: A. Millar, 1759.

Moore, John N. "John Adair's Contribution to the Charting of the Scottish Coasts: A Re-Assessment." *Imago Mundi* 52 (2000): 43–65.

Morton, Graeme. "Ethnic Identity in the Civic World of Scottish Associational Culture." In Bültmann, Hinson, and Morton, *Ties of Bluid, Kin and Countrie*, 33–50.

———. "What If? The Significance of Scotland's Missing Nationalism in the Nineteenth Century." In Broun, Finlay, and Lynch, *Image and Identity*, 157–76.

Mosse, George L. *Toward the Final Solution: A History of European Racism*. New York: Howard Fertig, 1978.

Muir, Edwin. *Scott and Scotland: The Predicament of the Scottish Writer*. 1936. Repr. Edinburgh: Polygon, 1982.

Murray, John. "Whistlers in the Dark: The Hielan Picture Postcard." In Carrell and Maclean, *From the Land*, 87–91.

Murray, Stuart, and Alan Riach, eds. "Celtic Nationalism and Postcoloniality," special issue, *SPAN: Journal of the South Pacific Association for Commonwealth Literature and Language Studies* 41 (1995).

Murray, W. H. *Rob Roy MacGregor: His Life and Times*. 1982. Repr. Edinburgh: Canongate, 1995.

Nairn, Tom. *The Break-Up of Britain: Crisis and Neo-Nationalism*. 1977. Expanded 2nd ed. London: Verso, 1981.

"The National Covenant." 1638. In *A Source Book of Scottish History*, ed. William Croft Dickinson, Gordon Donaldson, and Isabel A. Milne, 3 vols., 3:95–104. London: Thomas Nelson, 1952–54, rev. 2nd ed., 1958–61.

Nemoianu, Virgil. "Absorbing Modernization: The Dilemmas of Progress in the Novels of Walter Scott and in *Faust II*." In *Interpreting Goethe's "Faust" Today*, ed. Jane K. Brown, Meredith Lee, and Thomas P. Saine, 1–16. Columbia, S.C.: Camden House, 1994.

Newton, Michael. "'Becoming Cold-Hearted like the Gentiles around Them': Scottish Gaelic in the United States 1872–1912." *e-Keltoi: Journal of Interdisciplinary Celtic Studies* 2 (2003): 63–131, www4.uwm.edu/celtic/ekeltoi/volumes/vol2/2_3/newton_2_3.pdf.

———. "Celtic Cousins or White Settlers? Scottish Highlanders and First Nations." In Nilsen, *Rannsachadh na Gàidhlig 5*, 221–37.

———, ed. *Celts in the Americas*. Sydney, Nova Scotia: Cape Breton University Press, 2013.

———. "Cò a dhìthich clann Ghàidheal? Cnuasachd air ìmpireachd, fèin-aithne is ceartas sòisealta ann am fuadach nan Gàidheal / Bury My Heart at Culloden:

Reflections on Empire, Identity and Social Justice in the Gaelic Diaspora." In *Struileag: Shore to Shore / Cladach gu cladach*, ed. Kevin MacNeill / Caoimhin MacNèill. Edinburgh: Polygon, 2015.

———. "'Did You Hear about the Gaelic-Speaking African?': Scottish Gaelic Folklore about Identity in North America." In "The Celtic Nations and the African Americans," special issue, *Comparative American Studies* 8, no. 2 (2010): 88–106.

———. "How Scottish Highlanders Became White: The Introduction of Racialism to Gaelic Literature and Culture." In Newton, *Celts in the Americas*, 283–97.

———. "Jacobite Past, Loyalist Present." *e-Keltoi: Journal of Interdisciplinary Celtic Studies* 5 (2003): 31–62, www4.uwm.edu/celtic/ekeltoi/volumes/vol5/5_2/newton_5_2.pdf.

———. "Paying for the Plaid: Scottish Gaelic Identity Politics in Nineteenth-Century North America." In I. Brown, *From Tartan to Tartanry*, 63–81.

———. *Warriors of the Word: The World of the Scottish Highlanders*. Edinburgh: Birlinn, 2009.

Ngũgĩ wa Thiong'o. *A Grain of Wheat*. 1967. Rev. repr. Oxford: Heinemann, 1987.

Nicolson, Alexander, ed. *A Collection of Gaelic Proverbs and Familiar Phrases*. 1881. 3rd ed., abr. and repr. Edinburgh: Birlinn, 1996.

———. "Preface." In *A Collection of Gaelic Proverbs and Familiar Phrases*, xvii–xxxvi.

Nikro, Norman Saadi, ed. "Postcolonial Trauma Studies." Special issue, *Postcolonial Text* 9, no. 2 (2014), www.postcolonial.org.

Nilsen, Kenneth E., ed. *Rannsachadh na Gàidhlig 5 / Fifth Scottish Gaelic Research Conference*. Sydney, Nova Scotia: Cape Breton University Press, 2010.

Ó Baoill, Colm, ed., and Meg Bateman, trans. *Gàir nan clàrsach / The Harps' Cry: An Anthology of 17th Century Gaelic Poetry.* Edinburgh: Birlinn, 1994.

———. "Introduction." *The Harps' Cry*, 1–39.

Ó Dálaigh, Briain, ed. *The Strangers Gaze: Travels in County Clare, 1534–1950*. Ennis, Ireland: Clasp, 1998.

Ogilvie, John. *Rona, a Poem, in Seven Books*. London: J. Murray, 1777.

Ohlmeyer, Jane H. "'Civilisinge of Those Rude Partes': Colonization within Britain and Ireland, 1580s–1640s." In *The Oxford History of the British Empire*, ed. Roger Louis, vol. 1, *The Origins of Empire: British Overseas Enterprise to the Close of the Seventeenth Century*, ed. Nicholas Canny, 124–47. New York: Oxford University Press, 1998.

Ordnance Survey. "Gaelic Place Name Web Site." September 29, 2004, www.ordnancesurvey.co.uk/about/news/2004/gaelicplacenames.html.

———. "Putting Gaelic back on the Map." November 28, 2000, www.ordnancesurvey.co.uk/about/news/2000/gaelic.html.

Osterhammel, Jürgen. *Die Entzauberung Asiens: Europa und die asiatischen Reiche im 18. Jahrhundert.* Munich: Beck, 1998.

Oxford English Dictionary. Oxford: Oxford University Press. Online edition, www.oed.com.

Pagden, Anthony. "The Savage Critic: Some European Images of the Primitive." In "Colonial and Imperial Themes," ed. G. K. Hunter and C. J. Rawson, special issue, *Yearbook of English Studies* 13 (1983): 32–45.

Palmeri, Frank. "The Capacity of Narrative: Scott and Macaulay on Scottish Highlanders." *CLIO: A Journal of Literature, History and the Philosophy of History* 22, no. 1 (1992): 37–52.

Petersen, Kirsten Holst, and Anna Rutherford, eds. *A Double Colonization: Colonial and Post-Colonial Women's Writing*. Mundelstrup, Denmark: Dangaroo, 1986.

Phillipson, Nicholas. "The Scottish Enlightenment." In *The Enlightenment in National Context*, ed. Roy Porter and Mikuláš Teich, 19–40. Cambridge: Cambridge University Press, 1981.

Pinkerton, John. *A Dissertation on the Origin and Progress of the Scythians or Goths: Being an Introduction to the Ancient and Modern History of Europe*. London: George Nicol, 1787.

———. *An Enquiry into the History of Scotland, Preceding the Reign of Malcolm III, or the Year 1056*. 1790. Repr., 2 vols., Edinburgh: Bell and Bradfute, 1814.

Pittock, Murray G. H. *Celtic Identity and the British Image*. New York: Manchester University Press, 1999.

———. *The Invention of Scotland: The Stuart Myth and the Scottish Identity, 1638 to the Present*. New York: Routledge, 1991.

———. "Plaiding the Invention of Scotland." In I. Brown, *From Tartan to Tartanry*, 32–47.

———. *Poetry and Jacobite Politics in Eighteenth-Century Britain and Ireland.* Cambridge: Cambridge University Press, 1994.

———. "Scott as Historiographer: The Case of *Waverley*." In Alexander and Hewitt, *Scott in Carnival*, 145–53.

Ponzanesi, Sandra. *The Postcolonial Cultural Industry: Icons, Markets, Mythologies*. New York: Palgrave Macmillan, 2014.

Pratt, Mary Louise. "Arts of the Contact Zone." *Profession* 91 (1991): 33–40.

———. *Imperial Eyes: Travel Writing and Transculturation*. New York: Routledge, 1992. Rev. 2nd ed. 2008.

———. "Scratches on the Face of the Country; or, What Mr. Barrow Saw in the Land of the Bushmen." In Gates, "Race, Writing, and Difference," 119–43.

Prebble, John. *The King's Jaunt: George IV in Scotland, August 1822. 'One and Twenty Daft Days.'* London: Collins, 1988.

Price, Martin. "The Restoration and the Eighteenth Century." In Hollander and Kermode, *Oxford Anthology of English Literature*, 1:1549–60.

Pulsifer, Cameron. "A Highland Regiment in Halifax: The 78th Highland Regiment of Foot and the Scottish National/Cultural Factor in Nova Scotia's Capital, 1869–1871." In Harper and Vance, *Myth, Migration and the Making of Memory*, 141–56.

Ramazani, Jahan. *The Hybrid Muse: Postcolonial Poetry in English*. Chicago: University of Chicago Press, 2001.

Reay, George (3rd Lord Reay). Letter to an unknown addressee, probably a government official, September 2, 1746. Publ. in Angus Mackay, *The Book of Mackay*, 456–57. Edinburgh: Norman MacLeod, 1906.

Richards, David. "'Injured by Time and Defeated by Violence': Prospects of Loch Tay." In Sassi and van Heijnsbergen, *Within and without Empire*, 14–28.

Richards, Eric. *A History of the Highland Clearances*. 2 vols. London: Croom Helm, 1982 and 1985.

Ritz, Hans. *Die Sehnsucht nach der Südsee: Bericht über einen europäischen Mythos*. Göttingen: Muriverlag, 1983.

Rogowski, Ronald, and Edward A. Tiryakian, eds. *New Nationalisms of the Developed West: Toward Explanation*. Boston: Allen and Unwin, 1985.

Royle, Trevor. "From David Stewart to Andy Stewart: The Invention and Reinvention of the Scottish Soldier." In I. Brown, *From Tartan to Tartanry*, 59–61.

———. *The Mainstream Companion to Scottish Literature*. Edinburgh: Mainstream, 1993.

Ryan, Ray. *Ireland and Scotland: Literature and Culture, State and Nation, 1966–2000*. Oxford: Clarendon, 2002.

Said, Edward W. *Orientalism*. 1978. Repr. with new afterword, New York: Penguin, 1995.

Sanders, Andrew. *The Short Oxford History of English Literature*. 1994. Rev. 2nd ed. Oxford: Clarendon, 1996.

Şandru, Cristina, Sarah Lawson Welsh, and Janet Wilson, eds. *Rerouting the Postcolonial: New Directions for the New Millennium*. New York: Routledge, 2010.

———. "General Introduction." In *Rerouting the Postcolonial*, 1–13.

Sassi, Carla. "Acts of (Un)willed Amnesia: Dis/appearing Figurations of the Caribbean in Post-Union Scottish Literature." In *Caribbean–Scottish Relations: Colonial and Contemporary Inscriptions in History, Language and Literature*, ed. Joan Anim-Addo, Giovanna Covi, Velma Pollard, and C. Sassi, 131–98. London: Mango, 2007.

———. *"Imagined Scotlands": Saggi sulla letteratura scozzese*. Trieste: Edizioni Parnaso, 2002.

———. *Why Scottish Literature Matters*. Edinburgh: Saltire Society, 2005.

Sassi, Carla, and Theo van Heijnsbergen, eds. *Within and without Empire: Scotland across the (Post)Colonial Borderline*. Newcastle, Eng.: Cambridge Scholars, 2013.

Schoene-Harwood, Berthold. "Emerging as the Others of Ourselves: Scottish Multiculturalism and the Challenge of the Body in Postcolonial Representation." *Scottish Literary Journal* 25, no. 1 (1998): 54–72.

Schulze-Engler, Frank. "Exceptionalist Temptations—Disciplinary Constraints: Postcolonial Theory and Criticism." In "Current Critical Theories in Europe," ed. Catherine Bernard, Claire Connolly, and Ansgar Nünning, special issue, *European Journal of English Studies* 6, no. 3 (2002): 289–305.

———. "Introduction." In Helff and Schulze-Engler, *Transcultural English Studies*, ix–xvi.

———. "Theoretical Perspectives: From Postcolonial to Transcultural World Literature." In *English Literatures across the Globe: A Companion*, ed. Lars Eckstein, 20–32. Paderborn: Wilhelm Fink, 2007.

"Scotland and the Colonial Experience." Special issue, *Scotlands* 2, no. 1 (1995).

Scott, Jamie S. "Postcolonial Cultures and the Jewish Imaginary." Paper presented at the conference "Transcultural English Studies" hosted by the Association for the Study of the New Literatures in English (ASNEL), Frankfurt a.M., May 20, 2004.

Scott, P[aul] H[enderson]. "'A Severed and Withered Branch': The Rise and Fall of Britishness." In *Scotland to Slovenia: European Identities and Transcultural Communication: Proceedings of the Fourth International Scottish Studies Symposium*, ed. Horst W. Drescher and Susanne Hagemann, 19–31. Frankfurt a.M.: Peter Lang, 1996.

———. "An English Invasion Would Have Been Worse: Why the Scottish Parliament Accepted the Union." *Scottish Studies Review* 4, no. 2 (2003): 9–16.

———, ed. *Scotland: An Unwon Cause: An Anthology with a Commentary.* Edinburgh: Canongate, 1997.

Scott, Tania. "The Fantasy of the Celtic Revival: Lord Dunsany, Fiona Macleod and W. B. Yeats." In *Border Crossings: Narration, Nation and Imagination in Scots and Irish Literature and Culture*, ed. Colin Younger, 127–41. Newcastle, Eng.: Cambridge Scholars, 2013.

Scott, Walter. "General Preface" to the 1829 ed. of the Waverley novels. Repr. in the Penguin ed. of *Waverley*, 519–33. Harmondsworth, Eng., 1985.

———. *The Letters of Sir Walter Scott*. Ed. H. J. C. Grierson. 12 vols. London: Constable, 1932–37.

———, ed. *Minstrelsy of the Scottish Border: Consisting of Historical and Romantic Ballads, Collected in the Southern Counties of Scotland; with a Few of Modern Date Founded upon Local Tradition*. 1802. Repr., ed. T. F. Henderson, 4 vols. New York: Charles Scribner's Sons, 1902.

———. *Waverley; or, 'Tis Sixty Years Since*. Begun 1805, 1st publ. 1814. Repr. Harmondsworth, Eng.: Penguin, 1985.

Sellar, Patrick. Letter to Lord Advocate Colquhoun, May 24, 1815. Publ. in Adam, *Papers on Sutherland Estate Management*, 1:155–61.

———. Note concerning Sutherland, May 1816. Publ. in Adam, *Papers on Sutherland Estate Management*, 1:175–87.

Sharp, William (under the pseudonym "Fiona Macleod"). "For the Beauty of an Idea." In *The Winged Destiny: Studies in the Spiritual History of the Gael*, 167–220. 1904. Repr. London: William Heinemann, 1927.

———(as "Fiona Macleod"). *Green Fire*. Westminster: Archibald Constable, 1896.

———. "Introduction." In *Lyra Celtica: An Anthology of Representative Celtic Poetry*, ed. Elizabeth A. Sharp, xix–li. Edinburgh: Patrick Geddes, 1896.

———(as "Fiona Macleod"). "Iona." In *The Divine Adventure / Iona / By Sundown Shores*, 91–250 and 415–31. 1900. Repr. London: William Heinemann, 1927.

———(as "Fiona Macleod"). *Pharais*. Derby, Eng.: Harpur and Murray, 1894.

———(as "Fiona Macleod"). *The Sunset of Old Tales*. Leipzig: Bernhard Tauchnitz, 1905.

———(as "Fiona Macleod"). *Wind and Wave*. Leipzig: Bernhard Tauchnitz, 1902.

Shaw, Michael. "William Sharp's Neo-Paganism: Queer Identity and the National Family." In *Queer Victorian Families: Curious Relations in Literature*, ed. Duc Dau and Shale Preston, 77–95. New York: Routledge, 2015.

Sher, Richard B. "Percy, Shaw, and the Ferguson 'Cheat': National Prejudice in the Ossian Wars." In Gaskill, *Ossian Revisited*, 207–45.

Shields, Juliet. *Sentimental Literature and Anglo-Scottish Identity, 1745–1820*. Cambridge: Cambridge University Press, 2010.

Sims-Williams, Patrick. "The Invention of Celtic Nature Poetry." In T. Brown, *Celticism*, 97–124.

———. "The Visionary Celt: The Construction of an Ethnic Preconception." *Cambridge Medieval Celtic Studies* 11 (1986): 71–96.

Slemon, Stephen. "Unsettling the Empire: Resistance Theory for the Second World." *World Literature Written in English* 30, no. 2 (1990): 30–41.

Smith, Adam. *An Inquiry into the Nature and Causes of the Wealth of Nations*. 1776. Repr., ed. R. H. Campbell and A. S. Skinner. 2 vols. Oxford: Clarendon, 1976.

Smith, Louise Z. "Dialectic, Rhetoric, and Anthropology in Scott's *Waverley*." *Studies in Scottish Literature* 21 (1986): 43–52.

Smith, Philippa Mein. *A Concise History of New Zealand*. Cambridge: Cambridge University Press, 2005.

Smollett, Tobias. *The Adventures of Roderick Random*. 1748. Repr. Athens: University of Georgia Press, 2012.

———. *The Expedition of Humphrey Clinker*. 1771. Repr. Athens: University of Georgia Press, 1990.

———. Review of James Macpherson's *Fingal*. In *Critical Review, or, Annals of Literature* 12 (1761): 405–18, and 13 (1762): 45–53.

———. Review of James Macpherson's *Temora*. In *Critical Review, or, Annals of Literature* 15 (1763): 200–209.

———. "The Tears of Scotland." 1746. Repr. in *Scotlands: Poets and the Nation*, ed. Douglas Gifford and Alan Riach, 86–87. Manchester: Carcanet, 2004.

Smyth, Gerry. *Decolonisation and Criticism: The Construction of Irish Literature*. London: Pluto, 1998.

Sorensen, Janet. *The Grammar of Empire in Eighteenth-Century British Writing*. New York: Cambridge University Press, 2000.

Spivak, Gayatri Chakravorty. "Can the Subaltern Speak?" 1985. Repr. in *Marxism and the Interpretation of Culture*, ed. Larry Grossberg and Cary Nelson, 271–313. Urbana: University of Illinois Press, 1988.

Stafford, Fiona J. "Hugh Blair's Ossian, Romanticism and the Teaching of Literature." In R. Crawford, *Scottish Invention of English Literature*, 68–88.

———. *The Last of the Race: The Growth of a Myth from Milton to Darwin*. Oxford: Clarendon, 1994.

———. "Primitivism and the 'Primitive' Poet: A Cultural Context for MacPherson's Ossian." In T. Brown, *Celticism*, 79–96.

———. *The Sublime Savage: James Macpherson and the Poems of Ossian*. Edinburgh: Edinburgh University Press, 1988.

State of the Society in Scotland, for Propagating Christian Knowledge, Giving a Brief Account of the Condition of the Highlands and Islands of Scotland. . . . Together with Some Account of the Society's Missionaries for Converting the Native Indians of America. Edinburgh: R. Fleming, 1741.

Stevenson, Robert Louis. *Kidnapped*. 1886. Repr., together with Stevenson's *Catriona*, ed. Emma Letley, xxxvii–208, 477–83. New York: Oxford University Press, 1986.

Stiùbhart, Domhnall Uilleam. "Highland Rogues and the Roots of Highland Romanticism." In *Crossing the Highland Line: Cross-Currents in Eighteenth-Century Scottish Writing: Selected Papers from the 2005 ASLS Annual Conference*, ed. Christopher MacLachlan, 161–93. Glasgow: ASLS, 2009.

———. "Martin, Martin." In *Oxford Dictionary of National Biography*. Oxford: Oxford University Press, 2004. Online ed. 2008.

Stroh, Silke. "Gaeldom and Multi-Ethnic Scotland: A Long History and a Short Story." *The Bottle Imp* 10 (November 2011), www.thebottleimp.org.uk.

———. "The Gaelic Voice in (Post)Colonial Discourse: An Alignment Illustrated by Case Studies of Neil Gunn, William Neill and Tormod Caimbeul." In Sassi and van Heijnsbergen, *Within and without Empire*, 77–91.

———. "The Long Shadow of Tacitus: Classical and Modern Colonial Discourses in the Eighteenth- and Early-nineteenth-century Scottish Highlands." In Helff and Schulze-Engler, *Transcultural English Studies*, 339–54.

———. "Postcolonialism, Celticity, and the Nation-State: Interrogating Old and New Multiculturalisms in Europe and Beyond." In *Contested Identities: Literary Negotiations in Time and Place*, ed. Roger Nicholson, Claudia Marquis, and Gertrud Szamosi, 3–30. Newcastle, Eng.: Cambridge Scholars, 2015.

———. "Revisioning Irish Postcolonialism: The Scottish Connection." In *Anglistentag 2012 Potsdam: Proceedings*, ed. Katrin Röder and Ilse Wischer, 35–46. Trier: WVT, 2013.

———. "Scotland as a Multi-Fractured (Post-)Colonial Go-Between? Ambiguous Interfaces between (Post-)Celticism, Gaelicness, Scottishness and Postcolonialism." In *Global Fragments: (Dis)Orientation in the New World Order*, ed. Anke Bartels and Dirk Wiemann, 181–95. Atlanta: Rodopi, 2007.

———. "Transperipheral Translations? Native North American / Scottish Gaelic Connections." In *Translation of Cultures*, ed. Petra Rüdiger and Konrad Gross, 255–71. Atlanta: Rodopi, 2009.

———. *Uneasy Subjects: Postcolonialism and Scottish Gaelic Poetry*. Amsterdam: Rodopi, 2011.

Strother, Z. S. "Display of the Body Hottentot." In *Africans on Stage: Studies in Ethnological Show Business*, ed. Bernth Lindfors, 1–61. Bloomington: Indiana University Press, 1999.

Tacitus, Cornelius. *Agricola*. Ca. 98 AD. In Tacitus, *Agricola and Germany*, trans. Anthony R. Birley, 3–34. Oxford: Oxford University Press, 1999.

Taylor, Anne. *The People's Laird: A Life of Robert Bontine Cunninghame Graham*. York, Eng.: Tobias, 2005.

Thieme, John, ed. *The Arnold Anthology of Post-Colonial Literatures in English*. New York: Arnold, 1996.

———. "Introduction." In *The Arnold Anthology of Post-Colonial Literatures in English*, 1–9.

Thomas, Nicholas. *Colonialism's Culture: Anthropology, Travel and Government*. Princeton, N.J.: Princeton University Press, 1994.

Thomson, Derick S., ed. *The Companion to Gaelic Scotland*. Oxford: Basil D. Blackwell, 1983.

———. *The Gaelic Sources of Macpherson's "Ossian."* Edinburgh: Oliver and Boyd, n.d. [1951].

———. "'Ossian' Macpherson and the Gaelic World of the Eighteenth Century." *Aberdeen University Review* 40 (1963): 7–20.

———. "Unpublished Letters by the Poet Ewen MacLachlan." *SGS* 11, no. 2 (1968): 202–36.

Thompson, F. G. "Gaelic in Politics." *TGSI* 47 (1971–72): 67–100.

Tomasch, Sylvia. "Postcolonial Chaucer and the Virtual Jew." In *The Postcolonial Middle Ages*, ed. Jeffrey Jerome Cohen, 243–60. New York: St. Martin's, 2000.

Toogood, Mark. "Decolonizing Highland Conservation." In *Decolonizing Nature: Strategies for Conservation in a Post-Colonial Era*, ed. William M. Adams and Martin Mulligan, 152–71. Sterling, Va.: Earthscan, 2003.

Trumpener, Katie. *Bardic Nationalism: The Romantic Novel and the British Empire*. Princeton, N.J.: Princeton University Press, 1997.

Visser, Irene. "Trauma Theory and Postcolonial Literary Studies." *Journal of Postcolonial Writing* 47, no. 3 (2011): 270–82.

Voltaire. *Essai sur les moeurs et l'esprit des nations*. 1756. Repr., ed. Rene Pomeau, 2 vols., Paris: Garnier, 1963.

Watson, Roderick. *The Literature of Scotland*. Basingstoke, Eng.: Macmillan, 1984.

———, ed. *The Poetry of Scotland: Gaelic, Scots and English 1380–1980*. Edinburgh: Edinburgh University Press, 1995.

———. "Postcolonial Subjects? Language, Narrative Authority and Class in Contemporary Scottish Culture." *The European English Messenger* 7, no. 1 (1998): 21–31.

———. "Visions of Alba: The Constructions of Celtic Roots in Modern Scottish Literature." In "Actes du Congrès international d'études écossaises, Grenoble, 1991," special issue, *Études Écossaises* 1 (1992): 253–64.

Weinbrot, Howard D. *Britannia's Issue: The Rise of British Literature from Dryden to Ossian*. Cambridge: Cambridge University Press, 1993.

Wickman, Matthew. *The Ruins of Experience: Scotland's "Romantick" Highlands and the Birth of the Modern Witness*. Philadelphia: University of Pennsylvania Press, 2007.

Williams, Daniel G. "Is the 'Pan-' in Pan-Celticism the 'Pan-' in Pan-Africanism? Language, Race and Diaspora." In Newton, *Celts in the Americas*, 317–34.

———. "Pan-Celticism and the Limits of Post-Colonialism: W. B. Yeats, Ernest Rhys and William Sharp in the 1890s." In *Nations and Relations: Writing across the British Isles*, ed. Tony Brown and Russell Stephens, 1–29. Cardiff: New Welsh Review, 2000.

Williams, Heather. "Writing to Paris: Poets, Nobles, and Savages in Nineteenth-Century Brittany." *French Studies* 57, no. 4 (2003): 475–90.

Willson, David Harris. *King James VI and I*. 1956. Repr. London: Jonathan Cape, 1959.

Winlow, Heather. "Anthropometric Cartography: Constructing Scottish Racial Identity in the Early Twentieth Century." *Journal of Historical Geography* 27, no. 4 (2001): 507–28.

Withers, Charles W. J. *Gaelic in Scotland 1698–1981: The Geographical History of a Language*. Edinburgh: John Donald 1984.

———. *Geography, Science and National Identity: Scotland since 1520.* New York: Cambridge University Press, 2001.

———. "The Historical Creation of the Scottish Highlands." In *The Manufacture of Scottish History*, ed. Ian Donnachie and Christopher Whatley, 143–56. Edinburgh: Polygon, 1992.

———. "Introduction" to Martin Martin's works. In *"A Description of the Western Islands of Scotland" ca 1695 and "A Late Voyage to St Kilda" [by] Martin Martin with "A Description of the Occidental i.e. Western Islands of Scotland" [by] Donald Monro*, 1–11. Edinburgh: Birlinn, 1999.

Womack, Peter. *Improvement and Romance: Constructing the Myth of the Highlands.* Basingstoke, Eng.: Macmillan, 1989.

Yadav, Alok. *Before the Empire of English: Literature, Provinciality, and Nationalism in Eighteenth-Century Britain.* New York: Palgrave Macmillan, 2004.

Young, John R. "The Scottish Parliament and National Identity from the Union of the Crowns to the Union of Parliaments, 1603–1707." In Broun, Finlay, and Lynch, *Image and Identity*, 105–42.

Young, Robert J. C. *Colonial Desire: Hybridity in Theory, Culture and Race.* New York: Routledge, 1995.

———. *The Idea of English Ethnicity*. Malden, Mass.: Blackwell, 2008.

———. *Postcolonialism: An Historical Introduction.* Oxford: Blackwell, 2001.

———. "Scots' Goal Must Be Postcolonial Nationhood." *The Scotsman*, August 15, 2010, www.scotsman.com/news/robert-jc-young-scots-goal-must-be-post colonial-nationhood-1–821303.

Zureik, Elia T. *The Palestinians in Israel: A Study in Internal Colonialism*. Boston: Routledge and Kegan Paul, 1979.

INDEX